A History of Illinois

Governor Thomas Ford. Reproduced from
an oil painting by William Camm.
(Illinois State Historical Library)

A History of Illinois

*From Its Commencement as a State
in 1818 to 1847*

Governor Thomas Ford /1800-1850/

Annotated and Introduced by
Rodney O. Davis

Bibliographical Note by
Terence A. Tanner

977.303
FOR
8 1

University of Illinois Press
Urbana and Chicago

Publication of this book was supported by the Illinois State Historical Society in observance of the 175th anniversary of statehood.

Annotations, Introduction to the 1995 Edition, and Bibliographical Note © 1995 by the Board of Trustees of the University of Illinois
Manufactured in the United States of America
C 5 4 3 2 1

This book is printed on acid-free paper.

Contents

Bibliographical Note *by Terence A. Tanner*   xiii

Introduction to the 1995 Edition *by Rodney O. Davis*   xvii

Introduction *by General James Shields*   1

Preface   3

I. The Achievement of Statehood, 1818–1821   7

Petition of the Territorial Legislature to Congress to be admitted into the Union—Bill reported by Judge Pope, the territorial Delegate—Amendments proposed by him—Boundaries of the State enlarged—Ordinance of 1787—Claim of Wisconsin to the fourteen northern counties—Reasons for extending the boundaries—Call of a Convention—Constitution adopted—E. K. Kane—Petition of the Covenanters—Organization of the State Government—Gov. Bond recommends the Canal to Lake Michigan—Judge Foster—Judge Thomas—Legislature of 1819—Code of Laws—Removal of the Seat of Government to Vandalia—Origin of the name Vandalia—Character of the people—Notice of the French villages and of the early American settlers—Schools, learned professions—The early preachers—Pursuits and business of the people—Their ingenuity—Anecdote of James Lemon—Commerce—Money—Speculation—Banks in Ohio and Kentucky—General indebtedness—Money crisis—Creation of the State Bank of 1821—Its history—Col. Menard—John M'Lean—Judge Young—First duel—Judge Lockwood.

II. The Pioneer State, 1821–1827   30

Governor Coles, Judges Philips and Brown, and Gen. Moore—The question of Slavery—The Missouri Question—Immigrants from the Slave States to Missouri—Growing desire for the introduction of Slavery—The Slavery party—Effort for a Convention to amend the Constitution—Hanson and Shaw—Resolution for a Convention passed—The riotous conduct of the Slave party—The free State party rally—Contest between them in the election of 1824—Principal men of each party—The Convention defeated—Character of early political contests—No measures; and no parties of Whig or Democrat, Federalist or Republican—Effect of regular political parties—Reorganization of the Judiciary—Circuit Courts established—First case of proscription—Causes the repeal of the Circuit Courts—Road law and School law providing for a tax; operated well but were repealed—Hatred of taxation—School law of 1840; of 1845—Wm. Thomas, H. M. Wood, John S. Wright, and Thompson Campbell—Present state of Schools—Revision of the laws by Judges Lockwood and Smith—Gov. Edwards—Mr. Sloe—Lieutenant Gov. Hubbard—His speech, as a candidate for Governor—His speech about Wolf scalps—The old State Bank again—Effort to investigate its management—Resisted by the Bank officers—Gov. Edwards' messages—A packed committee report against the Governor—Power of a broken Bank—Combinations to commit crime or resist law—Daniel P. Cook—Gov. Duncan—Change of political parties—Gen. Jackson's defeat, and subsequent election—Influence of this upon parties—Gov. Duncan's change—Winnebago War—Galena—"Suckers"—"Pukes"—The chief, Red Bird—Gov. Edwards' claim to the public lands—Sale of School lands—Borrowing of the School fund.

III. Political and Social Development, 1827–1830   52

Review—Election of State Treasurer in 1827—Election and defalcation of Sheriffs—Courts—Judges—Sentence of Green—Instructions to juries—The hung jury—Law of 1846—Eminent lawyers—Character of litigation—Election by ballot—The keep-dark system—The "butcher-knife boys"—Influences in the Legislature—Greasing and swallowing, &c—Aims of politicians and the people—Anecdote of Senator Crozier—Good and bad self-government—Rule to test the capacity of the people for either—Educated ministers of the Gospel—Ill-will towards them of some of the old ministers—Room enough for both—Benevolent institutions and education—Colleges—Change of dress among young people—Regrets of the old folks—Effects of attending church on Sundays—Effects of not attending church on Sundays upon young people—Progress in commerce—Character of first merchants—Selling for money supplied by emigration—Nothing raised for or shipped to foreign markets—Flat-boats—Farmers taking their own crops to market, and bad effects of it—Foreign markets—Steamboats and high rates of exchange encourage the merchants to become exporters—Bad effects of farmers holding their produce from market, expecting a higher price—This practice contrasted with the New England practice of selling at the market price—Good effects of this practice—Prosperity of northern Illinois in a great measure owing to this.

IV. The Black Hawk War, 1831–1832   67

Extent of settlements in 1830—Election for Governor that year—Judge John Reynolds—William Kinney—Further development of party—Description of an election of contest—Reynolds elected by Jackson and anti-Jackson men—Legislature of 1831 bound to redeem the notes of the old State bank—Horror of increasing taxes—Fears of the Legislature—The Wiggins' loan—All the members broke down—The little bull law—Penitentiary punishments—Curious contest for State Treasurer—Indian disturbances—Treaties with the Indians—Black Hawk's account of them—His character—He invades the Rock river country—Call for volunteers—March to Rock Island—Escape of the Indians—New treaty with them—Next year Black Hawk returns—Volunteers again called for—March of Gov. Reynolds and Gen. Whiteside—Burning of Prophet's town—Arrival at Dixon—Majors Stillman and Bailey—Route at Stillman's Run—Account of it by a volunteer Colonel—Council of war—Gen. Whiteside marches in pursuit of the Indians—Massacre of Indian Creek—Two young ladies captured and restored—Gen. Whiteside buries the dead and marches back to Dixon—Meets Gen. Atkinson—Dissatisfaction of the men—Marches to Ottawa—Army discharged—New call for volunteers—Volunteer regiment left as a guard of the frontiers—Col. Jacob Fry—Capt. Snyder—Battle with the Indians—Bravery of Gen. Whiteside—Gen. Semple and Capt. Snyder—Indian murders—St. Vrain and others—Siege of the Apple-river Fort—Col. Strode—

Galena—Martial law there—Gen. Dodge's successful attack—Capt. Stephenson—
Martial spirit of the Indians—Major Dement—Defence of Kellogg's Grove—Gen.
Posey's march—Gen. Alexander—Gen. Atkinson—Gen. Henry—March up Rock
river—Turtle village—Burnt village—Lake Keshkonong—Search for the Indians—
Two regular soldiers fired on—Expeditions to the "trembling lands"—Army dis-
persed in search of provisions.

V. Conclusion of the War, 1832   91

Gen. Posey marches to Fort Hamilton—Gens. Henry and Alexander, and Major
Dodge, to Fort Winnebago—Gen. Atkinson remained behind to build a fort—Description of the country and the rivers at Fort Winnebago—Gen. Henry informed
as to the position of Black Hawk—Council of War—Agreement to violate orders
and march after the Indians—Alexander's men refuse to march—Dodge's horses broke down—Arrival of Craig's company—Protest of officers and signs of mutiny—Put down by Gen. Henry—His character as a military man—March for Rock
river—Description of Rock river—March for Cranberry lake—Express to Gen. Atkinson—Discovery of the retreat of Black Hawk to the Wisconsin—Thunder
storm—Privations of the men—Arrival at the four lakes—False alarm—Description of the four lakes—Gen. Ewing and the spies—Major Dodge—Ardor of the
men—Come close upon the Indians—Battle of the Wisconsin heights—Defeat of
the Indians—Their retreat across the river—Reasons why Gen. Henry and the
Illinois volunteers never received credit abroad for what they deserved—Gen.
Henry's death—His singular modesty—Return of the troops to the Blue Mounds—
Bad treatment of Henry and his brigade by Gen. Atkinson—Gen. Atkinson pur-
sues the Indians across the Wisconsin—Order of march—Henry's men put in
charge of the baggage—They resent, but submit—Gen. Atkinson in front decoyed
by the Indians—Drawn off on a false scent—Henry advances on the main trail—
Comes upon the main body of the Indians, and again defeats them before Gen.
Atkinson arrived with the rest of the army—Retreat of Black Hawk Indians—Sent
in pursuit of him—The one-eyed Decori—Capture of Black Hawk and the Prophet—Description of the Prophet—Indian speeches—Gen. Scott—Discharge of the
volunteers—Treaty of peace—Black Hawk and other prisoners taken to Washington—Makes the tour of the Union, and are returned to their own country, west
of the Mississippi.

VI. The Internal Improvement Era, 1833–1840   112

First efforts for a Railroad system—Central Railroad—Impeachment of Judge
Smith—Benjamin Mills—Other efforts to impeach judges—Effect on the public
mind—Election of Governor—Gov. Duncan—Creation of a new State Bank—Conrad Will—Means of passing its charter—Road tax—Hooking timber—Preachers
employed to preach against trespasses—Veto power—Banking in Illinois—Increase
of the Bank Stock—Stock readily taken—Intrigues of the subscribers—State Bank
goes into the hands of Thomas Mather and his friends—Effort to build up Alton—
The Lead trade—Unfortunate speculations—Real estate fund—Hostility of the
Democrats—Illinois and Michigan canal—George Forquer's report—Bill to borrow
money—Passed with an amendment to borrow on the credit of canal lands—Great
speculation in 1835–'36—Internal Improvement system—Means of passing it—
Calculations of its funds—Election of Governor in 1838—Thomas Carlin—Cyrus

Edwards—Maxim of politicians—Explosion of the Internal Improvement system—Presidential election of 1840—Further history of parties—Work on the canal—Payment of interest—Mr. Cavarly's bill.

VII. Judicial and Financial Issues, 1838–1842   145

Reform of the Supreme Court—Chief Justice Wilson—Justices Lockwood and Brown—Secretary of State and alien questions—Alexander P. Field—John A. McClernand—Decision of the Supreme Court—Popular excitement—Decision of a Circuit Judge on the alien question—Commotion among the Democrats—Suspicions of the Supreme Court—Mode of deciding political questions—Mode of reforming the Court—Violence of the measure—Reluctance of some Democrats—Obstinacy of others—How a politician must work in a party—Judge Douglass's speech in the lobby—Evasive decision of the Court—Judge Smith's intrigues and character—Passage of the bill—Motives of both parties—Prejudice against the Supreme Court—Moral power with the people of the Judges of the Supreme and Circuit courts—Breaking of the banks—Causes which lead to it—Bank suspensions—Power of the State Bank over the Legislature—Special session—Struggle to forfeit the Bank Charters—Whigs secede—Call of the House—Jumping out of the windows—Democratic victory—Thrown away before the end of the session—New suspensions—Small bills—Fierceness of parties against each other—Views of both parties concerning banking, and of each other.

VIII. Civil and Religious Discord, 1841–1842   157

Progress of settlements—Colleges—Education—Society—Religion—Literature—John M. Peck—James Hall—John Russell—Newspapers—Effects of speculation—Plenty of money—Credit—Debts—Usury—High rates of interest—History of mobs—Alton—Mob—Lovejoy—Abolitionists—Mobs in Pope county—Mobs in the north—Ogle county mob—Cause of mobs in free countries—Joe Smith—Origin of the Mormons—Their settlement in Missouri—Troubles there—Settlement in Ohio—Kirtland Bank—Mormons return to Missouri—Mormon war there—Expulsion from Missouri—Settlement of the Mormons in Illinois—Politics of the Mormons—Martin Van Buren—Henry Clay—John T. Stuart—Dr. Bennett—Senator Little—Stephen A. Douglass—Mormon Charters—Nauvoo Legion—Popular clamor against the Mormons—Arrest of Joe Smith—Trial before Judge Douglass—Nomination of Mr. Snyder as the democratic candidate for Governor—Gov. Duncan again a candidate—The Mormons declare for the Democrats—Gov. Duncan attacks the Mormons and the Mormon Charters—Death of Snyder—His character—Nomination of the author in his place—Reasons for this nomination—Further examination into the practical operations of government—Election of the author—The Governor, Auditor, and Treasurer forbid the receipt of Bank paper for Taxes—Condition of the State in 1842.

IX. Financial Ills and Legislative Remedies, 1842   194

Character of the people—North and South—Causes of discord—Principle on which elections were made—Character of candidates—Reasons for preference—Further maxims of politicians—John Grammar—Want of unity in the democratic party—Want of great leaders—Members of the Legislature—Legislative elections—Neglect of other business—Love of popularity—Account of lobby members—Their motives and influence—Professional politicians—Ultraists and "Milk and water men" tending to repudiation—Plans for public relief—Illinois Canal—Justin Butterfield—Michael Ryan—Arthur Bronson—Compromise with the Banks—Proposed repeal of their Charters—Gov. Carlin's message—Arguments for compromise and for repeal—Ayes and Noes in the House—John A. McClernand—Lyman Trumbull—James Shields—Feuds among politicians growing out of the appointment of Secretary of State—Amalgamation of the co-ordinate branches of government—Opposition to the Compromise Bill in the Senate—Character of the leader of this opposition—Removal of Trumbull from the office of Secretary of State—Humbug set off against humbug—Improvement of public affairs—Execution laws; debtor and creditor.

X. Politics and Mormonism, 1843–1844 219

Mormons—New warrant for the arrest of Joe Smith—Tried before Judge Pope—Intrigues of the Whigs—The Mormons determine to vote for Whig candidates for Congress—Cyrus Walker—Joseph P. Hoge—Dr. Bennett—Prejudices against the Mormons—New demand for the arrest of Joe Smith—Arrest and discharge by the Municipal Court—Walker's speech—Walker's and Hoge's opinion—Mormons always prefer bad advice—Demand for a call of the Militia—Reasons for not calling them—Intrigues of the Democrats—Backenstos—Hiram Smith—William Law—Revelation in favor of Hoge—Joe Smith's speech—Hoge elected—Indignation of the Whigs—Determination to expel the Mormons—Stephen A. Douglass—City ordinances—Insolence of the Mormons—Joe Smith a candidate for President—Conceives the idea of making himself a Prince—Danite band—Spiritual wives—Attempt on William Law's wife—Tyranny of Joe Smith—Opposition to him—"Nauvoo Expositor"—Trial of the press as a nuisance—Its destruction—Secession of the refractory Mormons—Warrant for Joe Smith and Common Council—Their arrest and discharge by the Municipal Court—Committee of anti-Mormons—Journey to Carthage—Militia assembled—Complaints against the Mormons—Cause of popular fury—False reports and camp news—Pledge of the troops to protect the prisoners—Martial law—Conduct of a Constable and Civil Posse—Council of officers—The great flood of 1844—Surrender of Joe Smith and the Common Council—Warrant for treason—Commitment of Joe and Hiram Smith—Preparations to march into Nauvoo—Council of officers—Militia disbanded—Journey to Nauvoo—Guard left for the protection of the prisoners—Further precautions—The leading anti-Mormons by false reports undermine the Governor's influence—Governor's speech in Nauvoo—Vote of the Mormons—News of the death of the Smiths—Preparation for defence of the country—Mischievous influences of the press.

XI. The Downfall of Joseph Smith, 1844–1845 248

Account of the assassination of the Smiths—Done by the forces at Warsaw—Treachery of the Carthage Greys—Franklin A. Worrell—Attack on the Jail—Murder of Joe and Hiram Smith—Character of Joe Smith—Character of the leading Mormons—Character of the Mormon people—Affairs of the Church—Sidney Rigdon's prophecies—The Twelve Apostles—Triumph of the Twelve—Increase of Mormonism—Causes of it—Gov. Ford and Herod and Pilate—The Mormons quit preaching to the Gentiles—Character of their preaching—Increased hostility of the "Saints"—Determination to expel the Mormons—Both parties ready to set aside free government—Natural inclination to despotism—Presidential election of 1844—Infatuation of the people—State elections—Col. Taylor's visit to the Mormons induces them to vote the democratic ticket—The fault laid on the Governor—Fresh determination to expel the Mormons—Conduct of the Whig press—Pusillanimity of politicians—Gen. Hardin—Col. Baker—Col. Weatherford—Col. Merriman—Anti-Mormon wolf-hunt—Military expedition to Hancock—Militia infected with anti-Mormonism—Surrender of two persons accused of the Murder—Terms of surrender arranged by Col. Baker—Incompetency of a Militia force in such cases—Prosecution of the murderers—Riotous trials—Constitution in relation to changes of venue—Trial of the Mormons for destroying the press—Both parties get a Jury to suit them—All acquitted—Anarchy in Hancock.

XII. The Canal Problem and Its Solution, 1843–1845   260

Canal Negotiations—Appointment of Oakley and Ryan to go to Europe—Factiousness of the letter-writers and newspapers—Proceedings of the Commissioners—David Leavitt—Meeting of American Bond-holders—Journey to Europe—Conditional agreement there—Appointment of Gov. Davis and Capt. Swift to examine and report on the Canal—Gov. Davis attacked by the Globe newspaper—Ryan's answer and attack on the Globe—Favorable Report—Ryan's second trip to Europe—Gov. Davis sent for—Failure of the negotiation—Ryan's attack on Gov. Davis—Letter from Baring, Brothers & Co. to Ryan—Letter of Wm. S. Wait, Esq., against taxation—Answer thereto—Visit of Mr. Leavitt and Col. Oakley to Europe—New negotiations successful—Opposition to the Governor likely to defeat the Canal—Nature of this opposition—How to get up an opposition to any Administration—Scandalous conduct of a Committee of Investigation—Trumbull and others—Conduct of the opposition—All their projects defeated—Visit of Gov. Davis and Mr. Leavitt to Springfield—Jealousy of the Legislature against monied men and foreign influence—They are well received—Propositions of the public creditors—Opposition arrayed—Miserable intrigues of George T. M. Davis and other Whigs—Patriotic conduct of Judge Logan and other Whigs—North and South again—Messrs. Strong, Adams, Janney, and Dunlap—The Canal Bill defeated in the Senate—Talk of bribery—Votes reconsidered and divided—Good management of Senator Kilpatrick—The Canal bill passed—The money for the Canal obtained—Election and organization of the Board of Trustees—Rate of Interest reduced to six per cent—Repeal of the Mormon Charters—Resolution calling on the Governor and Judges to relinquish their Salaries—The Governor's answer—Mistaken notions of Economy—Buncomb resolutions and speeches on the subject—Shawneetown Bank—Conditional contract with that Institution—Dr. Anderson—The true art of riding hobbies.

XIII. Expulsion of the Mormons, 1845–1846   284

The city of Nauvoo—The Temple—New causes of quarrel—The *"Oneness"*—Anti-Mormon meeting fired at by themselves—Character of the anti-Mormons—New mobs—House burning—Sheriff's posse—Backenstos—Plundering—McBratney—Death of Worrell—Daubenyer—Durfee—Trial of the Sheriff for murder—Gen. Hardin sent over with 500 men—Stops the disorders on both sides—Anti-Mormon Convention—The Mormons agree to leave the State—Maj. Warren with two companies left as a Guard—Good conduct of Major Warren—Indictments against the Twelve Apostles for counterfeiting—Exodus of the Mormons—Anti-Mormons anxious to expel the few that were left—Cause of a new quarrel—Writs sworn out—Old trick of calling the posse—The matter adjusted—Mormon vote in 1846—New excitements—New writs sworn out—The posse again—The new citizens petition for protection—Order to Major Parker—Order to Mr. Brayman—Treaty between the parties—Not agreed to by the Anti-Mormons—Mr. Brayman's letter—James W. Singleton—Thomas S. Brockman—Order to Major Flood—His proceedings under it—Numbers of each party—Battles—Not many hurt—The Mormons surrender the City—Triumphant entry of the anti-Mormons—Their brutal conduct—Sufferings of the Mormons—Excitement against the anti-Mormons—Moderate men not to be relied on in times of excitement—Difficulties of the Executive—Expedition to Nauvoo—The anti-Mormon posse dispersed—Violence of the anti-Mormons against the Governor—Anti-Mormon meetings—Their resolutions—Anti-Mormon committee of rogues and blackguards—The Irish Justice and Constable—Capt. Allen's expedition to Carthage—Major Webber—Attempts to arrest a Spy—Writs sworn out to arrest him and Capt. Allen—The old trick of the posse again—Instability of popular feeling—No disposition anywhere to assist, but a disposition everywhere to censure government, for not performing impossibilities—Popular notions of Martial Law—Like master like man—Anarchy and despotism—Liberty and slavery.

XIV. Crime and Violence in Massac County, 1846   309

Riots in Massac County in 1846—Robbery in Pope County—The regulators—Their proceedings—Arrests made by them—The torture and confession of their prisoners—The rogues vote for the county officers of Massac in 1846—Extorted and bribed evidence to implicate the sheriff and others, by the opposing candidates—The sheriff and others ordered to leave the county—Many whipped, tarred and feathered, and some drowned—Arrest of the rioters—They are rescued by the regulators—Judge Scates' charge to the grand jury—Indictments against the regulators—Threats to lynch the judge and the grand jury—Order to Dr. Gibbs, and reason for such an order—His proceedings under it—The Militia refuse to turn out—Inefficiency of well-disposed moderate men in such times—A few bold, violent men can govern a county, and how they do it—The reasons why the Militia would not turn out—Attack on old Mathis, his wife shot, he is carried away, supposed to have been murdered—The regulators arrested, given up by the sheriff, prisoners taken to Kentucky—Some of them drowned—Proceedings of the new Governor and the Legislature, then in session—District Courts provided to evade the Constitution against changes of the venue in criminal cases—The disturbances die away of themselves—The situation in 1842 compared with its condition in December, 1846.

Notes   317

Index   331

Bibliographical Note

Terence A. Tanner

The Chicago *Daily Democratic Press* of September 29, 1853, announced that James Shields had entered into an agreement with S. C. Griggs & Co. of Chicago to publish Thomas Ford's *History of Illinois*. Griggs, partially owned by the New York firm of Ivison & Phinney, sent the manuscript to New York to have it stereotyped and printed. Although Griggs had originally planned for publication in February 1854, the Chicago *Daily Democratic Press* on April 12, 1854, reported that the book "will be laid before the public in a few weeks." Seven weeks later, on May 29, 1854, the Chicago *Daily Democratic Press* announced that the "anxiously expected book . . . is now on sale at their [Griggs's] bookstore in this city." Reflecting Griggs's relationship with Ivison & Phinney, the book was published over the imprint "CHICAGO: | PUBLISHED BY S. C. GRIGGS & CO., | 111 LAKE STREET | NEW YORK: IVISON & PHINNEY. | [short rule] | 1854." and was advertised as available in cloth at $1.25 or full calf at $2.50. Later, Griggs advertised that copies could be obtained in half morocco for $1.50.

An annotated copy of the first printing (in the Illinois State Historical Library), probably corrected by James Shields, contains a pencil note on the rear free endpaper: "Ivison & Phinney | Booksellers | April, 1854 N. York," indicating that printing was probably completed by April 1854. Publication seems to have been delayed until May, however, by the effort involved in altering portions of the text to soften Ford's judgments of some of his contemporaries, in accordance with Shields's corrections. In order to accomplish this, six leaves (pages 153–54, 191–92, 203–4, 213–14, 387–88, and 431–32) were canceled in copies of the first printing and replaced with inserted leaves with the altered text, creating a second state of the first printing. These changes are outlined in Rodney Davis's notes to the text. Some copies either had been distributed before cancellation took place or were overlooked at the time of cancellation because, in addition to the copy at the Illinois State Historical Library, copies of the uncanceled first state of the first printing can be found at the University of Minnesota Library and at the Southern Illinois University Library at Carbondale.

Sales of the book proved brisk. The Chicago *Daily Democratic Press* on June 8, 1854, reported that a thousand copies had been sold in three days. In preparation for the second printing, the publishers altered the stereotype plates to incorporate the textual changes introduced into the second state of the first printing. At this time, the third line of the title page was corrected from "COMMENCEMENT AS A STATE IN 1814 TO 1847." to "COMMENCEMENT AS A STATE IN 1818 TO 1847.". The copyright notice was also altered to indicate that the book had been entered for copyright in the "Northern District of Illinois" instead of the "Northern District of New York," and the slug "PRINTED BY JOHN F. TROW, | 49 Ann St." was deleted from the copyright page. Thirty-one minor typographical errors identified in the annotated copy of the first state of the first printing at the Illinois State Historical Library were also corrected in the stereotype plates at the time of this printing, including one alteration that created an error where one did not exist. The spelling of Piatt County in line 5 on page 103 was incorrectly changed to "Platt." This error appeared in all subsequent printings of the first edition and was repeated by Milo Quaife in the Lakeside Classics edition of 1945–46 as well. Curiously, the publishers overlooked the misprint "INTERESING" for "INTERESTING" in the eighth line of the title, and that misprint appeared in every printing of the first edition.

The second printing is known in two states, identical in every respect except that one has the imprint on the title page as noted above and the other has an imprint reading: "NEW YORK: | IVISON & PHINNEY, 178 FULTON STREET; | (SUCCESSORS OF NEWMAN & IVISON, AND MARK H. NEWMAN & CO.) | CHICAGO: S. C. GRIGGS & CO., 111 LAKE STREET. | AUBURN: J. C. IVISON & CO. DETROIT: A M'FARREN. | CINCINNATI: MOORE, ANDERSON & CO. | [short rule] | 1854.". No priority between these states of the second printing has been established.

A third printing quickly followed. At the time of this printing, the stereotype plates were altered to change the advertisements that appeared at the back of the book. In the first and second printings, the last four leaves of the final gathering in the book contain six unnumbered pages of advertisements for Ivison & Phinney's publication of "Day & Thomson's Mathematical Series," followed by a blank leaf. In the third printing, these final four leaves were changed to contain illustrated advertisements, paginated 1–8, for Ivison & Phinney's publication of "Sanders' New Series of Readers."

Copies from this printing show a number of signs of deterioration to the stereotype plates. In all copies examined, the period has disappeared after Ivison & Phinney's name on the title page, the *a* in "abolitionists" in the eleventh line from the bottom on page 236 is broken, and the hyphen at the end of line six on page 237 is missing. In all but four of the copies examined, the type is broken in the first several lines on page 155.

Sometime before the end of 1854, a fourth printing was required. This printing is identical with the third printing, including the eight pages of advertisements for "Sanders' New Series of Readers" and the absence of the period after Ivison & Phinney's name on the title page, except that the additional line "SIXTH THOUSANDTH." appears above the imprint on the title page. All of the signs of deterioration to the stereotype plates are present in this printing. Copies of this printing were apparently still available as late as 1857 and were advertised by Griggs in the Chicago *Record* on July 1, 1857.

Griggs published a fifth printing of the first edition in 1859. Although the stereotype plates had to be altered to reflect the change in the date from 1854 to 1859, and a change in the publisher's address to "39 & 41 LAKE STREET.", Griggs didn't bother to remove the line "SIXTH THOUSANDTH" from the title page, nor replace the lost period after Ivison & Phinney's name in the imprint. The paper used for this printing is inferior to that used for earlier printings.

This was probably the only printing of the first edition actually printed in Chicago. The partnership between S. C. Griggs & Co. and Ivison & Phinney had been dissolved in 1858, although the two firms continued a working relationship, and it is reasonable to assume that Ivison & Phinney would have sent the stereotype plates for Ford's *History* to Griggs in Chicago after the dissolution of the partnership. For this printing, the stereotype plates were altered to remove the advertisements for Ivison & Phinney's publications, although one copy at the University of Chicago Library has an inserted twelve-page catalog for A. O. Moore & Co. of New York.

No other printing of Ford's *History* appeared until the second edition, edited by Milo M. Quaife for R. R. Donnelley & Co.'s annual Christmas series known as the "Lakeside Classics." Because of its size, the text was divided into two volumes, the first published for Christmas 1945, and the second for Christmas 1946. In 1968, University Microfilms of Ann Arbor published a facsimile of the first edition (technically the sixth printing of the first edition).

This University of Illinois Press printing is the third edition.

NOTE

This summary is based upon my continuing research into the bibliographical history of Ford's *History of Illinois*. To date, 110 copies of the first edition have been personally examined by me, or by librarians who responded to my bibliographical questionnaire.

Introduction to the 1995 Edition

Rodney O. Davis

The Illinois State Historical Society has chosen to observe the 175th anniversary of Illinois statehood by sponsoring this new edition of Thomas Ford's classic *History of Illinois*. There could not be a more appropriate commemoration than this account of the state's first thirty years. The book deserves being made readily available again, and its author is entitled to be introduced anew to an Illinois audience.

Few once-prominent men drop as precipitately from public view as Thomas Ford had fallen by the time of his tragic death in Peoria on November 3, 1850. Ford had come to the governorship of Illinois from a situation of relative obscurity in the state's judiciary, and in perhaps deeper obscurity did he die. More embattled than any of his predecessors, as governor of Illinois Ford had also been more effective than any of them; it was largely through his vision and legislative leadership that the state had been saved from bankruptcy. But he was constitutionally unable to succeed himself, and so controversial had his term been that he had little hope of an immediate political appointment. And, in accordance with the standards of the times, neither he nor his constituents gave any thought to public obligation to him as a retiree. Thus, after failing in private law practice in Peoria, suffering a long illness, and enduring the death of his wife, Ford died penniless less than four years after leaving the governorship. Indeed, his poverty, it was said at his death, "speaks well for the official integrity of the deceased."[1] Rather more grateful to Ford in death than in life, his fellow lawyers memorialized him across the state, and early in 1851 with near unanimity the General Assembly appropriated $500 in behalf of an eighteen-foot marble shaft to be erected in Ford's memory at his grave. Completed in 1853, that pillar in turn was destroyed in a windstorm five years later, leaving as more lasting monuments to Ford's life and services a good state credit rating, the Illinois and Michigan Canal, and, most significantly to us, his *History of Illinois*.[2]

* * *

Thomas Ford had a better opportunity than most to reflect on the early history of his state, for not only had he governed the state of

Illinois and pursued a legal and judicial career there, he had grown up with Illinois. He was brought to the Illinois country as a child five years before the creation of the Territory of Illinois by Congress, and he lived in Illinois continuously thereafter. Essentially, he had moved from one frontier to another, having been born in 1800 at Uniontown, Pennsylvania, near the pioneer landing at Brownsville on the Monongahela. Ford's widowed and obviously remarkable mother had set out in 1804 with her numerous family, the issue of two marriages, for free land and a new future in Spanish Louisiana, being apprised only upon arrival at St. Louis that Louisiana was now American and its real estate no longer so readily available. Hence the family was obliged to relocate, in Illinois, on a rented farm near New Design on the American Bottom, where Thomas Ford acquired his earliest schooling and, as a youth, hired himself out to labor.[3]

Six years older than Ford was his half-brother George Forquer, who was able upon attaining adulthood to leave the farm at New Design and to prosper as a house carpenter at St. Louis, then as a merchant and land speculator. With Forquer's support, Thomas Ford was able to spend a year at Transylvania University in Lexington, Kentucky, in 1818–19, returning when Forquer's business failure after the Panic of 1819 made it impossible for him to continue. Thereafter, the aspiring Forquer studied law and entered the wide-open politics of the early state of Illinois, becoming associated with Edward Coles, Ninian Edwards, and the latter's son-in-law, Congressman Daniel Pope Cook.

Eventually, Forquer held a range of offices, elective and appointive, in the General Assembly and as secretary of state, attorney general, and, at the time of his death in 1837, register of the Federal Land Office at Springfield. Forquer's connections and ambition for his younger half-brother made it possible for Ford also to study law, with Cook among others, and to be invited by Duff Green to help edit a Jacksonian campaign sheet in St. Louis in 1824. Ford's Jacksonian allegiance, although ambiguous in the preparty years of the 1820s, was to be constant thereafter. And for four years, between 1825 and 1829, Forquer and Ford shared a law office in Edwardsville.[4]

While at Edwardsville in 1828, Ford married Frances Hambaugh, whose parents' home was to provide a domestic anchor for Ford and his family, for beginning in 1829 Ford's career became decidedly peripatetic.[5] Together, Thomas and Frances Ford had five children, four of whom were born at the Hambaugh farm east of Quincy in what became Brown County. In 1829, Forquer became Illinois attorney general, and Ford and his wife moved to Galena, where Ford edited the *Miners' Journal* and tried unsuccessfully to begin a new law practice in that expansive community.[6] The next year, certainly helped by Attorney General Forquer's intervention with Governor Ninian Edwards, Ford was named state's attorney for Illinois's Fifth Judicial Circuit in the Military Tract of Western Illinois, and he continued in that capacity until he was elected judge of the Sixth Circuit, in the northern part of the state, in 1836. Thereafter, he served briefly as a municipal judge in Chicago, then as judge of the Ninth Circuit in the Rock River Country, and finally as a justice of the state supreme court in 1841–42.

The judicial positions were elective by the invariably Democratic General Assembly, at whose sessions Ford was normally in attendance; most lawyers of note in the state descended upon Vandalia or Springfield in December of even-numbered years to attend its sessions and the concurrent ones of the state supreme court. Not until 1836 does Ford seem to have had a home of his own, in the new town of Oregon, Illinois, the seat of Ogle County, which was on the Sixth and later the Ninth Judicial circuits, and not until 1839 does it appear that his family's presence in Oregon was continuous.[7] Even here his itinerant judgeship kept Ford constantly on the move from county seat to county seat, which probably helps explain the absence of any collection of Ford's private papers, a matter of great frustration to any potential biographer. The best record of this long period of Ford's life is yet to be tapped, for what remains of it must reside in the court files of counties in the judicial circuits where he served.

Ford acquired a favorable reputation on the bench, where he was respected by his peers and the attorneys who practiced before him; there is almost no disagreement about his learning, competence, and honesty as a judge.[8] It was with this reputation for judicial probity and party loyalty that he was picked by Democratic party leaders to replace Adam W. Snyder as gubernatorial candidate after Snyder's death in May 1842. Indeed, it is a credit to the organization and discipline of that party in Illinois that so difficult a situation could be met so well so near the August election day. Ford defeated the able Whig Joseph Duncan in the gubernatorial race that followed, and thus assumed his first and only popularly elective office.

As governor, Ford was obliged to find a way to salvage the state's credit after the wreck of the Internal Improvement System, to oversee the winding up of failed state-chartered banks, and to expedite the completion of the Illinois and Michigan Canal. Unanticipated distractions included the overwhelming problem involving the Mormons in Hancock County and the civil disturbances in the far south in Massac County. Ford's handling of all these matters elicits more respect now than it did from many of his contemporaries; indeed, some felt that his entry into politics was an egregious mistake, that he had exceeded his limits, and that he should have remained a judge.

More than one observer further claimed that Ford, while governor, lacked the resolve to contend with conflicting factions and pressures, indeed, that "to fortify his feeble animation, and acquire artifical courage, he had recourse to stimulants, which . . . grew to a confirmed and ruinous habit." Although the cause of his death was probably tuberculosis, it is further hinted that he was weakened by the "bad habits" acquired at Springfield, which might also have contributed to his inability to establish himself as a lawyer in Peoria after retiring from the governorship.[9] One can consider these allegations with some skepticism; it is hard to understand how the personal courage that must have sustained Ford as a judge on rough backwoods Illinois circuits would have deserted him as governor, although it is a fact that he was more able to contend with political adversaries in Springfield than he was with armed and numerous vigilantes in western and southern Illinois.

Compounding the tragedy of Ford's obscure demise was the death of his wife from cancer just three weeks earlier and the later unhappy destinies or early deaths of his children. Only one of his three daughters had a stable and fulfilling domestic life; of the other two one died young and unmarried, and the other friendless and the object of charity. Most ironic, considering the concern of Ford in his *History* and in his career with vigilantism and lawlessness, is the fact that both of his sons were lynched as outlaws in Kansas during the 1870s.[10]

*   *   *

It had been known before he left the governor's office that Thomas Ford was preparing a history of Illinois. He had apparently circulated portions of it in manuscript and discussed it with friends, and the governor had read publicly from the Black Hawk War chapters in Springfield early in 1847. Plans to publish it by subscription were announced shortly after Ford's retirement, but those plans aborted.[11] After his death it became apparent that Ford's principal and perhaps only asset had been that manuscript history, which the dying former governor had given to James Shields to find a publisher and to ensure that the book's proceeds would be used to help support Ford's five orphaned children.

It has been alleged that Shields suppressed as much as half of the original manuscript on account of its inflammatory and scurrilous content, and that the four-year delay in publication came from Shields's inability to find a publisher willing to take on the whole. But the allegation of suppression of that magnitude before publication seems dubious and is impossible to verify.[12] What has very recently become known is that after the manuscript was accepted for publication and the printer had run off some copies, some overdue proofreading was done and six alterations of the text were made, perhaps at the behest of Shields. These alterations, although indicative of the differing perspectives of 1847, when this book was written, and 1854 when it was published, were substantively relatively minor and are explained in the bibliographical note to this edition by Terence Tanner and in the appropriate footnotes. At all events, because of the well-known delay the appearance of Ford's book was widely anticipated, and it, along with the Kansas-Nebraska Act and the onset of the Crimean War, first became a matter of public discussion in Illinois in the spring of 1854.[13]

A reader of the immediate newspaper notices of Ford's *History*, by noting also the adjacent columns, can realize how much the state had changed in the few years since the governor's death.[14] Projects that had been mere speculations during Ford's term in office or even during his lifetime were now realities, as telegraph lines connected the state to the East and therefore the world, the canal was open, and railroads were beginning to provide rapid transportation to all sections of the commonwealth. Illinois was rapidly modernizing, and Ford's *History*, extending as it does only to late 1846, is very much a history of premodern, pioneer Illinois. Nearly half the book deals with Ford's administration as governor and all of it with Illinois history during his own lifetime; hence large parts of the volume constitute an apologia and come very close to autobiography. As is common in that form, the *History* is replete with Ford's frank, even abrasive, assessments of men and events. Many of the central figures lived into the new age, and many of *them* reacted strongly and personally to Ford's book. Indeed, the earliest responses to it tended to be piecemeal, to those specific portions of the volume that were of special interest to living individuals.

Former Governor John Reynolds had delivered a generous eulogy of Ford at Belleville in November of 1850, but he later found himself handled ambiguously at best in the *History*. Reynolds took particular offense at Ford's description of his very informal and even silly courtroom demeanor as a judge in the Madison County murder trial of Eliphalet Green in 1823 (52–53). In one of his own books on early

Illinois, Reynolds in turn dubbed Ford "heartless and superficial" for his treatment of the affair. John Francis Snyder later suggested that Reynolds detested Ford's memory thereafter.[15] Snyder was a very young man when Ford's *History* was published, but throughout his long life he never got over the condescending sketch that Ford rendered of his father, Adam W. Snyder, the Democratic candidate for governor in 1842 whose death propelled Ford into politics and the governorship (185–88). Although he tried to be charitable to Ford in his history of the same period, that Snyder was still livid and unforgiving sixty years later is obvious. He thought Ford "honorable, and conscientiously honest in every motive and deed, but totally wanting in penetration and tact."[16]

Ford's treatment of the convention issue of 1823–24 in chapter 2 was also immediately controversial upon the *History*'s publication. Although Governor Edward Coles and Editor Hooper Warren of the Edwardsville *Spectator* had each been leaders of the antislavery cause during that struggle over whether Illinois would amend its constitution to become a slave state, Warren disliked Coles so intensely as to have nearly compromised his own position in opposition to the peculiar institution. Editorially, it was not always clear which he liked least. Both men were still living in 1854, and Ford's book touched off a new round of extremely petty recriminations lasting more than a year, most of them originated by Warren and rejoined by Coles's friend and supporter the Reverend John Mason Peck. An Illinois historian himself, Peck agreed with Warren in one instance, that Ford wrote most accurately about things he knew most directly, of which the convention issue was not one.[17]

In writing of the Black Hawk War (chapters 4 and 5), Ford produced a reasonably comprehensive account, but one in which he was at pains to emphasize the significant military role of General James Dougherty Henry, who was from Illinois and died immediately after the war, and to denigrate the contribution of the Regular Army General Henry Atkinson and especially that of Colonel Henry Dodge of Wisconsin. Because Ford's version of the war had first been presented in the lecture that he read in 1847 and was therefore somewhat known before publication, Dodge's letter of inquiry about it is included as a footnote in the *History* itself. That letter was followed up in 1856 by published complaints from Dodge supporters in the Badger State, who also questioned the authority of Ford, a nonparticipant in the struggle, to even write about it.[18]

One of the few unqualified laudatory notices of Ford's book was circulated shortly after its publication by John Wentworth's Chicago *Democrat*, which praised Ford as much for his career accomplishments as for his *History*. In two newspaper columns the *Democrat* recounted the governor's struggle against the possible repudiation of the state's enormous internal improvement debt, carefully delineated by Ford in his book, and it emphasized the vital importance to Chicago of Ford's successful endeavor to rescue the Illinois and Michigan Canal. These, along with the concurrent uncoupling of the state from its banks, were the most politically difficult issues that Ford had to contend with as governor. They were also the achievements that gratified Ford most, and of the problems of his term they have been historiographically the least controversial. They required the conciliation or neutralization of partisan or sectional factions within the General Assembly, as well as confronting the bitter opposition of such powerful political leaders in Ford's own party as Lyman Trumbull and House Speaker William A. Richardson. Even the *Democrat* was silent, however, about the series of episodes that account for almost a quarter of Ford's *History*, those having to do with the Mormons in Hancock County.[19]

The governor had retired from office expressing satisfaction that the Mormons had left Illinois during his term. But the public silence of others suggests the existence of considerable embarrassment in the state over the matter and over Ford's handling of it.[20] Both Mormon and anti-Mormon writers came to view the appropriate chapters of Ford's *History* as mostly self-justification; ironically, he was accused by each of tilting excessively toward the opposing side, both as governor and as historian. Thomas Gregg's anti-Mormon *History of Hancock County* contains a contemptuous treatment of Ford's official activity relating to the Mormons and claims that the *History* purveys "many distortions of facts in order to make a case against the old citizens," whereas what for years was the Mormon Ur-text on events in Hancock County, B. H. Roberts's edition of Joseph Smith's *History of the Church of Jesus Christ of Latter Day Saints*, blames Ford for weakness and double-dealing as governor and for gross misrepresentation as historian.[21]

What is most controversial here is Ford's official and unofficial behavior in Hancock County after local officials had activated the militia as a posse comitatus following the destruction of the anti-Mormon *Expositor* newspaper press by order of the Nauvoo municipal court. Both Mormon and anti-Mormon historians cited the recollection of Thomas Geddes that at the peak of the crisis, while Joseph and Hyrum Smith were in Carthage Jail, Ford had remarked to Geddes that "it's all nonsense; you will have to drive the Mormons out yet," evidence either of Ford's wishes or, worse, of his duplicity.[22]

Roberts and his Mormon contemporaries were further influenced by affidavits taken from Porter Rockwell and William G. Sterrett that suggested that Ford knew in advance of the plans to murder the Smiths and probably approved of them. Perhaps most telling to Mormon scholars, and incriminating Ford of complicity with the assassins, was the governor's urging that the Smiths come to extremely turbulent Carthage to face the charges against them for ordering the *Expositor* press's destruction, then his leaving them guarded by the hostile Carthage Greys while he went to Nauvoo on June 27, 1844.

On these grounds, the Mormon compilers of Joseph Smith's *History* systematically rejected or rebutted Ford's arguments in the latter's *History* in defense of the actions that he took with regard to the Smiths or their murderers.[23] At best, it seemed to Mormon observers that Ford could either be blamed for truckling to the violent anti-Mormons or for utter executive incompetence, incompetence further compounded by his failure as governor after the Smiths' deaths to protect Mormons from their neighbors, inside Hancock County and out, until their departure from Illinois.

There can be no doubt that Thomas Ford disliked the Mormons; he makes no bones of that in the *History*. Although he is not charitable in his depiction of the anti-Mormons either, he devotes far more space to his vilification of the Mormons and their leaders. Actually, he allows grudging respect for Joseph Smith, "the most successful impostor in modern times," who possessed some "great natural parts" (249). The governor admits that he had actually contemplated permitting Joseph and Hyrum Smith to escape, presuming that they would then leave the state and that their followers would accompany them, as they had when the Mormons fled from Missouri to Illinois (237–38). Ford felt that the Mormons' continued presence could only be a perpetual source of trouble in the state. Throughout the controversy and even before, however, he acknowledged his obligation to them and to their leaders as citizens.[24] Although the issues of his collusion with anti-Mormon conspirators, or his intimidation by them, or his incompetence, will always be controversial, we should take Ford seriously when he writes of the Smiths, "I was determined, if possible, that the form of law should not be the catspaw of a mob, to seduce these people to a quiet surrender, as the convenient victims of popular fury" (232).

Ford's account of affairs in Hancock County is undoubtedly self-serving, but one must also recognize the utter difficulty of peacekeeping in so volatile a situation in June of 1844 or in subsequent crises in the autumns of 1844 and 1845 and the dreadful endgame in 1846. Peacekeeping of the scale required in Hancock County was a militia function, and the militia employed there invariably were, or quickly became, partisan and therefore useless if not actually vicious. Anti-Mormonism was the dominant sentiment in the counties surrounding Hancock, and it invariably came to be dominant in the militia raised in those counties, regardless of the proper disinterestedness of such militia leaders as John J. Hardin. In such a case, "The people cannot be used to put down the people," Ford wrote in some despair in the *History* in a different context but one also involving mob violence in Illinois (172). In the Mormon controversy the governor was practically alone in his avowed effort to stand dispassionately above faction. It should be added that some Mormon scholars have come to acknowledge these institutional and personal problems of Ford's and have therefore been more cognizant of and sympathetic toward his difficult situation.[25] They are consequently more inclined to use the *History* objectively as a primary source than were many of their forebears.

Ford's difficulty in maintaining order may well have been compounded by his strict construction of his authority as militia commander-in-chief, for as chief executive he professed to be unable to interfere in some of the questionable judicial maneuvers that went on in Carthage before the Smiths were murdered. He complained further of his lack of influence over militia officers, deriving from his constitutional powerlessness to appoint or remove them. But at this time and also later, he lacked moral authority too, as he freely admits: "Officers, men, and all under me, were so infected with the anti-Mormon prejudice that I was made to feel severely the want of moral power to control them" (257). That liability may have derived, at least in part, at a time when male physicality was much prized, from Ford's small stature and unprepossessing physical presence. One is struck by the frequent references his contemporaries made to these negative attributes and by what might be taken as a kind of compensatory assertiveness on Ford's own part in the *History*.[26]

It is obvious that Ford in the *History* maximizes his personal roles in the Mormon controversy and also in the political crisis involving the state's banks and internal improvement debt and the Illinois and Michigan Canal. He underscores his participation in other events, too. Although he was not a participant in the Black Hawk War in 1832, for instance, he makes it well known to readers that he was a member of a spy battalion of volunteers called out by Governor Reynolds the year before on the occasion of Black Hawk's earlier nominally illegal crossing of the Mississippi (75–76). But there are instances in the *History* in which Ford's significant connection with men or events is simply *not* stated. In chapter 2, his description of Governor Ninian Edwards can be interpreted as rendering that long-dead Illinois founder a bit ridiculous, yet the truth is that Ford had early in life been considerably indebted to Edwards. His long career in the state's judicial branch derived from an initial appointment as circuit attorney by Edwards in 1830, an appointment that had been earnestly solicited by Ford's half-brother, George Forquer. Forquer was an active member of Edwards's faction in preparty Illinois politics.[27] In chapter 6, Ford neglects to acknowledge his role as defense counsel in the 1833 impeachment trial of Supreme Court Justice T. W. Smith, a partisan judge whom Ford later describes as "an active, bustling, ambitious and turbulent member of the Democratic party" who "never lacked a plot to advance himself, or to blow up some other person" (150).[28] And although Ford writes rather disapprovingly in chapter 7 of the Judiciary Act of 1841, a partisan measure in which a Jacksonian legislature punished a previously Whig supreme court for allegedly partisan decisions by packing it with Democrats, he was one of those fortunate Democrats. One would not learn it from reading the *History*, but Ford's elevation to the supreme bench was a consequence of that act.[29]

But these in the end are rather minor matters, however much they may suggest about the personality of Thomas Ford. Much more important in this catalog of omissions is Ford's treatment of vigilante violence against outlaws in Ogle County in 1841 and the trial of the accused mob members that followed the next year (170–72). This episode falls within a longer reflection in the *History* on mob violence in a democratic society, a reflection that begins with a discussion of Elijah Lovejoy's murder at Alton and ends with Ford's first mention of the Mormons. The consideration of Lovejoy is one of the few accounts of his career in Alton that is unsympathetic to the martyr; indeed, it is rather hostile to his friend and earliest biographer Edward Beecher. Both men were guilty, Ford believed, of rendering religion "the mere ally and auxiliary of fanaticism," the governor's definition of abolitionism (164).

He seems to have considered overt antislavery activity as utterly irresponsible in a community that was at best ambivalent about the slavery issue. Ford's thoughts concerning a self-governing populace taking the law into its own hands given sufficient provocation are

worth reading, reflecting as they do a time when constitutional guarantees were perhaps generally less enforceable than at present and
when local communities were considered to be correspondingly more
sovereign (172–73). But what is missing from this account is Ford's
acknowledgment that he himself had presided at the trial of the Ogle
County Regulators, a trial so conducted to suggest that as judge he
was so disgusted with what seemed like outlaw rule that he collud-
ed with members of that unlawful group.[30] That he appeared to be
sympathetic to vigilantes in 1842 under such circumstances will
probably long reinforce the suspicion that despite his protestations
to the contrary, Ford was also quite capable of partisanship against
the Mormons in Hancock County later in the decade. It seems certain, however, that the truth can never be fully known about his intentions during the latter period.

As personal and sectarian passions have diminished over time,
more recent commentators on Ford's *History* have undertaken anal-
yses that incline to be more general or more related to twentieth-century interests. Marvin Meyers, for example, has noted the usefulness
of Ford's *History* to twentieth-century historians of social change in
the Jacksonian era. Meyers found Ford's treatment of positive change
in the state in the 1820s and 1830s, reflected in habits of dress and
the increase in churchgoing, to have been undertaken "with the in-
stincts of a gifted anthropologist" (60–63).[31] Paul Angle and Mark
Neely have also written about Ford as one who depicted the Illinois
political environment that produced Abraham Lincoln. Neely suggests
that Ford's cynical treatment of that environment, and those who
acted in it, was skewed by what Neely views as Ford's political na-
iveté until he was thrust into that arena. Disillusionment followed and
found its way into Ford's *History*, Neely writes, and that disillusionment subsequently induced historians to view Lincoln's early career
in Illinois politics as narrowly partisan, and unprincipled.[32] Angle acknowledges Ford's cynicism, as one must, but he emphasizes the
rarity of Ford's critical stance on American institutions in the nineteenth century. Such a position would be more expected among the
crabby observers who came to these shores from Europe in the first
half of the century, most of whom found little to admire.[33] Angle's
insight is a fruitful one; it suggests some more global and less specific considerations of Ford's *History*.

Most nineteenth-century American writers were simply laudatory
about the nation's people and institutions or those of the individual
states. But Ford's style and substance carry a muckraking modernity
that makes the *History* seem utterly out of place in premodern Illinois

or America. The book is full of readily quotable one-liners that are frequently caustic about the state's politics; in the end, Ford's book is a political history written by one acutely aware of the social bases of political behavior. And this is not surprising. Although Ford's active political career was brief, he knew politicians well and had taken the measure of many while in the state's judiciary. Furthermore, his mentor was his politically ambitious half-brother, whom he worshiped; more mundanely, he tells us in his Preface that he attended every session of the General Assembly between 1825 and 1847. In addition, one as astute as he would be especially sensitive to the significance of the experiment in popular government in which he and other Americans were participating in the nineteenth century.

Thomas Schwartz has suggested how widespread was the concern for civic responsibility and the preservation of republican institutions among participants in small-town debating societies in nineteenth-century America.[34] We must presume that concern to have been shared by Ford, if not eloquently stated in the *History* in the style that Ford's younger acquaintance, Abraham Lincoln, was later to perfect. However Ford was also a provincial, limited by location and circumstance. We do not know that he ever traveled east of Cincinnati after coming to Illinois in his extreme youth, and he was essentially self-taught. We cannot, therefore, expect him to render Tocquevillian insights into the problems of politics and society managed by a self-governing people on a new frontier of settlement. But we do Tocqueville no disservice by saying that Ford's reflections were of a similar tendency as those of the discerning Frenchman.

Certain political themes recur in the *History*. Ford reveals his awareness of the uneasy tension between liberty and authority in a democracy in his treatments of mob violence in Madison, Ogle, Hancock, and Massac counties. In each case, to secure public liberty by depriving government of power had led to popular attacks upon life and liberty. In his lengthy and mordant description of the General Assembly's passage of the Internal Improvements Act of 1837, he meditates upon the legislature's apparent surrender to putative popular instruction (122–29). He says of lawmakers who either opposed the act or approved it against their better judgment, "A public man will scarcely ever be forgiven for being right when the people are wrong" (132). The death of Elijah Lovejoy also afforded the governor an opportunity to discuss minority rights and their safety from the majority will however much he personally disapproved of Lovejoy: "Men engaged in unpopular projects expect more protection from the laws than the laws are able to furnish in the face of a popular excitement" he wrote rather sadly in this connection (173). From his experience in Hancock County and (less visibly in the *History*) Ogle County, Ford knew all too well the baneful impact of vigilantism and a politicized militia and court system. He also ensures that readers are conscious of the feeble authority given the executive by the 1818 constitution, although that weakness, ironically, would be somewhat rectified by the convention that drew up a new constitution the year the governor left office, seven years before the *History*'s publication.[35]

Ford thought that a government could be no better than the people who were governed by it: "Indifferent, selfish and ignorant people will be known by selfish and corrupt politicians" (59). He was appalled at the influence that groups of tough "butcher-knife boys" had wielded over some Illinois elections. But he also saw the possibility of people moving out of this benightedness and by implication becoming more fit to exercise the privileges of liberty. Indeed, in Ford's view this had begun to happen in the state as early as the 1820s and 1830s. Ford also professed a cheerful contempt for the General Assembly, which was made up of members constantly taking the public pulse and preoccupied with being reelected. Fickle if potentially educable, as Ford considered the electorate to be, and responsive, as the legislature tried to be to that fickle electorate, Ford saw the General Assembly as "a great fire in the boundless prairies of the State; it consumed everything. And again, it was like the genial breath of Spring, making all things new" (16). But he more than once suggests a remedy for legislative inconstancy. He thought that political parties should be more principled and better disciplined than parties in the state actually were and, by implication, less toadying to popular whim. "They cannot be very far from wrong if they disagree to everything proposed by their adversaries," he observed of parties. "It is safest for the minority to compel the majority to take the undivided responsibility of government," thus ensuring that a countervailing interest group would always be available to expose the inadequacies and blunders of those who governed (116, 155). In short, Ford was critical of Illinois—and American—politics and politicians but did not despair about them. His critique of the state's mechanisms of self-government was well considered and derived from more than "a tenderfoot's pique at the methods of state legislators."[36] Furthermore, it simply did not occur to him to suggest alternative political systems.

To an astonishing degree, then, Thomas Ford's *History of Illinois* touches on the major topics of the early statehood history of Illinois and on many of the larger issues that the nation faced at the same time. That it deals with matters still deemed vital, involving popular self-government, entitles it to be considered a minor classic, however opinionated or partial the author's treatment of those matters might be. We should not be surprised that a man so controversial as governor would produce a comparably controversial book. Readers must certainly make allowances for the author's position, his intentions, or even his authority to discourse on certain subjects. Ford's *History* must be read as any primary historical source is read—with care. But its stature as the major text for this period in Illinois history remains secure.

A Note on the Text and Annotation

The text of this reprinted volume has been electronically generated through the scanning of the 1945–46 edition of Ford's *History*, which was produced by Milo M. Quaife. The original 1854 edition proved unamenable to electronic reproduction or photoduplication. The text has been further altered by the restoration of material on six pages that appeared in the first printing of the 1854 edition, with the changes made in the second printing relegated to footnotes. It has seemed that this restored material brings readers closer to Ford's original manuscript.

Notes are of three types: Ford's own footnotes, which are designated by asterisks at the end of the appropriate paragraphs; some notes from Quaife's edition, which have been carried over to this edition as endnotes; and notes that I have generated. Quaife's notes are identified as his; those with no authorial identification are mine.

I have not identified all the persons Ford mentions because there are literally hundreds of them. The intention that governs this annotation has been to explain and amplify, and occasionally correct, instances where it has seemed to me that Ford's text required such treatment. I have chosen to identify persons only when Ford's indication is partial or when he has seemed disposed to conceal identity. That I found rather few instances requiring annotation according to these criteria is probably a tribute to Ford's accuracy and comprehensiveness, although I acknowledge that it can also reflect less than total acuity on my part. The notes by Milo Quaife that I have retained seem also to meet these qualifications. The long chapter headings on the Contents pages are based on Ford's headings in the 1854 edition, but the chapter titles originated with Milo Quaife in his 1945–46 version. The index is based on that in Quaife's 1945 edition; the original edition contained no index.

NOTES

1. Ford's friend William B. Ogden had unsuccessfully lobbied for Ford's appointment as master of the Illinois and Michigan Canal in the Fifteenth General Assembly. Ford to Ogden, February 8, 1847, William B. Ogden Papers, Chicago Historical Society. The quotation is from the Alton *Telegraph*, November 13, 1850.

2. *Weekly Chicago Democrat*, November 13, 1850; Belleville *Republican*, November 13, 1850; *Illinois Daily Journal* (Springfield), February 4, 1851, January 4, 1853, May 29, 1853; David McCulloch, "Governor Thomas Ford," in *Historical Encyclopedia of Illinois and History of Peoria County* (Chicago, 1902), 453; Illinois *House Journal*, 1851, 155–56; Illinois *Senate Journal*, 1851, 190–91. The General Assembly created Ford County, on the Grand Prairie, in 1859 and saw to the erection of another monument in Peoria in 1895.

3. McCulloch, "Governor Thomas Ford," 451. This sketch is based on Ford's brief autobiography. See also Charles Ballance, *History of Peoria* (Peoria, 1870), 246–47, and Edwin C. McReynolds, *Missouri: A Brief History of the Crossroads State* (Norman, 1962), 27–28.

A useful biographical sketch of Thomas Ford is in Robert P. Howard, *Mostly Good and Competent Men: Illinois Governors, 1818–1988* (Springfield, 1988), 79–88. An earlier one by Milo Quaife in Thomas Ford, *A History of Illinois*, 2 vols. (Chicago, 1945–46), 1:xv–xliii, is inadequate in some particulars.

4. John Reynolds, *My Own Times* (Chicago, 1879), 374; John Francis Snyder, "Governor Ford and His Family," *Journal of the Illinois State Historical Society* 3 (1910): 46; McCulloch, "Governor Thomas Ford," 451–52; Ballance, *History of Peoria*, 249.

5. John Francis Snyder, "The Two Sons of Governor Ford," typescript in John Francis Snyder Collection, Illinois State Historical Library, Springfield.

6. Douglas C. McMurtrie, "The First Printers of Illinois," *Journal of the Illinois State Historical Society* 26 (1933): 217.

7. James V. Gale Journal, typescript at the Oregon, Illinois, Public Library, 3–4, 7–8, 105–6; Henry R. Boss, *Sketches of the History of Ogle County* (Polo, 1859), 55; John Wentworth, "Early Chicago," *Fergus Historical Series* 7 (1876): 40, 56.

8. Jeriah Bonham, *Fifty Years' Recollections* (Peoria, 1883), 61–62; Reynolds, *My Own Times*, 376–77; Wentworth, "Early Chicago," 39; Snyder, "Governor Ford and His Family," 48–49.

9. Ballance, *History of Peoria*, 250–51, 254–55; Snyder, "Governor Ford and His Family," 48–49. The quotation is from Snyder.

10. "Death of Governor Ford's Daughter," *Journal of the Illinois State Historical Society* 3 (1910): 105–6; Snyder, "Governor Ford and His Family," 50–51; Snyder, "The Two Sons of Governor Ford."

11. [James Wellington] Norris and [George W.] Gardner, eds., *Illinois Annual Register and Western Business Directory* (Chicago, 1847), 5; Thomas Ford, *A History of Illinois* (Chicago, 1854), 148. The *Western Citizen* (Chicago) announced the proposed publication of Ford's history by Samuel H. Davis of Peoria, on May 4, 1847, and on July 1, 1847, Ford applied for a copyright for a book with the following daunting and yet defining title: *The State of Illinois, its Government, public men and people, with many amusing anecdotes of the early settlers; an account of the progress of society, public opinion, law, religion, politics and legislation, factions and political parties, from the year 1818, until December 1847; embracing a complete history of the Indian Wars in the State, a history of numerous mobs and of the Mormons and Mormon disturbances, and a running commentary upon the whole, showing the practical operation of Free Government in a newly settled country, by Thomas Ford, Esq., late Governor of the State.* See Douglas C. McMurtrie, *Early Illinois Copyright Entries, 1821–1850* (Evanston, 1943), 16–17. I am grateful to Terence Tanner for calling the last two references to my attention. His bibliographical assistance on this project has been invaluable.

12. "Death of Governor Ford's Daughter," 102–6. Milo Quaife doubted this story in 1945. See Ford, *History of Illinois*, ed. Quaife, 1:xxxix. No suppressed manuscript pages survive in existing collections of Shields materials in or outside Illinois. It is my opinion that the *History* simply holds together too well to have been so barbarously edited. Tanner argues that the delay arose from Shields's difficulty in finding a publisher willing to take the book on speculation. Terence A. Tanner, "Non-Periodical Printing in Illinois, 1814–1858," read at the Illinois Historical Symposium in Springfield, December 5, 1992.

13. Chicago *Democrat*, December 10, 1850; *Illinois Daily Journal* (Springfield), January 15, 1851, August 9, August 13, October 1, 1853, January 30, 1854; Charles Ballance, "Ford's History of Illinois," undated clipping from Peoria *Republican*, Ballance Scrapbook, 229–30, John Ballance Collection, Illinois State Historical Library, Springfield.

14. *Illinois Daily Journal* (Springfield), May 30, 1854; *Illinois Daily Register* (Springfield), May 30, 1854; Quincy *Whig*, June 17, July 19, July 20, 1854; *Weekly Chicago Democrat*, June 24, July 8, 1854.

15. Belleville *Advocate*, November 14, 1850; Reynolds, *My Own Times*, 219, 376–77; John Francis Snyder to Charles Manfred Thompson, March 25, 1911, John Francis Snyder Collection, Illinois State Historical Library, Springfield.

16. John Francis Snyder, *Adam W. Snyder and His Period in Illinois History* (Virginia, Ill., 1906), 402–18. See also Snyder, "Governor Ford and His Family," 45–51.

17. A compilation of the letters and editorials comprising this unedifying dialogue is in Clarence W. Alvord, "Governor Edward Coles," *Collections of the Illinois State Historical Library* 15 (1920): 310–64.

18. Peter Parkinson, Jr., "Strictures upon Ford's Black Hawk War,"

Wisconsin Historical Collections 2 (1856): 393–401; Charles Bracken, "More Strictures on Ford's Black Hawk War," *Wisconsin Historical Collections* 2 (1856): 402–13.

19. *Weekly Chicago Democrat,* July 8, 1854. Although Wentworth was away serving in Congress, the interval between publication and the *Democrat's* review of Ford's book suggests that he may have written the review. In later years, Wentworth professed to have been on cordial terms with Ford. See his "Early Chicago," 39–40.

The best secondary account of Ford's administration is in Evarts B. Greene and Charles M. Thompson, "Governors' Letter-Books, 1840–1853," *Collections of the Illinois State Historical Library* 7 (1911): xxix–cxvii. See also Daniel J. Elazar, "Gubernatorial Power and the Illinois and Michigan Canal," *Journal of the Illinois State Historical Society* 58 (1965): 415–16, 421–23.

20. Ford's final message to the General Assembly, December 7, 1846, in Illinois *Senate Journal,* 1846–47, 1–3.

21. Thomas Gregg, *History of Hancock County* (Chicago, 1880), 296–378; Joseph Smith, *History of the Church of Jesus Christ of Latter-Day Saints,* ed. Brigham H. Roberts, 7 vols. (Salt Lake City, 1902–12), vol. 6, chaps. 20–35, vol. 7, parts 1–4. The Gregg quotation is from 320.

22. Gregg, *History of Hancock County,* 372; Roberts, *History of the Church of Jesus Christ of Latter-Day Saints,* 7:94. The anecdote is not mentioned in Ford's *History.*

23. Roberts, *History of the Church of Jesus Christ of Latter-Day Saints,* 6:588–90; 7:18–29, 113–16. The first citation from volume 7 is a long quotation from Ford's *History* with footnote commentary by the editor; the second is from John Taylor's reminiscences.

24. Thomas Ford to "Dear Sir" (apparently a non-Mormon citizen of Hancock County), January 29, 1844, Mormon Collection, Chicago Historical Society.

25. Keith Huntress's article, "Governor Thomas Ford and the Murderers of Joseph Smith," *Dialogue* 4 (1969): 40–52, seems to have made a difference in this respect. Huntress understands Ford's main concern to have been the prevention of a civil war in Hancock County, rather than immediately with the Smiths. Harold Schindler, *Orrin Porter Rockwell: Man of God, Son of Thunder* (Salt Lake City, 1966), 134–35, cites the Rockwell affidavit and presumes Ford's connivance with Smith's assassins. Two more recent volumes by Latter Day Saint historians do not make such a presumption and are more inclined to be understanding of Ford; see Dallin H. Oaks and Marvin S. Hill, *Carthage Conspiracy: The Trial of the Accused Assassins of Joseph Smith* (Urbana, 1975), 30–42, and Donna Hill, *Joseph Smith, the First Mormon* (New York, 1977), 405–20. Furthermore, Richard D. Poll acknowledges that Joseph Smith's *History* "does not stand in the same light with historians as it did when B. H. Roberts and his contemporaries based their volumes upon it." See his "Nauvoo and the New Mormon History," *Journal of Mormon History* 6 (1978): 108.

26. See, for example, Simeon Francis to John J. Hardin, December 8, 1844, Hardin Family Collection, Chicago Historical Society; David Davis to F. W. Rockwell, December 17, 1845, David Davis Papers, Chicago Historical Society; Joseph Gillespie, "Recollections of Early Illinois and Her Noted Men," *Fergus Historical Series* 3 (1880): 26; Snyder, "Governor Ford and His Family," 45–49; Ballance, *History of Peoria*, 250–55.

27. George Forquer to Ninian Edwards, December 1, 1829, March 18, 1830, June 17, 1830, Ninian Edwards Papers, Chicago Historical Society.

28. Illinois *Senate Journal*, 1832–33, Appendix 71–91. Ford delivered the closing argument in behalf of Smith, which was later published as a twenty-page pamphlet, "Speech of Thomas Ford, in Defence of the Hon. Theophilus W. Smith, before the Senate of Illinois, Sitting as a Court of Impeachment, January 29 and 30, 1833."

29. Arnold Shankman, "Partisan Conflicts, 1839–1841, and the Illinois Constitution," *Journal of the Illinois State Historical Society* 63 (1970): 337–67.

30. Rodney O. Davis, "Judge Ford and the Regulators, 1841–1842," *Selected Papers in Illinois History* (1981): 25–36.

31. Marvin Meyers, *The Jacksonian Persuasion: Politics and Belief* (New York, 1960), 4, 131–32. The quotation is from 131.

32. Mark Neely, "A Great Fraud?: Politics in Thomas Ford's *History of Illinois,*" *Lincoln Lore* (September 1978): 1–4.

33. Paul M. Angle, "The Illinois Bookshelf," *Journal of the Illinois State Historical Society* 38 (1945): 99–104.

34. Thomas F. Schwartz, "The Springfield Lyceum and Lincoln's 1838 Speech," *Illinois Historical Journal* 83 (1990): 45–49.

35. Emil Joseph Verlie, ed., "Illinois Constitutions," *Collections of the Illinois State Historical Library* 13 (1919): Article IV, 66–67; Arthur Charles Cole, ed., "The Constitutional Debates of 1847," *Collections of the Illinois State Historical Library* 14 (1919): 404–42.

36. Neely, "A Great Fraud?" 4.

A History of Illinois

Introduction

General James Shields

In 1850 while the author of this work was on his death-bed he placed in my hands a manuscript, with the contents of which I was then wholly unacquainted, with the injunction that after his decease I should have it published for the benefit of his family. He soon after departed this life, leaving his orphan children in a destitute condition.

In compliance with his dying request I made repeated efforts to have the work published on terms that might secure some percentage to the orphans, but until my arrangements with the present publishers all these efforts proved unsuccessful. By this arrangement the children will receive a liberal percentage on the sales of the work.

The author during his whole life had very favorable opportunities for observing events and collecting information connected with the history of his State. He was yet a child when his parents emigrated to Illinois. On arriving at maturity he was there admitted to the bar, and practised his profession for many years with very considerable success. He was afterwards elected an Associate Justice of the Supreme Court of the State and discharged the duties of that responsible station with distinguished ability. Subsequently he was chosen Governor of the State, which was the last public office he held. From this office he retired to private life, and during his retirement prepared this history for publication. His opinions of men and measures are very freely and unreservedly expressed; but they may be regarded as the opinions of a man of strong feelings, who took such an active part in many of the scenes which he represents that it was impossible for him to describe them with ordinary moderation.

I regret the severity of some of the author's judgments and the censure with which he assails the character of some of our public men who are both my personal and political friends; but I feel it to be incumbent upon me by the very nature and circumstances of the trust not only to have the work published according to his injunction, for the purpose intended by him, but also to abstain from making any alteration in the text. I therefore give it to the public just as

I received it from the hands of the author and with the sincere hope, for the sake of his destitute children, that it may meet with an indulgent and generous reception.

Washington, Feb. 3d, 1854

Preface

To the Public

The author of this history has lived in Illinois from the year 1804 up to this time; he attended the first session of the Legislature under the State government at Kaskaskia in 1818–'19; and has been present at every session from 1825 up to 1847. He has not only had the means of becoming acquainted with events and results, but with the characters and motives of those who were the most active in bringing them about, which is the hidden soul and most instructive part of history. The events of such a government as that of Illinois and the men of its history must necessarily be matters of small interest in themselves. But the author has been encouraged to give some account of them by remembering that history is only philosophy teaching by examples; and may, possibly, teach by small as well as large ones. Observation of the curious habits of small insects has thrown its light upon science, as much as the dissection of the elephant. Therefore, if any one is curious to see what very great things may be illustrated by very small matters this book will give him some aid.

The author has written about small events and little men for two reasons: first, there was nothing else in the history of Illinois to write about; secondly, these small matters seemed best calculated to illustrate what he wanted to promulgate to the people. The historical events and personages herein recorded and described are related and delineated gravely and truthfully; and by no means in a style of exaggeration, caricature, or romance, after the fashion of Knickerbocker's amusing history of New York; but like a tale of romance they are merely made a kind of thread upon which to string the author's speculations; being his real, true, and genuine views, entertained as a man, not as a politician, concerning the practical operation of republican government and the machinery of party in the new States of the West. He has not ventured to call his book a *history* for the reason that much heavy lumbering matter necessary to constitute it a complete history, but of no interest to the general reader, has been omitted. Indeed, every history is apt to contain much matter not only tiresome to read but mischievous to be remembered; and it is often the unprofitable task of the antiquarian to busy himself in raking and carefully saving from oblivion some stupid or mischievous piece of knowledge which the good sense of the contemporary generation of mankind had made them forget.

The account of our very unimportant mobs and wars, and particularly the Mormon wars—in which the author had the misfortune to figure in a small way himself—is here introduced with the single remark that little events are recorded with a minuteness and particularity which, it is hoped, will not tire, but will certainly astonish the reader, until he sees the great principles which they illustrate. The author has earnestly endeavored to be as faithful and impartial as he well could, considering that he was himself an actor in some of the scenes described. For the history of the last four years, embracing the term of his own administration of the State government, the most difficult period of our history, he must bespeak some forbearance. The internal improvement system, the banks, the great plenty of money, had made every one morally drunk. The failure of all these brought about a sobering process, which just began when the author came into office. The different modes of relief for unparalleled calamity, brought about by unparalleled folly, which were proposed; the hideous doctrine of repudiation, and its opposite of increasing the taxes to pay our just debts; the everlasting intrigues of politicians with the Mormons; the serious disturbances and mobs which these led to; and the strife between the north and the south about the canal, and their contests for power, were difficult subjects to deal with. The author aimed to act positively, and not negatively, in all these matters, which brought him into fierce collision with many prominent men. He will go down to the grave satisfied in his own mind that he was right, and they wrong; and therefore it may be that he has not spoken so flatteringly of some of them as they may have wished. But he has set nothing down in malice. It is believed that many public men in Illinois aim to succeed only for the present, and have acted their parts with no idea of being responsible to history; and of course they have acted much worse than they would have done had they dreamed that history some time or other would record their selfish projects and hand them down to another age. They were encouraged by their insignificance to hope for oblivion; and it is, perhaps, after all, not very fair to take them by surprise by recording their miserable conduct, giving a small immortality to their littleness.

In all those matters in which the author has figured personally it will be some relief to the reader to find that he has not attempted to blow himself up into a great man. He has no vanity of that sort; and no one thinks more humbly of him than he does of himself. If he has been solicitous about anything concerning himself it has been to be considered "a well-meaning sort of person;" though he knows that this, of all others, is the most uncommon character in public life, and is the most despised by your men of rampant ambition. Insignificant as he may be, yet during his public life many volumes of billingsgate in the newspaper style have been written against him; but he has all the time had the satisfaction of knowing his own errors and imperfections better than did his revilers. And, like an Indian warrior about to be tortured, he could have pointed out vulnerable places and modes of infliction which even the active, keen eye of malice itself failed to discover. He has effectually abandoned all aim to succeed in public life in the future, having learned by long experience that in the pursuit of public honors "the play is not worth the candle." He will therefore but little regard malicious criticisms which may be the effect of the remains of bad feelings excited by former contests; being assured that no such criticisms can in any wise affect injuriously any of his plans for the future.

Peoria, Illinois, April 12, 1847

I

The Achievement of Statehood, 1818–1821

In the month of January, 1818 a petition was received from the territorial Legislature of Illinois by Nathaniel Pope, the delegate in Congress (now district judge) praying for the admission of the territory into the Union as an independent State. Judge Pope immediately brought the subject before Congress; and at an early day thereafter was instructed by the proper committee to report a bill in pursuance of the petition. Owing to the great amount of business which had matured, this bill was not acted on until the month of April, when it became a law, with certain amendments proposed by Judge Pope. The amendments were, 1st, to extend the northern boundary of the new State to the parallel of 42° 30' north latitude; and, 2d, to apply the three per cent. fund arising from the sales of the public lands to the encouragement of learning, instead of the making of roads leading to the State, as had been the case on the admission of Ohio and Indiana. These important changes were proposed and carried through both houses of Congress by Judge Pope upon his own responsibility. The territorial Legislature had not petitioned for them; no one at that time having suggested or requested the making of them; but they met the unqualified approbation of the people of Illinois.

By the Ordinance of 1787 there were to be not less than three nor more than five States in the territory north-west of the Ohio river. The boundaries of these States were defined by that law. The three States of Ohio, Indiana, and Illinois were to include the whole territory, and were to be bounded by the British possessions in Canada on the north. But Congress reserved the power, if they thereafter should find it expedient, to form one or two States in that part of the territory which lies north of an east and west line drawn through the southerly bend of Lake Michigan. That line, it was generally supposed, was to be the north boundary of Illinois. Judge Pope, seeing that the port of Chicago was north of that line and would be excluded by it from the State; and that the Illinois and Michigan canal (which was then contemplated) would issue from Chicago to connect the great northern lakes with the Mississippi, and thus be partly within and partly without the State of Illinois, was thereby led to a critical examination of the Ordinance, which resulted in a clear and satisfactory conviction that it was competent for Congress to extend the boundaries of the new State as far north as they pleased; and he found no difficulty in convincing others of the correctness of his views.

As it is now understood that the new State of Wisconsin puts in a claim under the Ordinance to the fourteen northern counties in Illinois, embracing the richest and most populous part of the State, it may be worth while to examine a little whether Judge Pope and the Congress of 1818 were right in their conclusions.

It appears that Congress retained the power under the Ordinance, if they should thereafter deem it expedient, to establish a State north of Illinois in that part of the north-western territory which lies north of the parallel running through the southern bend of the Lake.[1] Upon this provision is founded the claim of Wisconsin. But there is nothing in the Ordinance requiring such additional State to be formed *of* the territory north of that line. Another State might be formed *in* that district of country, but not *of* it; it need not necessarily include the whole. By extending the limits of Illinois north of the disputed line, Congress still had the power to make a new State *in* that district of country north of it, not including the portion given to Illinois. But the fallacy of the claim for Wisconsin is further apparent from the facts that the Ordinance established the northern limits of Illinois to extend to the British possessions in Canada, in other words, to the northern boundary of the United States; that the creation of a new State north of it was made to depend upon the subsequent discretion of Congress, and upon their ideas of expediency. Undoubtedly, Illinois could have been limited to the southern bend of Lake Michigan. But Congress has never as yet established that line; but, on the contrary, has established one upwards of fifty miles north of it, which line so established by Congress the people of Wisconsin say is void, as being against the Ordinance. If we take the ground assumed by Wisconsin as the true one, and admit that the line of 42° 30' is void, as being against the Ordinance, then it is plain that there is no northern limit to Illinois except the British possessions in Canada; thus making Illinois include all Wisconsin. If the people of Wisconsin can show that the line of 42° 30' is void, they do not establish any other; their line was not established by the Ordinance; that law merely authorized Congress to establish it if they saw proper and deemed it expedient. But Congress has never deemed it expedient to establish it. If, therefore, the only line which Congress ever did establish is void, then Illinois cannot be limited by a line which has never been established, but must extend to the northern boundary of the Union, including all Wisconsin. Premises from which such arguments can fairly be drawn must necessarily be suicidal to the claim of the new State of Wisconsin, as they inevitably result in its annihilation, and in extending the jurisdiction of Illinois over the whole of its territory.

But there were other and much more weighty reasons for this change of boundary which were ably and successfully urged by Judge Pope upon the attention of Congress. It was known that in all confederated republics there was danger of dissolution. The great valley of the Mississippi was filling up with a numerous people; the original confederacy had already advanced westward a thousand miles across the chain of mountains skirting the Atlantic; the adjoining States in the western country were watered by rivers running from every point of the compass, converging to a focus at the confluence of the Ohio and Mississippi at Cairo; the waters of the Ohio, Cumberland and Tennessee rivers carried much of the commerce of Alabama and Tennessee, all of Kentucky, considerable portions of that of Virginia, Pennsylvania, and New York; and the greater portion of the commerce of Ohio and Indiana, down by the Point at Cairo (situate in the extreme south of Illinois) where it would be met by the commerce to and from the lower Mississippi with all the States and territories to be formed in the immense country on the Missouri, and extending to the head waters of the Mississippi. Illinois had a coast of 150 miles on the Ohio river and nearly as much on the Wabash; the Mississippi was its western boundary for the whole length of the State; the commerce of all the western country was to pass by its shores, and would necessarily come to a focus at the mouth of the Ohio, at a point within this State and within the control of Illinois, if, the Union being dissolved, she should see proper to control it. It was foreseen that none of the great States in the west could venture to aid in dissolving the Union without cultivating a State situate in such a central and commanding position.

What then was the duty of the national government? Illinois was certain to be a great State with any boundaries which that government could give. Its great extent of territory, its unrivalled fertility of soil and capacity for sustaining a dense population, together with its commanding position, would in course of time give the new State a very controlling influence with her sister States situate upon the western rivers, either in sustaining the federal union as it is, or in dissolving it and establishing new governments. If left entirely upon the waters of these great rivers, it was plain that in case of threatened disruption the interest of the new State would be to join a southern and western confederacy. But if a large portion of it could be made dependent upon the commerce and navigation of the great northern lakes, connected as they are with the eastern States, a rival interest would be created to check the wish for a western and southern confederacy.

It therefore became the duty of the national government not only to make Illinois strong, but to raise an interest inclining and binding her to the eastern and northern portions of the Union. This could be done only through an interest in the lakes. At that time the commerce on the lakes was small, but its increase was confidently expected, and indeed it has exceeded all anticipations, and is yet only in its infancy. To accomplish this object effectually it was not only necessary to give to Illinois the port of Chicago and a route for the canal, but a considerable coast on Lake Michigan, with a country back of it sufficiently extensive to contain a population capable of exercising a decided influence upon the councils of the State.

There would, therefore, be a large commerce of the north, western, and central portions of the State afloat on the lakes, for it was then foreseen that the canal would be made; and this alone would be like turning one of the many mouths of the Mississippi into Lake Michigan at Chicago. A very large commerce of the centre and south would be found both upon the lakes and the rivers. Associations in business, in interest, and of friendship would be formed, both with the north and the south. A State thus situated, having such a decided interest in the commerce and in the preservation of the whole confederacy, can never consent to disunion; for the Union cannot be dissolved without a division and disruption of the State itself. These views, urged by Judge Pope, obtained the unqualified assent of the statesmen of 1818; and this feature of the bill for the admission of Illinois into the Union met the unanimous approbation of both houses of Congress.

These facts and views are worthy to be recorded in history as a standing and perpetual call upon Illinoisians of every age to remember the great trust which has been reposed in them as the peculiar champions and guardians of the Union by the great men and patriot sages who adorned and governed this country in the earlier and better days of the republic.

In pursuance of this Act of Congress a Convention was called in Illinois in the summer of 1818 which formed our present Constitution. The principal member of it was Elias K. Kane, late a senator in Congress and now deceased, to whose talents we are mostly indebted for the peculiar features of the Constitution. Mr. Kane was born in the State of New York and was bred to the profession of the law.

He removed in early youth to Tennessee, where he rambled about for some time, and finally settled in the ancient village of Kaskaskia in Illinois about the year 1815, when he was about twenty years of age. His talents were both solid and brilliant. After being appointed Secretary of State under the new government he was elected to the Legislature, from which he was elected and again re-elected to the United States Senate. He died a member of that body in the autumn of 1835; and in memory of him the County of Kane on Fox river was named, as was also the County of Pope on the Ohio river in honor of Judge Pope, the able and faithful delegate in Congress from the Illinois territory. During the sitting of the Convention of 1818 the Reverend Mr. Wiley and his congregation, of a sect called Covenanters, in Randolph county, sent in their petition asking that body to declare in the Constitution about to be made that "Jesus Christ was the head of the government, and that the Holy Scriptures were the only rule of faith and practice." It does not appear by the journals of the Convention that this petition was treated with any attention; wherefore the Covenanters have never yet fully recognized the State government. They have looked upon it as "an heathen and unbaptized government" which denies Christ; for which reason they have constantly refused to work the roads under the laws, serve on juries, hold any office, or do any other act showing that they recognize the government. For a long time they refused to vote at the elections; and never did vote until the election in 1824, when the question was, whether Illinois should be made a slave State, when they voted for the first time and unanimously against slavery. In the election of members to the Convention the only questions made before the people were, the right of the constituent to instruct his representative, and the introduction of slavery, which were debated with great earnestness during the canvass.

The Constitution as formed required the Governor and Lieutenant Governor to have been citizens of the United States for thirty years before their election. It also gave power to the governor to nominate, and the Senate to confirm, all officers whose appointments were not otherwise provided for by the Constitution; the only exceptions to this rule being the judges of the supreme and inferior courts, State treasurer, and public printer. But motives of favor to particular persons who were looked to to hold office under the new government induced the Convention to make exceptions in both these cases, which in the case of appointments to office in the hands of the legislature became the general rule.

Col. Pierre Menard, a Frenchman and an old settler in the country, was generally looked to to fill the office of lieutenant governor; but as he had not been naturalized until a year or so before, the Convention declared in a schedule to the Constitution that any citizen of the United States who had resided in the State for two years might be eligible to this office.

It was expected that Shadrach Bond would be the first governor; and the Convention wished to have Elijah C. Berry for the first auditor of public accounts, but as it was believed that Governor Bond would not appoint him to the office, the Convention again declared in the schedule that "an auditor of public accounts, an attorney general, and such other officers of the State as may be necessary, may be appointed by the General Assembly." The Constitution as it stood vested a very large appointing power in the governor; but for the purpose of getting one man into office a total change was made, and the power vested in the legislature. It was for many years a question what was an "officer of the State." Were States' attorneys of the circuits? Were the canal commissioners officers for the State? The legislature afterwards decided that all these were State offices and passed laws from time to time vesting in their own body all the appointing powers they could lay their hands on. In this mode they appointed canal commissioners, fund commissioners, commissioners of the board of public works, bank directors for the principal banks and branches, canal agents, States' attorneys, and all sorts of agencies which seemed to be necessary. Sometimes such agents were appointed by election, then again the legislature would pass a law enacting them into office by name and surname. They contrived to strip the governor of all patronage not positively secured to him by the Constitution; such as the appointment of a secretary of State, and the filling of vacancies during the recess of their sessions. At first the legislature contented themselves with the power to elect an auditor and attorney general. The governor appointed all the States' attorneys, the recorders of counties, all State officers and agents occasionally needed, and many minor county officers. But in the administration of Governor Duncan he was finally stripped of all patronage except the appointment of notaries public and public administrators. Sometimes one legislature, feeling pleased with the governor, would give him some appointing power which their successors would take away if they happened to quarrel with him. This constant changing and shifting of powers from one co-ordinate branch of the government to another, which rendered it impossible for the people to foresee exactly for what purpose either the governor or legislature were elected, was one of the worst features of the government. It led to innumerable intrigues and corruptions, and for a long time destroyed the harmony between the executive and legislative departments. And all this was caused by the Convention of 1818, in the attempt to get one man into an office of no very considerable importance.

According to general expectation, Shadrach Bond was elected the first governor, and commenced his term of four years in October, 1818. Governor Bond was a native of Maryland, was bred a farmer, and was a very early settler amongst the pioneers of the Illinois territory. He settled on a farm in the American Bottom, in Monroe County, near the Eagle Creek. He was several times elected to the territorial legislature, and once a delegate to represent the territory in Congress. He was also receiver of public moneys at Kaskaskia, but was never elected or appointed to any other office after his term as governor. Indeed, of the seven first governors of Illinois only one has ever held any office since the expiration of their respective terms of service; though I believe they have all, except myself, tried to obtain some other office. Governor Bond was a substantial, farmerlike man, of strong, plain common sense, with but little pretensions to learning or general information. He was a well-made, well-set, sturdy gentleman, and what is remarkable at this day his first message to the legislature contains a strong recommendation in favor of the Illinois and Michigan canal. At that early day the people north of Kaskaskia, then the seat of government, were northern people, and in favor of northern interests. The inhabited parts of the State then extended north a little above Alton; and at that time the people of Randolph, Monroe, St. Clair and Madison, then northern but now southern counties, were as anxious for the canal as the people of Lasalle have been since. In like manner when the seat of government was removed, first to Vandalia and afterwards to Springfield, the people north of those places, respectively, whilst the seat of government remained at them, were in favor of the canal and northern interests; but the northern men between Springfield and Vandalia were immediately converted into Southerners, and most of them ever afterwards opposed the canal. It seems that an imaginary east and west line will, in the imagination of politicians, be drawn through the seat of government, and all north of it will be north and all south of it will be south, with some trifling exceptions. Governor Bond died about the year 1834; and for him was named the county of Bond, lying on the waters of Shoal Creek.

The legislature was convened at Kaskaskia in October, 1818 and organized the government by the election of Joseph Philips to be chief justice, Thomas C. Brown and John Reynolds and William P. Foster associate justices of the Supreme Court. Judges Brown and Reynolds will be spoken of hereafter. Philips had been a captain in the regular army and was afterwards appointed secretary of State of the territory; and being a lawyer and a man of high order of talent, was therefore elected chief justice. Being afterwards a candidate for governor and defeated, he left the State in such disgust as defeat is apt to inspire and went to reside in Tennessee, where he is yet alive. Foster, who was elected one of the judges, was almost a total stranger in the country. He was a great rascal but no one knew it then, he having been a citizen of the State only for about three weeks before he was elected. He was no lawyer, never having either studied or practised law; but he was a man of winning, polished manners, and was withal a very gentlemanly swindler, from some part of Virginia. It might be said of him, as it was of Lambro, "he was the mildest mannered man that ever scuttled ship or cut a throat, with such true breeding of a gentleman that you never could divine his real thought." He was believed to be a clever fellow in the American sense of the phrase, and a good-hearted soul. He was assigned to hold courts in the circuit on the Wabash; but being fearful of exposing his utter incompetency, he never went near any of them. In the course of one year he resigned his high office, but took care first to pocket his salary, and then removed out of the State. He afterwards became a noted swindler, moving from city to city and living by swindling strangers and prostituting his daughters, who were very beautiful.

Ninian Edwards, now no more, and Jesse B. Thomas, who at this time resides in the State of Ohio, were elected our first senators in Congress. Elias K. Kane was appointed secretary of State, Daniel P. Cook was elected the first attorney general, Elijah C. Berry auditor of public accounts, and John Thomas State treasurer. Under the auspices and guidance of these names was Illinois launched on her career of administration as an independent State of the American Union. Among these gentlemen I will at this time speak of Judge Thomas only. He is first distinctly known when he resided in the territory of Indiana, and was a member of the territorial legislature at the time Indiana territory included all the Illinois country. William Biggs and John Messenger of St. Clair county represented the Illinois country in that legislature, and were desirous to obtain a division of that territory and to erect a separate territorial government for Illinois. The Indiana legislature then met at Vincennes, a town on the Wabash, for which reason it was long afterwards, by the vulgar, known by the name of the *"vinsan legislater;"* and the laws of the territory during that period were called the laws of the "Vinsan legislater." The Illinoisians wanted a legislature of their own to meet at Kaskaskia, then vulgarly known by the name of "Kusky," a corruption and contraction of the real name. Whether the territory could be divided or not depended upon the election of a delegate to Congress. The Illinoisians were anxious to elect one favorable to a division and they selected Mr. Thomas for this purpose. But being determined not to be cheated, they made him give his bond to be in favor of a division. With the aid of the Illinois vote and his own Mr. Thomas had a bare majority and was elected. True to his pledges and his bond, Mr. Thomas procured a division of the territory, the erection of a separate territorial government for Illinois, and came home with the appointment of one of the judgeships of the supreme court of the new territory for himself. Judge Thomas then removed to Illinois, where he continued to be one of the judges during the existence of the territory. He was elected from St. Clair county a member of the Convention which formed the Constitution, and had the honor to be chosen president of that body. He was twice elected to the United States Senate, and in the year 1827 left the State to reside in Ohio. During his senatorial career he was a great favorite with William H. Crawford, the secretary of the treasury, and was a warm advocate of Mr. Crawford's election to the presidency; but after Mr. Adams was declared to be elected by the House of Representatives he came over to the support of Mr. Adams' administration. He was a large, affable, good-looking man, with no talents as a public speaker; but he was a man of tact, an adroit and winning manager. It was a maxim with him that no man could be talked down with loud and bold words, "but any one might be whispered to death."

It appears by the journals of this first legislature that a committee was appointed to contract for stationery, who reported that they had purchased a sufficient stock at the cost of $13.50. For every dollar then paid we now pay hundreds for the same articles; but this was in the days of real frugality and economy, and before any of the members had learned the gentlemanly art of laying in from the public stock a year or two's supply at home. The assembly having organized the State government and put it in motion, adjourned to meet again in the winter of 1818–'19. At this adjourned session a code of statute law was passed, mostly borrowed from the statutes of Kentucky and Virginia. Upon examining the laws of that day it will be seen that they are generally better drawn up than those which were passed at a later and more enlightened period. The members were mostly ignorant and unpretending men; there was then some reverence for men of real knowledge and real abilities; the world was not then filled with audacious and ignorant pretenders; and the sensible and unpretend-ing members were content to look to men of real talents and learn-ing to draw their bills. But in these days of empiricism and quackery in all things, when every ignorant pretender who has the luck to *"break"* into the legislature imagines himself to be a Lycurgus or a Moses, very few good laws have been made; and those which have, were drawn by men of talents who were not members, for the most part.

But this code as a whole did not stand long. For many sessions afterwards, in fact until the new revision in 1827, all the standard laws were regularly changed and altered every two years to suit the taste and whim of every new legislature. For a long time the rage for amending and altering was so great that it was said to be a good thing that the Holy Scriptures did not have to come before the Legislature; for that body would be certain to alter and amend them so that no one could tell what was or was not the word of God, any more than could be told what was or was not the law of the State. A session of the legislature was like a great fire in the boundless prairies of the State; it consumed everything. And again, it was like the genial breath of spring, making all things new.

One of the most remarkable laws of this first code was the act concerning negroes and mulattoes. It is to be observed that the or-dinance of Congress of the year 1787 and the deed of cession of the country from Virginia were interpreted so as to secure the French settlers in a right to their slaves, and the legislatures of the Indiana and Illinois territories had passed laws allowing a qualified introduc-tion of slavery. For instance, it had been enacted that emigrants to the country might bring their slaves with them, and if the slaves, being of lawful age to consent, would go before the clerk of a county and voluntarily sign an indenture to serve their master for a term of years they should be held to a specific performance of their contracts. If they refused to give such consent, their masters might remove them out of the territory in sixty days. The children of such slaves, being under the age of consent, might be taken before an officer and regis-tered; and then they were bound by those laws to serve their mas-ters until they were thirty-two years old. Such slaves were then called indentured and registered servants; the French negroes were called slaves. Many servants and slaves were held under these laws, but the number of negroes was very small compared with the number of the white inhabitants. Nevertheless, this first legislature reenacted in Illinois all the severe and stringent laws to be found in a slave State, where the number of negroes was equal to or greater than the number of white people, and where such severity might be necessary to prevent rebellion and servile war. For instance, it was enacted that no negro or mulatto should reside in the State until he had produced a certificate of freedom and given bond, with security, for good behavior and not to become a county charge. No person was to harbor or hire a negro or mulatto who had not complied with the law, under the penalty of five hundred dollars fine. All such free negroes were to cause their families to be registered. Every negro or mulatto not having a certificate of freedom was to be deemed a runaway slave; was liable to be taken up by any inhabitant; committed by a justice of the peace; imprisoned by the sheriff; advertised; sold for one year; and, if not claimed within that time was to be considered a free man unless his master should afterwards reclaim him. Any person bringing a negro into the State to set him free was liable to a fine of two hundred dollars. Riots, routs, unlawful assemblies, and seditious speeches of slaves were to be punished with stripes, not exceeding thirty-nine, at the discretion of any justice of the peace; also, slaves were to be punished with thirty-five lashes for being found ten miles from home without a pass from their master; also, it was made lawful for the owner of any dwelling or plantation to give or order to be given to any slave or servant coming upon his plantation ten lashes upon his bare back; and persons who should permit slaves and servants to assemble for dancing or revelling, by night or day, were to be fined twenty dollars. It was made the duty of all sheriffs, coroners, judges, and justices of the peace, on view of such an assemblage, to commit the slaves to jail, and to order each one of them to be whipped, not exceeding thirty-nine stripes, on the bare back, to be inflicted the next day unless the same should be Sunday, and then on the next day after. In all cases where free persons were punishable by fine under the criminal laws of the State servants were to be punished by whipping, at the rate of twenty lashes for every eight dollars fine. No person was to buy of, sell to, or trade with a slave or servant, without the consent of his master; and for so doing, was to forfeit four times the value of the article bought, sold, or traded. Lazy and disorderly servants were to be corrected by stripes, on the order of a justice of the peace.

These provisions have been continued in all the revisions of the law since made, and are now the law of the land. It was partly the object of these laws to prevent free negroes from becoming numerous in the State by discouraging their settlement here, and discouraging runaway slaves from coming to Illinois to become free; and when we consider the importance, for the purposes of harmony and good government, of preserving a homogeneous character amongst the people, such an object was a wise one. But for what purpose such severities were denounced against slaves and servants when their numbers were so few that they could not be dangerous can only be conjectured. The most plausible account of the matter may be that as the early legislators were from the slave States; they imported this law, as they did others, without considering its want of application to the condition of the country. In the same manner we find early laws imported from the slave States for the inspection of hemp and tobacco when there was neither hemp nor tobacco raised in the country. And no doubt the feeling and habit of domination over the slave acquired in a slave State and brought by the settlers into a free one had its full share of influence. These laws would have been modified or repealed long ere this if it had not been for the abolition excitement of modern times which has made it dangerous to the popularity of politicians to propose their repeal, since such a proposition might indicate a leaning to that unpopular party. But as it is, the severe points of them are now, and for a long time past have been, a dead letter upon the pages of the statute book, there being no instance, within the memory of the present generation of putting them in force.

This legislature also provided for the removal of the seat of government from the town of Kaskaskia, the ancient seat of empire for more than one hundred and fifty years, both for the French and American inhabitants. Commissioners were appointed to select a new site, who made choice of a place then in the midst of the wilderness, on the Kaskaskia river north-east of the settlements, which they called "Vandalia." After the place had been selected it became a matter of great interest to give it a good sounding name, one which would please the ear and at the same time have the classic merit of perpetuating the memory of the ancient race of Indians by whom the country had first been inhabited. Tradition says that a wag who was present suggested to the commissioners that the "Vandals" were a powerful nation of Indians who once inhabited the banks of the Kaskaskia river, and that "Vandalia," formed from their name, would perpetuate the memory of that extinct but renowned people. The suggestion pleased the commissioners, the name was adopted, and they thus proved that the name of their new city (if they were fit representatives of their constituents) would better illustrate the character of the modern than the ancient inhabitants of the country.

In the year 1818, the whole people numbered about forty-five thousand souls. Some two thousand of these were the descendants of the old French settlers in the villages of Kaskaskia, Prairie Du

Rocher, Prairie Du Pont, Cahokia, Peoria, and Chicago. These people had fields in common for farming, and farmed, built houses, and lived in the style of the peasantry in old France one hundred and fifty years ago. They had made no improvements in anything, nor had they adopted any of the improvements made by others. They were the descendants of those French people who had first settled the country more than one hundred and fifty years before under LaSalle, Ibberville, and the priests Alvarez, Rasles, Gravier, Pinet, Marest, and others, and such as subsequently joined them from New Orleans and Canada; and they now formed all that remained of the once proud empire which Louis XIV., king of France, and the regent Duke of Orleans, had intended to plant in the Illinois country. The original settlers had many of them intermarried with the native Indians, and some of the descendants of these partook of the wild, roving disposition of the savage, united to the politeness and courtesy of the Frenchman. In the year 1818, and for many years before, the crews of keel boats on the Ohio and Mississippi rivers were furnished from the Frenchmen of this stock. Many of them spent a great part of their time in the spring and fall seasons in paddling their canoes up and down the rivers and lakes in the river bottoms on hunting excursions, in pursuit of deer, fur, and wild fowl, and generally returned home well loaded with skins, fur, and feathers, which were with them the great staples of trade. Those who stayed at home contented themselves with cultivating a few acres of Indian corn in their common fields for bread, and providing a supply of prairie hay for their cattle and horses. No genuine Frenchman in those days ever wore a hat, cap, or coat. The heads of both men and women were covered with Madras cotton handkerchiefs which were tied around in the fashion of night-caps. For an upper covering of the body the men wore a blanket garment called a "capot," (pronounced cappo) with a cap to it at the back of the neck, to be drawn over the head for a protection in cold weather, or in warm weather to be thrown back upon the shoulders in the fashion of a cape. Notwithstanding this people had been so long separated by an immense wilderness from civilized society they still retained all the suavity and politeness of their race. And it is a remarkable fact, that the roughest hunter and boatman amongst them could at any time appear in a ballroom or other polite and gay assembly with the carriage and behavior of a well bred gentleman. The French women were remarkable for the sprightliness of their conversation and the grace and elegance of their manners. And the whole population lived lives of alternate toil, pleasure, innocent amusement, and gaiety.

Their horses and cattle, for want of proper care and food for many generations, had degenerated in size, but had acquired additional vigor and toughness; so that a French pony was a proverb for strength and endurance. These ponies were made to draw, sometimes one alone sometimes two together, one hitched before the other to the plough, or to carts made entirely of wood, the bodies of which held about double the contents of the body of a common large wheel-barrow. The oxen were yoked by the horns instead of the neck, and in this mode were made to draw the plough and cart. Nothing like reins were ever used in driving; the whip of the driver, with a handle about two feet, and a lash two yards long, stopped or guided the horse as effectually as the strongest reins.

The French houses were mostly built of hewn timber set upright in the ground or upon plates laid upon a wall, the intervals between the upright pieces being filled with stone and mortar. Scarcely any of them were more than one story high, with a porch on one or two sides and sometimes all around, with low roofs extending with slopes of different steepness from the comb in the centre to the lowest part of the porch. These houses were generally placed in gardens, surrounded by fruit-trees of apples, pears, cherries, and peaches; and in the villages each enclosure for a house and garden occupied a whole block or square, or the greater part of one. Each village had its Catholic church and priest. The church was the great place of gay resort on Sundays and holidays, and the priest was the adviser and director and companion of all his flock. The people looked up to him with affection and reverence, and he upon them with compassion and tenderness. He was ever ready to sympathize with them in all their sorrows, enter into all their joys, and counsel them in all their perplexities. Many good Protestant ministers who stoutly believed these Catholic priests to be the emissaries of Satan would have done well to imitate their simple-hearted goodness to the members of their flocks.

The American inhabitants were chiefly from Kentucky, Virginia, and Pennsylvania. Some of them had been the officers and soldiers under General George Rogers Clark, who conquered the country from the British in 1778 and they, with others who afterwards followed them, maintained their position in the country during the Indian wars in Ohio and Indiana in the times of Harmar, St. Clair, and Wayne. This handful of people, being increased in the whole to about twelve thousand souls by subsequent emigration, with the aid of one company of regular soldiers defended themselves and their settlements during the war of 1812 against the then numerous and powerful nations of the Kickapoos, Sacs and Foxes, Pottawattomies, and Shawnees, and even made hostile expeditions into the heart of their territories, burning their villages and defeating and driving them from the country. In the year 1818 the settled part of the State extended a little north of Edwardsville and Alton; south, along the Mississippi to the mouth of the Ohio; east, in the direction of Carlysle to the Wabash; and down the Wabash and the Ohio, to the mouth of the last-named river. But there was yet a very large unsettled wilderness tract of country within these boundaries, lying between the Kaskaskia river and the Wabash; and between the Kaskaskia and the Ohio, of three days' journey across it. There were no schools in the country except for reading, writing, and arithmetic, and one school for surveying and book-keeping. The lawyers and professional men came from abroad. Preachers of the gospel frequently sprung up from the body of the people at home, without previous training except in religious exercises and in the study of the Holy Scriptures. In those primitive times it was not thought to be necessary that a teacher of religion should be a scholar. It was thought to be his business to preach from a knowledge of the Scriptures alone, to make appeals warm from the heart, to paint heaven and hell to the imagination of the sinner, to terrify him with the one and to promise the other as a reward for a life of righteousness. However ignorant these first preachers may have been, they could be at no loss to find congregations still more ignorant, so that they were still capable of instructing some one. Many of them added to their knowledge of the Bible a diligent perusal of Young's Night Thoughts, Watts' hymns, Milton's Paradise Lost, and Hervey's Meditations, a knowledge of which gave more compass to their thoughts, to be expressed in a profuse, flowery language, and raised their feelings to the utmost height of poetical enthusiasm.

Sometimes their sermons turned upon matters of controversy; unlearned arguments on the subject of free grace, baptism, free will, election, faith, good works, justification, sanctification, and the final perseverance of the saints. But that in which they excelled was the earnestness of their words and manner, leaving no doubt of the strongest conviction in their own minds, and in the vividness of the pictures which they drew of the ineffable blessedness of heaven and the awful torments of the wicked in the fire and brimstone appointed for eternal punishment. These, with the love of God to sinful men, the sufferings of the Saviour, the dangerous apathy of sinners, and exhortations to repentance, furnished themes for the most vehement and passionate declamations. But above all they continually inculcated the great principles of justice and sound morality.

As many of these preachers were nearly destitute of learning and knowledge they made up in loud hallooing and violent action what they lacked in information. And it was a matter of astonishment to what length they could spin out a sermon embracing only a few ideas. The merit of a sermon was measured somewhat by the length of it, by the flowery language of the speaker, and by his vociferation and violent gestures. Nevertheless, these first preachers were of incalculable benefit to the country. They inculcated justice and morality, and to the sanction of the highest human motives to regard them, added those which arise from a belief of the greatest conceivable amount of future rewards and punishments. They were truly patriotic also; for at a time when the country was so poor that no other kind of ministry could have been maintained in it they preached without charge to the people, working week days to aid the scanty charities of their flocks in furnishing themselves with a scantier living. They believed with a positive certainty that they saw the souls of men rushing to perdition; and they stepped forward to warn and to save, with all the enthusiasm and self-devotion of a generous man who risks his own life to save his neighbor from drowning. And to them are we indebted for the first Christian character of the Protestant portion of this people.

The long, loud, and violent declamations of these early preachers seemed to be well adapted to the taste of the inhabitants. In course of time their style became the standard of popular eloquence. It was adopted by lawyers at the bar and by politicians in their public harangues; and to this day in some of the old settled parts of the State no one is accounted an orator unless he can somewhat imitate thunder in his style of public speaking. From hence, also, comes the vulgar notion that any bellowing fellow with a profusion of flowery bombast is a "smart man," a man of talents, fit to make laws, govern the country, and originate its policy. The public exercises in religion were greatly aided by the loud and wild music made by the singing of untutored voices. He was considered the best singer who could wake up the echoes to his voice from the greatest distance in the deep woods around; so that in process of time, when the New England singing masters began to establish singing schools, many people looked upon their scientific and chastened performances with perfect scorn. One of these itinerant teachers of music called his scholars together, they being large, loud voiced young men and women, trained to sing at camp meetings. As he stood out in their midst and began a tune in a low, melodious voice, sawing the air with his hand to beat the time, sliding gracefully about the room, after the fashion of a singing master, his scholars lifted up their loud voices and struck into the tune before him, overwhelming him with a horrible din of sound such as he had never heard before; drowning his feeble voice and his fine music both together. The scholars were vastly pleased with their own performance and held that of their teacher in utter contempt. Whereupon they all concluded with one accord that each one of them was already far superior to his teacher, and the school broke up.

The pursuits of the people were agricultural. A very few merchants supplied them with the few necessaries which could not be produced or manufactured at home. The farmer raised his own provisions; tea and coffee were scarcely used, except on some grand occasions. The farmer's sheep furnished wool for his winter clothing; he raised cotton and flax for his summer clothing. His wife and daughters spun, wove, and made it into garments. A little copperas and indigo, with the bark of trees, furnished dye stuffs for coloring. The fur of the raccoon made him a hat or a cap. The skins of deer or of his cattle, tanned at a neighboring tan yard or dressed by himself, made him shoes or moccasins. Boots were rarely seen even in the towns. And a log cabin made entirely of wood, without glass, nails, hinges, or locks, furnished the residence of many a contented and happy family. The people were quick and ingenious to supply by invention, and with their own hands, the lack of mechanics and artificers. Each farmer as a general thing built his own house, made his own ploughs and harness, bedsteads, chairs, stools, cupboards, and tables. The carts and wagons for hauling were generally made without iron, without tires or boxes, and were run without tar, and might be heard creaking as they lumbered along the roads for the distance of a mile or more.

As an example of the talents of this people to supply all deficiencies and provide against accidents by a ready invention the following anecdote is related of James Lemon, one of the old sort of baptist preachers, formerly of Monroe county but now deceased. Mr. Lemon was a farmer, and made all his own harness. The collars for his horses were made of straw or corn husks, plaited and sewed together by himself. Being engaged in breaking a piece of stubble ground and having turned out for dinner, he left his harness on the beam of his plough. His son, a wild youth, who was employed with a pitch fork to clear the plough of the accumulating stubble, staid behind and hid one of the horse collars. This he did that he might rest whilst his father made a new collar. But the old man, returning in the afternoon and missing his collar, mused for a few minutes and then, very much to the disappointment of his truant son, he deliberately pulled off his leather breeches, stuffed the legs of them with stubble, straddled them across the neck of his horse for a collar, and ploughed the remainder of the day as bare legged as he came into the world. In a more civilized country, where the people are better acquainted with the great laws which control the division of labor, a half day would have been lost in providing for such a mishap.

Such a thing as regular commerce was nearly unknown. Until 1817 everything of foreign growth or manufacture had been brought from New Orleans in keel boats towed with ropes or pushed with poles by the hardy race of boatmen of that day up the current of the Mississippi; or else wagoned across the mountains from Philadelphia to Pittsburgh, and from thence floated down the Ohio to its mouth in keel boats; and from there shoved, pushed, and towed up the Mississippi, as from New Orleans. Upon the conclusion of the war of 1812 the people from the old States began to come in and settle in the country. They brought some money and property with them and introduced some changes in the customs and modes of living. Before the war such a thing as money was scarcely ever seen in the country, the skins of the deer and raccoon supplying the place of a circulating medium. The money which was now brought in, and which had before been paid by the United States to the militia during the war, turned the heads of all the people and gave them new ideas and aspirations; so that by 1819 the whole country was in a rage for speculating in lands and town lots. The States of Ohio and Kentucky, a little before, had each incorporated a batch of about forty independent banks. The Illinois territory had incorporated two at home, one at Edwardsville and the other at Shawneetown; and the territory of Missouri added two more at St. Louis. These banks made money very plenty; emigrants brought it to the State in great abundance. The owners of it had to use it in some way; and as it could not be used in legitimate commerce in a State where the material for commerce did not exist, the most of it was used to build houses in towns which the limited business of the country did not require, and to purchase land which the labor of the country was not sufficient to cultivate. This was called "developing the infant resources of a new country."

The United States government was then selling land at two dollars per acre; eighty dollars on the quarter section to be paid down on the purchase, with a credit of five years for the residue. For nearly every sum of eighty dollars there was in the country, a quarter section of land was purchased; for in those days there were no specie circulars to restrain unwarrantable speculations but, on the contrary, the notes of most of the numerous banks in existence were good in the public land offices. The amount of land thus purchased was increased by the general expectation that the rapid settlement of the country would enable the speculator to sell it for a high price before the expiration of the credit. This great abundance of money also, about this time, made a vast increase in the amount of merchandise brought into the State. When money is plenty every man's credit is good. The people dealt largely with the stores on credit, and drew upon a certain fortune in prospect for payment. Every one was to get rich out of the future emigrant. The speculator was to sell him houses and lands; and the farmer was to sell him everything he wanted to begin with and to live upon until he could supply himself. Towns were laid out all over the country and lots were purchased by every one on a credit; the town maker received no money for his lots, but he received notes of hand which he considered to be as good as cash; and he lived and embarked in other ventures, as if they had been cash in truth. In this mode, by the year 1820 nearly the whole people were irrecoverably involved in debt. The banks in Ohio and Kentucky broke, one after another, leaving the people of those States covered with indebtedness and without the means of extrication. The banks at home and in St. Louis ceased business. The great tide of immigrants from abroad, which had been looked for by every one, failed to come. Real estate was unsaleable; the lands purchased of the United States were unpaid for, and likely to be forfeited. Bank notes had driven out specie, and when these notes became worthless there was no money of any description left in the country. And there was absolutely no commerce by means of which a currency could be restored. For in those days we exported nothing; and if there had been any property fit for exportation there was no market for it abroad, and if there had been a market there was no capital with which to purchase it and take it to market. The people began to sue one another for their debts; and as there was absolutely no money in the country it was evident that scarcely any amount of property would pay the indebtedness.

To remedy these evils the legislature of 1821 created a State Bank. It was founded without money, and wholly on the credit of the State. It was authorized to issue one, two, three, five, ten and twenty dollar notes in the likeness of bank bills, bearing two per cent. annual interest and payable by the State in ten years. A principal bank was established at Vandalia and four or five branches in other places; the legislature elected all the directors and officers; a large number of whom were members of the legislature, and all of them professional politicians. The bank was directed by law to lend its bills to the people to the amount of one hundred dollars on personal security; and upon the security of mortgages upon land for a greater sum. These bills were to be receivable in payment of all State and county taxes, and for all costs and fees and salaries of public officers; and if a creditor refused to endorse on his execution his willingness to receive them in payment of debt, the debtor could replevy or stay its collection for three years by giving personal security. So infatuated were this legislature with this absurd bank project that the members firmly believed that the notes of this bank would remain at par with gold and silver; and they could readily prove their belief to be well-founded; for the most difficult argument to answer is one founded partly upon fact, but mostly upon guess work and conjecture. As an evidence of the belief of the legislature to this effect the journals show that a resolution was passed requesting the secretary of the treasury of the United States to receive these notes into the land offices in payment for the public lands. When this resolution was put to the vote in the Senate, the old French lieutenant-governor, Col. Menard, presiding over that body, did up the business as follows: "Gentlemen of *de* Senate, it is moved and seconded *dat de* notes of *dis* bank be made land office money. All in favor of *dat* motion, say aye; all against it, say no. It is decided in *de* affirmative. And now, gentlemen, *I bet you one hundred dollar he never be made land office money.*" The county of Menard on the Sangamon river was named in honor of him; and the name could not have been more worthily bestowed.

John McLean of Shawneetown was then the speaker of the House of Representatives. He was opposed to this bank, and was possessed of a fertility of genius and an overpowering eloquence of which the bank party were justly afraid. For this reason that party being in the majority in the House refused to go into committee of the whole so as to allow Mr. McLean to participate in the debate. Mr. McLean, indignant at such treatment, resigned his office of speaker and in a speech remarkable for its ability and eloquence predicted all the evil consequences which resulted from the bank, and put in motion an opposition to the prevailing policy of crippling creditors in the collection of their debts which thereafter prevented the repetition of such measures during that generation. But the majority were for the bill. The governor and judges, acting as a council of revision,[2] objected to it as being unconstitutional and inexpedient, but it was afterwards repassed through both houses by the constitutional majorities. It was passed in the spirit of brute force triumphing over the power of intellect. The Supreme Court of the United States afterwards decided in the case of Craig against the State of Missouri that the bills payable at a future day of all such banks representing a State only were bills of credit, and prohibited by the constitution.

The most distinguished advocate for the creation of this bank amongst the members of the House of Representatives was Judge Richard M. Young, who has since been so prominent in Illinois; and who is one of the very many examples in our history of the forgiving disposition of the people to such of their public servants as have been so unfortunate as to be in favor of bad measures, or opposed to good ones. Mr. McLean was also afterwards, as long as he lived, very prominent in the politics of Illinois. He was several times elected to the legislature, once elected to the lower house of Congress, and twice to the United States Senate, and died a member of the Senate in 1830. He was naturally a great, magnanimous man, and a leader of men. The county of McLean was named in honor of him.

In the summer of 1821, the new bank went into operation. Every man who could get an endorser borrowed his hundred dollars. The directors, it is believed, were all politicians; and either were then, or expected to be, candidates for office. Lending to everybody, and refusing none, was the surest road to popularity. Accordingly, three hundred thousand dollars of the new money was soon lent without much attention to security or care for eventual payment. It first fell twenty-five cents, then fifty, and then seventy cents below par. And as the bills of the Ohio and Kentucky banks had driven all other money out of the State, so this new issue effectually kept it out. Such a total absence was there of the silver coins that it became utterly impossible, in the course of trade, to make small change. The people, from necessity, were compelled to cut the new bills into two pieces, so as to make two halves of a dollar. This again further aided to keep out even the smallest silver coins, for the people must know that good money is a very proud thing and will not circulate, stay, or go where bad money is treated with as much respect as the good. For about four years there was no other kind of money but this uncurrent State bank paper. In the meantime very few persons pretended to pay their debts to the bank. More than half of those who had borrowed considered what they had gotten from it as so much clear gain, and never intended to pay it from the first.

By the year 1824 it became impossible to carry on the State government with such money as the bills of this bank. The State revenue varied from twenty-five to thirty thousand dollars per annum, which was raised almost exclusively by a tax on lands then owned by non-residents in the military tract lying north-west of the Illinois river. The resident land tax in other parts of the State was paid into the county treasuries. The annual expenditures of the State government were about equal to the annual revenues; and as the taxes were collected in the bills of the State bank, the legislature, to carry on the government, were compelled to provide for their own pay and that of all the public officers and the expenses of the government by taking and giving enough of the depreciated bills to equal in value the sums required to be paid. So that each member instead of receiving three dollars per day received nine dollars per day. The salaries of the governor and judges, and all other expenses, were paid in the same way. So that if $30,000 were required to pay the expenses of government for a year, under this system it took $90,000 to do it. And thus, by the financial aid of an insolvent bank, the legislature managed to treble the public expenses without increasing the revenues or amount of service to the State. In fact, this State lost two-thirds of its revenue and expended three times the amount necessary to carry on the government. In the course of ten years it must have lost more than $150,000 by receiving a depreciated currency, $150,000 more by paying it out, and $100,000 of the loans, which were never repaid by the borrowers and which the State had to make good by receiving the bills of the bank for taxes, by funding some at six per cent interest, and paying a part in cash in the year 1831.

The year 1820 was signalized by the first and last duel which was ever fought in Illinois. This took place in Belleville, St. Clair county, between Alphonso Stewart and William Bennett, two obscure men. The seconds had made it up to be a sham duel to throw ridicule upon Bennett, the challenging party. Stewart was in the secret; but Bennett, his adversary, was left to believe it a reality. They were to fight with rifles; the guns were loaded with blank cartridges; and Bennett, somewhat suspecting a trick, rolled a ball into his gun without the knowledge of the seconds, or of the other party. The word to fire was given and Stewart fell mortally wounded. Bennett made his escape, but two years afterwards he was captured in Arkansas, brought back to the State, indicted, tried and convicted of murder. A great effort was made to procure him a pardon; but Governor Bond would yield to no entreaties in his favor; and Bennett suffered the extreme penalty of the law by hanging, in the presence of a great multitude of people. This was the first and last duel ever fought in the State by any of its citizens. The hanging of Bennett made duelling discreditable and unpopular, and laid the foundation for that abhorrence of the practice which has ever since been felt and expressed by the people of Illinois. The present Judge Lockwood was then the Attorney General of the State, and prosecuted in this case. To his talents and success as a prosecutor the people are indebted for this early precedent and example, which did more than is generally known to prevent the barbarous practice of duelling from being introduced into this State.

II

The Pioneer State, 1821–1829

In the year 1822 another Governor was elected and this resulted in again agitating the question of the introduction of slavery. There were four candidates for the office, Joseph Philips, the chief Justice; Thomas C. Brown, one of the judges of the Supreme Court; Major-General James B. Moore, and Edward Coles, who was at that time Register of the Land office at Edwardsville. Mr. Coles was a Virginian, had been private secretary to Mr. Madison, had travelled in Europe, was well informed, well bred, and voluble in conversation; had emancipated his slaves in Virginia, was appointed to a land office in Illinois through the influence of Mr. Crawford, the Secretary of the Treasury, had brought his slaves with him to Illinois and settled them on farms, and was a thorough opponent of slavery. At that early day Mr. Crawford and John C. Calhoun of South Carolina and others were looking forward as candidates for the Presidency. Ninian Edwards, one of our Senators, favored Mr. Calhoun; and Jesse B. Thomas, our other Senator, was in favor of Mr. Crawford. To counteract the influence of Edwards Mr. Coles was sent out to Illinois. Philips and Brown were from the slave States and were in favor of slavery. General Moore run also as an opponent to slavery. Mr. Coles was elected by a mere plurality vote over Philips, his highest competitor; and, of course, was so unfortunate as to have a majority of the legislature against him during his whole term of service.

This election took place not long after the settlement of the great Missouri question; a question which convulsed the whole nation and came near dissolving the Union. The Illinois Senators in Congress had voted for the admission of Missouri into the Union as a slave State, without restriction, whilst Mr. Cook, then our only representative in the lower House, voted against it. This all helped to keep alive some questions for or against the introduction of slavery. About this time, also, a tide of immigrants was pouring into Missouri through Illinois, from Virginia and Kentucky. In the fall of the year every great road was crowded and full of them, all bound to Missouri with their money and long trains of teams and negroes. These were the most wealthy and best educated immigrants from the slave States. Many of our people who had land and farms to sell looked upon the good fortune of Missouri with envy; whilst the lordly immigrant, as he passed along with his money and droves of negroes, took a malicious pleasure in increasing it by pretending to regret the short-sighted policy of Illinois which excluded him from settlement amongst us; and from purchasing the lands of our people. In this mode a desire to make Illinois a slave State became quite prevalent. Many persons had voted for Brown or Philips with this view; whilst the friends of a free State had rallied almost in a body for Coles.

Notwithstanding the defeat of the party at this election they were not annihilated. They had only been beaten for Governor by a division in their own ranks; whilst they had elected a large majority in each house of the Assembly and were now determined to make a vigorous effort to carry their measure at the session of the legislature to be held in 1822–3. Governor Coles, in his first message, recommended the emancipation of the French slaves. This served as the spark to kindle into activity all the elements in favor of slavery.

Slavery could not be introduced, nor was it believed that the French slaves could be emancipated, without an amendment of the constitution; the constitution could not be amended without a new convention; to obtain which, two-thirds of each branch of the legislature had to concur in recommending it to the people; and the voters at the next election had to sanction it by a majority of all the votes given for members of the legislature. When the legislature assembled it was found that the Senate contained the requisite two-thirds majority; but in the House of Representatives, by deciding a contested election in favor of one of the candidates, the slave party would have one more than two-thirds; but by deciding in favor of the other they would lack one vote of having that majority. These two candidates were John Shaw and Nicholas Hanson, who claimed to represent the county of Pike, which then included all the military tracts, and all the country north of the Illinois river to the northern limits of the State.

The leaders of the slave party were anxious to re-elect Jesse B. Thomas to the United States Senate. Hanson would vote for him, but Shaw would not; Shaw would vote for the Convention, but Hanson would not. The party had use for both of them and they determined to use them both, one after the other. For this purpose they first decided in favor of Hanson, admitted him to a seat, and with his vote elected their United States Senator; and then, towards the close of the session, with mere brute force and in the most barefaced manner they reconsidered their former vote, turned Hanson out of his seat and decided in favor of Shaw, and with his vote carried their resolution for a convention.

The night after this resolution passed the convention party assembled to triumph in a great carousal. They formed themselves into a noisy, disorderly, and tumultuous procession headed by Judge Philips, Judge Smith, Judge Thomas Reynolds, late governor of Missouri, and Lieutenant Governor Kinney, followed by the majority of the legislature and the hangers-on and rabble about the seat of government; and they marched, with the blowing of tin horns and the beating of drums and tin pans, to the residence of Governor Coles and to the boarding houses of their principal opponents, towards whom they manifested their contempt and displeasure by a confused medley of groans, wailings, and lamentations. Their object was to intimidate and crush all opposition at once.

But they were mistaken: the anti-convention party took new courage and rallied to a man. They established newspapers to oppose the convention; one at Shawneetown edited by Henry Eddy; one at Edwardsville edited by Hooper Warren with Gov. Coles, Thomas Lippincott, George Churchill, and Judge Lockwood for its principal contributors; and finally, one at Vandalia edited by David Blackwell, the secretary of State. The slave party had established a newspaper at Kaskaskia under the direction of Mr. Kane and Chief Justice Reynolds; and one at Edwardsville edited by Judge Smith; and both parties prepared to appeal to the interests, the passions, and the intelligence of the people. The contest was mixed up with much personal abuse; and now was poured forth a perfect lava of detraction, which, if it were not for the knowledge of the people that such matters are generally false or greatly exaggerated, would have overwhelmed and consumed all men's reputations. Morris Birkbeck, an Englishman who settled an English colony in Edwards' county, Gov. Coles, David Blackwell, George Churchill, and Thomas Lippincott wrote fiery hand-bills and pamphlets, and the old preachers preached against a convention and slavery. Elias K. Kane, Judge Thomas Reynolds, Judge Samuel McRoberts, Judge Smith, and others wrote handbills and pamphlets in its favor. These missive weapons of a fiery contest were eagerly read by the people. The State was almost covered with them; they flew everywhere, and everywhere they scorched and scathed as they flew. This was a long, excited, angry, bitter, and indignant contest. It was to last from the spring of 1823 until the August election of 1824; the rank and file of the people were no less excited than their political leaders. Almost every stump in every county had its bellowing, indignant orator on one side or the other; and the whole people for the space of eighteen months did scarcely anything but read newspapers, hand-bills and pamphlets, quarrel, argue, and wrangle with each other whenever they met together to hear the violent harangues of their orators.

The principal partisans in favor of a convention were Judges Philips, Brown, and John Reynolds, Jesse B. Thomas and Gov. Edwards, our senators in Congress, Lieut. Gov. Kinney, Judge Smith, Chief Justice Thomas Reynolds, John McLean, Elias K. Kane, Judge M' Roberts, and Gov. Bond. And the principal men opposed to a convention and slavery were Morris Birkbeck, Gov. Coles, Daniel P. Cook, our member of Congress, David Blackwell, George Churchill, Samuel D. Lockwood, Thomas Lippincott, Hooper Warren, George Forquer,[1] Thomas Mather, and Henry Eddy. The odds in the array of great names seemed to be in favor of the convention party. The question of slavery was thoroughly discussed. The people took an undivided and absorbing interest in it; they were made to understand it completely; and as this was long before the abolition excitement of modern times the introduction of slavery was resisted not so much upon the ground of opposition to it in general as simply upon the grounds of policy and expediency. The people decided by about two thousand majority in favor of a free State. Thus, after one of the most bitter, prolonged, and memorable contests which ever convulsed the politics of this State the question of making Illinois a slave State was put to rest, as it is hoped, forever.

Nothing of any interest occurred after this struggle until the session of the legislature in 1824–'5. The people had been so long under the influence of an intense excitement that they required rest. And as a general thing they had not then become inured to a political warfare which has latterly become interminable. The contests in those days were of short duration and were scarcely ever repeated on the same grounds or questions. There were no parties of Whig and Democrat, Federalist and Republican. The contests were mostly personal, and for men. As for principles and measures, with the exception of the convention question there were none to contend for. Every election turned upon the fitness and unfitness, the good and bad qualities of the candidates. The only mode of electioneering for a friend then known was to praise one set of men and blacken the characters of the other. The candidates were not announced until within a few weeks of the election; the contest was soon over, and then peace and quiet reigned until the next election, two years afterwards.

There are those who are apt to believe that this mode of conducting elections is likely to result in the choice of the best materials for administering government. But experience did not prove the fact to be so. The idea of electing men for their merit has an attractive charm in it to generous minds; but in our history it has been as full of delusion as it has been attractive. Nor has the organization of regular parties and the introduction of the new principle in elections of "measures not men," fully answered the expectation of its friends. But if the introduction of such parties, supposed to be founded on a difference in principles, has done no other good, it has greatly softened and abated the personal rancor and asperity of political contests, though it has made such contests increasing and eternal. It is to be regretted, however, if there be evils attending the contests of party, that society cannot receive the full benefit from them by the total extinction of all mere personal considerations, personal quarrels, and personal crimination not necessary to exhibit the genius and tendency of a party as to measures, and which are merely incidental to contests for office. The present doctrine of parties is measures, not men, which if truly carried out would lead to a discussion of measures only. But parties are not yet sufficiently organized for this; and, accordingly we find at every election much personal bitterness and invective mingled with the supposed contests for principle. The political world is still full of those men who believe, and perhaps believe correctly, that the attachment to principle is not yet so general and perfect as to destroy all chance of overthrowing the principles of a candidate by overwhelming his reputation with falsehood. Perhaps the time may come when all these personal contests will be confined to the bosom of one party, in selecting the best candidates to carry out its principles.

At the session of 1824–'5 the legislature, under the provisions of the Constitution, reorganized the judiciary by creating five circuit court judges who were to hold all the circuit courts in the State; and the supreme court, composed of four judges, was to be held twice a year at the seat of government. William Wilson was elected chief justice; Thomas C. Brown, Samuel D. Lockwood, and Theophilus W. Smith were elected associate judges of the supreme court; John York Sawyer, Samuel McRoberts, Richard M. Young, James Hall, and James O. Wattles were elected judges of the circuits; and James Turney to be attorney general. Of these ten great officers it is believed that Wilson, Brown, Smith, Sawyer, M'Roberts, Young, Hall, and Turney had belonged to the convention party; but such was the nature of party at that day that they had not lost their popularity even with the party opposed to them. The anti-convention party had a large majority in this legislature; but upon the principle of men, not measures, they put their opponents into office.

Proscription for opinion's sake was then but little known. The first instance of it was shortly afterwards put in practice by one of the circuit judges. Judge McRoberts removed Joseph Conway, an opponent, and appointed Emanuel J. West, a friend of his own, to be clerk of the circuit court of Madison county. Mr. Conway was well known and popular in several of the adjacent counties. The people of his own county elected him to the Senate without opposition, and kept him there, by re-election, for eight years. A great outcry was raised against the extravagance of the judiciary system, the prodigal waste of the public money to pension unnecessary life officers upon the people; and a talented young lawyer of stirring eloquence in the southern part of the State, a man possessing many qualities which admirably fitted him for a demagogue of the highest order, mounted the hobby and rode it in a storm of passion through several counties in the south.[2] The legislature of 1826–'7 repealed the circuit system, turned the circuit judges out of office, and required the judges of the supreme court to hold the circuit courts. The chief reasons for the repeal of the system were its cost and the proscription of a popular clerk. It was thought to be the height of extravagance to maintain nine judges, though the salaries of all of them together amounted only to six thousand two hundred dollars. The salary of a judge of the supreme court was eight hundred dollars and that of a circuit judge was six hundred dollars. Such were then the popular notions of economy and extravagance in public expenditures.

The effort to repeal the circuit judges out of office was aided by a decision of Judge McRoberts on the circuit. It has been said before that Gov. Coles had emancipated his negroes. The law required him to give a bond for their good behavior, and that they should not become a county charge. This he omitted to do and thereby subjected himself to a penalty of two hundred dollars for each negro, to be sued for by the county in which they were set free. The county commissioners of Madison county during the convention contest were instigated to bring a suit against him for this penalty and obtained the verdict of a jury in the suit for two thousand dollars; but before any judgment was rendered the legislature, by law, released him from the penalty. At the next term of the court Gov. Coles, in pursuance of the act of the legislature for his relief, pled it in bar of a judgment on the verdict. But Judge McRoberts, being under the erroneous belief that the legal doctrine of vested rights was applicable to municipal corporations created solely for purposes of government, decided that the law was unconstitutional and void. The decision made a great noise at the time, as it naturally would directly after a fierce contest about slavery. It was taken to the supreme court and reversed, as a matter of course.

At the session of 1825, also, William S. Hamilton[3] introduced a new road law, which passed the legislature. Hitherto the law had required every able-bodied man to work on the roads five days in the year. The new law levied a tax in proportion to property, to be applied in money or labor to the construction and repair of roads. Gov. Duncan, then a member of the Senate, introduced a bill which became a law for the support of schools by a public tax. Both of these laws worked admirably well. The roads were never, before nor since, in such good repair, and schools flourished in almost every neighborhood. But it appears that these valuable laws were in advance of the civilization of the times. They were the subject of much clamorous opposition. The very idea of a tax, though to be paid in labor as before, was so hateful that even the poorest men preferred to work five days in the year on the roads rather than to pay a tax of twenty-five cents, or even no tax at all. For the same reason they preferred to pay all that was necessary for the tuition of their children, or to keep them in ignorance, rather than submit to the mere name of a tax by which their wealthier neighbors bore the brunt of the expense of their education. Both of these laws were repealed and the old systems restored by the legislature of 1826–'7. Since then the legislature has been constantly engaged in making and amending laws for roads and schools, but there has been no good system of either. Each subsequent attempt has been only a vain effort to accomplish its purpose by inadequate means. To come forward a little, in 1840 Judge William Thomas of Jacksonville prepared a school bill which became a law, but for want of the taxing power, which the legislature refused to grant, it had but little effect. In the summer of 1844 John S. Wright of Chicago, H. M. Weed of Lewiston, Thomas M. Kilpatrick of Winchester, and others got up a common school convention at Peoria which prepared a very enlightened memorial to the legislature in favor of common schools; and as a means of furthering the common object the governor, at the session of 1844 recommended the appointment of a superintendent of common schools to stir up the people and to collect information for the use of the legislature.[4] The whole resulted in a new school law making the secretary of State *ex officio* the superintendent of common schools and authorizing a school tax to be levied in each district.

Mr. Thompson Campbell, the secretary of State, made an able report to the legislature of 1846–'7, from which it appears that information had been collected from fifty-seven counties only out of the ninety-nine in the State, and that with the exception of Chicago and some other places the common schools were nowhere in a very flourishing condition. The school commissioners and other agents of schools in the counties, receiving no compensation for their services, were generally negligent of their duties, or not qualified to perform them. Almost everywhere the people had refused to tax themselves under the law; and in almost all the south part of the State there were complaints that the legal standard of qualifications for teachers was too high, the law requiring a knowledge of reading, writing, and arithmetic, English grammar, geography, and history; and the people, being scarce of materials for such learned teachers, were desirous of getting back to the old standard of reading, writing, and ciphering, to the rule of three, or at farthest through the arithmetic.

And now to go back again; at the session of 1824–'5 the judges of the supreme court were appointed to prepare a revision of the laws and present it at the next session. At the session of 1826–'7 Judges Lockwood and Smith presented the result of their labor, which was adopted, and the laws then presented by them have been standard laws in every revision since. It is believed that they were the authors of the laws in the revised code under the titles Abatement, Account, Amendments and Jeofails, Apprentices, Attachments, Attorneys, Bail, Bills of Exchange, Chancery, Conveyances, Courts, Criminal Code, Depositions, Detinue, Dower, Evidence, Forcible Entry and Detainer, Fugitives from Justice, Habeas Corpus, Jails and Jailors, Limitations, Mandamus, Minors and Orphans, Ne Exeat and Injunctions, Oaths and Affirmations, Practice, Promissory Notes, Replevin, Right of Property, and Sheriffs and Coroners. Judge McRoberts prepared the act concerning frauds and perjuries; Judge Sawyer, the act concerning insolvent debtors; Judge Young, the act concerning wills and testaments; and Henry Starr, Esq., now of Cincinnati, prepared the act concerning judgments and executions. It is most probable that all these laws were more perfect when they came from the hands of their authors than after they were amended somewhat out of shape and system by the legislature.

A new election for governor took place in 1826, for which office there were three candidates. Thomas C. Sloe, now of New Orleans, was one of them. He was a well-informed merchant and a man of good character and strong sense, and withal was a well-bred, courteous gentleman. Ninian Edwards and the then lieutenant-governor, Adolphus Frederick Hubbard, were the other two candidates. As a part of a picture of the times, and as illustrative of what a candidate for governor thought of himself and the people, I preserve a few words of one of Mr. Hubbard's public addresses during the canvass. In his speeches he said: "Fellow-citizens, I offer myself as a candidate before you for the office of governor. I do not pretend to be a man of extraordinary talents; nor do I claim to be equal to Julius Caesar or Napoleon Bonaparte, nor yet to be as great a man as my opponent, Governor Edwards. Nevertheless, I think I can govern you pretty well. I do not think that it will require a very extraordinary smart man to govern you; for to tell you the truth, fellow-citizens, I do not think you will be very hard to govern, no how." Mr. Hubbard could not have made his last assertion with much show of truth for several years past.

This gentleman had made himself famous for a number of odd sayings, and by a speech in the legislature on a bill to pay a bounty on wolf-scalps. Tradition has preserved this speech as follows: "Mr. Speaker, I rise before the question is put on this bill to say a word for my constituents. Mr. Speaker, I have never seen a wolf. I cannot say that I am very well acquainted with the nature and habits of wolves. Mr. Speaker, I have said that I had never seen a wolf. But now I remember that once on a time as Judge Brown and I were riding across the Bonpas prairie we looked over the prairie about three miles and Judge Brown said, Hubbard! look! there goes a wolf! And I looked, and I looked, and I looked, and I said, Judge, where? And he said there; and I looked again, and this time, in the edge of a hazel thicket about three miles across the prairie I think I saw the wolf's tail. Mr. Speaker, if I did not see a wolf this time, I think I never saw one. But I have heard much and read more about this animal. I have studied his natural history. By-the-bye, history is divided into two parts; there is, first, the history of the fabulous, and secondly, of the non-fabulous, or unknown ages. Mr. Speaker, from all these sources of information I learn that the wolf is a very noxious animal; that he goes prowling about seeking something to devour; that he rises up in the dead and secret hours of the night, when all nature reposes in silent oblivion, and then commits the most terrible devastations upon the rising generation of hogs and sheep. Mr. Speaker, I have done, and return my thanks to the house for their kind attention to my remarks." These speeches are truly characteristic of the man; and they are given as being illustrative of the state of civilization which existed when such a man could be elected to the office of lieutenant-governor, and gain such popularity in his office as to be encouraged to become a candidate for governor.

Ninian Edwards, the other candidate at this election, was born in Maryland and brought up in Kentucky. He was bred to the legal profession, and became attorney general of Kentucky at an early age. At the age of twenty-eight he was appointed chief justice of the High Court of Appeals. He held this office when the late Chief Justice Boyle of Kentucky was appointed the first governor of the Illinois territory in 1809. Mr. Edwards preferred to be governor of the territory and Mr. Boyle preferred to be chief justice; so in the end they exchanged offices. Edwards was sent out to Illinois by the president as first governor of the territory, and Boyle was made chief justice by the Governor of Kentucky. Edwards was a large, well-made man, with a noble, princely appearance, which was a circumstance greatly in his favor as governor over a rude people, of whom it may be said that the animal greatly predominated over the intellectual man. In fact it may well be questioned whether mankind ever will become so intellectual and spiritual that mere size, vigor of muscle, and consequent animal spirits will cease to have more influence with the multitude than mere intellect, unaided by these fleshly advantages. Gov. Edwards had been governor of the Illinois territory for nine years, and was then elected to the United States Senate. In this office he showed an extensive knowledge of public affairs and became distinguished as a man of fine talents throughout the Union. Whilst in the Senate he was appointed by Mr. Monroe to be minister to Mexico, and shortly after this appointment, whilst on his way home to Illinois to prepare for his mission, he wrote out and sent back to the House of Representatives in Congress various charges against William H. Crawford, secretary of the treasury, accusing him of a corrupt administration of the treasury department in aid of his election to the presidency. A committee of investigation was appointed, a messenger of the House was sent after Mr. Edwards, with whom he was required to return to Washington. Mr. Edwards failed to make good his charges to the satisfaction of the committee, and as this happened just before the presidential election of 1824, when the whole country was convulsed with excitement, it resulted in prostrating his character abroad and very much affected his standing at home. Public opinion was so much against him in the nation that he resigned his mission to Mexico. Gov. Edwards has often informed me himself that he made the charges against Mr. Crawford under a promise of support from President Monroe, Gen. Jackson, John C. Calhoun, and John Quincy Adams. I merely give his words without pretending to know whether he spoke the truth or not. But one thing makes his statement the more probable. Mr. Crawford had been nominated for the presidency by a caucus of fifty or sixty of the republican members of Congress. Before that time this had been the usage of the republican party. But Gen. Jackson, John Quincy Adams, and Henry Clay were independent candidates; John C. Calhoun had been one and declined; and many people, believing caucus nominations by members of Congress to be utterly corrupt and corrupting, a powerful party was formed to break up the usage. Upon this principle all the other candidates and their friends were rallied against Mr. Crawford.

This defeat very much injured the influence of Gov. Edwards, and now, when, as a candidate for Governor he attacked the financial system which had hitherto prevailed; and committed himself to press an investigation into the corruptions of the old State bank he was not listened to or confided in to the extent required by a reformer in the work of reforming public abuses. He was opposed by all the old members of the legislature who had supported the many unwise measures of finance, and by the whole bank influence, from the Presidents down to the lowest agents, who had in anywise cause to fear an investigation. But his great talents and fine personal appearance enabled him to triumph over his adversaries. He was elected by a mere plurality vote over Mr. Sloe, his principal opponent. It is worthy of remark here that he never condescended to the common low arts of electioneering. Whenever he went out among the people he arrayed himself in the style of a gentleman of the olden times, dressed in fine broadcloth, with short breeches, long stockings, and high, fair-topped boots; was drawn in a fine carriage driven by a negro; and for success he relied upon his speeches, which were delivered with great pomp and in a style of diffuse and florid eloquence.

When he was inaugurated in 1826 he appeared before the General Assembly wearing a gold-laced cloak, and with great pomp he pronounced his first message to the two houses of the legislature. In this address he merely repeated the grounds which he had taken as a candidate. But in several messages afterwards he pointed out to the House of Representatives specific acts of mismanagement and corruption on the part of the officers of the old bank. A committee of investigation was appointed. The bank directors and officers, new and old, were sent for from every quarter. The charges of corruption were directed more particularly against Judge Smith, who as cashier had administered the Edwardsville branch. Smith was a sagacious, active and blustering politician, and managed to make all persons who had been connected with the bank believe that they were all involved in a common danger. A powerful combination of influential men was thus formed to thwart the investigation and ensure their common safety from impeachment. And now commenced such a running to and fro about the seat of government by day and night as can only be equaled by a swarm of bees when rudely attacked in their hive. The Governor was openly and boldly charged with base motives; and that kind of stigma was attempted to be cast on him which is apt to fix itself upon a common informer. His charges against Mr. Crawford were remembered; and he was now charged with being influenced by hostility towards Judge Smith, who had been a friend to Mr. Crawford's election. Judge Smith, with others involved in the charges, as a sure mode of defence raised a cry of persecution and alleged that the whole weight of the executive power and influence, directed by the spirit of revenge, had been pointed to overwhelm them. Without pronouncing here upon either the guilt or innocence of the accused it may be remarked that it is no uncommon thing for rogues, when about to be held accountable for crime, to seek sympathy and aid by raising a cry of persecution. And as strength is supposed to be on the side of men in high office and weakness on the side of private persons it is sure to happen that in contests between them the public sympathy inclines in favor of the weakest party; so that the strength of the one is apt to make him weak, and the weakness of the other makes him strong. And now, at this day, if a politician can get up a cry of persecution to operate in his favor it is a tower of strength; although in truth he be only suffering an exposure of his folly or villainy.

The evidence before the committee undoubtedly showed great mismanagement of the bank. But a committee of investigation had been packed for the purpose, and such was the influence of a combination of the officers of even an insolvent bank that a report was made without hesitation against the Governor's charges. Such was the influence of a bank conducted by public officers, being the first but not the last time in the history of Illinois in which it was proved that any considerable number of men of influence, acting in combination, to whom the monied affairs of the State are entrusted are above all accountability; for which reason it has not as yet been safe for the State to have any great complicated interests to be managed by public officers; nor was it the last time when it has been proved that any considerable combination of men are irresistible, and not to be made accountable when associated to commit crime, or to procure immunity from punishment. See future chapters upon the history of banking in this State, fund commissioners, internal improvements, mobs and Mormons, for this proof.

It was during Gov. Edwards' administration in the summer of 1827 that the first Indian disturbances occurred since the war of 1812. This was called the Winnebago war. The Winnebagoes, Sacs and Foxes, Sioux, Menominies, and other northern nations towards the head waters of the Mississippi had been at war with each other most of the time for more than a century; and the United States had undertaken to act as mediators between them and restore peace. In fact it has been the policy of the United States government latterly to compel the Indian tribes to live in peace with one another; for experience has shown that war cannot exist amongst the Indians without its being inconvenient and dangerous to white people. But despite all the remonstrances of the United States government, hostilities were continued and murders frequently committed. In the summer of this year a party of twenty-four Chippeways were surprised by a war party of the Winnebagoes and eight of them were killed or wounded. The United States commander at Saint Peter's caused four of the offending Winnebagoes to be arrested and delivered to the Chippeways, by whom they were shot for the murder. The white people had also a little before begun to overrun the Winnebago lands in the lead mines above Galena; many of the miners having pushed their searches for mineral as far as the Wisconsin river. This was a further source of irritation to the Winnebagoes. Red Bird, a Winnebago chief, was determined to revenge the shooting of the four Winnebagoes, and for this purpose he led a war party against the Chippeways, by whom he was defeated; and now returning disgraced and disappointed of his vengeance, he resolved to repair his disaster by an attack on the white people who had abetted his enemies, and, as he believed, invaded his country. On the 27th of June two white men were killed and another wounded near Prairie Du Chien; and on the 30th of July two keel-boats carrying supplies to Fort Snelling, situate at the mouth of the St. Peter's, were attacked by the Indians and two of the crew were killed and four wounded.

The intelligence of these murders alarmed the frontier settlements at Galena and in the mining country around it. Galena, as a town, had been settled about eighteen months before. Col. James Johnson of Kentucky had gone there with a party of miners in 1824 and had opened a lead mine about one mile above the present town.[5] His great success drew others there in 1825; and in 1826 and 1827 hundreds and thousands of persons from Illinois and Missouri went to the

Galena country to work the lead mines. It was estimated that the number of miners in the mining country in 1827 was six or seven thousand. The Illinoisans ran up the Mississippi river in steamboats in the spring season, worked the lead mines during warm weather, and then ran down the river again to their homes in the fall season; thus establishing, as was supposed, a similitude between their migratory habits and those of the fishy tribe called "Suckers." For which reason the Illinoisans were called "Suckers," a name which has stuck to them ever since. There is another account of the origin of the nickname "Suckers," as applied to the people of Illinois. It is said that the south part of the State was originally settled by the poorer class of people from the slave States, where the tobacco plant was extensively cultivated. They were such as were not able to own slaves in a slave State, and came to Illinois to get away from the imperious domination of their wealthy neighbors. The tobacco plant has many sprouts from the roots and main stem, which if not stripped off suck up its nutriment and destroy the staple. These sprouts are called "suckers," and are as carefully stripped off from the plant and thrown away as is the tobacco worm itself. These poor emigrants from the slave States were jeeringly and derisively called "suckers," because they were asserted to be a burthen upon the people of wealth; and when they removed to Illinois they were supposed to have stripped themselves off from the parent stem and gone away to perish like the "sucker" of the tobacco plant. This name was given to the Illinoisans at the Galena mines by the Missourians. Analogies always abound with those who desire to be sarcastic; so the Illinoisians by way of retaliation called the Missourians "Pukes." It had been observed that the lower lead mines in Missouri had sent up to the Galena country whole hordes of uncouth ruffians, from which it was inferred that Missouri had taken a "Puke" and had vomited forth to the upper lead mines all her worst population. From thence forth the Missourians were regularly called "Pukes;" and by these names of "Suckers" and "Pukes" the Illinoisans and Missourians are likely to be called, amongst the vulgar, forever.

The miners in all the surrounding country upon the alarm of Indian hostilities collected into Galena. By order of Gov. Edwards Gen. Tom M. Neale marched there with a regiment of volunteers from Sangamon county; a considerable mounted force was raised amongst the miners, which elected Gen. Dodge to be their commander. The inhabitants fortified the town of Galena and Gen. Atkinson of the U. S. army with a body of regulars and volunteers marched into the Winnebago country of the Wisconsin river in pursuit of the offending

Indians. The chief called Red Bird, with six other Indians of the tribe, voluntarily surrendered themselves prisoners to save their nation from the miseries of war. They were kept in jail a long time at Prairie Du Chien awaiting their trials for murder. Some of them were acquitted and some were convicted and executed. It was the fate of Red Bird, who is described as having been a noble-looking specimen of the savage chieftain, to pine away and die in prison, not from the fear of death, but by a gradual wasting away, the victim of regret and sorrow for the loss of his liberty as he had been accustomed to enjoy it in the fresh green woods.

By the session of the legislature of 1828–'9 the excitement of the politicians at the previous session had somewhat subsided, as men had time to forget and forgive each other for the causes of their animosity. Gov. Edwards, in the electioneering campaign previous to his election, had run athwart the views and conduct of many of his best friends by attacking the various public abuses; and his attempt to impeach the managers of the old State bank had resulted in a signal failure. The lieutenant-governor, Kinney, one of his opponents, truly said of him "that he was like unto an old crippled horse which being no longer able to jump a fence had fallen over into a cornfield, but was hurt so much by the fall that he was not able to eat the corn after he had thus broken into it." So the governor sought to repair this disaster by starting a new hobby at this session. It is true that there was but little of political party in those days but this did not prevent great men from having their hobbies, or rather from proposing measures upon the consideration of which they preferred the elections should turn, rather than on their own merits; and it was singular that Gov. Edwards, the gifted and eminent man of talents with every personal advantage necessary to command success, should think it necessary to ride a hobby. With a person and manner well calculated to win popular admiration and favor and talents acknowledged by all to be superior to any of his competitors, it was somewhat strange that he could not be content to throw himself before the people upon his own merits, upon his reputation for talents, as an aspirant for office. As it was, his course could not be sensibly justified upon any ground except that of pointing the public attention to matters with which he stood connected, and thereby diverting it from himself.

Generally it is the men without merit, the men of small pretensions without natural gifts to conciliate favor, who ride hobbies and most insist upon measures as artificial helps to distinction. But if such appliances are necessary to make small things great, so they may be used to lift great weights from the low level of bad character to high and respectable positions in government.

The hobby which Gov. Edwards selected on this occasion was to claim for the State all the public lands of the United States lying within its limits. This claim was put forth in his message at this session with great earnestness, and is elaborately sustained upon the ground of State sovereignty, to which eminent domain it must necessarily belong; and upon the ground that Illinois had been admitted into the Union upon an equal footing with the original States.

I have been informed on good authority that the governor put forth this claim without having any confidence in its validity, and that it was fabricated in the first instance only to embarrass his enemies. The question was new; it had never been discussed before the people and it was unknown whether they would regard it with favor or otherwise. However, the governor's enemies were not to be entrapped; they were too cunning to oppose what might be a popular measure out of mere spite against its author. It is believed that no one had any confidence in the claim and yet the legislature were nearly unanimous in sustaining it. But this resulted in breaking down the opposition to Gov. Edwards' administration, for the members, thinking themselves compelled to support his humbug, were more than ordinarily docile and obsequious, supporting all his measures and electing all his candidates to office. Having laid a broad foundation to enrich the State with the public lands, they returned to their constituents swelling with importance and high expectations of future favor. But the people were not such big fools as they were believed to be, for many of them were indifferent on the subject and most of them laughed at their representatives in very scorn of their pretensions. Governor Edwards died of the cholera in Belleville in the year 1833. The county of Edwards in the Wabash country and the town of Edwardsville in Madison county were named in honor of him; and I had forgotten to mention in its proper place that the county of Coles on the head waters of the Embarrass river (pronounced Embraw) was named in honor of Governor Coles.

In looking back over this period of time and calling to mind the prominent actors in the scenes of that day, the fierce struggles and quarrels amongst them, the loves and the hatreds, the hopes, fears, successes and disappointments of men recently but now no more on the stage of action, one cannot but be struck with the utter nothingness of mere contests for office. Of the men who then figured, Jesse B. Thomas, Gov. Coles, Chief Justice Philips, Henry Starr, and Judge

Hall have left the State; John McLean, Morris Birkbeck, Governor Bond, Elias K. Kane, Governor Edwards, Daniel P. Cook, Governor Duncan, Chief Justice Reynolds, George Forquer, Samuel McRoberts, and John York Sawyer are dead, reposing in their graves. But whilst they lived they were full of bustle and agitation, contending with each other for pre-eminence and place as if they divided the earth amongst them and office was immortal. Since their time they have had successors in the contest who have fluttered and shone for a few years and then disappeared forever, either by death, removal from the country, or loss of popularity. It is somewhat melancholy but highly instructive to look back upon the long list of popular names of those who for a time rioted in power, with a fair prospect of continued pre-eminence, but who have gone the way of all flesh to the grave or to oblivion, the way of the great mass of politicians.

About these times political parties began to form in Illinois. Hitherto Governor Edwards, Daniel P. Cook, and Judge Pope had constituted the heads of one party; whilst Governor Bond, Elias K. Kane, John McLean, Judge Thomas, and Judge Smith constituted the heads of the other. The parties which called forth their struggles were merely personal, and for men; measures and principles of national politics had nothing to do with them. Upon the election of Mr. Monroe in 1816 and during his long, successful, and glorious administration the angry elements of party were quelled and the nation rested in peace. The noise of the battle between federalist and republican had never reached Illinois. It is true that during the war of 1812 we had heard a rumor of the existence of such a people as the federalists in the old States. We had heard of their opposition to the war, of the Hartford Convention, and of the burning of blue lights in Connecticut as a signal to the enemy, and the unsophisticated republicans of the territory, being at war with and surrounded by thousands of hostile savages, naturally concluded that the federalists were second in atrocity only to the great beast with the seven heads and ten horns. A federalist was hated with a most fervent hatred as being an enemy to his country and an aider and abettor of the savages in slaughtering defenceless women and children; but as there were none of them in Illinois it was impossible to rally parties here upon the principles of federalists and republicans. I have already mentioned Daniel P. Cook as being the first attorney general.[6] He was elected to Congress in 1819 and was re-elected biennially until 1826 when he was beaten by the late Gov. Duncan. Mr. Cook was a man of eminent talents and accomplishments. In person he was small and erect. He was a man of great social powers, wholly without guile, and kindness, sincerity, and truth animated every motion of his body, making his face to shine and giving his manners a grace and a charm which the highest breeding will not always give. He was a complete gentleman, and in all his electioneering intercourse with the people he had the rare talent of making himself singularly acceptable and agreeable, without stooping to anything low or relaxing in the slightest degree the decorum or the carriage of a high-bred gentleman. His mind was uncommonly supple, wiry, and active and he could, as he pleased, shoot his thoughts readily over the great field of knowledge. As a speaker his voice, though not strong, was soft, melodious, and of great compass and variety of tone. He rose to a high reputation in Congress, and the last session he was there he acted as chairman of the important committee of Ways and Means of the lower house. To his services at this last session the people of Illinois are indebted for the donation by Congress of 300,000 acres of land for the construction of the Illinois and Michigan canal. For him the county of Cook was appropriately named, as more than half of its great prosperity is owing to his exertions in Congress in favor of the canal.

The defeat of Mr. Cook in 1826 by Gov. Duncan, marks a kind of turning point in the politics of Illinois. It is a new era in our elections, and marks the origin, though not the completion, of a great revolution in men's motives for political action. It is the point where the old system of electing public officers upon merit and personal preference was about to terminate, and the new principle of "measures, not men," was to begin. The opponents of Mr. Cook had run a candidate against him at every election; first John McLean, after him Elias K. Kane, and after him Gov. Bond. They had even endeavored to make Illinois a slave State, somewhat with a view to this eventual defeat. But they had failed on every occasion. Defeat only inspired new courage, and prompted them to the use of additional energy. They kept up their organization from year to year, and as parties were founded on the principle of personal affection to one set of men and personal hatred of another, and as men are more attached to their friends than to their principles, it followed that there was less defection and treachery in the ranks and more fidelity and devotion to leaders than have been since under the new system.

At last the time came for the Cook and Edwards party to go down and their enemies to rise. And this was the occasion of the revolution. Gen. Jackson, John Quincy Adams, William H. Crawford, and Henry Clay were candidates for President of the United States at the election of 1824. No one of the candidates received a majority of the electoral votes. The election, therefore, came into the House of Representatives in Congress. Mr. Cook gave the vote of Illinois to Mr. Adams, by which he was elected. Gen. Jackson had received more of the electoral votes than any other candidate. He had received two in Illinois, and Mr. Adams had received but one. The people believed that Gen. Jackson had been cheated out of his election by bargain, intrigue, and corruption; and whether their belief was well or ill-founded, they resented his defeat with a generous indignation which consumed all opposition, and which has continued to burn and consume until this day. The old opposition to the Cook and Edwards party and all the Crawford men now rallied in favor of Gen. Jackson. They brought out the late Gov. Duncan as a candidate against Mr. Cook, and by means of Gen. Jackson's great popularity and the resentment of the people against the vote for Mr. Adams he was elected by a small majority.

At this time Gov. Duncan was a thorough Jackson man, as the friends of Gen. Jackson were then called. He was what was called an original Jackson man, that is, he had been for Gen. Jackson the first time Gen. Jackson was a candidate. He was attached to Gen. Jackson from admiration of his character and the glory of his military achievements. As yet there were no principles or measures, nor even the names of federalist and republican, involved in the election. Gen. Jackson had not as yet declared his opinions on the tariff, except that he was in favor of "a judicious tariff;" nor upon internal improvements by Congress, the bankrupt law, the distribution of the proceeds of the sales of the public lands; nor upon the constitutionality or expediency of a United States Bank. Nor did parties in Illinois rally upon these subjects for some years afterwards. A few years after Gov. Duncan's first election Gen. Jackson attacked the United States Bank, vetoed its charter, and removed from it the deposits of the public moneys. He also vetoed appropriations for the Maysville road, and for the improvement of the Wabash river. Gov. Duncan now, differing from him in opinion on these subjects, began to withdraw from his support; and his aversion to Gen. Jackson's administration was finally completed by his objections to Mr. Van Buren, an influential favorite of the President, likely to succeed him in office and in the control of the Jackson party. A public man has a perfect right to his own opinions and predilections. Gov. Duncan was a brave, honest man, a gentleman in his intercourse with society, and possessed a rare talent for conciliating affection and inspiring confidence. But his great error was in becoming attached to a party and a cause in the first instance without knowing the principles by which he was to be governed. Thousands of others were in the same predicament, many of whom, both before and after Gov. Duncan, left as he did when the Jackson policy began to be developed; and many, equally ignorant when they began in favor of Gen. Jackson, finding themselves suited by his measures and principles adhered to him with more devotion than ever. Afterwards, when Gov. Duncan had thoroughly identified himself with the opponents of Gen. Jackson, an old friend of his rebuked him and lamented over him as follows: "Now, Gov. Duncan, we Jackson men took you up when you was young, poor, and friendless; we put you into high office and enabled you to make a fortune; and for all this you have deserted us and gone over to the Adams men. You was like a poor colt. We caught you up out of a thicket, fed you on the best, combed the burrs out of your mane and tail, and made a fine horse of you; and now you have strayed away from your owners." Such were, and are likely to be, the opinions of mankind upon changes of political relations. No allowance is made for the altered circumstances of the times, for the oblivion of old questions of dispute, or the springing up of new ones not dreamed of in former contests. Neither is any allowance made amongst fierce partisans for the fallibility of human judgment, nor for the results of a more matured, careful, and candid examination of political questions. Mankind adopt their principles when they are young, when the passions are strong, the judgment weak, the mind misinformed, and are generally influenced in their adoption by mere prejudice arising from attachment to friends. The mind has nothing to do with it. If afterwards they attain to more knowledge and capacity they are required to persevere in their first impressions or to be branded with inconsistency. Without asserting that Gov. Duncan was right in his change, for such would not be my opinion, yet it would seem from his example and that of many others that it would be better for politicians if they could reverse the order of their existence, come into the world in their old age and go out when they are young. As it really is, a man comes into the world without knowledge, experience, or capacity to think, and before he gets them, under the influence of his attachments to men, he is required to make up his opinions upon all the grave questions which are to affect himself or his country. He is to take a party name, and however much he may afterwards become enlightened, or parties shift grounds, he is never to change, under the penalty of being branded as a traitor to his party. But perhaps this is one of the means appointed by providence and implanted in man's nature to keep the opinions of the men of the governing or majority party united and give some stability to the councils of republican government. The fact that there is such a number who even down to old age are never capable of forming opinions of their own would seem to favor such a conclusion.

In the year 1828 and afterwards the policy of selling the school lands and borrowing the school fund was adopted. From the very first organization of the State government the legislature had been too fearful of its popularity to provide adequate revenues by taxation. At first the State treasury relied upon taxes upon lands in the military tract, then unsettled and owned by non-residents. The land tax in other parts was given to the counties to aid them in building court-houses and jails and paying county expenses. This system kept the State treasury in debt. But it so happened that Congress had donated to the State a township of land for a seminary of learning; three per cent. of the net proceeds of the sale of the public land, and the sixteenth section in every township for the support of common schools; that is, they had granted to the State one whole township of six miles square, and the thirty-sixth part of all the residue of the land in the State, and three per cent. of the net proceeds of the sales of the remainder to promote education in this new country. This was a most magnificent provision for education. The sixteenth section, amounting to near a million of acres, is destined to be worth a large sum of money. The man is now alive and full grown who will see the day when these lands will be worth from fifteen to twenty millions of dollars. So far as the sales have proceeded it may be judged that the whole of them will not sell for more than one million and-a-half, or two millions of dollars; and before the end of this generation it is to be feared that under the system adopted of selling and then lending out the price, most frequently on personal security, there will be no trace or vestige of this beneficent donation remaining either in money or lands.

Laws were first made for leasing out these lands, the rents to be paid in improvements; but the lessees soon desired a more permanent title. Every township throughout the inhabited parts had settlers on the school section, either as lessees or squatters, who were entitled to a vote at elections; and in a newly-settled country where the whole people came merely to better their individual fortunes as to property, with but little devotion to the public interest or to that of posterity, these lessees and squatters were likely to have great influence in government. And this is only one instance out of a thousand in Illinois in which a very small minority united by interest, passion, prejudice, or clanship and acting with bold vigor, has controlled the majority and sacrificed the public interest to individual interest. I speak what I know when I say that the laws to sell school lands were passed to please the people who were settled on them, who wanted to purchase them at the Congress price, whilst the other inhabitants being divided into little factions and thinking more of success at one election than the interest of all posterity; and acting upon the principle that what is everybody's business is nobody's business, aided or suffered the mischief to be done. It is true that other reasons were alleged in the legislature. It was said that if these lands were not sold the children of that generation must lose all benefit from them, and their value would be destroyed by being stripped of their timber. These were the reasons assigned in debate, but they were not the true reasons for these laws. It has been often the case in an Illinois legislature that a majority of the members for secret and selfish reasons of their own first resolve upon a measure and then invent the reasons to be given to the public for it afterwards; and these invented and artificial reasons are always the reasons assigned in debate. So, too, to relieve the State treasury from debt the legislature, to save the popularity of members by avoiding the just and wholesome measure of levying necessary taxes, passed laws for the sale of the seminary township and for borrowing the proceeds of the sale and the three per cent. school fund; and for paying them out as other public moneys and for paying an annual interest thereon to the several counties for the use of schools. By which means the debt of the State for these moneys alone amounted in 1842 to $472,493. Thus, as I conscientiously believe, was a township of land sacrificed at low prices; the school fund robbed, and a debt of near half a million of dollars fixed upon the State, rather than that the members would run the risk of not getting back to the legislature, or of being defeated for some other office. This money was paid into the treasury in sums averaging $20,000 per annum. The annual interest now paid on it is $28,000. And so to save the popularity of members of the legislature the State has received about $20,000 a year for about twenty-five years; by which she has become bound to pay $28,000 per annum, forever; the difference against the State being the difference between twenty thousand dollars borrowed, and twenty-eight thousand dollars annual interest; and the difference between eternity and twenty-five years. The only good which can result from these unwise and selfish measures is that they will inevitably compel the State into a system of taxation for the support of schools; and the payment of interest on these borrowed moneys will furnish the pretext and excuse for it.[7]

III

Political and Social Development, 1827–1830

Nothing more of importance occurred in the history of the State than what is related in the last chapter, until 1830. A few miscellaneous facts and a slight review of the progress of society and the workings of government during this time may not be uninteresting.

In 1827 there was a very excited election before the legislature for a State treasurer, in which the former incumbent of the office was defeated. After the election was over the Assembly immediately adjourned; but before the members got out of the house the unsuccessful candidate walked into their chamber and administered personal chastisement upon four of the largest and strongest of his opponents who had voted against him.[1] The members generally broke one way or another out of the house and fled like sheep from a fold invaded by a wolf. No steps were ever taken to bring the offender to punishment, but the same session he was appointed clerk of the circuit courts and recorder for Jo Daviess county.

During all this time from 1818 to 1830 a very large number of sheriffs elected by the people were defaulters to the State or to counties for taxes, or to individuals for moneys collected on execution. The practice was to take the moneys collected on execution and with them pay up for taxes, for without getting certificates of having paid all moneys charged to them for taxes the sheriffs were not allowed to be commissioned when re-elected. The people generally felt but little interest in the collection of moneys for debt and paying it over, so that a defalcation here was not apt to injure the popularity of an officer who would lend the people money to pay their taxes, and who was compelled by his official duty to be constantly around among them, giving him ample opportunity to make friends, contradict charges, and thus secure his election.

In those days justice was administered without much show, parade, or ceremony. In some countries the people are so ignorant and stupid that they have to be humbugged into a respect for the institutions and tribunals of the State. The judges and lawyers wear robes and gowns and wigs, and appear before them with all the "excellent gravity" described by Lord Coke. Wherever means like these are really necessary to give authority to government it would seem that the bulk of the people must be in a semi-barbarous state at least, and must so lack intelligence and capacity as to be influenced more by mere outside show than by the realities of wisdom and real dignity of character in the judge. The judges in early times in Illinois were gentlemen of considerable learning and much good sense, and held their courts mostly in log-houses or in the bar-rooms of taverns fitted up with a temporary bench for the judge and chairs or benches for the lawyers and jurors. At the first circuit court in Washington county, held by Judge John Reynolds, the sheriff, on opening the court went out into the court-yard and said to the people: "Boys, come in, our John is going to hold court." This was the proclamation for opening the court. In general the judges were averse to deciding questions of law if they could possibly avoid doing so. They did not like the responsibility of offending one or the other of the parties, and preferred to submit everything they could to be decided by the jury. They never gave instructions to a jury unless expressly called for; and then only upon the points of law raised by counsel in asking for them. They never commented upon the evidence or undertook to show the jury what inferences and presumptions might be drawn from it; for which reason they delivered their instructions hypothetically, stating them thus: "If the jury believe from the evidence that such a matter is proved, then the law is so and so." This was a clear departure from the practice of the judges in England and most of the United States; but the new practice suited the circumstances of the country. It undoubtedly requires the highest order of talent in a judge to "sum up" the evidence rightly to a jury so as to do justice to the case and injustice to neither party. Such talent did not exist to be put on the bench in these early times; or at least the judges must have modestly believed that they did not possess it.

I knew one judge who when asked for instructions would rub his head and the side of his face with his hand as if perplexed and say to the lawyers, "Why, gentlemen, the jury understand the case; they need no instructions; no doubt they will do justice between the parties." This same judge presided at a court in which a man named Green was convicted of murder; and it became his unpleasant duty to pronounce sentence of death upon the culprit. He called the prisoner before him, and said to him: "Mr. Green, the jury in their verdict say you are guilty of murder, and the law says you are to be hung. Now I want you and all your friends down on Indian Creek to know that it is not I who condemns you, but it is the jury and the law. Mr.

Green, the law allows you time for preparation, and so the court wants to know what time you would like to be hung." To this the prisoner replied, "May it please the court, I am ready at any time; those who kill the body have no power to kill the soul; my preparation is made, and I am ready to suffer at any time the court may appoint." The judge then said, "Mr. Green, you must know that it is a very serious matter to be hung; it can't happen to a man more than once in his life, and you had better take all the time you can get; the court will give you until this day four weeks. Mr. Clerk, look at the almanac and see whether this day four weeks comes on Sunday." The clerk looked at the almanac, as directed, and reported that "that day four weeks came on Thursday." The judge then said, "Mr. Green, the court gives you until this day four weeks, at which time you are to be hung." The case was prosecuted by James Turney, Esq., the attorney-general of the State, who here interposed and said: "May it please the court, I on solemn occasions like the present when the life of a human being is to be sentenced away for crime by an earthly tribunal it is usual and proper for courts to pronounce a formal sentence, in which the leading features of the crime shall be brought to the recollection of the prisoner, a sense of his guilt impressed upon his conscience, and in which the prisoner should be duly exhorted to repentance, and warned against the judgment in a world to come." To this the judge replied: "O! Mr. Turney, Mr. Green understands the whole matter as well as if I had preached to him a month. He knows he has got to be hung this day four weeks. You understand it in that way, Mr. Green, don't you?" "Yes," said the prisoner; upon which the judge ordered him to be remanded to jail and the court then adjourned.

If some judges were unwilling to risk censure by giving instructions to juries, there was at least one who was very positive in his mode of instructing them. This one, being more ambitious to show his learning and ability, gave very pointed instructions on one occasion; but the jury could not agree on a verdict. The judge asked to know the cause of their difference, whereupon the fore man answered with great apparent honesty and simplicity, "Why, judge, this *'ere* is the difficulty. The jury want to know whether that *ar* what you told us when we first went out was *raly* the law, or whether it was *ony jist* your notion." The judge of course informed them that it was really the law, and they found a verdict accordingly.

Some other judges through fear of doing wrong, or feeling a timid anxiety to avoid censure if they were compelled to give instructions which might decide the verdict on one side, were careful to accompany them with such exceptions and explanations as served to mystify what they had previously said, and destroy its force with the jury. Others again were accused of partiality, and when a principle of law was in favor of the party whom they desired to lose the case they took this mode, when compelled to give instructions, of rendering them of no force or value. To this day some of the judges are reluctant to give proper instructions to juries. This arises from a want of confidence felt by the judge in his own capacity; from a pusillanimous fear of giving offence, or a desire to avoid doing anything in favor of a side which the judge has determined shall not win if he can help it. It appears that this practice must have continued down to a late period, for the legislature of 1846 passed a law requiring all instructions to juries to be given in writing, and that there should be no exceptions or explanations but such as should be given in writing also. Whether this will be an improvement of the law remains to be seen.

In this period there were many eminent lawyers in the State. Messrs. Cook, McLean, Starr, Mears, Blackwell, Kane, Lockwood, Mills, and Chief Justice Thomas Reynolds would have ranked respectably as lawyers at any bar in the United States. The character of the litigation was somewhat different from what it has been since. Except during one time of general indebtedness the law suits were principally small appeal cases, actions of trespass, trover replevin, slander, indictments for assault and battery, affrays, riots, selling liquor without license, and card playing; but there was a natural leaning on the part of jurors against convictions for these minor offences, and so it was a rare thing that any one was convicted. There was now and then an indictment for murder or larceny and other felonies, but in all cases of murder arising from heat of blood or in fight it was impossible to convict. The juries were willing enough to convict an assassin or one who murdered by taking a dishonorable advantage, but otherwise if there was a conflict and nothing unfair in it. This same spirit prevailed in Kentucky and Tennessee, and was the cause of the great success of Clay, Rowan, and Grundy in defending trials for murder.

During a part of this time all elections were by ballot. This mode of voting has always been most insisted on in old settled countries in which wealth is accumulated in the hands of the few, where there are a few landlords, and the great body of the people tenants, where some are capitalists and employers, and others laborers and dependents. In such countries the ballot is supposed to preserve the independence of the poor and make them irresponsible to their wealthy superiors. But in Illinois the ballot mode of voting came near destroying all manly independence and frankness. As there were no measures to be contended for in elections, suffrage was bestowed as a matter of favor. To vote against a candidate was equivalent to an insult, by telling him that he was not so worthy or so well qualified as his opponent. Therefore many of the voters never let it be known how they voted at elections. And this was the origin of the "keep dark" system of former times, which is thus explained. Each candidate for office and his more immediate friends kept their preference for other candidates for other offices to be filled at the same election a profound secret. There were many offices to be filled at each election, and the candidates made secret combinations amongst each other for mutual support a few days before or on the day of election. But as these engagements for mutual support were secret and could only be carried out and fulfilled in secret many were the frauds and breaches of faith among the candidates and their friends. That candidate who was the most intriguing and unprincipled, in common cases was the most likely to be elected. In the course of a few years' practice under the system it was difficult to find any aspirant for office who would risk the expression of an opinion about any person or thing. Each one sought to keep himself in a position of non-committalism, in which he would be at liberty to make the best bargains for himself, to fulfil such engagements as would result most to his advantage, and to cheat such other candidates as he might be obliged to sacrifice. This "keep dark" system less or more pervaded the whole office-seeking tribe from the highest to the lowest, so that it was a rare thing to find amongst the humble expectants of the office of constable any degree of frankness of conversation or independence in the expression of opinion. No doubt this result was as much produced by the want of the influence of "measures," the want of party lines, as by the ballot mode of voting; but the two together made an election, so far as the candidates and their immediate friends were concerned, one great fraud, in which honor, faith, and truth were freely sacrificed and politicians were debased below the standard of the popular idea of that class of men. The ballot system of voting was repealed in 1828-'9.

In the primary elections by the people many influences were at work to thwart the establishment of a wise policy. In almost every county there was a race of the original pioneers, many of whom were ignorant, illiterate, and vicious. These were apt to be such as wore the hunting-shirt, the buckskin trousers, the raccoon skin cap, and leather moccasins. These delighted to wear a butcher knife as an appendage of dress. They claimed unbounded liberty, and were naturally hostile to any action of government tending to their improvement and civilization. It is true that this class of people formed but a small minority, but the better informed and more civilized portion were so divided by faction and split up by contests amongst themselves for power and office that these "butcher knife boys," as they were called, made a kind of balance of power party. These people, from their propensity to fight and to lead uproarious lives, were also called "the half horse and half alligator men." In all elections and in all enactments of the legislature great pains were taken by all candidates and men in office to make their course and measures acceptable to these "butcher knife boys;" and most of the elections in early times were made under "butcher knife influence;" not that these instruments were actually wielded to force an election, but only the votes of those who carried them. The candidate who had the "butcher knife boys" on his side was almost certain to be elected. Since the butcher knife has been disused as an article of dress, the fashion has been to call this class of people "the bare-footed boys," "the flat-footed boys," and "the huge-pawed boys," names with which they seem to be greatly tickled and pleased, and their influence is yet considerable in all elections.

Personal politics, intrigue, and a disregard of the public welfare were carried from the primary elections into the legislature. Almost everything there was done from personal motives. Special legislation for the benefit of friends occupied members and diverted their attention from such measures as were for the general benefit. The man of the most tact and address, who could make the most friends and the most skilful combinations of individual interests, was always the most successful in accomplishing his purposes. A smooth, sleek, supple, friendly manner, which by gaining favor imposed upon credulity, made a politician formidable. Truly, the man who could approach another with a graceful and friendly impudence and readily conciliate good-will, was potent indeed. The genius and humor of the times invented or imported a slang language very expressive of the achievements of these political heroes. Such an operator in politics was said to carry "a gourd of *possum fat*" with which to "grease" the members. It is not known why the fat of the opossum was selected for the emblem of this kind of tact, unless because it was the most fluid and slippery of oils then known in the country. The easy, facile, credulous fool who was the victim of artful fascination was said to be *"greased and swallowed."* A man was" greased" when he was won over to the purposes of another by a feigned show of friendship and condescension; and he was "swallowed" when he was made to act to suit the purposes of "the intrigue," whatever it might be. Sometimes the act of lubrication by which a man was fitted to be "swallowed" was supposed to be performed with *"soft soap."* It was no uncommon thing to hear that such a one "had a great deal of soft soap about him," and was a "great hand to swallow people." Gov. Edwards was said to be the greatest hand to swallow people in all the country; and when he was last a candidate for governor it was charged on him that he had not only swallowed a great many of his former enemies, but that he had actually performed the grand operation of swallowing himself. The simpleton who suffered himself to be made a mere instrument in the hands of another to do something discreditable or unpopular, whereby he was unable to be elected again, was said to be "used up," meaning that he had been used like the aforesaid soft soap or other household article until there was no more of him left.

During this period of twelve years neither the people nor their public servants ever dreamed that government might be made the instrument to accomplish a higher destiny for the people. There seemed to be no aim to advance the civilization and real happiness of the human family. Government was supposed to be necessary not because any one understood or cared for its true object but because men had been in the habit of living under government. The people looked around and they saw that everybody, everywhere else, lived under some kind of government, and they merely submitted to it to be in the fashion with other States and nations; but they did not want government to touch them too closely or in too many places: they were determined upon the preservation and enjoyment of their liberties. So that government made no encroachment upon liberty, they inquired no further into its true aim and object. But not so with politicians; they had a definite destiny to accomplish, not for the people but for themselves. In fact the great mass of the people, politicians and all, had a mere selfish destiny in view. The people were, most of them, pioneers and adventurers, who came to a new country hoping to get a living with more ease than they had been accustomed to, or to better their condition as to property. Such persons cared but little for matters of government except when stirred up by their demagogues; and then they had no definite object to accomplish except to punish their representatives for a single act or vote which was, nine times out of ten, a good one. The politicians took advantage of this lethargic state of indifference of the people to advance their own projects, to get offices and special favors from the legislature, which were all they busied their heads about. The people asked nothing and claimed nothing but to be let alone, and the politicians usually went to work to divide out the benefits and advantages of government amongst themselves; that is, amongst the active men who sought them with most tact and diligence. Offices and jobs were created, and special laws of all kinds of individual, not general benefit, were passed, and these good things were divided out by bargains, intrigues, and log-rolling combinations, and were mostly obtained by fraud, deceit, and tact.

It is related of Mr. Samuel Crozier, a former Senator from Randolph county, who was a remarkable example of the most pure, kind, and single-hearted honesty, that after serving two sessions in the Senate, at the close of the second, and after he had been bought and sold a hundred times without knowing it, he said he "really did believe that some intrigue had been going on." So little as this are honest men aware of the necessity of keeping their eyes open in sleepless watchfulness, or otherwise the few will monopolize all the advantages of government, and it will be done in the most unfair and corrupt manner. Thus it was that a corrupt, cunning, and busy activity blinded the eyes of the people and their representatives, governed in the name of the people, and divided out amongst those who practiced it nearly all the benefits and advantages of government. In every government the administration of it will, in the long run, reflect the true character of the people; and this is one thing which I desire to illustrate in this history. Many persons erroneously believe that good laws will make a good government; whereas, if the genius of the people will permit it, the best laws will be badly administered and will make a bad government. Reformation is not to begin with the laws or with the politicians, but with the people themselves; and when they are reformed, they will reform everything else. An indifferent, selfish, and ignorant people will be made known by selfish and corrupt politicians who administer their government and pervert the best of laws to the worst of purposes. If we could find a people truly wise, incapable of being misled, deceived, or humbugged, we should find statesmen instead of intriguing politicians, and a government where all the people enjoyed equal benefits and advantages arising from it, and where none would be permitted by fraud, tact, deceit and humbug to exceed their just share. If this rule be observed, it will be the true test by which to judge of the capacity of a people for a good or bad self-government. Up to the year 1840, I can say with perfect truth that considerations of mere party, men's condescensions, agreeable carriage, and professions of friendship had more influence with the great body of the people than the most important public services. The capacity to be grateful for public services, short of fighting the battles of the country, existed to but a limited extent. But some could be grateful for individual benefits and all resented individual injury.

About the year 1820 and perhaps a little before, one or two educated ministers of the gospel removed to this State. The Rev. John M. Peck of Rock Spring in St. Clair county, I believe, was the first one. By the year 1830 quite a number of them had come in from other States. They were either sent or encouraged to come by the missionary societies at the North and East; and being animated themselves by the principles of charity which have formed the religious world into benevolent societies of various sorts, they immediately began to make active efforts to get up Bible societies, tract societies, missionary societies, and Sunday schools in Illinois. For a long time they were looked upon with jealousy and bad feeling by some of the old race of uneducated preachers. These last had been the pioneers of the gospel at a time when educated ministers with salaries could not have been supported. They had preached the doctrine of a free salvation, truly and literally without money and without price. At their own expense had they traversed the wilderness, slept in the open air, swam rivers, suffered cold and hunger, travelled on horseback and on foot to preach the gospel and establish churches. They were now about to be superseded, as some of them feared, and thrown aside for nice, well-dressed young men from college, whom they stigmatized as having no religion in their hearts and with knowing nothing about it except what they had learned at school. A daintier taste for preaching had grown up in the towns, which could be satisfied only by a more polished and intellectual ministry. The new preachers settled themselves mostly in the villages and towns, where a more enlightened preaching was most in demand. They obtained here what little salary the people were willing and able to pay; but drew their chief support from the contributions of charitable societies in the old States; and from the towns they occasionally made short excursions to preach in the country places. They were charged by some of the old ministers with exercising their ministry for the lucre of gain; with selling the gospel to those who were able to pay for it; with desiring the salvation of the genteel, well-dressed, rich people who lived in the towns, and with being utterly unconcerned about the salvation of the rough poor people in the country, who were unable to pay them a salary. Nevertheless the new ministers persevered in their labors without taking any notice of these persecutions, and rapidly succeeded in forming congregations, organizing churches, and building places of worship. And now at this day the truth is apparent that both sorts of preachers were needed. Competition between them was not called for by the interest of either. The educated minister of the town with his learning and better information and his more chaste and subdued style of eloquence would have been but an indifferent teacher of religion in many country places; whilst the unlearned, rough and boisterous speaker of former times was as little suited to carry the message of grace to "ears polite" in town.

I have said already that these new ministers were active in establishing all those kinds of societies which have been made to illustrate the spirit of benevolent enterprise characteristic of the first part of the nineteenth century. Everywhere they endeavored to promote education among the people, and in a few years they undertook to build colleges and seminaries of learning; and to obtain acts of incorporation for them from the legislature. But such was the prejudice against them on the part of the people that they did not succeed in getting any charters for several years, and when they did get them each charter contained a prohibition of a theological department, so determined were the people that no institution should be encouraged by law for educating a sectarian ministry at home.

A most remarkable change occurred during this period and a little before in the habits of dress and appearance of the people. After the year 1830 a man dressed in the costume of the territory, which was a raccoon-skin cap, linsey hunting-shirt, buckskin breeches and moccasins, with a belt around the waist, to which the butcher-knife and tomahawk on the side and back were appended, was rarely to be seen. The blue linsey hunting shirt with red or white fringe had given place to the cloth coat; the raccoon-skin cap with the tail of the animal dangling down behind had been thrown aside for hats of wool or fur. Boots and shoes had supplanted the deer-skin moccasin, and the leather breeches strapped tight around the ankle had disappeared before unmentionables of more modern material. The female sex had made a still greater progress in dress. The old sort of cotton or woolen frocks, spun, wove and made with their own fair hands and striped and crossbarred with blue dye and turkey red had given place to gowns of silk and calico. The feet, before in a state of nudity, now charmed in shoes of calfskin or slippers of kid; and the head formerly unbonnetted but covered with a cotton handkerchief now displayed the charms of the female face under many forms of bonnets of straw, silk or leghorn. The young ladies instead of walking a mile or two to church on Sunday, carrying their shoes and stockings in their hands to within a hundred yards of the place of worship as formerly, now came forth arrayed complete in all the pride of dress, mounted on fine horses, and attended by their male admirers.

With the pride of dress came ambition, industry, the desire of knowledge, and a love of decency. It has been said that civilization is a forced state of man to which he is stimulated by a desire to gratify artificial wants; and it may be truly said that the young people of that day were powerfully advanced in the way of civilization by the new wants created by the new spirit by which they were animated. But the old people regretted the change. They would have been better contented to live in their old log cabins, go bare-footed, and eat hog and hominy. From such were heard complaints that the spinningwheel and the loom were neglected and that all the earnings of the young people were expended in the purchase of finery. The old world political economist foretold the ruin of the country. He was certain that all these new trappings and ornaments should be disused or manufactured at home; for if purchased from other States, all the money which came in must be sent out of the country as fast as it came.

But to the philosophical observer it appeared that those who adopted the new habits were more industrious and thrifty than those were who held on to the old ones. For this advancement in civilization the young people were much indebted to their practice of attending church on Sundays. Here they were regularly brought together at stated times; and their meeting, if it effected no better end, at least accustomed them to admire and wish to be admired. Each one wanted to make as good a figure as he could; and to that end came to meeting well-dressed and clean, riding on a fine horse elegantly caparisoned. This created in them a will to exert more than the old measure of industry; and taught them new notions of economy and ingenuity in business, to get the means of gratifying their pride in this particular. This again led to settled habits of enterprise, economy and tact in business, which once acquired and persevered in were made the cause of a thriftiness unknown to their fathers and mothers.

As to the practice of attending church on Sunday I am confident that it produced these effects I have observed very carefully in the course of thirty-five years spent on the extreme frontiers; that in those neighborhoods where the people habitually neglect to attend public worship on Sundays such improvements rarely, if ever, take place. In such places the young people feel no pride and do not desire improvement. They scarcely ever throw aside their every-day rough apparel to dress up neat and clean on Sunday. On that day the young men are seen with uncombed heads, unshorn beards, and unwashed linen, strolling in the woods hunting; or on the race-course, or at a grocery contracting habits of intoxication, or lounging sullenly and lazily at home. The young women in appearance, dress, manners and intelligence, are the fit companions for their brothers. Sunday to them brings no bright skies, no gladness, no lively and cheerful thoughts, and no spirits renovated by mixing in the sober, decent, quiet, but gay assemblage of youth and beauty. Their week of labor is not cheered by anticipations of the gay and bright fête with which it is to close. Labor through the week to them is a drudgery; and is performed with surliness and grudging; and their Sabbaths are spent in heedless sleepy stupidity. The young people of both sexes are without self-respect and are conscious of not deserving the respect of others. They feel a crushing and withering sense of meanness and inferiority mingled with an envious malignity towards all excellence in others who exhibit an ambition for improvement. Such neighborhoods are pretty certain to breed up a rough, vicious, ill-mannered and ill-natured race of men and women.

Commerce from 1818 to 1830 made but small progress. Steamboats commenced running the western waters in 1816 and by the year 1830 there were one or two small ones running on the Illinois river as far up as Peoria, and sometimes farther. The old keel-boat navigation had been disused; but as yet there was so little trade as not to call for many steamboats to supply their place. The merchants of the villages, few in number at first, were mere retailers of dry-goods and groceries; they purchased and shipped abroad none of the productions of the country except a few skins, hides and furs, and a little tallow and beeswax. They were sustained in this kind of business by the influx of immigrants, whose money being paid out in the country for grain, stock and labor, furnished the means of trade. The merchant himself rarely attempted a barter business and never paid cash for anything but his goods. There was no class of men who devoted themselves to the business of buying and selling, and of making the exchanges of the productions at home for those of other States and countries. The great majority, in fact nearly all the merchants, were mere blood-suckers, men who with a very little capital, a small stock of goods, and with ideas of business not broader than their ribbands nor deeper than their colors sold for money down, or on a credit for cash, which when received they sent out of the country. Since their time a race of traders and merchants has sprung up who use the money they receive for goods in purchasing the wheat, corn, beef, and pork of the farmers; and ship these articles to the eastern cities. Mather Lamb & Co., late of Chester in Randolph county, but now of Springfield, were the first to engage in this business; and they were led to it by the refusal of the United States Bank at St. Louis to grant them the usual facilities of trade. As they could get no accommodation from the bank, they fell upon this course to avoid going to St. Louis to purchase eastern exchange.

The money which they received, being again paid out, remained in the country and the produce went forward in its place to pay for stocks of goods. The traders in this way made a profit on their goods which they brought into the State and another profit on the produce which they sent out of it.

But, as yet the merchants generally had neither the capital nor the talents for such a business; and it was not until a more recent period, upon the going down of the United States Bank, the consequent withdrawal of facilities for exchange in money, and the high rates of exchange which came in with local banks of doubtful credit that they have been very extensively forced into it. When they could no longer get either money for remittance to their eastern creditors or bills of exchange except at ruinous rates of premium, they at once saw the advantage of laying out the local currency received for their goods in purchasing the staples of the country and forwarding them in the place of cash. In very early times there were many things to discourage regular commerce. A want of capital, a want of capacity for the business, the want of a great surplus of productions, the continual demand for them created by immigrants, and facility of carrying on a small commerce with the money supplied by emigration alone, all stood in the way of regular trade. New Orleans at that time was our principal market out of the State. It was then but a small city and shipped but a trifle of the staple articles of Illinois to foreign countries. Such shipments as were made to it were intended for the supply of the local market; and here the Illinoisans had to compete with Kentucky, Ohio, Indiana, Tennessee, and Missouri. Any temporary scarcity in this market was soon supplied and the most of the time it was completely glutted.

For want of merchants or others who were to make a business of carrying our staples to market our farmers undertook to be their own merchants and traders. This practice prevailed extensively in the western country. A farmer would produce or get together a quantity of corn, flour, bacon, and such articles. He would build a flat-bottomed boat on the shore of some river or large creek, load his wares into it, and, awaiting the rise of water, with a few of his negroes to assist him would float down to New Orleans. The voyage was long, tedious, and expensive. When he arrived there he found himself in a strange city, filled with sharpers ready to take advantage of his necessities. Everybody combined against him to profit by his ignorance of business, want of friends or commercial connexions; and nine times out of ten he returned a broken merchant. His journey home was performed on foot through three or four nations of Indians inhabiting the western parts of Mississippi, Tennessee, and Kentucky. He returned to a desolate farm which had been neglected whilst he was gone. One crop was lost by absence and another by taking it to market. This kind of business was persevered in astonishingly for several years to the great injury and utter ruin of a great many people.

In later times, after the steamboat had taken the place of other species of navigation, after regular dealers and business men had made their appearance on the theatre of trade, and after New Orleans had become a great city and a great mart of foreign commerce, there were still other difficulties to be encountered of a very formidable character. These were the disposition of the people not to sell their produce for the market price and to raise no surplus whatever unless the prices were high. If the trader offered one price the farmer would ask a little more, and more than the trader could afford to give and make a reasonable profit. Let the price be what it might, many would hold up their commodity a whole year, expecting a rise in the market; and if the price was low they would cease producing. If a farmer had a surplus of corn, wheat, hogs, or cattle in the fall season and could not sell them for the full price he demanded he would keep them until next year, expecting to get more for them then. In the meantime he would lose more by the natural loss and waste of his property than he could possibly gain by increased prices the next season. I have known whole stacks of wheat and whole fields of corn to rot or to be dribbled out and wasted to no purpose; and whole droves of hogs to run wild in the woods so as never to be reclaimed, whilst the owner was saving them for a higher price. He suffered, also, by laying out of the present use of the money, and by being compelled to purchase many necessary articles on a credit, at a higher price than they could be bought for with cash. By holding back for a higher price he suffered loss by the natural waste of his property, by laying out of the use of his money, by losing the many good bargains he could have made with it in the meantime, and by being compelled to purchase dear on a credit and pay a high interest on the debt if not paid when due. In all these ways he lost more than he would by borrowing money on compound interest. And yet he could never be persuaded that it was for his advantage to sell as soon as his article became marketable, and at the market price.

This practice of holding up property from the market unless the owner can receive more than the market price still prevails extensively in the southern and some of the eastern parts of the State, and fully accounts for much of the difference in the degree of prosperity which is found there and in the middle and northern part of the State.

The New England population make it a rule to sell all their marketable property as soon as it becomes fit for market, and at the market price. By this means the farmer avoids the loss and expense of keeping it on hand. He has the present use of its value in money and makes many good bargains and speculations which could not be made without a little ready money. He avoids buying on credit, or rather, paying interest on his debts after they become due. Money is more plenty and the whole people are enabled to be more punctual in the payment of their debts. The local merchant is enabled to do an active business. He is always sure that he can purchase to the extent of his capital and at rates which will put it in his power to sell at a profit. In this manner the farmer prospers, the local merchant prospers, the miller and manufacturer prosper. Towns grow up rapidly. Employment is furnished for mechanics and laborers. By such means our northern people are enabled to build up a country village in three or four years as large as a country seat in the south of twenty years' standing.*

*The people in many parts of the State have another practice which they must abandon before money can be plenty among them. They make their contracts to be paid in "trade at trade rates." This practice, by dispensing with the use of money in business, discourages its presence: whereas the opposite course, by creating a necessity for money, is the means of forcing it into the country. And accordingly, in all those countries where debts are punctually paid in cash, bargains all made to be paid in cash, laborers all paid in cash at short intervals, say at the end of the week, money is always the most plenty; and in those countries where the contrary course is pursued it is the most scarce. It is useless to say that plenty of money enables one country to do a cash business and that scarcity prevents it in the other. Money will go where it is most prized, used, and needed in business, and will refuse to go where its use is dispensed with, or to be used only to be hoarded. If any people want to be prosperous and have plenty of money, let them remember this.

IV

The Black Hawk War, 1831–1832

The population of the State had increased by the year 1830 to 157,447; it had spread north from Alton as far as Peoria, principally on the rivers and creeks; and in such places there were settlers sparsely scattered along the margin of the Mississippi river to Galena, sometimes at the distance of an hundred miles apart; also on the Illinois to Chicago, with long intervals of wilderness; and a few sparse settlements were scattered about all over the southern part of the military tract.[1] The country on the Sangamon river and its tributaries had been settled and also the interior of the south; leaving a large wilderness tract yet to be peopled between Galena and Chicago; the whole extent of the Rock river and Fox river countries, and nearly all the lands in the counties of Hancock, McDonough, Fulton, Peoria, Stark, Warren, Henderson, Knox, Mercer, Henry, Bureau, Livingston, Champaign, Platt, and Iroquois, comprising one-third of the territory of the State. As yet but few settlements had been made anywhere in the open wide prairies, but were confined to the margins of the timber in the vicinity of rivers and streams of water.

A new election for governor was to be held in August, 1830. The candidates for the office were John Reynolds, late a judge of the supreme court, and William Kinney, then lieutenant governor, both of them of the dominant party. All general elections since 1826, had resulted in favor of the friends of Gen. Jackson. The legislature always contained a large majority of Jackson men; but parties were not as yet thoroughly drilled and consolidated. On the one side there was a kind of idolatrous devotion to General Jackson; on the other, a mere personal opposition and dislike, with but little reference on either side to the principles of government. When the great popular movement commenced which resulted in the elevation of General Jackson to power many politicians ranged themselves under his banner as that of a popular and fortunate leader, upon whose shoulders they themselves could climb into power and office. Such persons were influenced in but a small degree by the spite and malice of party; so that if they could provide for themselves they were disposed to be kind and tolerant to their opponents. With many such it was the height of ambition to get to the legislature; and when they got there the sleek, smooth, pleasant men of tact and address in the minority seduced them from the majority; and so the legislative acts of public officers were as likely to result in favor of one party as the other. This was a matter of wonder and astonishment to the new immigrants from the older States, who came blazing hot like brands plucked from the burning, heated with the fiery contests in the States from whence they came between the old organized parties of federalists and republicans.

But party lines were so far drawn that no anti-Jackson man could be elected to Congress, to the United States Senate, or to be governor of the State. For this reason the anti-Jackson party proposed no candidate for governor at this election; some of them preferred one candidate of the dominant party and some the other; but the great body of the anti-Jackson party supported Governor Reynolds. Mr. Kinney was one of the old sort of Baptist preachers; his morality was not of that pinched up kind which prevented him from using all the common arts of a candidate for office. It was said that he went forth electioneering with a Bible in one pocket and a bottle of whiskey in the other; and thus armed with "the sword of the Lord and the spirit," he could preach to one set of men and drink with another, and thus make himself agreeable to all. In those days the people drank vast quantities of whiskey and other liquors; and the dispensation of liquors, or "treating," as it was called, by candidates for office was an indispensable element of success at elections. In many counties the candidates would hire all the groceries at the county seats and other considerable villages, where the people could get liquor without cost for several weeks before the election. In such places during the pending of elections the voters in all the neighboring country turned out on every Saturday to visit the county seat to see the candidates and hear the news. They came by dozens from all parts and on every road, riding on their ponies, which they hitched up or tied to the fences, trees, and bushes in the village. The candidates came also, and addressed the people from wagons, benches, old logs, or stumps newly cut, from whence comes the phrase "stump speeches," used to signify a popular harangue to the people by a candidate for office. The stump speeches being over, then commenced the drinking of liquor, and long before night a large portion of the voters would be drunk and staggering about town, cursing, swearing, hallooing, yelling, huzzaing for their favorite candidates, throwing their arms up and around, threatening to fight, and fighting. About the time of this election I have seen hundreds of such persons in the town of Springfield, now the polished seat of government of the State. Towards evening they would mount their ponies, go reeling from side to side, galloping through town, and throwing up their caps and hats, screeching like so many infernal spirits broke loose from their nether prison, and thus they departed for their homes.

This had been the case for many years in many counties at all the circuit courts, elections, and public gatherings; but thank God, such scenes are no more to be witnessed in Illinois.

Mr. Kinney had the name of being a whole hog, thorough-going original Jackson man. Politicians in those days of the Jackson party were divided into whole hog men and nominal Jackson men. Mr. Kinney belonged to the first division; he possessed a vigorous understanding, an original genius, and was a warm and true friend and a bitter enemy. He was a witty, merry and jovial man, who studied fun and was highly esteemed by his neighbors and acquaintances. The anti-Jackson men hated him more than they did Reynolds, and hence their preference for the latter. They did not so much vote *for* Reynolds as *against* Kinney. They were like the man who said that he had not voted for any candidate for the last ten years, nevertheless he had always voted at every election; but instead of voting *for* any one person, he had always voted *against* some rascal.

Judge Reynolds was made of more good-natured, easy and pliable materials. He had received a classical education and was a man of good talents in his own peculiar way; but no one would suppose from hearing his conversation and public addresses that he had ever learned more than to read and write and cypher to the rule of three; such acquisitions being supposed to constitute a very learned man in the times of his early life. He had been a farmer, a lawyer, and a soldier, a judge, and a member of the legislature. He had passed his life on the frontiers among a frontier people; he had learned all the bye-words, catch-words, old sayings and figures of speech invented by vulgar ingenuity and common among a backwoods people; to these he had added a copious supply of his own, and had diligently compounded them all into a language peculiar to himself, which he used on all occasions, both public and private. He was a man of remarkably good sense and shrewdness for the sphere in which he chose to move, and possessed a fertile imagination, a ready eloquence, and a continual mirthfulness and pleasantry when mingling with the people. He had a kind heart, and was always ready to do a favor and never harbored resentment against any human being. Such a man was certain to be successful against the Baptist preacher, and sure enough he was elected by a most triumphant majority.

A new legislature was elected at the same time; it contained a majority of Jackson men; a majority of whom again had been opposed to Reynolds' election; but the union of Reynolds' Jackson friends with the anti-Jackson members constituted a small majority of the legislature. It is not remembered that the new governor put forth or advocated any measure of public policy as a measure of his administration. But during this first session the legislature had to make provision for the redemption of the notes of the old State Bank, which became due in the course of the next summer.[2] No former legislature had dared to risk their popularity by providing for the redemption of these notes, by taxation or otherwise.

The subject had been put off from time to time, each legislature willing to shift the odious task upon their successors in office, until further delay would amount to a breach of the public faith. Something must now be done, and that immediately. The popularity-loving members of this legislature came up to the work with fear and trembling. They feared to be denounced as a band of perjured and faithless men if they neglected their duty, and they dreaded to meet the deep roar of indignant disapprobation from their angry constituents by performing it. But a majority in each house acted like men. They passed a law authorizing the celebrated Wiggins' loan of one hundred thousand dollars. The money was obtained and the notes of the bank were redeemed, the honor of the State was saved, but the legislature was damned for all time to come. The members who voted for the law were struck with consternation and fear at the first sign of the public indignation. Instead of boldly defending their act and denouncing the unprincipled demagogues who were inflaming the minds of the people, these members, when they returned to their constituents, went meanly sneaking about like guilty things, making the most humble excuses and apologies. A bolder course by enlightening the public mind might have preserved the standing of the legislature and wrought a wholesome revolution in public opinion, then much needed.

But as it was, the destruction of great men was noticeable for a great number of years. The Wiggins' loan was long a by-word in the mouths of the people. Many affected to believe that Wiggins had purchased the whole State, that the inhabitants for generations to come had been made over to him like cattle; and but few found favor in their sight who had anything to do with the loan. There has never been anything like this destruction of great men in Illinois except on a subsequent occasion when the legislature passed a law for the improvement of the breed of cattle by which small bulls were prohibited under *severe* penalties from running at large.[3] On this last occasion no one dreamed that a hurricane of popular indignation was about to be raised, but so it was: the people took sides with the little bulls. The law was denounced as being aristocratic and intended to favor the rich, who, by their money, had become possessed of large bulls, and were to make a profit by the destruction of the small ones; and besides this there was a generous feeling in the hearts of the people in favor of an equality of privileges even among bulls. These two laws overthrew many a politician, never to recover again or be seen in the public councils. The "Wiggins' loan" and "the little bull law" will be long remembered by numerous aspirants for office who were sunk by them so low in the public favor that the "hand of resurrection has never reached them."

At this session of 1830–'1, the criminal code was first adapted to penitentiary punishment, and ever after the old system of whipping and pillory for the punishment of crimes has been disused. In the course of fifteen years' experience under the new system I am compelled to say that crime has increased out of all proportion to the increase of inhabitants.

At this session there was a curious contest in the election of a State Treasurer. Judge Hall was the candidate of the Kinney men; John Dement was the candidate of Governor Reynolds. Hall was a violent anti-Jackson man, but had been editor of a newspaper in favor of Kinney. Dement was an original Jackson man, but had warmly supported Governor Reynolds. The Kinney men were the ultraists, the proscriptionists, and the whole-hog-men of the party, but yet they fought manfully for Hall, whilst the anti-Jackson members fought as manfully for Dement. On this question the two parties exchanged positions and candidates.

Not long after the adjournment of this session news came of disturbances by the Indians in the Rock river country. It appears that a treaty had been made by Gen. Harrison at St. Louis in November, 1804 with the chiefs of the Sac and Fox nations of Indians by which those Indians had ceded to the United States all their land on Rock river, and much more elsewhere. This treaty was confirmed by a part of the tribe in a treaty with Gov. Edwards and Auguste Chouteau in September, 1815 and by another part in a treaty with the same commissioners in May, 1816. The United States had caused some of these lands situate at the mouth of Rock river to be surveyed and sold. These lands included the great town of the nation near the mouth of the river. The purchasers from the government moved on to their lands, built houses, made fences and fields, and thus took possession of the ancient metropolis of the Indian nation. This metropolis consisted of about two or three hundred lodges made of small poles set upright in the ground upon which other poles were tied transversely with bark at the top so as to hold a covering of bark peeled from the neighboring trees, and secured with other strips of bark with which they were sewed to the transverse poles. The sides of the lodges were secured in the same manner. The principal part of these Indians had long since moved from their town to the west of the Mississippi.

But there was one old chief of the Sacs, called Mucata Muhicatah, or Black Hawk, who always denied the validity of these treaties. Black Hawk was now an old man. He had been a warrior from his youth. He had led many a war party on the trail of an enemy, and had never been defeated. He had been in the service of England in the war of 1812 and had been aid-de-camp to the great Tecumseh. He was distinguished for courage and for clemency to the vanquished. He was an Indian patriot, a kind husband and father, and was noted for his integrity in all his dealings with his tribe and with the Indian traders. He was firmly attached to the British and cordially hated the Americans. At the close of the war of 1812 he had never joined in making peace with the United States, but he and his band still kept up their connection with Canada and were ever ready for a war with our people. He was in his personal deportment grave and melancholy, with a disposition to cherish and brood over the wrongs he supposed he had received from the Americans. He was thirsting for revenge upon his enemies and at the same time his piety constrained him to devote a day in the year to visit the grave of a favorite daughter buried on the Mississippi river, not far from Oquaka. Here he came on his yearly visit and spent a day by the grave, lamenting and bewailing the death of one who had been the pride of his family and of his Indian home. With these feelings was mingled the certain and melancholy prospect of the extinction of his tribe and the transfer of his country, with its many silvery rivers, rolling and green prairies, and dark forests, the haunts of his youth, to the possession of a hated enemy; whilst he and his people were to be driven as he supposed into a strange country, far from the graves of his fathers and his children.

Black Hawk's own account of the treaty of 1804 is as follows. He says that some Indians of the tribe were arrested and imprisoned in St. Louis for murder, that some of the chiefs were sent down to provide for their defence; that whilst there, and without the consent of the nation, they were induced to sell the Indian country; that when they came home it appeared that they had been drunk most of the time they were absent, and could give no account of what they had done except that they had sold some land to the white people and had come home loaded with presents and Indian finery. This was all that the nation ever heard or knew about the treaty of 1804.*

Under the pretence that this treaty was void he resisted the order of the government for the removal of his tribe west of the Mississippi. In the spring of 1831 he recrossed the river with his women and children and three hundred warriors of the British band, together with some allies from the Potawatomie and Kickapoo nations, to establish himself upon his ancient hunting-grounds and in the principal village of his nation. He ordered the white settlers away, threw down their fences, unroofed their houses, cut up their grain, drove off and killed their cattle, and threatened the people with death if they remained. The settlers made their complaints to Governor Reynolds. These acts of the Indians were considered by the governor to be an invasion of the State. He immediately addressed letters to Gen. Gaines of the United States army and to Gen. Clark the superintendent of Indian affairs, calling upon them to use the influence of the government to procure the peaceful removal of the Indians, if possible; at all events to defend and protect the American citizens who had purchased those lands from the United States and were now about to be ejected by the Indians. Gen. Gaines repaired to Rock Island with a few companies of regular soldiers and soon ascertained that the Indians were bent upon war. He immediately called upon Governor Reynolds for seven hundred mounted volunteers. The governor obeyed the requisition. A call was made upon some of the northern and central counties, in obedience to which fifteen hundred volun-

---

*It may be well here to mention, that some historians of the Black Hawk war have taken much of the matter of their histories from a life of Black Hawk written at Rock Island in 1833 or 1834, purporting to have been his own statements written down on the spot. This work has misled many. Black Hawk knew but little, if anything, about it. In point of fact it was got up from the statements of Mr. Antoine Le Clere and Col. Davenport and was written by a printer, and was never intended for anything but a catch-penny publication. Mr. Le Clere was a half-breed Indian interpreter, and Col. Davenport an old Indian trader, whose sympathies were strongly enlisted in favor of the Indians and whose interest it was to retain the Indians in the country for the purposes of trade. Hence the gross perversion of facts in that book, attributing this war to the border white people, when in point of fact these border white people had bought and paid for the land on which they lived from the government, which had a title to it by three different treaties. They were quietly and peaceably living upon their lands when the Indians under Black Hawk attempted to dispossess them. As yet I have seen no excuse for Black Hawk's second invasion of the State in breach of his own treaty with Gen. Gaines in 1831; but the sympathizers with the Indians skip over and take no notice of that treaty, so determined have they been to please their own countrymen at all hazards.

teers rushed to his standard at Beardstown, and about the 10th of June were organized and ready to be marched to the seat of war. The whole force was divided into two regiments, an odd battalion and a spy battalion. The 1st regiment was commanded by Col. James D. Henry, the 2d by Col. Daniel Lieb, the odd battalion by Major Nathaniel Buckmaster, and the spy battalion by Major Samuel Whiteside. The whole brigade was put under the command of Major General Joseph Duncan of the State Militia. This was the largest military force of Illinoisans which had ever been assembled in the State, and made an imposing appearance as it traversed the then unbroken wilderness of prairie.

The army proceeded in four days to the Mississippi at a place now called Rockport, about eight miles below the mouth of Rock river, where it met Gen. Gaines in a steamboat, with a supply of provisions. Here it encamped for one night, and here the two generals concerted a plan of operations. Gen. Gaines had been in the vicinity of the Indian town for about a month, during which time it might be supposed that he had made himself thoroughly acquainted with the localities and topography of the country. The next morning the volunteers marched forward with an old regular soldier for a guide. The steamboat with Gen. Gaines ascended the river. A battle was expected to be fought that day on Vandruff's Island, opposite the Indian town. The plan was for the volunteers to cross the slough on to this island, give battle to the enemy if found there, and then to ford the main river into the town, where they were to be met by the regular force coming down from the fort. The island was covered with bushes and vines so as to be impenetrable to the sight at the distance of twenty feet. General Gaines ran his steamboat up to the point of the island and fired several rounds of grape and canister shot into it to test the presence of an enemy. The spy battalion formed in line of battle and swept the island; but it was soon ascertained that the ground rose so high within a short distance of the bank that General Gaines's shot could not have taken effect one hundred yards from the shore. The main body of the volunteers in three columns came following the spies; but before they had got to the northern side of the island they were so jammed up and mixed together, officers and men, that no man knew his own company or regiment or scarcely himself. Gen. Gaines had ordered the artillery of the regular army to be stationed on a high bluff which looked down upon the contemplated battlefield a half mile distant, from whence, in case of battle with the Indians in the tangled thickets of the island their shot were likely to kill more of their friends than their enemies. It would have been impossible for the artillerists to distinguish one from the other. And when the army arrived at the main river they found it a bold, deep stream, not fordable for a half mile or more above by horses, and no means of transportation was then ready to ferry them over. Here they were in sight of the Indian town, with a narrow but deep river running between, and here the principal part of them remained until scows could be brought to ferry them across it.

When the volunteers reached the town they found no enemy there. The Indians had quietly departed the same morning in their canoes for the western side of the Mississippi. Whilst in camp twelve miles below the evening before, a canoe load of Indians came down with a white flag to tell the General that they were peaceable Indians, that they expected a great battle to come off next day, that they desired to remain neutral and wanted to retire with their families to some place of safety, and they asked to know where that was to be. General Gaines answered them very abruptly, and told them to be off and go to the other side of the Mississippi. That night they returned to their town and the next morning early the whole band of hostile Indians re-crossed the river and thus entitled themselves to protection.

It has been stated to me by Judge William Thomas of Jacksonville, who acted as quartermaster of the brigade of volunteers, that Gaines and Duncan had reason to believe before the commencement of the march from the camp on the Mississippi that the Indians had departed from their village, that measures had been taken to ascertain the fact before the volunteers crossed to Vandruff's Island, that Gen. Duncan in company with the advanced guard following the spies preceded the main army in crossing, and that this will account for the want of order and confusion in the march of the troops.

I was myself in company with the spies, I arrived at the river a mile in advance of the army, I saw Gen. Gaines ascend with his boat to the point of the island, was within one hundred yards of him when he fired into the island to test the presence of the Indians; I marched ahead with the spies across the island, saw with my own eyes the elevation of the land near the shore, which would have prevented cannon-shot taking effect more than one hundred yards. I also know the condition of the island as to bushes and vines, and saw the artillery force from the fort stationed on the high bluff on the opposite side of the river. I was on the bank of the main river when Gen. Duncan came up, followed soon after by his brigade in the utmost confusion, and heard him reprimand John S. Miller, a substantial and worthy citizen of Rock Island, for not letting him know that the main river was on the north side of the island; and I heard Miller curse him to his face at the head of his troops for refusing his services as guide when offered the evening before; and then censuring him for not giving information which he had refused to receive. I give the facts as I personally know them to be true, and leave it to others to judge whether the two Generals knew of the departure of the Indians; had taken proper measures to ascertain the presence of an enemy, or had made the best disposition for a battle if the Indians had been found either at their village or on the island. Much credit is undoubtedly due to Gov. Reynolds and Gen. Duncan for the unprecedented quickness with which the brigade was called out and organized and marched to the seat of war, and neither of them are justly responsible for what was arranged for them by Gen. Gaines.

The enemy having escaped, the volunteers were determined to be avenged upon something. The rain descended in torrents and the Indian wigwams would have furnished a comfortable shelter; but notwithstanding the rain the whole town was soon wrapped in flames, and thus perished an ancient village which had once been the delightful home of six or seven thousand Indians; where generation after generation had been born, had died and been buried; where the old men had taught wisdom to the young; whence the Indian youth had often gone out in parties to hunt or to war, and returned in triumph to dance around the spoils of the forest or the scalps of their enemies; and where the dark-eyed Indian maidens by their presence and charms had made it a scene of delightful enchantment to many an admiring warrior.

The volunteers marched to Rock Island next morning and here they encamped for several days, precisely where the town of Rock Island is now situated. It was then in a complete state of nature, a romantic wilderness. Fort Armstrong was built upon a rocky cliff on the lower point of an island near the centre of the river, a little way above; the shores on each side formed of gentle slopes of prairie extending back to bluffs of considerable height, made it one of the most picturesque scenes in the western country. The river here is a beautiful sheet of clear, swift-running water, about three quarters of a mile wide, its banks on both sides were uninhabited except by Indians from the lower rapids to the fort, and the voyager up-stream after several days' solitary progress through a wilderness country on its borders came suddenly in sight of the white-washed walls and towers of the fort, perched upon a rock surrounded by the grandeur and beauty of nature, which at a distance gave it the appearance of one of those enchanted castles in an uninhabited desert, so well described in the Arabian-Nights Entertainments.

General Gaines threatened to pursue the Indians across the river, which brought Black Hawk and the chiefs and braves of the hostile band to the fort to sue for peace. A treaty was here formed with them by which they agreed to remain forever after on the west side of the river, and never to recross it without the permission of the president or the governor of the State. And thus these Indians at last ratified the treaty of 1804 by which their lands were sold to the white people, and they agreed to live in peace with the government.

But notwithstanding this treaty, early in the spring of 1832 Black Hawk and the disaffected Indians prepared to reassert their right to the disputed territory.

The united Sac and Fox nations were divided into two parties. Black Hawk commanded the warlike band and Keokuk, another chief, headed the band which was in favor of peace. Keokuk was a bold, sagacious leader of his people, was gifted with a wild and stirring eloquence rare to be found even among Indians, by means of which he retained the greater part of his nation in amity with the white people. But nearly all the bold, turbulent spirits, who delighted in mischief, arranged themselves under the banners of his rival. Black Hawk had with him the chivalry of his nation, with which he recrossed the Mississippi in the spring of 1832. He directed his march to the Rock river country and this time aimed, by marching up the river into the countries of the Pottawattomies and Winnebagoes, to make them his allies. Governor Reynolds upon being informed of the facts made another call for volunteers. In a few days eighteen hundred men rallied under his banner at Beardstown. This force was organized into four regiments and a spy battalion. Col. DeWitt commanded the 1st regiment, Col. Fry the 2d, Col. Thomas the 3d, Col. Thompson the 4th, and Col. James D. Henry commanded the spy battalion. The whole brigade was put under the command of Brigadier Gen. Samuel Whiteside of the State militia, who had commanded the spy battalion in the first campaign.

On the 27th of April Gen. Whiteside, accompanied by Gov. Reynolds, took up his line of march. The army proceeded by way of Oquaka on the Mississippi to the mouth of Rock river, and here it was agreed between Gen. Whiteside and Gen. Atkinson of the regulars that the volunteers should march up Rock river about fifty miles to the Prophet's town and there encamp to feed and rest their horses and await the arrival of the regular troops in keel boats with provisions.

Judge William Thomas, who again acted as quartermaster to the volunteers, made an estimate of the amount of provisions required until the boats could arrive, which was supplied, and then Gen. Whiteside took up his line of march. But when he arrived at the Prophet's town instead of remaining there his men set fire to the village, which was entirely consumed, and the brigade marched on in the direction of Dixon, forty miles higher up the river. When the volunteers had arrived within a short distance of Dixon orders were given to leave the baggage wagons behind so as to reach there by a forced march. And for the relief of the horses, the men left large quantities of provisions behind with the wagons. At Dixon Gen. Whiteside came to a halt to await a junction with Gen. Atkinson, with provisions and the regular forces; and from here parties were sent out to reconnoitre the enemy and ascertain his position. The army here found upon its arrival two battalions of mounted volunteers, consisting of 275 men, from the counties of McLean, Tazewell, Peoria, and Fulton under the command of Majors Stillman and Bailey. The officers of this force begged to be put forward upon some dangerous service in which they could distinguish themselves. To gratify them they were ordered up Rock river to spy out the Indians. Major Stillman began his march on the 12th of May, and pursuing his way on the south-east side he came to "Old Man's" creek, since called "Stillman's Run," a small stream which rises in White Rock Grove in Ogle county and falls into the river near Bloomingville. Here he encamped just before night; and in a short time a party of Indians on horseback were discovered on a rising ground about one mile distant from the encampment. A party of Stillman's men mounted their horses without orders or commander and were soon followed by others, stringing along for a quarter of a mile, to pursue the Indians and attack them. The Indians retreated after displaying a red flag, the emblem of defiance and war, but were overtaken and three of them slain. Here Major Samuel Hackelton, being dismounted in the engagement, distinguished himself by a combat with one of the Indians in which the Indian was killed, and Major Hackelton afterwards made his way on foot to the camp of Gen. Whiteside. Black Hawk was near by with his main force, and being prompt to repel an assault soon rallied his men, amounting then to about seven hundred warriors, and moved down upon Major Stillman's camp, driving the disorderly rabble, the recent pursuers, before him. These valorous gentlemen, lately so hot in pursuit when the enemy were few, were no less hasty in their retreat when coming in contact with superior numbers. They came with their horses in a full run, and in this manner broke through the camp of Major Stillman, spreading dismay and terror among the rest of his men who imme-diately began to join in the flight, so that no effort to rally them could possibly have succeeded. Major Stillman, now too late to remedy the evils of insubordination and disorder in his command, did all that was practicable by ordering his men to fall back in order and form on higher ground; but as the prairie rose behind them for more than a mile, the ground for a rally was never discovered; and besides this, when the men once got their backs to the enemy they commenced a retreat, without one thought of making a further stand. A retreat of undisciplined militia from the attack of a superior force is apt to be a disorderly and inglorious flight; and so it was here, each man sought his own individual safety and in the twinkling of an eye the whole detachment was in utter confusion. They were pursued in their flight by thirty or forty Indians for ten or twelve miles, the fugitives in the rear keeping up a flying fire as they ran, until the Indians ceased pursuing.

But there were some good soldiers and brave men in Stillman's detachment whose individual efforts succeeded in checking the ca-reer of the Indians, whereby many escaped that night who would otherwise have been the easy victims of the enemy. Amongst these were Major Perkins and Captain Adams, who fell in the rear, bravely fighting to cover the retreat of their fugitive friends. But Major Still-man and his men pursued their flight without looking to the right or the left until they were safely landed at Dixon. The party came strag-gling into camp all night long, four or five at a time, each fresh arriv-al confident that all who had been left behind had been massacred by the Indians. The enemy was stated to be just behind in full pur-suit, and their arrival was looked for every moment. Eleven of Still-man's men were killed, and it is only astonishing that the number was so few.

It is said that a big, tall Kentuckian with a very loud voice, who was a colonel of the militia but a private with Stillman, upon his ar-rival in camp gave to Gen. Whiteside and the wondering multitude the following glowing and bombastic account of the battle: "Sirs," said he, "our detachment was encamped amongst some scattering tim-ber on the north side of Old Man's creek, with the prairie from the north gently sloping down to our encampment.[4] It was just after twi-light, in the gloaming of the evening, when we discovered Black Hawk's army coming down upon us in solid column; they deployed in the form of a crescent upon the brow of the prairie and such ac-curacy and precision of military movements were never witnessed by man; they were equal to the best troops of Wellington in Spain. I have said that the Indians came down in solid column and deployed in the form of a crescent; and what was most wonderful, there were large squares of cavalry resting upon the points of the curve, which squares were supported again by other columns fifteen deep, extending back through the woods and over a swamp three-quarters of a mile, which again rested upon the main body of Black Hawk's army bivouaced upon the banks of the Kishwakee. It was a terrible and a glorious sight to see the tawny warriors as they rode along our flanks attempting to outflank us with the glittering moonbeams glistening from their polished blades and burnished spears. It was a sight well calculated to strike consternation into the stoutest and boldest heart, and accordingly our men soon began to break in small squads for tall timber. In a very little time the rout became general, the Indians were upon our flanks and threatened the destruction of the entire detachment. About this time Major Stillman, Col. Stephenson, Major Perkins, Capt. Adams, Mr. Hackelton, and myself with some others threw ourselves into the rear to rally the fugitives and protect the retreat. But in a short time all my companions fell, bravely fighting hand to hand with the savage enemy, and I alone was left upon the field of battle. About this time I discovered not far to the left a corps of horsemen which seemed to be in tolerable order. I immediately deployed to the left, when leaning down and placing my body in a recumbent posture upon the mane of my horse, so as to bring the heads of the horsemen between my eye and the horizon, I discovered by the light of the moon that they were gentlemen who did not wear hats, by which token I knew they were no friends of mine. I therefore made a retrograde movement and recovered my former position, where I remained some time meditating what further I could do in the service of my country, when a random-ball came whistling by my ear and plainly whispered to me, 'stranger, you have no further business here.' Upon hearing this I followed the example of my companions in arms and broke for tall timber, and the way I run was not a little, and quit."

This colonel was a lawyer, just returning from the circuit with a slight wardrobe and Chitty's Pleadings packed in his saddle-bags, all of which were captured by the Indians. He afterwards related with much vexation that Black Hawk had decked himself out in his finery, appearing in the wild woods amongst his savage companions dressed in one of the colonel's ruffled shirts drawn over his deer-skin leggings, with a volume of Chitty's Pleadings under each arm.

Major Stillman and his men were for a long time afterwards the subject of thoughtless merriment and ridicule, which were as undeserved as their battle, if so it may be called, had been unfortunate.

The party was raw militia; it had been but a few days in the field; the men were wholly without discipline and as yet without confidence in each other or in their officers.

This confidence they had not been long enough together to acquire. Any other body of men under the same circumstances would have acted no better. They were as good material for an army, if properly drilled and disciplined, as could be found elsewhere.[5]

In the night after their arrival at Dixon the trumpet sounded a signal for the officers to assemble at the tent of Gen. Whiteside. A council of war was held in which it was agreed to march early the next morning to the fatal field of that evening's disaster. In consequence of the ill-advised and misjudged march from the Prophet's town, the wastefulness of the volunteers, and leaving the baggage wagons behind to make a forced march without motive or necessity, there were no provisions in the camp except in the messes of the most careful and experienced men. The majority had been living upon parched corn and coffee for two or three days. But Quartermaster Thomas, anticipating the result of the council, went out in search of cattle and hogs, which were obtained of Mr. John Dixon, then the only white inhabitant on Rock river above its mouth. By this means, before daylight the next morning the army was supplied with some fresh beef, which they ate without bread, and now they began their march for the scene of the disaster of the night before. When the volunteers arrived there the Indians were gone. They had scattered out all over the country, some of them farther up Rock river and others towards the nearest settlements of white people.

A party of about seventy Indians made a descent upon the small settlement of Indian creek, a tributary of Fox river, and there within fifteen miles of Ottawa they massacred fifteen persons, men, women, and children, of the families of Messrs. Hall, Davis, and Pettigrew and took two young women prisoners. These were Sylvia and Rachel Hall, the one about seventeen and the other about fifteen years old.

This party of Indians immediately retreated into the Winnebago country, up Rock river, carrying the scalps of the slain and their prisoners with them. Indian wars are the wars of a past age. They have always been characterized by the same ferocity and cruelty on the part of the Indians. To describe this massacre is only to repeat what has been written a hundred times; but the history of this war would be imperfect without some account of it. The Indians approached the house in which the three families were assembled in the day time. They entered it suddenly, with but little notice. Some of the inmates were immediately shot down with rifles, others were pierced through with spears or despatched with the tomahawk. The Indians afterwards related with an infernal glee how the women had squeaked like geese when they were run through the body with spears, or felt the sharp tomahawk entering their heads. All the victims were carefully scalped; their bodies were mutilated and mangled; the little children were chopped to pieces with axes; and the women were tied up by the heels to the walls of the house; their clothes falling over their heads, left their naked persons exposed to the public gaze.

The young women prisoners were hurried by forced marches beyond the reach of pursuit. After a long and fatiguing journey with their Indian conductors through a wilderness country, with but little to eat and being subjected to a variety of fortune, they were at last purchased by the chiefs of the Winnebagoes, employed by Mr. Gratiot for the purpose, with two thousand dollars in horses, wampum, and trinkets, and were safely returned to their friends.[6]

Gen. Whiteside, finding no Indians in the vicinity of the recent battle-field and being destitute of provisions, contented himself with burying the dead. He gathered up their mutilated bodies as well as he could and buried them in a common grave on a ridge of land on the old trace south of "Stillman's run," and put up a rude board, hewn from a tree, as a memorial of the slain. He then returned to Dixon, where on the next day Gen. Atkinson arrived with provisions and the regular forces. The army now amounted to twenty-four hundred, and had the men been willing to serve longer the war could have been ended in less than a month by the capture or destruction of all Black Hawk's forces. But the volunteers were anxious to be discharged. Their term of service had nearly expired. Many of them had left their business in such a condition as to require their presence at home; and besides this there was much dissatisfaction with the commanding general. To require further service from unwilling men was worse than useless, for a militia force will never do any good unless their hearts prompt them to a cheerful alacrity in performing their duty. The militia can never be forced to fight against their will. Their hearts as well as their bodies must be in the service; and to do any good they must feel the utmost confidence in their officers. They were first marched back to the battle-field in pursuit of the Indians and then by Pawpaw Grove and Indian creek to Ottawa, where the whole at their urgent request were discharged by Governor Reynolds on the 27th and 28th of May.

The governor had previously issued orders for raising two thousand additional volunteers to rendezvous at Beardstown and Hennepin. In the meantime he called for a volunteer regiment from amongst those recently discharged to remain in defence of the country until the new forces could be assembled. Such a regiment was readily raised, of which Jacob Fry was elected colonel, James D. Henry lieutenant-colonel, and John Thomas major. Whiteside, the late commanding general, volunteered as a private. The different companies of this regiment were so disposed of as to guard all the frontiers. Captain Adam W. Snyder was sent to range through the country between Rock river and Galena; and whilst he was encamped not far distant from Burr Oak Grove on the night of the 17th of June his company was fired upon by the Indians; the next morning he pursued them, four in number, and drove them into a sink-hole in the ground, where his company charged on them and killed the whole of the Indians, with the loss of one man mortally wounded. As he returned to his camp, bearing his wounded soldier, the men suffering much from thirst scattered in search of water, when they were sharply attacked by about seventy Indians who had been secretly watching their motions and awaiting a good opportunity. His men, as usual in such cases, were taken by surprise and some of them commenced a hasty retreat. Captain Snyder called upon Gen. Whiteside, then a private in his company, to assist him in forming his men; the general proclaimed in a loud voice that he would shoot the first man who attempted to run. The men were soon formed into rank. Both parties took position behind trees. Here General Whiteside, an old Indian fighter and a capital marksman with a rifle, shot the commander of the Indians, and they from that moment began to retreat.[7] As they were not pursued the Indian loss was never ascertained; but the other side lost two men killed and one wounded. Captain Snyder, General Whiteside, and Colonel (now General) Semple are particularly mentioned as having behaved in the most honorable and courageous manner in both these little actions.

On the 15th of June the new levies had arrived at the places of rendezvous and were formed into three brigades; General Alexander Posey commanded the 1st, General Milton K. Alexander the 2d, and General James D. Henry commanded the 3d. On the march each brigade was preceded by a battalion of spies commanded by a major. The whole volunteer force this time amounted to three thousand two hundred men, besides three companies of rangers under the command of Major Bogart, left behind to guard the frontier settlements. The object in calling out so large a force was to overawe the Pottawattomie and Winnebago Indians, who were hostile in their feelings to the whites and much disposed to join Black Hawk's party.

But before the new army could be brought into the field the Indians had committed several murders. One man was killed on Bureau creek some seven or eight miles above Princeton; another in Buffalo Grove; another between Fox river and the Illinois; and two more on the east side of Fox river on the Chicago road about six miles north-east of Ottawa. On the 22d of May Gen. Atkinson had despatched Mr. St. Vrain, the Indian agent for the Sacs and Foxes at Rock Island, with a few men as an express to Fort Armstrong.[8] On their way thither they fell in with a party of Indians led by a chief well known to the agent. This chief was called "The little bear," he had been a particular friend of the agent, and had adopted him as a brother. Mr. St. Vrain felt no fear of one who was his friend, one who had been an inmate of his house, and who had adopted him as a brother, and approached the Indians with the greatest confidence and security. But the treacherous Indian, untrue in war to the claims of gratitude, friendship, and brotherhood, no sooner got him in his power than he murdered and scalped him and all his party with as little compassion as if he had never known him or professed to be his friend.

Not long after the new forces were organized on the Illinois river, Black Hawk with a hundred and fifty warriors made an attack on Apple River Fort, situate about a quarter of a mile north of the present village of Elizabeth within twelve miles of Galena, and defended by twenty-five men under the command of Captain Stone. This fort was a stockade of logs stuck in the ground with block-houses at the corners of the square by way of towers and bastions. It was made for the protection of a scattering village of miners who lived in their houses in the vicinity during the day and retired into the fort for protection at night. The women and children, as usual in the daytime, were abroad in the village when three men on an express from Galena to Dixon were fired on by the Indians lurking in ambush within a half mile of the village, and retreated into the fort. One of them was wounded; his companions stood by him nobly, retreating behind him and keeping the Indians at bay by pointing their guns first at one and then at another of those who were readiest to advance. The alarm was heard at the fort in time to rally the scattered inhabitants; the Indians soon came up within firing distance; and now commenced a fearful struggle between the small party of twenty-five men in the fort against six times their number of the enemy. The Indians took possession of the log-houses, knocked holes in the walls through which to fire at the fort with greater security to themselves, and whilst some were firing at the fort others broke the furniture, destroyed the provisions, and cut open the beds and scattered the feathers found in the houses. The men in the fort were excited to the highest pitch of desperation; they believed that they were contending with an enemy who never made prisoners; and that the result of the contest must be victory or death, and a horrid death too, to them and their families; the women and children moulded the bullets and loaded the guns for their husbands, fathers, and brothers and the men fired and fought with a fury required by desperation itself. In this manner the battle was kept up about fifteen hours, when the Indians retreated. The number of their killed and wounded, supposed to be considerable, was never ascertained, as they were carried away in the retreat. The loss in the fort was one man killed and one wounded. One of the men who first retreated to the fort immediately passed on to Galena and there gave the alarm. Col. Strode of the militia, who commanded in Galena, lost no time in marching to the assistance of the fort, but before his arrival the Indians had raised the siege and departed. Galena itself had been in imminent danger of attack; at that time it was a village of four hundred inhabitants, surrounded on every side by the enemy. Col. Strode, like a brave and prudent commander, took every possible measure for its defence. Even here in this extremity of danger a number of the inhabitants yielded their assistance unwillingly and grudgingly. There were a number of aspirants for office and command; and quite a number refused obedience to the militia commander of the regiment; but Col. Strode took the most effectual mode of putting down these discontents. He immediately declared martial law; the town was converted into a camp; men were forced into the ranks at the point of the bayonet; and a press warrant from the colonel in the hands of armed men procured all necessary supplies; preparations for defence were kept up night and day; and the Indian spies seeing no favorable opportunity for attack, no considerable body of Indians ever came nearer the town than Apple Fort.

About the time of the siege of the fort a party of Indians made an attack on three men near Fort Hamilton in the lead mines, two of the men were killed and the other escaped. Gen. Dodge of Wisconsin, who happened to arrive at the fort soon after with twenty men under his command, made quick pursuit after these Indians, who were chased to the Pekatonica and there took shelter under the high bank of the river. General Dodge and his party charged upon them in their place of concealment and shelter and killed the whole party, eleven in number, with the loss of three of his own brave men mortally wounded and one who afterwards recovered. This little action will equal any for courage, brilliancy and success in the whole history of Indian wars.

About this time also, Capt. James W. Stephenson of Galena with a part of his company pursued a party of Indians into a small dense round thicket in the prairie.[9] He commenced a severe fire upon them at random within firing distance of the thicket, but the Indians having every advantage succeeded in killing a few of his men, he ordered a retreat. Neither he nor the men were willing to give up the fight; and they came to the desperate resolution of returning and charging into the thicket upon the Indians. The command to charge was given; the men obeyed with ardor and alacrity; the captain himself led the way; but before they had penetrated into the thicket twenty steps the Indians fired from their covert; the fire was instantly returned; the charge was made a second and third time, each time giving and receiving the fire of the enemy, until three more of his men lay dead on the ground and he himself was severely wounded. It now became necessary to retreat, as he had from the first but a small part of his company along with him. This attack of Capt. Stephenson was unsuccessful and may have been imprudent; but it equalled anything in modern warfare in daring and desperate courage.

The Indians had now shown themselves to be a courageous, active and enterprising enemy. They had scattered their war parties all over the north, from Chicago to Galena and from the Illinois river into the territory of Wisconsin; they occupied every grove, waylaid every road, hung around every settlement, and attacked every party of white men that attempted to penetrate the country. But their supremacy in the field was of short duration; for on the 20th, 21st and 22d of June the new forces assembled on the Illinois river were put in motion by Gen. Atkinson of the regular army, who now assumed the command over the whole. Maj. John Dement with a battalion of spies attached to the first brigade was sent forward in advance whilst the main army was to follow and concentrate at Dixon. Maj. Dement pushed forward across Rock river and took position at Kellogg's Grove in the heart of the Indian country.

Major Dement, hearing by express on the 25th of June that the trail of about five hundred Indians leading to the south had been seen within five miles the day before, ordered his whole command to saddle their horses and remain in readiness whilst he himself with twenty men started at daylight next morning to gain intelligence of their movements. His party had advanced about three hundred yards when they discovered seven Indian spies; some of his men immediately made pursuit but their commander, fearing an ambuscade, endeavored to call them back. In this manner he had proceeded about a mile; and being followed soon after by a number of his men from the camp, he formed about twenty-five of them into line on the prairie to protect the retreat of those yet in pursuit. He had scarcely done this before he discovered three hundred Indians issuing from the grove to attack him. The enemy came up firing, hallooing and yelling to make themselves more terrific, after the Indian fashion; and the major seeing himself in great danger of being surrounded by a superior force slowly retired to his camp, closely pursued by the Indians. Here his whole party took possession of some loghouses which answered for a fort, and here they were vigorously attacked by the Indians for nearly an hour. There were brave soldiers in this battalion, among whom were Major Dement himself and Lieut. Gov. Casey, a private in the ranks, who kept up such an active fire upon their assailants and with such good aim that the Indians retreated with the certain loss of nine men left dead on the field, and probably five others carried away. The loss on the side of the whites was five killed and three wounded. Major Dement had previously sent an express to Gen. Posey, who marched with his whole brigade at once to his relief; but did not arrive for two hours after the retreat of the Indians. Gen. Posey moved next day a little to the north in search of the Indians, then marched back to Kellogg's Grove to await the arrival of his baggage-wagons; and then to Fort Hamilton on the Pekatonica.

When the news of the battle at Kellogg's Grove reached Dixon, where all the volunteers and the regular forces were then assembled under command of Gen. Atkinson, Alexander's brigade was ordered in the direction of Plum river, a short stream with numerous branches falling into the Mississippi thirty-five miles below Galena, to intercept the Indians if they attempted in that direction to escape by recrossing the river. Gen. Atkinson remained with the infantry at Dixon two days and then marched, accompanied by the brigade of Gen. Henry, towards the country of the four lakes,[10] farther up Rock river. Colonel Jacob Fry with his regiment was despatched in advance by Gen. Henry to meet some friendly Indians of the Pottawattomie tribe commanded by Caldwell, a half-breed, and Shaubanie, the war-chief of the nation.

Gen. Atkinson having heard that Black Hawk had concentrated his forces at the four lakes and fortified his position with the intention of deciding the fate of the war by a general battle, marched with as much haste as prudence would warrant when invading a hostile and wilderness country with undisciplined forces, where there was no means of procuring intelligence of the number or whereabouts of the enemy.

On the 30th of June he passed through the Turtle village,[11] a considerable town of the Winnebagoes then deserted by its inhabitants, and encamped one mile above it in the open prairie near Rock river. He believed that the hostile Indians were in that immediate neighborhood and prepared to resist their attack if one should be made. That night the Indians were prowling about the encampment till morning. Continual alarms were given by the sentinels and the whole command was frequently paraded in order of battle. The march was continued next day and nothing occurred until the army arrived at Lake Kuskanong except the discovery of trails and Indian signs, the occasional sight of an Indian spy, and the usual abundance of false alarms amongst men but little accustomed to war. Here the army was joined by Gen. Alexander's brigade; and after Major Ewing and Col. Fry with the battalion of the one and the regiment of the other had thoroughly examined the whole country round about and had ascertained that no enemy was near, the whole force again marched up Rock river on the east side to the Burnt village, another considerable town of the Winnebagoes on the White Water river, where it was joined by the brigade of Gen. Posey and a battalion of a hundred men from Wisconsin commanded by Major (now General) Dodge.

During the march to this place the scouts had captured an old blind Indian of the hostile band, nearly famished with hunger, who had been left behind by his friends, (for want of ability to travel) to fall into the hands of his enemies or to perish by famine. Being, as he said, old, blind, and helpless, he was never consulted or advised with by the other Indians, and could give no account of the movements of his party except that they had gone farther up the river. One historian of the war says that the army magnanimously concluded not to kill him, but to give him plenty to eat and leave him behind to end his life in a pleasant way by eating himself to death. The old man, however, was denied this melancholy satisfaction; for falling in the way of Posey's men as they were marching to the camp, he was quickly despatched even before he had satisfied his natural hunger. This barbarous action is an indelible stain upon the men of that brigade. At this place, also, Captain Dunn, at present a judge in Wisconsin, acting as officer of the day of one of the regiments, was shot by a sentinel and dangerously wounded.

Up to the time of reaching the burnt village the progress of the command had been slow and uncertain. The country was comparatively an unexplored wilderness of forest and prairie. None in the command had ever been through it. A few who professed to know something of it volunteered to act as guides and succeeded in electing themselves to be military advisers to the commanding general. The numbers of the hostile party were unknown; and a few Winnebagoes who followed the camp, and whose fidelity was of a very doubtful character, were from necessity much listened to but the intelligence received from them was always delusive. Short marches, frequent stoppages, and explorations always unsatisfactory were the result, giving the enemy time to elude the pursuing forces and every opportunity of ascertaining their probable movements and intentions.

The evening the army arrived at the Burnt village Captain Early with his company of spies returned from a scout and reported the main trail of the Indians, not two hours old, to be three miles beyond. It was determined to pursue rapidly next morning. At an early hour next day, before the troops were ready to march, two regular soldiers, fishing in the river one hundred and fifty yards from camp, were fired upon by two Indians from the opposite shore and one of them dangerously wounded. A part of the volunteers were immediately marched up the river in the direction indicated by Captain Early and Col. Fry's regiment, with the regulars, were left behind to construct bridges and cross to the point from which the Indians had shot the regular soldier. A march of fifteen miles up and across the river (fordable above) proved Captain Early's report to be incorrect: no trail was discoverable. On crossing the river the troops entered upon the trembling lands, which are immense flats of turf extending for miles in every direction, from six inches to a foot in thickness, resting upon water and beds of quicksand. A troop or even a single horseman passing over produced an undulating and quivering motion of the land, from which it gets its name. Although the surface is quite dry, yet there is no difficulty in procuring plenty of water by cutting an opening through the stratum of turf. The horses would sometimes, on the thinner portions, force a foot through and fall to the shoulder or ham; yet so great is the tenacity of the upper surface that in no instance was there any trouble in getting them out. In some places the weight of the earth forces a stream of water upwards, which carrying with it and depositing large quantities of sand, forms a mound. The mound, increasing in weight as it enlarges, increases the pressure upon the water below, presenting the novel sight of a fountain in the prairie pouring its stream down the side of a mound, then to be absorbed by the sand and returned to the waters beneath.

Discovering no sign of an enemy in this direction, the detachment fell back to the Burnt village, and the bridges not being yet completed it was determined to throw over a small force on rafts the next day. The Winnebagoes had assured the general that the shore beyond was a large island and that the whole of Black Hawk's forces were fortified on it. In consequence of this information Captain Early's company were crossed on rafts, followed and supported by two companies of regulars under the command of Captain Noel of the army, which last were formed in open order across the island while Captain Early proceeded to scour it, reporting afterwards at Head Quarters that he had found the trail of a large body of Indians; but Col. William S. Hamilton having crossed the main river three miles below with a party of Menominies, reported the trail of the whole tribe on the main west shore, about ten days old, proceeding northward; and it was afterwards ascertained that no sign had been seen upon the island but that of the two Indians who had fired upon the regular soldiers.

Eight weeks had now been wasted in fruitless search for the enemy, and the commanding general seemed farther from the attainment of his object than when the second requisition of troops was organized. At that time Posey and Alexander commanded each a thousand men, Henry took the field with twelve hundred and sixty-two, and the regular force under Col. Taylor, now Major General, amounted to four hundred and fifty more. But by this time the volunteer force was reduced nearly one half. Many had entered the service for mere pastime and a desire to participate in the excellent fun of an Indian campaign, looked upon as a frolic; and certainly but few volunteered with well-defined notions of the fatigues, delays, and hardships of an Indian war in an unsettled and unknown country. The tedious marches, exposure to the weather, loss of horses, sickness, forced submission to command, and disgust at the unexpected hardships and privations of a soldier's life produced rapid reductions in the numbers of every regiment. The great distance from the base of operations; the difficulties of transportation either by land or water, making it impossible at anytime to have more than twelve days' provisions beforehand, still further curtailed the power of the commanding general. Such was the wastefulness of the volunteers that they were frequently one or two days short of provisions before new supplies could be furnished.

At this time there were not more than four days' rations in the hands of the commissary, the enemy might be weeks in advance; the volunteers were fast melting away, but the regular infantry had not lost a man. To counteract these difficulties Gen. Atkinson found it necessary to disperse his command for the purpose of procuring supplies.

V

Conclusion of the War, 1832

According to previous arrangements the several brigades took up their lines of march on the 10th of July for their respective destinations. Col. Ewing's regiment was sent back to Dixon as an escort for Captain Dunn, who was supposed to be mortally wounded; Gen. Posey marched to Fort Hamilton on the Peckatonica as a guard to the frontier country. Henry, Alexander, and Dodge, with their commands, were sent to Fort Winnebago, situate at the Portage between the Fox and the Wisconsin rivers; whilst Gen. Atkinson himself, fell back with the regular forces near to Lake Kush-Konong and erected a fort, which he called by the name of the lake. There he was to remain until the volunteer generals could return with supplies. Henry and Alexander made Fort Winnebago in three days, Major Dodge having preceded them a few hours by a forced march which so fatigued and crippled his horses that many of them were unable to continue the campaign. Their route had been in a direct line a distance of eighty miles through a country which was remarkably swampy and difficult. On the night of the 12th of July a *stampede* occurred amongst the horses. This is a general wild alarm, the whole body of them breaking loose from their fastenings and coursing over the prairie at full speed, their feet all striking the ground with force and sounding like rolling thunder, and by this means an hundred or more of them were lost or destroyed in the swamps or on a log causeway three miles in length near the fort.

A view of the country from the camp at Fort Winnebago presented the most striking contrariety of features. Looking towards the fort, a neat and beautiful erection among the green hills east of Fox river, were seen the two streams, the Fox and the Wisconsin, with sources several hundred miles apart, the former in the east the latter in the north, gliding as if to mingle their waters until when within three miles of each other they sweep, the one to the northeast the other to the southwest, as if they had met only to take a gallant adieu before parting in their adventurous journey, the one to deposit his sweet and limpid waters in the gulf of St. Lawrence, the other to contribute his stained and bitter flood to the gulf of Mexico. The course of the Fox is short, crooked, narrow and deep, and abounds with the finest varieties of fish; whilst the Wisconsin is long, wide, and comparatively straight and is said to have no fish; this, perhaps, is owing to its passage through the cypress swamps which render it unwholesome to the finny tribes, and is also the cause of the discoloration of its waters. This river is shallow and abounds in sand bars, which by constant shifting renders its navigation by steam-boats dangerous, if not impracticable. Besides the rivers, the face of the country is no less remarkable. The strip of land between the two rivers is low, flat, and swampy with no other growth but a coarse variety of rush, and at high water so completely overflowed by the two streams as to convert all that part of the United States east of the Mississippi into a great island; a wisp of straw being thrown into the flood where the two currents meet will be divided and one portion floated to the northern, the other to the southern sea. East of Fox river the land is gently undulating, presenting an equable distribution of prairie of the richest mould and timber of the finest growth, unobstructed by underbrush, and furnishing an abundance of a plant called pea-vine, an excellent food for cattle. West of the Wisconsin, at the water's edge commence those frowning steps of rugged and barren rock, garnished with black and bristling pines and hemlock, which, as the hunter progresses towards the Mississippi he finds to terminate in a region mountainous, dreary, terrific, and truly alpine in all its features.[1]

Two days were occupied at the fort in getting provisions; on the last of which the Winnebago chiefs there reported that Black Hawk and his forces were encamped at the Manitou village thirty-five miles above Gen. Atkinson on Rock river. In a council held between Alexander, Henry, and Dodge it was determined to violate orders by marching directly to the enemy, with the hope of taking him by surprise; or at least putting him between them and Gen. Atkinson; thus cutting off his further retreat to the north. Twelve o'clock on the 15th was appointed as the hour to march. Gen. Henry proceeded at once to reorganize his brigade with a view to disencumber himself of his sick and dismounted men, that as little as possible might impede the celerity of his march. Gen. Alexander soon announced that his men were unwilling and had refused to follow; and Major Dodge reported his horses so much disabled by their late march that he could not muster a force worth taking along. Gen. Henry was justly indignant at the insubordination and defection of his companions in arms, and announced his purpose to march in pursuit of the enemy alone if he could prevail upon but fifty men to follow him. But directly after this a company of mounted volunteers under the command of Capt. Craig from Apple river and Galena in Illinois, with fresh horses, arrived at Fort Winnebago to join Major Dodge's battalion, which now made his force of men and horses fit for service one hundred and twenty in the whole. General Henry's brigade, exclusive of Dodge's battalion, amounted to between five and six hundred men, but not more than four hundred and fifty had horses fit for service. On returning to his own brigade Gen. Henry discovered that his own men, infected by association with those of Gen. Alexander, were on the point of open mutiny.

Lieutenant-colonel Jeremiah Smith of Fry's regiment presented to Gen. Henry a written protest signed by all the officers of the regiment except the colonel against the intended expedition; but these mutineers had to deal with an officer of rare abilities as a commander of militia. General Henry was a complete soldier; he was gifted with the uncommon talent of commanding with sternness without giving offence; of forcing his men to obey without degrading them in their own estimation; he was brave without rashness, and gave his orders with firmness and authority, without any appearance of bluster. In his mere person he looked the commander; in a word he was one of those very rare men who are gifted by nature with the power to command militia; to be at the same time feared and loved: and with the capacity of inspiring the soldiery with the ardor, impetuosity, and honorable impulses of their commander. General Henry made no other reply to this protest than to order the officers under arrest for mutiny; appointing at the same time Collins' regiment as a guard to escort them to Gen. Atkinson. Colonel Smith in great trepidation protested that he did not know what the paper contained when he signed it, and implored the general's permission to consult a few moments with the officers before further steps were taken. This being accorded, in less than ten minutes they were all collected at the general's quarters, manifesting the utmost contrition, many of them with tears, and pledging themselves, if forgiven, to return to their duty and never be guilty of the like offence again. The general, than whom none better understood human nature or had more capacity to act on it, made them a few remarks, tempered with dignity and kindness; the officers returned to their duty and it is but doing them justice to say that from that hour no men ever behaved better. Alexander's brigade marched back to General Atkinson.

From this place Gen. Henry took up his line of march on the 15th of July, accompanied by Paquette, a half-breed, and the "White Pawnee," a Winnebago chief, as guides, in quest of the Indians. On the route to the head waters of Rock river he was frequently thrown from a direct line by intervening swamps extending for miles. Many of them were crossed, but never without difficulty and the loss of horses. After three days' hard marching his forces encamped upon the beautiful stream of Rock river. This river is not exceeded by any other in natural beauty. Its waters are clear; its bottom and banks rocky or pebbly. The country on each side is either rolling, rich prairie or hills crowned with forests free from undergrowth, and its current sweeps to the Mississippi, deep and bold. Here three Winnebagoes gave intelligence that Black Hawk was encamped at Cranberry lake, farther up the river. Relying upon this information, it was settled by Gen. Henry to make a forced march in that direction the next morning. Doctor Merryman of Springfield and W. W. Woodbridge of Wisconsin were despatched as expresses to Gen. Atkinson. They were accompanied by a chief called Little Thunder as guide; and having started about dark and proceeded on their perilous route about eight miles to the south-west they came upon the fresh main trail of the enemy, endeavoring to escape by way of the Four Lakes across the Wisconsin river. At the sight of the trail the Indian guide was struck with terror and without permission retreated back to the camp. Merryman and Woodbridge returned also, but not until Little Thunder had announced his discovery in the Indian tongue to his countrymen, who were in the very act of making their escape when they were stopped by Major Murray McConnell and taken to the tent of Gen. Henry, to whom they confessed that they had come into camp only to give false information and favor the retreat of the Indians; and then, to make amends for their perfidy and perhaps, as they were led to believe, to avoid immediate death, they disclosed all they knew of Black Hawk's movements. Gen. Henry prudently kept the treachery of these Indians a secret from his men for it would have taken all his influence and that of all his officers to save their lives if their perfidious conduct had been known throughout the camp.

The next morning (July 19th) by day-light everything was ready for a forced march, but first another express was despatched to Gen. Atkinson. All cumbrous baggage was thrown away. The tents and most of the camp equipage were left in a pile in the wilderness. Many of the men left their blankets and all their clothes except the suit they wore, and this was the case in every instance with those who had been so unfortunate as to lose their horses, such as these took their guns, ammunition, and provisions upon their backs and traveled over mountain and plain, through swamp and thicket, and kept up with the men on horseback. All the men now marched with a better spirit than usual. The sight of the broad, fresh trail inspired every one with a lively hope of bringing the war to a speedy end; and even the horses seemed to share somewhat in the general ardor. There was no murmuring, there was no excuse or complaining, and none on the sick report. The first day in the afternoon they were overtaken by one of those storms common on the prairies, black and terrific, accompanied by torrents of rain and the most fearful lightning and thunder; but the men dashed on through thickets almost impenetrable and swamps almost impassable and that day marched upwards of fifty miles. During this day's march Gen. Henry, Major McConnell, and others of the General's staff often dismounted and marched on foot, giving their horses to the footmen.

That night the storm raged till two o'clock in the morning. The men, exhausted with fatigue, threw themselves supperless upon the muddy earth, covered with water, for a little rest. The rain made it impossible to kindle a fire or to cook, so that both officers and men contented themselves with eating some raw meat and some of the wet flour which they carried in their sacks, and which was converted into a soft dough by the drenching rains. A similar repast served them next morning for breakfast. The horses had fared but little better than the men. The government furnished nothing for them to eat and they were obliged to subsist that night upon a scanty grazing, confined within the limits of the camp.

Next morning (July 20) the storm had abated and all were on the march by daylight, and after a march as hard as that on the day before the army encamped at night upon the banks of one of the four lakes forming the source of the Catfish river in Wisconsin, and near the place where the Indians had encamped the previous night.[2] At this place the men were able to make fires and cook their suppers and this they did with a hearty good will, having travelled about one hundred miles without tasting anything but raw food and without having seen a spark of fire. That night they again laid upon the ground, many of them with nothing but the sky for a covering, and slept soundly and sweetly, like men upon their beds at home. All were in fine spirits and high expectation of overtaking the Indians next day and putting an end to the war by a general battle. The night did not pass, however, without an alarm. One of the sentinels posted near the bank of the lake fired upon an Indian gliding in his canoe slyly and stealthily to the shore. Every man was aroused and under arms in an instant but nothing followed to continue the alarm. A small black speck could be seen by aid of the starlight on the surface of the lake but no enemy was visible.

The march was continued by early light in the morning (July 21) with unabated ardor; passing round the lake on the edge of the water; and after crossing a tongue of land running down between two of the lakes the army forded a considerable stream, the outlet of one lake running into another. After this they ascended a rising ground from whence could be seen, at one view three of these beautiful sheets of water. The lakes and the surrounding country of sloping prairies and wooded hills stretching away in the distance presented some very striking and beautiful scenery. The hand of civilization had not then disfigured its natural beauty. The smoke of the log cabin and the ragged worm fence were not then to be seen. All was wild and silent save the distant roar of surging waters lashed into motion by the constant but ever-varying winds. The men, however, had but little time to contemplate the beauty of the scenery around them. They were hurried forward by the continual cry of "Close up your ranks" as the officers, whose duty it was to direct and accelerate the march, rode along the lines admonishing them to keep up with the advanced guard. This day's march was still harder than any which preceded it. The men on foot were forced into a run to keep up with the advancing horsemen. The men on horseback carried their arms and baggage for them by turns.

Major William Lee D. Ewing (since a Major General) commanded the spy battalion, and with him was joined the battalion of Major Dodge of Wisconsin. These two officers with their commands were in the advance; but with all their ardor they were never able to get out of sight of the main body. Gen. Henry, who remained with the main body, despatched Major McConnell with the advance guard so as to get the earliest intelligence of any unusual occurrence in front. About noon of this day the advance guard was close upon the rear-guard of the retreating enemy. It is to be regretted that we have no account of the management, the perils, and hair-breadth escapes of the Indians in conducting their retreat. All that we know is that for many miles before they were overtaken their broad trail was strewn with camp kettles and baggage of various kinds which they had thrown away in the hurry of their flight. The sight of these articles encouraged Henry's men to press forward, hoping soon to put an end to this vexatious border war which had so much disturbed the peace of our northern frontier settlements. About noon, also, the scouts ahead came suddenly upon two Indians and as they were attempting to escape one of them was killed and left dead on the field. Doctor Addison Philleo, coming along shortly after, scalped this Indian and for a long time afterwards exhibited the scalp as an evidence of his valor. Shortly after this the rear guard of the Indians began to make feint stands, as if to bring on a battle. In doing so their design was merely to gain time for the main body to reach a more advantageous position. A few shots would be exchanged and the Indians would then push ahead, whilst the pursuing force would halt to form in the order of battle. In this way the Indians were able to reach the broken grounds on the bluffs of the Wisconsin river by four o'clock in the afternoon before they were overtaken.

About this time whilst the advance guard was passing over some uneven ground through the high grass and low timber they were suddenly fired upon by a body of Indians who had here secreted themselves. In an instant Major Ewing's battalion dismounted and were formed in front, their horses being removed into the rear. The Indians kept up a fire from behind fallen trees and none of them could be discovered except by the flash and report of their guns. In a few minutes Gen. Henry arrived with the main body. The order of battle was now formed. Col. Jones' regiment was placed on the right, Col. Collins' on the left, and Col. Fry's in the rear to act as a reserve. Major Ewing's battalion was placed in front of the line and Major Dodge's on the extreme right. In this order Gen. Henry's forces marched into battle. An order was given to charge upon the enemy, which was handsomely obeyed by Ewing's battalion and by Jones' and Collins' regiments.

The Indians retreated before this charge obliquely to the right and concentrated their main force in front of Dodge's battalion, showing a design to turn his flank. General Henry sent an order by Major McConnell to Major Dodge to advance to the charge; but this officer being of opinion that the foe was too strong for him requested a reinforcement. Col. Fry's regiment was ordered to his aid, and formed on his right. And now a vigorous charge was made from one end of the line to the other.

Colonel Fry's regiment made a charge into the bush and high grass where the Indians were concealed and received the fire of their whole body. This fire was briskly returned by Fry and Dodge and their men, who continued to advance, the Indians standing their ground until the men came within bayonet reach of them, then fell back to the west along the high broken bluffs of the Wisconsin, only to take a new position amongst the thickest timber and tall grass in the head of a hollow leading to the Wisconsin river bottom. Here it seemed they were determined to make a firm stand; but being charged upon in their new position by Ewing's battalion and by Collins' and Jones' regiments, they were driven out of it, some of them being pursued down the hollow and others again to the west along the Wisconsin heights until they descended the bluffs to the Wisconsin bottom, which was here about a mile wide and very swampy, covered with thick tall grass, above the heads of men on horseback. It being now dark night farther pursuit was stopped and Gen. Henry and his forces lay upon the field of battle. That night Henry's camp was disturbed by the voice of an Indian loudly sounding from a distant hill, as if giving orders or desiring a conference. It afterwards appeared that this was the voice of an Indian chief speaking in the Winnebago language, stating that the Indians had their squaws and families with them, that they were starving for provisions and were not able to fight the white people; and that if they were permitted to pass peaceably over the Mississippi they would do no more mischief. He spoke this in the Winnebago tongue in hopes that some of that people were with Gen. Henry and would act as his interpreter. No Winnebagoes were present, they having run at the commencement of the action; and so his language was never explained until after the close of the war.[3]

Next morning early Gen. Henry advanced to the Wisconsin river and ascertained that the Indians had all crossed it and made their escape into the mountains between that and the Mississippi. It was ascertained after the battle that the Indian loss amounted to sixty-eight left dead on the field and a large number of wounded, of whom twenty-five were afterwards found dead along the Indian trail leading to the Mississippi. General Henry lost one man killed and eight wounded. It appeared that the Indians, knowing that they were to fight a mounted force, had been trained to fire at an elevation to hit men on horseback; but as Gen. Henry had dismounted his forces and sent his horses into the rear the Indians overshot them; and this will account for the very few men killed and wounded by them.[4]

We have now to account for the fact that Gen. Henry never received abroad the credit which was due him as the commander in this battle, or in any other during the war. In the morning after the battle Col. Fry heard Major Dodge and Dr. Philleo consulting privately about writing an account of it to be published. He immediately conveyed this intelligence to Gen. Henry, suggesting that Dodge would claim all the credit and advising Gen. Henry, as the only means of securing his rightful claim, to send an express immediately to Galena with his own account of the battle. This prudent advice Henry neglected.

Doctor Philleo was the editor of a newspaper at Galena called "the Galenian," then the only newspaper published north of Springfield, either in Illinois or Wisconsin. The war news always appeared first in this paper. The editor belonged to Dodge's battalion and when he wrote home the news to be published in his paper he never mentioned Henry except as a subordinate, or any other officer but Dodge. His letters chronicled the doings of Gen. Dodge only, and by calling him *General* Dodge it was made to appear that he was the commander of the whole brigade instead of a single battalion attached to it. These letters were copied into all other newspapers throughout the United States as the authentic news of the war; and never having been contradicted, the people abroad were thus deluded into the belief that Dodge was the great hero of the war. Henry was lost sight of; and now in many histories we find it asserted that Dodge was the commander in this war; thus throwing out of sight both Generals Henry and Atkinson as well as General Zachary Taylor, who, as colonel, commanded the regular force. The world loves to be humbugged. This delusion was of immense advantage to Gen. Dodge; for although he was a man of very high merit, yet would he have been more fortunate than thousands of others equally meritorious if this delusion did not assist much in getting the great name he afterwards obtained. He was first appointed a colonel of dragoons; then to be governor of Wisconsin territory; then he was elected a delegate from the territory to Congress; and after this he was again appointed governor of the territory. And it is but just to say of him that independently of the renown he acquired in the Black Hawk war he enjoyed great popularity and influence.*

*DODGEVILLE, March 17th, 1847.

HON. THOMAS FORD,—

SIR—The enclosed paragraph taken from the "Milwakee Sentinel and Gazette" of the 17th ult. purports to have been a lecture read by you in the Senate chamber during the late session of the Illinois legislature giving the "true history of the Black Hawk war." Will you please inform me at your earliest convenience, if you made the statements attributed to you in the paragraph in question?

Respectfully, your servant,
HENRY DODGE.

VERSAILLES, BROWN COUNTY, ILLINOIS, April 13, 1847.

SIR,—After an absence of two weeks, on my return to this place I had the honor to receive your note of the 7th ult., which was forwarded to me from Springfield. The extract cut from the Wisconsin paper, endorsed in your letter, does not contain a correct account of my lecture on the Black Hawk war. It is erroneous in many important particulars. That lecture was prepared from my own personal knowledge of the campaign in 1831; and from information of the various operations in 1832 from various persons; more particularly from Maj. Gen. Jacob Fry of Lockport; Maj. Murray McConnell of Jacksonville; Dr. E. H. Merriman, of Springfield; Maj. Gen. Wm. Lee D. Ewing, late of Springfield, and the Hon. John J. Stewart, late a member of Congress. Gen. Fry commanded a regiment under Gen. Henry; Gen. Ewing commanded the spy battalion of Henry's brigade; Maj. McConnell was brigade-major of Henry's brigade; Dr. Merriman was adjutant of Collins' regiment in Henry's brigade; and Mr. Stewart commanded a battalion in it. I have not had an opportunity to see and converse with Cols. Collins and Jones, who commanded the other two regiments belonging to Henry's command in the battle of the Wisconsin. But Gen. Fry, Gen. Ewing and Maj. McConnell, were with Gen. Henry throughout the war. In collecting the facts and writing out the history of this war my only object has been to arrive at and state the truth; for history without truth is of but little value. I concluded, therefore, before publishing anything on the subject I would deliver this portion of the history of Illinois as a lecture, at Springfield during the session of the legislature, there being then many persons present who had been out in the war, and who might be able to correct me when I might be in error. Such corrections were invited; and accordingly I have received many, of which I have freely availed myself since.

It is my intention to publish a history of Illinois in the course of the summer, but as yet I have neither directly nor indirectly authorized any of the newspaper notices of it made last winter; nor have I given any sort of publicity to the matter more than a lecture can give. In the meantime I will be glad to avail myself of any information which you may have it in your power to communicate; and if I cannot consistently with other evidence follow your statements implicitly, they will be published entire, if not too voluminous.

According to my present information I have felt it to be my duty to insist that Gen. Henry was the principal man in this war; that he commanded and directed all the movements of the troops from Fort Winnebago to Rock river, and from thence to the Wisconsin, and throughout the battle which there ensued; that he commanded a brigade of three regiments and a spy battalion; and that you commanded but a single battalion of one hundred and twenty men. I have stated that on the march your command, and the spies commanded by the late Gen. Ewing, were in front as the advance guard; that in the battle you was stationed on the extreme right, but when a charge of the whole line was ordered by Gen. Henry, the Indians collected on the right in front of your battalion, showing a design to turn your flank, which caused Gen. Henry to order Col. Fry's regiment to form on your right; which being done, you and Gen. Fry charged upon and drove the Indians into the head of a hollow leading down from the bluffs of the Wisconsin, and from thence, upon the charge of the whole brigade they were routed, and fled down the bluffs and across the bottom to the Wisconsin river. Gen. Fry and Maj. McConnell say that your battalion did not come into the action until re-enforced by Fry's regiment. Maj. McConnell says that he bore the order from Gen. Henry to you to charge on the Indians but that you thought you was not strong enough. He returned with this answer to Gen. Henry, and then Henry sent Fry to re-enforce you. Gen. Fry says that when the Indians first began the attack you was in advance with Gen. Ewing's battalion, and that you and your battalion immediately fell back into line. This last fact I see that I omitted to state in my lecture. I have also been informed that you would not agree to march from Fort Winnebago in pursuit of the Indians, thereby disobeying the orders of Gen. Atkinson, without a written order from Gen. Henry. This, also, I see I have omitted in my lecture. I see upon examination that I said nothing whatever about written orders.

I have also stated that when Gen. Atkinson pursued the Indians across the Wisconsin your battalion was put in advance with the regulars; and that Gen. Henry's brigade was put in the rear with the baggage by way of degrading him and his men, as they understood the matter; that when Atkinson's advance reached within four or five miles of the Mississippi it was fired on by about twenty Indians; that he pursued them with all his forces (yours included) except Henry's brigade to a place on the river about two or three miles above the encampment of the main body of Indians; that Henry coming up in the rear, and as yet being without orders, pursued the main trail of the Indians directly to the river, where his brigade was the first to attack their main body, and had killed or driven the principal part of them into the river or over a slough on to a little willow island before Gen. Atkinson came up with his forces, including your battalion. These are the principal matters stated by me, so far as you and Gen. Henry are concerned.

I have been informed by Gen. Fry that directly after the battle of the Wisconsin he heard you and Dr. Philleo talking about writing out and sending away an account of the battle; that he mentioned the circumstance to Gen. Henry, and urged Henry immediately to write out his report and send it to Galena by express to be published, as the only mode of securing the credit due to himself; but Henry neglected to do so. This I have stated. I am informed also by Fry, Merriman, McConnell and Stuart that you did write a letter to Gen. Street or some other person, giving an account of the battle, in which you said nothing of Gen. Henry. But as I do not remember seeing the letter I have not attempted to speak of its contents. It is said that this letter was published in the St. Louis papers and from them was extensively copied throughout the Union. I have made no search as yet in St. Louis for it and do not intend to speak of its contents unless I can find it; and then they will be stated correctly.

I do not personally know that Doctor Philleo was with you in this campaign; but during the war I was a reader of the "Galenian" newspaper of which he was editor. It contained many letters from the Doctor giving accounts of your operations and saying but little of other officers. I remember, also, that these letters in the "Galenian" were extensively republished in other papers, from which I have inferred that this is the true cause why Gen. Henry and the Illinois volunteers have never received credit abroad for what they deserved in this war.

It is not true that I stated you were first brought into notice by this war, as is asserted in the Wisconsin paper; or that honors and offices were showered upon you and your family in consequence of your renown acquired in this war. But it is true that I have traced the parallel between your good fortune and that of Gen. Henry, and I stated expressly in my lecture that independently of the renown which you acquired in the Black Hawk war you have enjoyed great popularity and influence.

It has been stated to me that after the war you endeavored to get Doctor Philleo the appointment of surgeon in the army but that he could not pass an examination before the Medical Board. Will you allow me to ask you how this is?

Doctor Merriman has informed me in writing that when Henry, Alexander, and yourself were sent to Fort Winnebago for supplies you preceded the others a few hours by a forced march, by which most of your horses were disabled; that after agreeing to march with Henry in pursuit of the Indians and after Alexander's brigade had mutinied and refused to march you reported to Gen. Henry that you could raise no more than forty horses; that Henry insisted that you should go even with that number; that you replied you would see what you could do; and just at that time some fresh horsemen came up, making your command, which you took along, one hundred and twenty effective men. I would be pleased to have your statement concerning this.

I have noticed in the most flattering manner your engagement, or rather charge upon the Indians at Peckatonica. A short statement of this affair will be thankfully received.

The Illinois volunteers, when they returned from the war, unanimously gave Gen. Henry the credit of being the principal man in it, and such has been the current and universal belief in this State ever since—now nearly fifteen years. This has undoubtedly had its influence on my mind and as yet I perceive no good reason why it ought not to have an influence. Be pleased to direct your future correspondence to Peoria, to which place I intend to remove my family in a few days.

I am, most respectfully, your obedient servant,

THOMAS FORD.

HIS EXCELLENCY HENRY DODGE,
Dodgeville, Wisconsin.

I regret exceedingly that after waiting about five months nothing has been received from Gov. Dodge in answer to the foregoing letter. From the evidence before me I have been concientiously of opinion that Gov. Dodge was not, and that Gen. Henry was, entitled to the credit of being the hero of the Black Hawk war; that Dodge, whether designedly or not on his part, has been for the last fifteen years wearing the laurels due to Henry; and I have endeavored to set forth that opinion with manly independence. If, however, Gen. Dodge after commencing a correspondence on the subject had seen proper to continue it in answer to the foregoing letter, and had communicated any facts calculated to weaken the force of that opinion, he should have had the full benefit of his communications.

Since writing the foregoing I have found the following in Niles' Register of the 18th August, 1832: "INDIAN WAR. We have received the 'Missouri Republican' extra of the 1st instant confirming the intelligence published in our paper of Thursday of the defeat of the Indians by *General Dodge* at the Wisconsin. The following letter from *General Dodge* gives a hope that the remnant of the Indians may be overtaken:

"CAMP WISCONSIN, July 22, 1832

"*We* met the enemy yesterday near the wisconsin river, and opposite the old Sack village, after a close pursuit for near a hundred miles. *Our* loss was one man killed and eight wounded. From the scalps taken by the Winnebagoes as well as those taken by the whites, and the Indians carried from the field of battle, *we* have killed forty of them. The number of wounded is not known. We can only judge from the number of killed that many were wounded. From their crippled situation *I* think *we* must overtake them, unless they descend the Wisconsin by water. If you could place a field-piece immediately on the Wisconsin that would command the river you might prevent their escape by water. Gen. Atkinson will arrive at the Blue Mounds on the 24th with the regulars and a brigade of mounted men. *I* will cross the Wisconsin to-morrow, and should the enemy retreat by land he will probably attempt crossing some twenty miles above Prairie du Chien. In that event the mounted men would want some boats for the transportation of their arms, ammunition, and provisions. If you could procure for us some Mackinaw boats in that event, as well as some provision supplies, it would greatly facilitate our views. Excuse great haste. I am, with great respect, your obedient servant,

H. DODGE,
Col. commanding Michigan Volunteers."

The fact that Gen. Dodge wrote the foregoing letter beginning "*We* met the enemy," continuing "*Our* loss was," &c., "*We* have killed forty of them," "*I* think *we* must overtake them," "*I* will cross the Wisconsin," &c., the fact that he points out to the officer at Prairie du Chien what to do to intercept the Indians and aid the whites, as if Dodge was in reality the commander the fact that he signs himself "Col. commanding Michigan Volunteers," when he only commanded a small battalion, the fact that he says nothing of Gen. Henry who was present, but does speak of Gen. Atkinson who was absent, the fact that this letter was republished as war news in all the newspapers in the United States, and the fact that Henry himself never made any report of the battle will, whether Gen. Dodge designed it or not, sufficiently explain the reason why Gen. Henry did not get the credit abroad which was and is justly due him, and also the reason why Gen. Dodge did get credit which he never was entitled to of being the hero of the Black Hawk war.

General Henry's subsequent career was less brilliant, but this was because it was cut short by death. Although he was a man of very powerful and muscular make, not long after the war he was attacked with the consumption. He went to the South for his health and died at New Orleans on the 4th day of March, 1834. Such was the amiable modesty and unpretending merit of this man that he never let it be known to the strangers among whom he resided in his last sickness that he was Gen. Henry of the Black Hawk war. This fact was discovered to them only after his death. He left no family to inherit his honors and vindicate his fame. After his death the selfishness of the many suffered the matter to rest. No one felt interested to vindicate the rights of the dead against the false claims of the living. If I had not undertaken to write this history I am certain that I never should have thought of doing it. And now whilst I attempt it I wish to do General Dodge no injustice. That he is a brave, meritorious officer I make no doubt; and in this history I have cheerfully given him all the credit he is entitled to. But *I deny most positively* that he was the principal man, either in rank or merit, in the Black Hawk war. In doing so I have no motive but a generous one. It is simply to do justice to the memory of the great and meritorious dead—to the memory of him who, being removed from the scene of action, has no further power to do me either good or harm. And in doing so I may be fortunate not to expose myself to the enmity of the powerful living, who can do me both or either.

In Illinois, General Henry's merits have been always duly appreciated. He was the idol of the volunteers and the people, and if he had lived his numerous friends would never have permitted him to submit to the base larceny by which he was deprived[5] abroad and in history of his well-earned glory. If he had lived he would have been elected governor of the State in 1834 by more than 20,000 majority, and this would have been done against his own will, by the spontaneous action of the people.

The next day after the battle of the Wisconsin, for want of provisions it was determined to fall back to the Blue Mounds. The Winnebagoes who accompanied Henry during his forced march had displayed their usual treachery and cowardice by retreating at the commencement of the battle. No one then in the brigade knew enough of the country to act as guide. Henry had marched one hundred and thirty miles through an unknown and hitherto unexplored country, without roads or land-marks, and now found himself in a position from which no one with him could direct his way to the settlement. He was without provisions for his men, or surgeons or accommodations for the wounded; horses and men were worn down with fatigue, and they might be a week or more blundering through the wilderness before they found their way out. A council was called to consider these difficulties; and whilst it was debating the course to be pursued some Indians approached with a white flag who were ascertained to be friendly Winnebagoes. Their services were secured as guides. Litters were made for the wounded; and the army was soon on the march for the Blue Mounds, which were reached in two days. Here Gen. Henry met Gen. Atkinson with the regulars and Alexander's and Posey's brigades. It was soon apparent to Gen. Henry and all his officers that Gen. Atkinson and all the regular officers were deeply mortified at the success of the militia. They did not intend that the militia should have had any of the credit in the war. The success of Henry, too, was obtained by a breach of orders and in defiance of the counsels of those who professed exclusive courage and knowledge in the military art. The regular officers evidently envied those of the militia. General Atkinson had always relied most upon the regulars; they had all the time been kept in advance, and now it was too much to be borne that whilst they were forted at Lake Kushkonong the Indians had been discovered, pursued, overtaken, and victory obtained by the Illinois militia.

After spending two days in preparation at the Blue Mounds the whole force, now under the direction of Gen. Atkinson, was again on the march in pursuit of the Indians. The Wisconsin river was crossed at Helena and the trail of the Indians was struck in the mountains on the other side. And now again the regulars were put in front; Dodge's battalion and Posey's and Alexander's brigades came next; and Henry was placed in the rear in charge of the baggage, the commanding general thus making known the ungenerous envy which burned in his bosom against the brave men who had distinguished themselves in the previous battle. It was plain that if other laurels were to be won they were to be worn on other brows. Henry's brigade felt that they had been visited with undeserved insult, for they well knew that they deserved better treatment, and with one voice claimed the post of honor and of danger. But Henry was too good an officer to utter a word of complaint and his officers and men, though lately the victors in a well-fought field, following his noble example quietly trudged on in the rear, doing the drudgery of the army by taking charge of the baggage trains.

Day after day the whole force toiled in climbing and descending mountains covered with dense forests and passing through swamps of deep, black mud lying in the intervening valleys. But the march was slow compared with that preceding the battle of the Wisconsin. In this march were found, all along the route, the melancholy evidences of the execution done in that battle. The path of the retreating Indians was strewn with the wounded who had died on the march, more from neglect and want of skill in dressing their wounds than from the mortal nature of the wounds themselves. Five of them were found dead at one place where the band had encamped for the night.

About 10 o'clock in the morning of the fourth day after crossing the Wisconsin Gen. Atkinson's advance reached the bluffs on the east side of the Mississippi. The Indians had reached the bank of the river some time before. Some had crossed and others were now making preparations to cross it. The steamboat "Warrior," commanded by Captain Throckmorton, descended to that place the day before. As the steamboat neared the camp of the Indians they raised a white flag; but Captain Throckmorton, believing this to be treacherously intended, ordered them to send a boat on board, which they declined doing. In the flippant language of the Captain, after allowing them fifteen minutes to remove their squaws and children he let slip a six-pounder at them, loaded with canister shot, followed by a severe fire of musketry; "and if ever you saw straight blankets, you would have seen them there." According to the Captain's account the "fight" continued for an hour and cost the lives of twenty-three Indians and a large number wounded. The boat then fell down the river to Prairie du Chien; and before it could return the next morning the land forces under Gen. Atkinson had come up and commenced a general battle.

It appears that the Indians were encamped on the bank of the Mississippi some distance below the mouth of the Bad Axe river. They were aware that Gen. Atkinson was in close pursuit; and to gain time for crossing into the Indian country west of the Mississippi they sent back about twenty men to meet Gen. Atkinson, within three or four miles of their camp. This party of Indians were instructed to commence an attack and then to retreat to the river three miles above their camp. Accordingly when Gen. Atkinson, the order of march being as before, came within three or four miles of the river he was suddenly fired upon from behind trees and logs, the very tall grass aiding the concealment of the attacking party. Gen. Atkinson rode immediately to the scene of action and in person formed his lines and directed a charge. The Indians gave way and were pursued by Gen. Atkinson with all the army except Henry's brigade, which was in the rear and in the hurry of pursuit left without orders. When Henry came up to the place where the attack had been made he saw clearly that the wily stratagem of the untutored savage had triumphed over the science of a veteran general. The main trail of the Indians was plain to be seen leading to the river lower down. He called a hasty council of his principal officers and by their advice marched right forward upon the main trail. At the foot of the high bluff bordering the river valley, on the edge of a swamp densely covered with timber, drift-wood, and under-brush, through which the trail led fresh and broad, he halted his command and left his horses. The men were formed on foot and thus advanced to the attack. They were preceded by an advance guard of eight men, who were sent forward as a forlorn hope and were intended to draw the first fire of the Indians and to disclose thereby to the main body where the enemy was to be found, preparatory to a general charge. These eight men advanced boldly some distance until they came within sight of the river, where they were fired upon by about fifty Indians and five of the eight instantly fell wounded or dead. The other three, protected behind trees, stood their ground until the arrival of the main body under Gen. Henry, which deployed to the right and left from the centre. Immediately the bugle sounded a charge, every man rushed for ward, and the battle became general along the whole line. These fifty Indians had retreated upon the main body amounting to about three hundred warriors, a force equal if not superior to that now contending with them. It was soon apparent that they had been taken by surprise. They fought bravely and desperately but seemingly without any plan or concert of action. The bugle again sounded the inspiring music of a charge. The Indians were driven from tree to tree and from one hiding-place to another. In this manner they receded step by step, driven by the advancing foe, until they reached the bank of the river. Here a desperate struggle ensued but it was of short duration. The bloody bayonet in the hands of excited and daring men pursued and drove them for-ward into the waters of the river. Some of them tried to swim the river; others to take a temporary shelter on a small willow island near the shore.

About this time Gen. Atkinson with the regulars and Dodge's battalion arrived, followed by Posey's and Alexander's men. But the main work had been done before they came up. It had been determined that Henry's men should have no share in this day's glory, but the fates, taking advantage of a blunder of Gen. Atkinson, had otherwise directed. After the Indians had retreated into the river and on to the island Henry despatched Major McConnell to give intelligence of his movements to his commander, who whilst pursuing the twenty Indians in another direction had heard the firing where Henry was engaged. Gen. Atkinson left the pursuit of the twenty Indians and hastened to share in the engagement. He was met by Henry's messenger near the scene of action, in passing through which the dead and dying Indians lying around bore frightful evidence of the stern work which had been done before his arrival. He, however, lost no time in forming his regulars and Dodge's battalion for a descent upon the island. These forces together with Ewing's battalion and Fry's regiment made a charge through the water up to their armpits on to the island, where most of the Indians had taken their last refuge. All the Indians who attempted to swim the river were picked off with rifles or found a watery grave before they reached the opposite shore. Those on the island kept up a severe fire from behind logs and driftwood upon the men as they advanced to the charge; and here a number of regulars and of volunteers under Dodge were killed and wounded. But most of the Indians there secreted were either killed, captured, or driven into the water, where they perished miserably, either by drowning or by the still more fatal rifle. During these engagements a number of squaws were killed. They were dressed so much like the male Indians that, concealed as they were in the high grass, it was impossible to distinguish them. It is estimated that the Indian loss here amounted to one hundred and fifty killed and as many more who were drowned in the river, and fifty prisoners were taken, mostly squaws and children. The residue of the Indians had escaped across the river before the commencement of the action. The twenty men who first commenced the attack, led by Black Hawk in person, escaped up the river. The American loss amounted to seventeen killed, one of them a captain of Dodge's battalion and one a lieutenant of Fry's regiment, and twelve wounded.

It appears that Black Hawk with his twenty men, after the commencement of the battle by Gen. Henry and after Gen. Atkinson had ceased pursuit, retreated to the Dalles on the Wisconsin river. A number of Sioux and Winnebago Indians were sent in pursuit of him. These tribes, though sympathizing with the hostile band, were as accomplished in treachery to their friends when friendship was most needed as are a more civilized people. They had lately seen so striking a display of the strength of the white man that, like a more polished race, their mean and crafty natures clung to the side of power. Headed by the one-eyed Decori, a Winnebago chief, they went in pursuit of Black Hawk and his party and captured them high up on the Wisconsin river. The prisoners were brought down to Prairie du Chien and delivered up to Gen. Street, the United States Indian Agent. Amongst them was a son of Black Hawk and also the Prophet, a noted chief who formerly resided at Prophet's town in Whiteside county, and who was one of the principal instigators of the war. He has perhaps been correctly described as being about forty years old, tall, straight, and athletic; with a large, broad face; short, blunt nose; large, full eyes; broad mouth; thick lips; and an abundance of thick, coarse, black hair. He was the priest and prophet of his tribe and he mingled with his holy character the cruel feelings of a wild beast of the feline tribe; exhibiting in his looks a deliberate ferocity and embodying in his person all our notions of priestly assassination and clerical murder. He was dressed in a suit of very white deerskin, fringed at the seams, and wore a headdress of white cloth which rose several inches above his head, and held in one hand a white flag whilst the other hung carelessly down by his side.

The prisoners were presented by the two chiefs, Decori and Cheater. The Decori said to Gen. Street: "My father, I now stand before you; when we parted I told you we would return soon. We had to go a great distance, to the Dalles of the Wisconsin. You see that we have done what we went to do. These are the two you told us to get (pointing to Black Hawk and the Prophet). We always do what you tell us because we know it is for our good. My father, you told us to get these men, and it would be the cause of much good to the Winnebagoes. We have brought them but it has been very hard for us to do it. That one, Mucatah Muhicatah, was a great way off. You told us to bring them alive; we have done so. If you had told us to bring their heads alone, we would have done it. It would have been easier to do than what we have done. My father, we deliver these men into your hands; we would not deliver them even to our brother, the chief of the warriors, but to you, because we know you and believe you are our friend. We want you to keep them safe. If they are to be hurt we do not wish to see it. My father, many little birds have been flying about our ears of late and we thought they whispered to us that there was evil intended for us; but now we hope the evil birds will let our ears alone. My father, we know you are our friend, because you take our part; this is the reason we do what you tell us to do. My father, you say you love your red children; we think we love you more than you love us. My father, we were promised much good if we would take these people. We wait to see what good will be done for us. My father, we have come in haste and are tired and hungry; we now put these men in your hands."

The foregoing is not given as a specimen of Indian eloquence; but may serve as a fair example of the mean spirit, cringing, fawning, and flattering of these rude barbarians when their natural ferocity is overpowered by fear.

It may at this day be interesting to hear the answer of the great Gen. Taylor, who was then a colonel of the regulars, to this speech. He said: "The great chief of the warriors told me to take the prisoners, when you should bring them, and send them to him at Rock Island. I will take them and keep them safe and use them well; and will send them down by you and Gen. Street when you go down to the council, which will be in a few days. Your friend, Gen. Street, advised you to get ready and go down to the council. I advise you to do so too. I tell you again that I will take the prisoners, keep them safe, and do them no harm. I will deliver them to the great chief of the warriors and he will do with them and use them as he may be directed by your great father the president."

Cheater addressed Gen. Street as follows: "My father, I am young and don't know how to make speeches. This is the second time I have spoken to you before the people. My father, I am no chief, I am no orator, but I have been allowed to speak to you. My father, if I should not speak as well as others, still you must listen to me. My father, when you made the speech to the chiefs Waugh-kon Dacori, Caramanee, the one eyed Dacori and others the other day I was there and heard you. I thought what you said to them you also said to me. You said if these two (pointing to Black Hawk and the Prophet) were brought to you, a black cloud would never again hang over the Winnebagoes. My father, your words entered into my ears and into my heart. I left here that very night and you have not seen me since until now. My father, I have been a great way. I have had much trouble. But when I remember what you said, knowing you were right, I kept right on and did what you told me to do. Near the Dalles on the Wisconsin river I took Black Hawk. No one did it but me. I say this in the ears of all present; they know it to be true. My father, I am no chief, but what I have done is for the benefit of my nation; and I now hope for the good that has been promised us. My father, that one, Wabokishick (the prophet) is my kinsman. If he is hurt I do not wish to see it. The soldiers sometimes stick the ends of their guns into the backs of the Indian prisoners when they are going about in the hands of the guard. I hope this will not be done to these men." This is a more manly specimen of Indian oratory, showing much generous feeling, delicately expressed.

General Atkinson with the regulars had gone down to Prairie Du Chien in the steamboat Warrior; the volunteers had marched down by land. Here they met Gen. Scott, who had been ordered from the East to take the chief command in this war. In eighteen days Gen. Scott had transported a regular force from Fortress Monroe on the

Chesapeake Bay to Chicago. On their route up the lakes they were dreadfully afflicted with the Asiatic cholera, then a new and strange disease making its first appearance on the continent of America. It suddenly broke out among his troops at Detroit, about forty miles from which place two hundred and eight men were landed under the command of Colonel (now General) Twiggs, of whom it is said only nine survived. The main body under Gen. Scott came on to Chicago, but were attacked with the same disease at Mackinaw and by the time they arrived at Chicago the contagion was general; and within thirty days, ninety more were carried to their graves. Gen. Scott stayed at Chicago about a month, and reached the Mississippi at Rock Island some time in August 1832; but not until the decisive affair at the Bad Axe had terminated the war.

Upon the arrival of the troops at Prairie Du Chien. the volunteers were ordered to Dixon, where they were discharged, and then each merry, brave man hastened as he pleased to his home, his kindred and friends. Black Hawk and his son, Naapope, Wishick, and the Prophet were sent down to Rock Island; and with them went many of the Winnebago chiefs to meet Keokuk and the other chiefs of the Sacs and Foxes. But when they arrived at Rock Island, the place appointed for a treaty, the cholera had broken out there, so that Gen. Scott and Gov. Reynolds with the prisoners and other chiefs fell down to Jefferson Barracks; where a treaty was made by which the Sacs and Foxes ceded to the United States a large tract of land bordering on the Mississippi, from the Desmoine to Turkey river in the territory of Iowa. The prisoners named were held as hostages for the peaceable behavior of the hostile Indians. They were taken to Washington City, where they had an interview with President Jackson, to whom it is reported, Black Hawk said: "I am a man and you are another. We did not expect to conquer the white people. I took up the hatchet to revenge injuries which could no longer be borne. Had I borne them longer my people would have said, Black Hawk is a squaw; he is too old to be a chief. He is no Sac. This caused me to raise the war-whoop. I say no more of it. All is known to you. Keokuk once was here; you took him by the hand, and when he wanted to return you sent him back to his nation. Black Hawk expects that like Keokuk we will be permitted to return too." The President told him that when he was satisfied that all things would remain quiet they should return. He then took them by the hand and dismissed them. They were then sent to Fortress Monroe where Black Hawk became much attached to Col. Eustis, the commander at the fort. On parting with him Black Hawk said: "The memory of your friendship will remain until the Great Spirit says that it is time for Black Hawk to sing his death song;" then presenting him with a hunting-dress and some feathers of the white eagle, he said: "Accept these, my brother; I have given one like them to the White Beaver" (Gen. Atkinson.) "Accept them from Black Hawk, and when he is far away they will serve to remind you of him. May the Great Spirit bless you and your children. Farewell."

By order of the President, these Indian prisoners on the 4th day of June, 1833 were returned to their own country. They were taken to Baltimore, Philadelphia, New York, and other cities to show them the numbers and power of the white people. In all these places they attracted great attention; crowds everywhere collected to see them; and they even divided the attention and curiosity of the public with Gen. Jackson himself, who was then making the tour of the northern States. Amongst others, the ladies universally sought their acquaintance; and one young lady (said to be respectable) in her admiration of Black Hawk's son actually kissed him before crowds of people. In return for their politeness and sympathy Black Hawk told them that they were "very pretty squaws." They were returned by way of the New York canal and the northern lakes to their own people in the wilderness west of the Mississippi. Black Hawk lived until the 3d of October, 1840, when he was gathered to his fathers at the age of eighty years, and was buried on the banks of the great river where he had spent his life, and which he had loved so much.[6]

VI

The Internal Improvement Era, 1833–1840

fter the Black Hawk war nothing of importance occurred until the session of the legislature of 1832–'3; which was distinguished for the first efforts seriously made to construct railroads and to impeach one of the judges. Several charters passed to incorporate railroad companies; and an effort was made to procure a charter for a railroad from Lake Michigan to the Illinois river, in place of a canal. The stock in none of these companies was ever taken. At this session also were first proposed in the Senate surveys for a railroad across the State through Springfield; and the central railroad from Peru to Cairo. George Forquer proposed the first and the last was proposed by Lieutenant Governor Jenkins, though the central railroad had before been suggested in a newspaper publication by Judge Breese, now Senator in Congress.

Numerously signed petitions from the people were sent up to this legislature praying the impeachment of Theophilus W. Smith, one of the justices of the Supreme Court, for oppressive conduct and misdemeanors in office. Witnesses were sent for and examined by the House of Representatives. Articles of impeachment were voted and sent up to the Senate charging the judge with selling a clerk's office of one of the circuit courts; with swearing out vexatious writs returnable before himself for the purpose of oppressing innocent men by holding them to bail, and then continuing the suits for several terms in a court of which he was judge; with imprisoning a Quaker for not taking off his hat in court; and with suspending a lawyer from practice for advising his client to apply for a change of venue to some other circuit where Judge Smith did not preside. A solemn trial was had before the Senate, which sat as a high court of impeachment, and which trial lasted for several weeks. The judge was prosecuted by a committee of managers from the House of Representatives of which Benjamin Mills was chairman.[1] This highly-gifted man shone forth with uncommon brilliancy in three days summing up by way of conclusion on the side of the prosecution. At last the important day and hour came when a vote was to be taken, which was to be a sentence of doom to one of the magnates of the land or was to restore him to his high office and to the confidence of his friends. But during the progress of the trial Judge Smith procured some one to go into the Senate chamber regularly after every adjournment and gather up the scraps of paper on the desks of the senators upon which they had scribbled during the trial. From these much information was obtained as to the feelings of senators, their doubts and difficulties; and this enabled him and his counsel to direct their evidence and arguments to better advantage. The whole country looked with anxious expectation for the result of this trial. The vote being taken, it appeared that twelve of the senators concurred in believing him guilty of some of the specifications; ten were in favor of acquitting him; and four were excused from voting. It appears from the journals that fifteen senators, being a majority of two thirds of the senators voting, had voted him guilty of one or the other of the specifications; but as twelve was the highest vote against him on any one specification he was acquitted. The House of Representatives by a two-thirds vote immediately passed a resolution to remove him by address, but the resolution failed in the Senate.

Afterwards other efforts were made to impeach judges for misconduct, but without success. So that latterly the legislature has refused even to make an effort to bring a judge to trial; knowing that whether guilty or innocent such an effort can have no other result than to increase the length and expenses of the session. This conviction has been so general among intelligent men that it has had a wonderful effect in creating a feeling in favor of limiting the term of service of the judges.

In August, 1834 another election came on for Governor, which resulted in the choice of Governor Duncan. Lieutenant Governor Kinney was again the opposition candidate. By this time Governor Duncan had become thoroughly estranged from the friends and administration of Gen. Jackson. But as he was absent in Congress when he became a candidate and never returned until after the election the rank and file of the Jackson party had no means of ascertaining his defection. It was known to the anti-Jackson men and to the leading men of the Jackson party. These last had not credit enough with their party friends to make them believe it, nor would they believe it until the publication of the new governor's inaugural message, which took bold and strong ground against the measures of Gen. Jackson's administration. About this time the anti-Jackson party began generally to take the name of Whigs; and attempted to base it, as did the whigs of the revolution, upon opposition to the executive power. It may be well here to give some further account of Governor Duncan. He was a native of Kentucky; and when quite young obtained an ensign's commission during the war of 1812. He was with Col. Croghan and his handful of men at the defence of Fort Stephenson against ten times their number of British and Indians. This brilliant affair was the means of distinguishing all the inferior officers engaged in it, and immortalized their commander.

Governor Duncan was a man of genteel, affable, and manly deportment; with a person remarkably well adapted to win the esteem and affections of his fellow-citizens. He had not been long a citizen of this State before he was elected major-general of the militia and then a State Senator, where he distinguished himself in the session of 1824–'5 by being the author of the first common school law which was ever passed in this State. He was next elected to Congress, in which he continued as a member of the House of Representatives until he was elected governor in 1834. He was a man of but little education or knowledge except what he had picked up during his public services, and he had profited to the utmost by these advantages. He had a sound judgment, a firm confidence in his own convictions of right, and a moral courage in adhering to his convictions which is rarely met with.

A new legislature was elected at the same time with Governor Duncan, which met at Vandalia in Dec. 1834. At that time the State was in a very flourishing and prosperous condition. Population and wealth were pouring into it from all the old States. The great speculation in lands and town lots, shortly afterwards so rife, had made only a beginning, and that at Chicago alone. The people were industrious, and contented with the usual profits of labor, skill, and capital. They were free from debt; and the treasury of the State for once had become solvent, paying all demands in cash. If the prevalent speculations farther east had not commenced in Illinois, there were certainly very many persons who were anxious that they should begin; for at this session the legislature undertook to better the condition of public and private affairs by chartering a new State Bank with a capital of one million five hundred thousand dollars; and by reviving the charter of the bank at Shawneetown with a capital of three hundred thousand dollars, which had once broke, and had ceased to do business for twelve years. This was the beginning of all the bad legislation which followed in a few years, and which, as is well known, resulted in general ruin. At the commencement of this session no one could have anticipated the creation of a bank. The people with one accord, ever since the failure of the old State Bank of 1821, had looked upon local banks with disfavor. And the whigs at that time, contending as they were for a national bank, were thought to be hostile to banks of any other kind. But a large majority of them in both branches of the legislature voted for these bank charters. The United States Bank, vetoed by Gen. Jackson, was about to go out of existence. Mr. Woodbury, the United States secretary of the treasury, had encouraged the State and local banks to discount liberally with a view to supply the deficiency of currency anticipated upon the discontinuance of the United States Bank. From this, very many democrats inferred it to be the wish of Gen. Jackson's administration that State banks should be created where they did not exist; and with this view, these democrats were now in favor of the creation of banks. The intrigues practised to pass these charters are but imperfectly known to me. The charter for the State Bank was drawn by Judge Smith, and presented in the Senate by Conrad Will of Jackson county. It was in honor of him that the county of Will was subsequently named. He was not remarkable for anything except his good-humor and for having been long a member of the legislature. One member of the Senate who was bitterly hostile to all banks and was opposed to the Shawneetown Bank bill on constitutional grounds, as he declared from his place in the Senate, gave both the bank charters his hearty support in consideration of assistance in passing a law to levy a tax on land in the military tract for road purposes;[2] and a member of the House supported them because the bank men made him a State's attorney.[3]

It may be thought strange that an increase of taxes was so earnestly insisted on at that early day as to be made the subject of log-rolling in the creation of a bank. But it is to be remembered that the military lands were then owned principally by nonresidents, who were unwilling to sell except at high prices. Every town built, farm made, road opened, bridge or school-house erected by the settlers in their vicinity added to the value of these lands at no expense to the nonresident. The people persuaded themselves that in improving their own farms they were putting money into the pockets of men who did nothing for the country except to skin it as fast as any hide grew on it. This tax was called for to make the nonresident owner contribute his share to the improvement of the country, and thus by burdening his land with taxes render him more willing to sell it. A very bad state of feeling existed towards the non-resident land-owners; the timber on their land was considered free plunder, to be cut and swept away by every comer; the owners brought suits for damage, but where the witnesses and jurors were all on one side justice was forced to go with them. The non-residents at last bethought themselves of employing and sending out ministers of the gospel to preach to the people against the sin of stealing, or *hooking* timber, as it was called. These preachers each had a circuit, or district of country assigned them to preach in, and were paid by the sermon; but I have never learned that the non-resident land-owners succeeded any better in protecting their property by the gospel than they did at law.

But to return to the banks. How many other converts were made in their favor by similar means must remain forever a secret. The State Bank charter was passed in the House of Representatives by a majority of one vote; so that it may be said that making of a State's attorney made a State Bank. The vote in the legislature was not a party vote; the banks were advocated and supported upon grounds of public utility and expediency; and like on the vote upon the internal improvement system, which followed at the next session, both whigs and democrats were earnestly invited to lay party feelings aside and all go, at least once, for the good of the country. Whenever I have heard this cry since I have always suspected that some great mischief was to be done for which no party desired to be responsible to the people. As majorities have the power, so it is their duty to carry on the government. The majority, as long as parties are necessary in a free government, ought never to divide and a portion of it join temporarily with the minority. It should always have the wisdom and courage to adopt all the measures necessary for good government. As a general thing, if the minority is anything more than a faction, if it has any principles and is true to them, it will rally an opposition to all that is done by the majority; and even if it is convinced that the measures of the majority are right, it is safest for the minority to compel the majority to take the undivided responsibility of government. By this means there will always be a party to expose the faults and blunders of our rulers; and the majority will be more careful what they do. But if the minority mixes itself up with the majority in the support of great measures which prove unfortunate for the country, neither party can expose the error without prostrating its own favorites. In this way many persons now prominent as politicians in this State have gone unwhipped of justice, who otherwise would have been consigned to an unfathomable oblivion. Certain it is that if this course had been observed in the enactment of the disastrous measures of this and the succeeding session of the legislature the dominant party would never have dared, as it did not afterwards dare, to risk the continuance of popular favor by supporting such a policy.

These banks were brought into existence in violation of the plainest principles of political economy. The State was young. There was no social or business organization upon any settled principles. A large crowd of strangers, as it were, had met here for adventure. Our most sagacious citizens were of this sort. We had no cities, no trade, no manufactures, and no punctuality in the payment of debts. We exported little or nothing. We had no surplus capital, and consequently the capital for banking must come from abroad. Some few then foresaw, what proved true, that it would be difficult to find directors and officers for two banks and numerous branches who, from their known integrity and financial knowledge would be entitled to the public confidence. The stock-holders would (as they did) reside abroad in other States. They could not supervise the conduct of the directory in person. It was probable that many improvident loans would be made, and that the banks would be greatly troubled in making their collections.

It appears to me that banking cannot be successful in any country where the capital comes necessarily from abroad. The stockholders will be imposed on. They cannot conveniently meet in proper person to examine the banks, but must from year to year trust everything to agents, who, the whole world says, never manage other people's business as well as their own. Banking cannot succeed except in a state of settled, organized society, where honesty, truth, and fidelity are paramount; where the merchants and business men have all received a regular commercial training; where they have been educated from their youth upwards in the principles and practice of commercial honor and punctuality; where a bank protest, by breaking a man and closing his business, is more terrible than imprisonment; where the laws favor the collection of debts and the whole people are in the habit of prompt payment. In such a society honest and capable men may be readily found to manage banks and those who deal with them may be relied on for punctuality. I place great stress upon punctuality as the vital principle of safe banking. Because if the debtors of the bank do not pay the bank itself cannot.

Nor can banking succeed in a State where the great body of the people, or any considerable party of them, are opposed to banks. Some project to repeal their charter or harass them will be started at every session of the legislature, and they will be strongly tempted to extend their favors farther than safety will warrant for the purpose of silencing opposition. In a community like Illinois there are scores of men in every county who, from their business, or rather want of business and want of punctuality, cannot with safety be favored by a bank. Yet such men are not destitute of political importance and influence, and can give the banks great trouble if a loan is refused.

Favor to such persons is a fraud upon the stockholders and the community which credits the circulation. Nevertheless banks are driven to accommodate such persons, and, in fact, to absolute bribery for the purpose of buying their peace.

I aver without fear of contradiction that when these banks were chartered there was, in a manner, no surplus capital in the State; that the capital came mostly from abroad; that the stockholders resided at a distance and never had a meeting, in proper person, in this State; that we had no cities and but few large towns; that, in a manner, we exported nothing, but imported everything except meat and breadstuffs, and indeed much of these. We had no settled society. The business men were not generally men of commercial training and education. The laws did not favor the collection of debts nor did the public sentiment frown upon a want of punctuality.

After the internal improvement system was adopted at a subsequent session its friends increased the capital of these banks by making the State a stockholder in each. The capital of the State Bank was increased two millions of dollars, and the Illinois Bank one million four hundred thousand dollars.

The stock in the State Bank was readily and greedily taken, and the subscriptions greatly exceeded the amount allowed by the charter. Early in the spring of 1835 John Tillson, jr., then of Hillsboro; Thomas Mather, then of Kaskaskia; Godfrey Gilman & Co., then of Alton; Theophilus W. Smith, then one of the judges of the Supreme Court; and Samuel Wiggins of Cincinnati made arrangements to obtain large sums of money in the eastern cities, principally in New York and Connecticut, to be invested in this stock. The charter required the advance of five dollars on each share subscribed and gave a preference to citizens of the State. It also provided against the undue influence of large stockholders, by reducing their (proportional) vote for directors. These provisions made it desirable not only that all the stock should be subscribed by citizens of the State, but also that all subscriptions should be small in amount. Accordingly each of these gentlemen, with a view of monopolizing the stock and controlling the bank, employed men all over the country to obtain powers of attorney from any and all who were willing to execute them authorizing one or the other of these persons to act as their agents in subscribing for stock, and to transfer and control it afterwards.

Many thousands of such subscriptions were made in the names of as many thousands who never dreamed of being bankers, and who do not know to this day that they were ever, apparently, the owners of bank stock.

The contest for the control of the bank was between Judge Smith on the one side and the other gentlemen named on the other. When the commissioners met to apportion the stock a motion was made that all subscriptions by or for the use of citizens of the State should be preferred to subscriptions made for the use of persons residing abroad, and requiring all holders of proxies to make oath as to the fact of residence or nonresidence. This resolution was advocated by Judge Smith, who stood ready, as it was said, to swear that all the stock subscribed by him in his own name or by power of attorney, *bona fide* belonged to him and had been paid for by his own money. The other great operators could not make such an oath and consequently opposed the resolution, which was defeated. Tillson, Mather, Wiggins, and Godfrey Gilman & Co., combined against Smith. They obtained a controlling portion of the stock. Mather was made president and a directory was elected who were in the interest of the combination. The directors appointed were probably as good men for the trust as could have been found in the State.

As I have said, the stock in the State Bank having been taken it went into operation under the control of Thomas Mather and his friends in 1835. The Alton interest in it was very large. Godfrey Gilman & Co., merchants of Alton, had obtained control of a large part of the stock; enough, in case of division, to control the election of directors. To conciliate them the bank undertook to lend its aid to build up Alton in rivalry of St. Louis. At this time a strong desire was felt by many to create a commercial emporium in our own State; and it was hoped that Alton could be made such a place. As yet, however, nearly the whole trade of Illinois, Wisconsin, and of the Upper Mississippi was concentrated at St. Louis. The little pork, beef, wheat, flour, and such other articles as the country afforded for export were sent to St. Louis to be shipped. All the lead of the upper and lower lead-mines was shipped from or on account of the merchants of St. Louis. Exchange on the east to any amount could only be purchased at St. Louis; and many of the smaller merchants all over the country went to St. Louis to purchase their assortments.

The State Bank undertook to break up this course of things and divert these advantages to Alton. Godfrey Gilman & Co. were supplied with about $800,000 to begin on the lead business. By their agents they made heavy purchases of lead and had it shipped to Alton. Stone, Manning & Co., another Alton firm, were furnished with several hundred thousand dollars with which to operate in produce; and Sloo & Co. obtained large loans for the same purpose. The design of the parties, of course, was not accomplished. Instead of building up Alton, enriching its merchants, and giving the bank a monopoly of exchanges on the east these measures resulted in crushing Alton, annihilating its merchants, and breaking the bank. This result ought to have been foreseen. The St. Louis merchants had more capital in business than ten such banks and twenty such cities as Alton. They were intimately connected, either as owners or agents, in all the steamboats running on the Illinois and Upper Mississippi. These boats required an up-river as well as a down-river freight. The up-river freight could only be got in St. Louis and would not be furnished to boats known to be engaged in the Alton conspiracy. The merchants in Galena and throughout the Upper Mississippi and Illinois country were connected in trade with the St. Louis merchants, many of them owing balances not convenient to be paid and enjoying standing credits which could not be dispensed with.

The Alton merchants, however, commenced operations on the moneys furnished by the bank, and they were so anxious to obtain a monopoly of purchases that prices rose immediately. The price of lead rose in a short time from $2.75 to $4.25 per hundred. This did not appear to be the best way of monopolizing the lead trade. Therefore, Godfrey Gilman & Co. furnished their agent in Galena some two or three hundred thousand dollars to purchase lead-mines and smelting establishments.[4] This agent was a manly, frank, honorable, and honest man, but wild and reckless in the extreme. He bought all the mines and smelting establishments he could get and some lots in Galena. He scattered money with a profuse and princely hand. The effect was apparent in a short time. Property in Galena rose in a few months more than two thousand per cent. While such great exertions were making to divert the lead trade to Alton, and while such lavish expenditures at Galena raised its price there, they could not keep up the price in the eastern cities, its destined market. The lead was kept in store in New York a year or two in hopes the price would rise. The owners were at last compelled to sell at a great sacrifice and the operation ruined all concerned. Stone, Manning & Co. and Sloo & Co. were equally unfortunate.

I think the bank must have lost by all its Alton operations near a million of dollars, and was nearly insolvent before the end of the second year of its existence, though the fact was unknown to the people. This is an example of the danger of endeavoring to force trade, wholly against nature, out of its accustomed channels. Let it be a warning also to all banks not to engage, either by themselves or by their agents, in the ordinary business of trade and speculation.

The democrats helped to make the banks but the whigs controlled the most money, which gave them the control of the banks. The president and a large majority of the directors and other officers were whigs; just enough of democrats had been appointed to avoid the appearance of proscription. Thus the democrats were defeated at least once in the contest for the "spoils," and probably it will always be thus when long purses are to decide who are the "victors."

When the State Bank was created its projectors, to make it popular, attached to it a provision for a real estate fund to the amount of a million of dollars, to be lent out on mortgages of land. This was intended to conciliate the farmers, as thereby the bank would become a sort of farmers' bank, out of which the farmers could obtain money on a mortgage of their farms. But this was really the worst feature in the whole project. At this day it will be generally acknowledged that no farmer ought ever to borrow money to carry on his farm. The only mode in which a farmer can be benefited by a bank is for merchants and traders to borrow money and pay it out to farmers for their produce. But very many farmers did borrow and very few of them were able to pay. Their farms were taken away from them; and so this popular lure to the farmers operated like setting out huge steel traps to catch their plantations.

The fact that the presidents and cashiers of the principal bank and branches and a very majority of the directors and other officers were whigs was sufficient to dub the bank a whig concern. It was viewed with great jealousy by the democrats. Judge Smith headed an opposition to it; and although he had written the charter and urged its passage upon his friends in the legislature, he did not hesitate to declare it unconstitutional. He was joined by Judge McRoberts, Receiver of public moneys at Danville, and many other leaders of the party. The bank made an effort to get the deposits of public money, but it had become so odious to the democrats and such representations had been made at Washington that the Secretary of the Treasury refused its application. The consequence was that a continual run was made upon it for specie to enter Government land. To avoid this continual drain of specie the bank adopted the expedient of sending its notes, purporting to have been issued at one branch, to be loaned at another, and by this means keeping its circulation at a distance from the place of payment.

Here I will leave the subject of the bank for the present and notice another important matter acted upon by the legislature at the session of 1834–'5. This was the Illinois and Michigan canal. As early as 1821 the legislature appropriated $10,000 for a survey of the route of this canal. Judge Smith and others were appointed commissioners, and they again appointed René Paul of St. Louis and Justus Post, now of Alexander county, as engineers. A survey of the route was made. The work was reported eminently practicable, and the cost of construction was estimated at a sum near six or seven hundred thousand dollars. In 1826 Congress donated to the State about 300,000 acres of land on the route of the canal in aid of the work. In 1825 a law was passed incorporating a company to make the canal. The stock was never subscribed. And in 1828 another law was passed providing for the sale of lots and lands, for the appointment of a board of canal commissioners, and for the commencement of the work. Nothing was done under this law except the sale of some land and lots and a new survey of the route and estimate of costs by the new engineer, Mr. Bucklin. The estimate this time ran into millions instead of thousands but was yet too low, as experience has subsequently demonstrated. After that time there were various projects of giving the work to a company or of making a railroad instead of a canal. But nothing effectual was proposed to be done until the session of 1834-'5.

At this session of the legislature George Forquer, a senator for Sangamon county, as chairman of the committee on internal improvements prepared and made an elaborate report in favor of a loan of half a million of dollars on the credit of the State, to begin with. I call the report an elaborate one because it is so: perhaps more able than any similar document submitted to any of the western legislatures. It contains evidence of vast research and abundance of facts and probable conjectures, and is expressed in language at once pleasing, brilliant, and attractive. The report was accompanied by a bill authorizing a loan on the credit of the State, which passed the Senate and would certainly have passed the legislature but for the fact that the governor in his general message, and also in a special message, asserted with confidence that the money could be obtained upon a pledge of the canal lands alone. Amended in this particular, the bill passed, and has served as a model for all the subsequent laws on that subject. The report was justly liable to one criticism. The cost was estimated too low. The Senate ordered 5,000 copies of it to be published for the information of the people. This was the first efficient movement in favor of the canal. The loan under this law failed; but at a special session in 1835 a law was introduced by James M. Strode, then a senator representing all the country including and north of Peoria, authorizing a loan of half a million of dollars on the credit of the State. This loan was negotiated by Governor Duncan in 1836 and with this money a commencement was made on the canal in the month of June of that year. William F. Thornton, Gurdon S. Hubbard, and William B. Archer, all whigs, were appointed the first canal commissioners under this law.

In the spring and summer of 1836 the great land and town lot speculation of those times had fairly reached and spread over Illinois. It commenced in this State first at Chicago, and was the means of building up that place in a year or two from a village of a few houses to a city of several thousand inhabitants. The story of the sudden fortunes made there excited at first wonder and amazement, next a gambling spirit of adventure, and lastly an all-absorbing desire for sudden and splendid wealth. Chicago had been for some time only one great town market. The plats of towns for a hundred miles around were carried there to be disposed of at auction. The eastern people had caught the mania. Every vessel coming west was loaded with them, their money and means, bound for Chicago, the great fairy land of fortunes. But as enough did not come to satisfy the insatiable greediness of the Chicago sharpers and speculators they frequently consigned their wares to eastern markets. Thus, a vessel would be freighted with land and town lots for the New York and Boston markets at less cost than a barrel of flour. In fact, lands and town lots were the staple of the country, and were the only articles of export.

The example of Chicago was contagious. It spread to all the towns and villages of the State. New towns were laid out in every direction. The number of towns multiplied so rapidly that it was waggishly remarked by many people that the whole country was likely to be laid out into towns; and that no land would be left for farming purposes. The judgments of all our business men were unsettled and their minds occupied only by the one idea, the all-absorbing desire of jumping into a fortune. As all had bought more town lots and lands than many of them could pay for, and more than any of them could sell, it was supposed that if the country could be rapidly settled, its resources developed, and wealth invited from abroad that all the towns then of any note would soon become cities, and that the other towns, laid out only for speculation and then without inhabitants, would immediately become thriving and populous villages, the wealth of all would be increased, and the town lot market would be rendered stable and secure.

With a view to such a consummation a system of internal improvements began to be agitated in the summer and fall of 1836. It was argued that Illinois had all the natural advantages which constitute a great State; a rich soil, variety of climate, and great extent of territory. It only wanted inhabitants and enterprise. These would be invited by a system of improvements; timber would be carried by railroad to fence the prairies; and the products of the prairies by the same means would be brought to market. The people began to hold public meetings and pass resolutions on the subject; and before the next winter most of the counties had appointed delegates to an internal improvement convention to be assembled at the seat of government. This body of delegates assembled at the same time with the legislature of 1836–'7. It devised and recommended to the legislature a system of internal improvements; the chief feature of which was "that it should be commensurate with the wants of the people." Thus the general desire of sudden and unwarrantable gain; a dissatisfaction with the slow but sure profits of industry and lawful commerce, produced a general frenzy. Speculation was the order of the day and every possible means was hastily and greedily adopted to give an artificial value to property. In accomplishing this object as to the manner and means, our people surrendered their judgments to the dictates of a wild imagination. No scheme was so extravagant as not to appear plausible to some. The most wild calculations were made of the advantages of a system of internal improvements; of the resources of the State to meet all expenditures; and of our final ability to pay all indebtedness without taxation. Mere possibilities appeared highly probable; and probability wore the livery of certainty itself.

I have said that our people were moved by these influences; but only those are meant who attended these meetings and aided in sending and instructing delegates to the internal improvement convention. It is not true that the whole people were thus moved or thus acted. These meetings were generally held in the towns, and mostly attended by the town people. The great body of the people in the country treated the subject with indifference. But this silence was taken for consent. The voice of these meetings was considered as the voice of the people, and the voice of the people as "the voice of God," and many of the members of the legislature felt themselves instructed by it to vote for some system of internal improvements.

The legislature at this session took up the subject in full earnest; and in the course of the winter passed a system providing for railroads from Galena to the mouth of the Ohio; from Alton to Shawneetown; from Alton to Mount Carmel; from Alton to the eastern boundary of the State, in the direction of Terre Haute; from Quincy on the Mississippi through Springfield to the Wabash; from Bloomington to Pekin; and from Peoria to Warsaw; including in the whole about 1,300 miles of road. It also provided for the improvement of the navigation of the Kaskaskia, Illinois, Great and Little Wabash, and Rock rivers.

And besides this two hundred thousand dollars were to be distributed amongst those counties through which no roads or improvements were to be made. The legislature voted $8,000,000 to the system, which was to be raised by a loan.

As a part of the system also, the canal from Chicago to Peru was to be prosecuted to completion and a further loan of four millions of dollars was authorized for that purpose. The legislature had already established a board of canal commissioners. They now established a board of fund commissioners to negotiate the new loans for the railroads; and a board of commissioners of public works, one for each judicial circuit, then seven in number, to superintend construction. And as a crowning act of folly it was provided that the work should commense simultaneously on all the roads at each end and from the crossings of all the rivers.

It is very obvious now that great errors were committed. It was utterly improbable that the great number of public officers and agents for the faithful prosecution of so extensive and cumbrous a system could be found in the State; or if found, it was less likely that the best material would be selected. But the legislature went on to create a multitude of officers for a multitude of men who were all to be engaged in the expenditure of money and superintending improvements, as if there were a hundred De Witt Clintons in the State; but there is no limit to the conceit of aspiring ignorance. Indeed, our past experience goes far to show that it has not yet been safe for Illinois, as a government, to have any very complicated or extensive interests to manage, for the want of men to manage them; and for the want of an enlightened public will to sustain able and faithful public servants and to hold the unfaithful to a just and strict account. The legislature were to elect the members of the board of public works, and these offices were very near being filled by the election of members of the legislature. It is true that the constitution made them ineligible by providing that no member should be appointed to an office created during the term for which he had been elected. Governor Duncan announced his determination not to commission members of the legislature, if elected, to these offices. A law was attempted to be passed dispensing with a commission from the governor although the constitution provides that all civil officers shall be commissioned by him. It had been too much the case in the Illinois legislature that when a majority were set upon accomplishing their purpose no constitutional barriers were sufficient to restrain them. Ingenious reasons were never wanting to satisfy the consciences of the more timid; so that many regretted that there was any constitution at all, by the violation of which members were forced to commit perjury to accomplish their utilitarian views. A vigorous effort was made in the two houses to elect members to these offices; but not quite a majority could be obtained in favor of it. The joint meeting was adjourned for one day, and on the next persons were elected who were not members of the legislature.

No previous survey or estimate had been made, either of the routes, the costs of the works, or the amount of business to be done on them. The arguments in favor of the system were of a character most difficult to refute, composed as they were partly of fact but mostly of prediction. In this way I have heard it proved to general satisfaction by an ingenious orator in the lobby that the State could well afford to borrow a hundred millions of dollars and expend it in making internal improvements. The orators in favor of the system all aimed to argue their way logically, and the end has showed that the counsels of a sound judgment guided by common sense jumping at conclusions are to be preferred to ingenious speculation. Nothing is more delusive in public affairs than a series of ingenious reasonings. In this way John C. Calhoun in his report on the Memorial of the Memphis Convention proved condusively that it is constitutional to build a single pier on the lakes but it would be unconstitutional to build two of them close together and parallel, for then they would be a harbor. In the same manner he proved it to be constitutional to improve the channels of the great Western rivers, but utterly uncon- stitutional to improve them near shore so that boats could have a landing; and in the same manner he proved that it was constitutional to improve the navigation of rivers common to three or more States but unconstitutional to improve a river running through a single State, although it might be the channel of trade for half the nation.

The means used in the legislature to pass the system deserve some notice for the instruction of posterity. First, a large portion of the people were interested in the success of the canal, which was threatened if other sections of the State were denied the improvements demanded by them; and thus the friends of the canal were forced to log-roll for that work by supporting others which were to be ruinous to the country. Roads and improvements were proposed everywhere to enlist every section of the State. Three or four efforts were made to pass a smaller system, and when defeated the bill would be amend- ed by the addition of other roads until a majority was obtained for it. Those counties which could not be thus accommodated were to share in the fund of two hundred thousand dollars. Three roads were ap- pointed to terminate at Alton before the Alton interest would agree to the system. The seat of government was to be removed to Springfield. Sangamon county, in which Springfield is situated, was then represented by two senators and seven representatives, called "the long nine," all whigs but one. Amongst them were some dexterous jugglers and managers in politics, whose whole object was to obtain the seat of government for Springfield.[5] This delegation from the beginning of the session threw itself as a unit in support of or opposition to every local measure of interest, but never without a bargain for votes in return on the seat of government question. Most of the other counties were small, having but one representative, and many of them with but one for a whole district; and this gave Sangamon county a decided preponderance in the log-rolling system of those days. It is worthy of examination whether any just and equal legislation can ever be sustained where some of the counties are great and powerful and others feeble. But by such means "the long nine" rolled along like a snow-ball, gathering accessions of strength at every turn until they swelled up a considerable party for Springfield, which party they managed to take almost as a unit in favor of the internal improvement system, in return for which the active supporters of that system were to vote for Springfield to be the seat of government. Thus it was made to cost the State about six millions of dollars to remove the seat of government from Vandalia to Springfield, half which sum would have purchased all the real estate in that town at three prices; and thus by log-rolling on the canal measure, by multiplying railroads, by terminating three railroads at Alton that Alton might become a great city in opposition to St. Louis, by distributing money to some of the counties to be wasted by the county commissioners and by giving the seat of government to Springfield was the whole State bought up and bribed to approve the most senseless and disastrous policy which ever crippled the energies of a growing country.

The examples of Pennsylvania and Indiana in adopting a similar system were powerfully urged by the deluded demagogues of this legislature to delude their fellow members and to quiet the fears of the people. Now was developed for the first time a principle of government, or rather a destiny for government to aim at, which was to keep pace with the grand ideas which had seized upon the people of other States,—ideas having in view not the improvement of individual man by increasing his knowledge and power of thought, but merely by enriching his pockets.

It appears by a report of a committee of the House of Representatives that it was believed that the people were expecting and anxious for a system of internal improvements; that the system would be of great utility in multiplying population and wealth; that such a system was entirely practicable; that the cost of it could be easily guessed at without previous surveys; that even small sums could be profitably expended upon the rivers; that estimates for the railroads could be ascertained by analogy and comparison with similar works in other States; that the system would cause a great deal of land to be entered and increase the land tax, a part of which could go to form a fund to pay interest; that the tolls on parts of the roads as fast as they were completed both ways from the crossings of rivers and from considerable towns would yield the interest on their cost; that the water-power made by improvements on the rivers would rent for a large sum; that lands were to be entered along all the roads by the State, which were to be re-sold for a higher price; that eminent financiers were to be elected fund commissioners, whose high standing and eminent qualifications were to reflect credit upon the State and add to its resources; and with all these resources at command, that no great financial skill would be required in any future legislature to provide for paying the interest on the loans and carry the system to completion without burdening the people. Such were the ingenious devices of this legislature, in all of which they were totally mistaken, as experience afterwards proved. Not a solitary one of these propositions has borne the test of experiment; but all have resulted just contrary to what was predicted. I will mention also that it was confidently believed, in and out of the legislature, that the State stock to be issued would command a premium of 10 per cent, which would go to swell the interest fund; that the stock in the banks would yield enough to pay interest on the bank bonds and a surplus besides; and that in fact the system was to be self-acting and self-sustaining; to provide for its own liquidation and payment and enrich the State treasury into the bargain.

I mention these calculations, all of which so signally failed; all of which were once so confidently believed but which now appear so absurd and ridiculous, as a warning to all theoretical, visionary schemers in public affairs; and against the counsels of all impracticable, dreaming politicians. Let posterity remember it and engrave it upon their hearts as a lesson of wisdom that splendid abilities and the power of ingenious speculation are not statesmanship; but they may lead a country to the verge of ruin unless guided by solid judgment and plain common sense; by which they are rarely accompanied.

As no system could be passed except by log-rolling, and without providing for a simultaneous expenditure of money all over the State, it followed that none of the roads were ever completed. Detached parcels of them were graded on every road, the excavations and embankments of which will long remain as a memorial of the blighting-scathe done by this legislature; but nothing was finished except the road from the Illinois river to Springfield, which cost about $1,000,000 and which now is not worth one hundred thousand dollars.

I will here mention that this internal improvement law was returned by the Governor and council of revision with their objections, but afterwards passed both houses by the constitutional majority. It is a singular fact that all the foolish and ruinous measures which ever passed an Illinois legislature would have been vetoed by the governor for the time being if he had possessed the constitutional power. The old State Bank of 1821 which ruined the public finances and demoralized the people; and by which the State lost in various ways more than its entire capital, would have been vetoed by Governor Bond. The laws creating the late banks and increasing their capital by making the State a stockholder to a large amount, and the internal improvement system, would have been vetoed by Governor Duncan. In all these cases the veto power would have been highly beneficial. I am aware that demagogues and flatterers of the people have so far imitated the supple parasites in the courts of Monarchs, whose maxim is that the "king can do no wrong," as to steal the compliment and apply it to the people. They are contending everywhere that the people never err. Without disputing the infallibility of the people, we know that their representatives can and have erred; and do err most grievously. A qualified veto power in the executive is a wholesome corrective. It can only operate to delay a good and popular measure; for if the people desire it with any unanimity they will select representatives who will pass it notwithstanding the veto.

As I have already said, the capital stock of the State Bank was increased this session in the whole to the amount of $3,100,000 by making the State a stockholder. The stock of the Shawneetown Bank was increased to $1,700,000 in all. The Fund Commissioners were authorized to subscribe for this increase of stock, amounting to $3,400,000, a portion of which was to be paid for from the surplus revenues of the United States and the residue by a sale of State bonds. And although the State was to have the majority of stock in both banks, yet were the private stockholders to have a majority of the directors. The banks were made the fiscal agents of the canal and railroad funds; and upon the whole it was a mere chance that the State did not lose its entire capital thus invested. It was supposed that the State bonds would sell for a premium of about 10 per cent, which would go to swell the interest fund; and that the dividends upon stock would not only pay the interest on the bonds but furnish a large surplus to be carried, likewise, to the interest fund. However, when these bonds were offered in market they could not be sold even at par. The banks were accommodating, and rather than the speculation should fail they agreed to take the bonds at par as cash, amounting to $2,665,000. The Bank of Illinois sold their lot of $900,000, but the $1,765,000 in bonds disposed of to the State Bank, it is alleged, were never sold. They were, however, used as bank capital and the bank expanded its business accordingly.

In the spring of 1837 the banks through out the United States suspended specie payments. The banks of Illinois followed the example of others. I will not dwell upon the causes of this movement as they belong more to the history of the whole country than to that of a single State. The charter of the State Bank contained a provision that if the institution refused specie payments for sixty days together it should forfeit its charter. These banks were made the fiscal agents for the canal and the railroads. A large sum of public money was deposited in them and if they went down they would carry the canal and the internal improvement system in their train of ruin. Two of the canal commissioners visited Governor Duncan and requested a call of the legislature to avert the evil. A special session was called in July. The governor's message made a statement of the matter, without any direct recommendation to legalize the suspension, and did recommend a repeal or classification of the internal improvement system. The legislature did legalize the suspension of specie payments but refused to touch the subject of internal improvements. It was plain that nothing could be done to arrest the evil for near two years more. In the meantime all considerate persons hoped that the public insanity would subside, that the people would wake up to reflection and see the utter absurdity of the public policy.

They were disappointed. Loan after loan was effected, both in Europe and America. The United States Bank, then dealing in stocks, by which it was ruined, gave important aid to our negotiations. This bank itself took some of the loans and lent its great credit to effect others. The loans made in America were at par, but those in Europe were at 9 per cent discount. The banker paid 90 cents on the dollar to the State and, as is alleged, 1 per cent to the Fund Commissioners for brokerage. Rawlings, of Shawneetown, undoubtedly received it.[6] A large contract was made for railroad iron at an extravagant price. The work continued to be prosecuted upon all the improvements. A new governor and new legislature were to be elected in August, 1838, from whose second sober thoughts relief was to be expected, unless the State should be irretrievably ruined in the meantime.

At this election the question of the continuance of the railroad system was but feebly made. Cyrus Edwards, the whig candidate for governor, declared himself to be decidedly in favor of it. Thomas Carlin, the democratic candidate, was charged with secret hostility to it but never so sufficiently explained his views during the pendency of the election that he could be charged with entertaining an opinion one way or the other. A large majority of the legislature was for the system. And although Mr. Carlin was elected governor, and most probably was opposed to it, yet, finding that nothing could be done with such a legislature, he was at the first session forced to keep silence.

This legislature not only refused to repeal or modify the system but added other works to it requiring an additional expenditure of about $800,000. Thus was presented the spectacle of a whole people becoming infatuated, adopting a most ruinous policy, and continuing it for three years; in fact, until the whole scheme tumbled about their ears and brought down the State to that ruin which all cool, reflecting men saw from the first was inevitable.

A special session was again called in 1838–'9. This session repealed the system and provided for winding it up. By this time it became apparent that no more loans could be obtained at par. The Fund Commissioner and those appointed to sell canal bonds had adopted some ingenious expedients for raising money, all of which most signally failed. Upon the creation of the New York free banking system a demand was at once created for State stocks to set the swindling institutions under it in motion. The law required a deposit of State stocks of double the value of circulation and debt, together with a certain percentage in specie. Our commissioner enabled several of these swindling banks to start by advancing Illinois bonds on a credit, in hopes that when the banks came into repute they would receive payment in their notes. These banks all failed, I believe, in a short time, and the amount they received was nearly a total loss. Other State bonds to a large amount were left in various places on deposit, for sale, and others again freely sold on a credit, although the law required ready payment in cash at par. A large amount was left with Wright & Co. of London for sale. Some half a million was sold and then Wright & Co. failed, with the money and the residue of the bonds in their hands.

The residue of the bonds was returned but the State was obliged to come in as a creditor and share with others in their estate for the money received. The State received a few shillings on the pound.

I do not attempt to write a history of all the bungling, illegal and ill-advised negotiations of our commissioners. I mean to say enough to show that at the special session in 1838–'9 the legislature was compelled by inevitable necessity to stop the system. And in fact that nearly the whole people obstinately shut their eyes to the perception of plain truths until these truths burst upon them terrible as an army with banners.

It may be supposed that this revulsion, this disappointment of cherished hopes, came upon the people with a crushing effect. It did so. Nevertheless there was but little discontent. The people looked one way and another with surprise, and were astonished at their own folly. They looked about for some one to blame but there was no one. All were equally to be condemned.

It was a maxim with many politicians just to keep along even with the humor of the people, right or wrong. Any measure was to be considered right which was popular for the time being. The politician felt assured that if he supported a bad measure when it was popular or opposed a good one when it was unpopular he would never be called to account for it by the people. It was believed that the people never blame any one for misleading them; for it was thought that they had too good a conceit of themselves to suspect or admit that they could be misled. A misleader of the people, therefore, thought himself safe if he could give present popularity to his measures. In fact it is true that a public man will scarcely ever be forgiven for being right when the people are wrong. New contests, forever occurring, will make the people forget the cause of their resentment; but their resentment itself or rather a prejudice which it sinks into will be remembered and felt when the cause of it is forgotten. It is the perfect knowledge of this fact by politicians which makes so many of them ready to prostitute their better judgments to catch the popular breeze; and so it will always be until the people have the capacity and the will to look into their affairs more carefully. Any reform in this particular must begin with the people themselves and not with politicians. Reformation must work upwards from the people through the government, and not from the politicians down. For I still insist that as a general thing the government will be a type of the people. The following are the ayes and nays on the passage of the internal improvement system in the House of Representatives. The names of prominent men are given in full. Those in favor of it were: Able, Aldrich, Atwater, Ball,

Barnett, Charles, Courtright, Craig, *John Crain, John Dougherty, John Dawson, Stephen A. Douglas,* Dunbar, Edmondson, *Ninian W. Edwards, William F. Elkin, Augustus C. French,* Galbreath, Green of Clay, Green of St. Clair, Hankins, *William W. Happy,* Hinshaw, *John Hogan,* Lagow, Leary, *Abram Lincoln, U. F. Linder,* Logan, Lyons, McCormack, *John A. McClernand,* Madden, Morris, Minor, *John Moore,* Moore of St. Clair, Morton, Murphy of Perry, Murphy of Vermilion, *Joseph Naper, James H. Ralston,* Rawalt, Reddick, *James Shields, Robert Smith,* Smith of Wabash, *Dan Stone,* Stuntz, Turley, Turney, Voris, Walker of Cook, Walker of Morgan, Watkins, Wilson, Wood, and *James Semple, the Speaker.* Those opposed to it were: Bently, *Milton Carpenter,* Cullom, Davis, Dairman, Dollins, Dubois, English, Enloe, *John J. Hardin, John Harris,* Lane, McCown, *William McMurtry, William A. Minshall,* Adam, O'Neil, Pace, Paullen, *William A. Richardson,* Stuart, Thompson, Wheeler, Whitten, and Witt. And *John Dement* and *William A. Minshall* afterwards voted to concur in the amendments of the senate.

Of those who voted for the measure on the final passage, or by concurring with the senate, Messrs. Crain, Dougherty, Dawson, Edwards, Elkin, Happy, Hogan, Naper, and Minshall have been since often elected or appointed to other offices, and are yet all of them popular men. Hogan was appointed Commissioner of the Board of Public Works and run by his party for Congress; Moore was elected to the Senate and to be Lieut. Governor, and afterwards Lieut.-Colonel in the Mexican war; Stone and Ralston were elected to be Circuit Judges—Ralston afterwards to be a Senator, and then run by his party for Congress; Linder has been Attorney General and Member of the Legislature; Dement has been twice appointed Receiver of Public Moneys; Semple, to be Chargé des Affaires at New Grenada, Judge of the Supreme Court, and Senator in Congress; Shields, to be Auditor, Judge of the Supreme Court, Commissioner of the General Land office, and Brigadier-General in the Mexican war; French was elected Governor in August, 1846; Lincoln was several times elected to the Legislature and finally to Congress; and Douglas, Smith, and McClernand have been three times elected to Congress, and Douglas to the United States Senate. Being all of them spared monuments of popular wrath, evincing how safe it is to a politician but how disastrous it may be to the country, to keep along with the present fervor of the people.*

*These gentlemen have been excused upon the ground that they were instructed to vote as they did, and that they had every right to believe that they were tru-

But the only hope now was that the State might not be able to borrow the money. This was soon taken away; for the fund commissioners succeeded in negotiating a loan in the summer of 1837; and before the end of the year the work had begun at many points on the railroads. The whole State was excited to the highest pitch of frenzy and expectation. Money was as plenty as dirt. Industry instead of being stimulated actually languished. We exported nothing; and everything from abroad was paid for by the borrowed money expended amongst us. And if our creditors have found us slow of payment they have been justly punished for lending us the money. In doing so they disappointed the only hope of the cool, reflecting men of the State.

At the same time the work was going on upon the canal. The board of canal commissioners, in pursuance of law, projected a most magnificent work and completed portions of it in a manner most creditable to the engineers and contractors. But here again the spirit of over-calculation did infinite mischief. The United States in 1826 had donated about 300,000 acres of land to this work. This land was estimated at the most exaggerated price. It was thought that its value was illimitable. As the fund appeared to be so great a very large and deep canal was projected, to be fed by the waters of Lake Michigan. Governor Duncan had recommended the commencement of a steamboat canal, which according to our present experience would have cost some $20,000,000, as a means of improving the navigation of the Illinois river and rendering its shores more healthy; and confidently relied upon Congress for additional appropriations of money or land to complete it. Such a recommendation from a distinguished source bewildered and depraved the public intellect and contributed in no small degree to form the inflated and bombastic notions which led to the extravagances of the internal improvement system. The legislature refused to sanction a steamboat canal; but nevertheless projected the work after a style of grandeur far beyond the means of the State. Several magnificent canal basins and a steamboat canal and basin at the termination on the Illinois were provided for. To complete the whole about $9,000,000 would be required. This sum, however, was regarded as a mere nothing when compared with the then inflated ideas of the value of the canal lands. At the session of 1837 there were already great complaints of mismanagement on the part of the banks; committees were appointed to exam-

---

ly reflecting the will of their constituents. But it appears to me that members ought to resign such small offices, to sacrifice a petty ambition, rather than become the willing tools of a deluded people to bring so much calamity upon the country.

ine them but the examination resulted in no discovery of any importance. The only thing worthy to be remembered concerning it is that one of the committee to examine the Shawneetown Bank, after his return, being asked what discoveries he had made, verbally reported that he had seen plenty of good liquor in the bank and sugar to sweeten it with.

But to return to the internal improvement system. The fund commissioners by taking from the principal sums borrowed managed to pay interest on the State debt until the meeting of the legislature in 1840. During the interim between the fall of the system and this meeting there was a terrible contest between the whigs and the democrats for a President of the United States. Gen. Harrison was the candidate on one side and Mr. Van Buren on the other. Nothing was heard in this contest but United States Bank, subtreasury, tariff, free trade, patriots, friends of the country, spoilsmen, gold spoons, English carriages, extravagance, defalcations, petticoat-heroes, aristocrats, coons, log-cabins, and hard cider. Not one word of our local affairs. Thus was substituted in the public mind one species of insanity for another which had worn out; and thus it was that both parties cheated themselves into a forgetfulness of the dreadful condition of the State. For previous to the explosion of the internal improvement system a debt had been contracted for that and the canal of $14,237,348, not counting the debt to the school fund or for deposits of surplus revenues; all of which was to be paid by a population of 478,929 according to the State census of 1840.

And here is a proper place for some further account of political parties. In their origin such parties seem to be founded partly in the nature of man and much upon artifice. There is undoubtedly a difference in the mental and physical constitution of men, inclining them one way or the other in political affairs. Some distrust the people, others confide in their capacity for self-government. Some prefer a quiet government, others a stormy turbulence. The condition of men, also, has much to do with party; some are poor and lowly as to property but proud in their hearts; others rich and well born with a power to make their pride felt by others. Some are ignorant and feeble-minded, others shrewd and intelligent; some are rough and ill-bred, others polished and graceful. In a word some have superior advantages which create them into a caste of their own. That portion enjoying these superior advantages are apt to look down upon their less-gifted fellow-citizens with contempt or indifference; and to feel that as they are superior in some respects they ought to be in all. They can have but little patience with the idea that the rabble is to govern the country. The people in humble condition look up to them with resentment and detestation. These remarks are not invariably true of either side, but it will be accorded to me that almost every neighborhood has some one richer than the rest who puts on airs of importance and manifests such a want of sympathy with his fellows as to disgust his humbler neighbors; amongst whom there are those who, full of ill-nature, look upon such pretensions with envious resentment. These little big men on both sides, of the neighborhood sort, are apt to feel the most thorough hatred for each other; their malice often supplying the place of principle and patriotism. They think they are devoted to a cause when they only hate an opponent; and the more thoroughly they hate the more thoroughly are they partisans. Here originates the hostility between democracy and aristocracy, as it is said to exist in this country; and here originates the feeling of proscription which is more violent amongst mere neighborhood politicians, men who never expect an office, than among politicians who have risen to distinction. The eminent politicians on each side frequently feel a liberality personally to an adversary which cannot be manifested without losing the confidence of their humbler friends.

And this state of things is kept up by the party newspapers on each side, the editors of which well know that their most profitable harvest is during an excited contest. Newspapers are then more sought for and read; and then it is that an editor's funds best support him with money and patronage. It may be said with truth that a partisan editor is a continual candidate for the favor of his party; for which reason it is his interest to make political contests interminable. The great mass of the people who take newspapers at all generally content themselves with one political paper of their own party. This and no other, except in the towns, they read from week to week and from year to year until they become thoroughly enlisted in all the quarrels of the editor and imbued with all his malice and prejudice; and thus they become bound up in the most ill-natured, narrow-minded, pedantic conceits; fully convinced that their way, and no other, is right, and that all persons of the opposite party know it to be so. They feel assured that their political opponents, and particularly those of them who are elected to office, are a set of insufferable rogues, bent upon the enslavement of the people or the ruin of the country. The rascality of the whigs, in the opinion of the democrats, is to end in enslaving the people, or to transfer the government to some foreign power; and the rascality of the democrats, in the opinion of the whigs, is to ruin the country. It is probably true that in something like this is the natural difference founded upon which parties will continue to be built, and that all efforts to get up third parties not founded upon this difference, and all efforts to make new and merely temporary issues the permanent foundation of party, must be abortive.

Some men are attached to one and some to the other party from conviction, interest, or the prejudices of education. I have already said that there was no question of principle such as now divides parties involved in the first election of Gen. Jackson. I speak only of Illinois. But as the measures of Gen. Jackson's administration were unfolded it was discovered that he favored the doctrines of the old republican party. His attack upon the United States Bank, his veto of its charter in 1832, removal of the deposits in 1833, the expunging resolutions, and the specie circular rallied all to his party who were of a nature to be hostile to the power of wealth. This is not to say that all wealthy men were excluded from or all poor ones included in the democratic party. Many wealthy persons still remained democrats from principle, interest, or ambition; and many poor men attached themselves to the opposite party for like reasons. There is a class of the poor over whom it is natural for the wealthy to exercise an influence; this class most generally lack the boldness and vigor to think and feel for themselves. Some are attached to the "rich and well-born" on account of their accomplishments and virtues, and others find it their interest to adhere to them. And there is always a class of wealthy men who from pure benevolence or from the love of the importance their wealth gives them as leaders attach themselves to the democracy. The Jackson party had long called themselves democrats; the other party called themselves democratic republicans. The democrats began to call their opponents federalists; and these opponents in 1833 or '4 began to call themselves whigs, a popular name of the revolution. The whigs, to be even with the democrats for calling them federalists, which they greatly resented, about the year 1837 gave to the democrats the name of locofocos, which they had persisted in calling the democrats ever since.[7] The whigs, knowing the influence of mere words in all human affairs, gave this uncouth name to the democrats in hopes thereby to make them ashamed of it, disavow it, and prefer the name of whig. It has had no effect whatever on elections; but the whigs still keep it up as if it had a power in it to blister and destroy, and no consideration on earth can induce them to relinquish it. In all this there are just two things which are remarkable. It is remarkable that the whigs, by the mere influence of the newspapers, without any open agreement, have from one end of the Union to the other adopted this name for their opponents and have adhered to it now for nine years as the only name by which their opponents shall be known; and it is remarkable that the democratic party should have no squeamish men in its ranks to run away from, or be disgusted with a party having so uncouth a name.

Our old way of conducting elections required each aspirant for office to announce himself as a candidate. The more prudent, however, always first consulted a little caucus of select, influential friends. The candidates then travelled around the county or State in proper person, making speeches, conversing with the people, soliciting votes, whispering slanders against their opponents, and defending themselves against the attacks of their adversaries. But it was not always best to defend against such attacks. A candidate in a fair way to be elected should never deny any charge made against him; for if he does his adversaries will prove all they have said and much more. As a candidate did not offer himself as the champion of any party, he usually agreed with all opinions and promised everything demanded by the people; and most usually promised, either directly or indirectly, his support to all the other candidates for office at the same election. One of the arts was to raise a quarrel with unpopular men, who were odious to the people; and thus try to be elected upon the unpopularity of others, as well as upon his own popularity. These modes of electioneering were not true of all the candidates nor perhaps half of them, very many of them being gentlemen of first-rate integrity.

After party spirit arose so as to require candidates to come out on party grounds there was for a time no mode of concentrating the action of a party. A number of candidates would come out for the same office, on the same side. Their party would be split up and divided between them. In such a case the minority party was almost sure of success, this being the only case in which one is stronger than many. As party spirit increased more and more, the necessity of some mode of concentrating the party strength became more and more apparent. The large emigration from the old States, bringing with it the zeal and party organization in which it had been trained from infancy gave a new impulse to the consolidation of the strength of party. An attempt at this was early made by the New England and New York people living in the north part of the State, by introducing the convention system of nominating candidates.

This system was first tried in counties and districts in the north; but on account of the frauds and irregularities which first attended it, small progress was made in it from 1832 when its introduction was first attempted, until 1840, the people generally preferring the

election of independent candidates. In 1837 Judge Douglas was nominated for Congress in the Peoria district and in the winter of 1837
Col. James W. Stephenson was nominated by a State convention as
a candidate for governor; and upon his inability to serve on account
of sickness Thomas Carlin was nominated in the same way in the
summer of 1838.

At first the system encountered the furious opposition of the
whigs, who, being in the minority, were vitally interested to prevent
the concentration of the democratic strength. The western democrats
looked upon it with a good deal of suspicion. It was considered a
Yankee contrivance, intended to abridge the liberties of the people by
depriving individuals, on their own mere motion, of the privilege of
becoming candidates, and depriving each man of the right to vote for
a candidate of his own selection and choice. The idea of conventions
was first brought into the middle and lower part of the State by Ebenezer Peck, Esq., a member of the bar at Chicago, a man of plausible
talents, who had formerly resided in Canada. He had there been elected to the provincial parliament by the liberal party in opposition to
the ultra monarchy party. But he had not been long in parliament
before the governor of Canada appointed him King's Counsel, in return for which favor Mr. Peck left his old friends to support the ultra
monarchists. His position was an uneasy one; so before long he resigned his offices and removed to Chicago. Here he attached himself
to the democratic party but on account of his defection in Canada
anything coming from him was viewed with suspicion and prejudice
by many, who thought him, no doubt erroneously, a man who, if he
had lived in the days of the apostles, would have rivaled Judas Is-
cariot in betraying the Saviour of men, and undertook the job for
much less than thirty pieces of silver.[8]

At a great meeting of the lobby during the special session of 1835–
'6 at Vandalia, Mr. Peck made the first speech ever made in the lower part of the State in favor of the convention system.[9] He was answered by William Jefferson Gatewood, democratic senator from
Gallatin county, and some considerable interest was awakened on
the subject among politicians. From this time the system won its way
slowly, and now all the candidates for governor, lieutenant governor,
and members of Congress are brought before the people by conventions, and it pervades two-thirds of the State in nominating candidates for the legislature.

The system has some advantages and disadvantages in this country. Those in favor of it say that it furnishes the only mode of concentrating the action of a party and giving effect to the will of the

majority. They justly urge that since the organization of parties the old system of electing from personal preference is carried into each party in the mere selection of candidates, which distracts the harmony of a party by introducing competition amongst distinguished men for the mere privilege of becoming candidates, without any means of deciding between them except at the polls. Accordingly it is strictly true that where two or more men of the same party are candidates without a nomination they are apt to hate each other ten times as intensely as they do the prominent men of the opposite party. A whig is to be elected by whigs, a democrat by democrats. The success of either depends upon the number and strength of their respective parties; but an aspiring whig or democrat has still to seek support in his own party in opposition to his own prominent political friends by a canvass of his merits as a man. Such being the case it is not likely that the ambitious men of the same party who are excited against each other by mere personal contests will decline in favor of others so as to have but a single candidate for the same office in the same party. Without a nomination, a party may be greatly in the majority, but by being divided on men the minority may succeed in the elections and actually govern the majority. To remedy this evil it was proposed by conventions of delegates, previously elected by the people, to provide but a single set of candidates for the same party. It was also urged by some that these bodies would be composed of the best-informed and principal men of a party, and would be more competent than the people at large to select good men for candidates. This body to the people would be like a grand jury to a circuit court. As the court would have no power to try any one for crime without a previous indictment by the grand jury, so the people would have no right to elect any one to office without a nomination by a convention. In the one case innocent men could not be publicly accused and tried for crime without a private examination of their guilt and establishing a probability of its existence; so the people would be restrained from electing any one to office without a previous nomination of a body more fitted to judge of his qualifications. The convention system was said to be a salutary restraint upon universal suffrage, compelling the people to elect men of standing who alone could be nominated by conventions.

On the other side it was urged that the whole convention system was a fraud on the people; that it was a mere fungus growth engrafted upon the constitution; that conventions themselves were got up and packed by cunning, active, intriguing politicians to suit the wishes of a few. The mode of getting them up was for some active man to procure a few friends in each precinct of a county to hold primary meetings where delegates were elected to county conventions, who met at the county seats and nominated candidates for the legislature and for county offices; and appointed other delegates to district and State conventions to nominate candidates for Congress and for governor. The great difficulty was in the primary meetings in the precincts. In the Eastern States, where conventions originated, they had township governments, little democracies, where the whole people met in person at least once a year to lay taxes for roads and for the support of schools and the poor. This called the whole people of a township together, enlightened their minds, and accustomed them to take a lively interest in their government; and whilst assembled they could and did elect their delegates to conventions. In this mode a convention reflected the will of a party as much as the legislature reflected the will of the whole people. But how is it in Illinois? We had no township governments, no occasions for a general meeting of the people, except at the elections themselves; the people did not attend the primary meetings; a few only assembled who were nearest the places of meeting, and these were too often mere professional politicians, the loafers about the towns, who having but little business of their own were ever ready to attend to the affairs of the public. This threw the political power out of the hands of the people, merely because they would not exercise it, into the hands of idlers—of a few active men who controlled them. If any one desired an office he never thought of applying to the people for it; but passed them by and applied himself to conciliate the managers and idlers about the towns, many of whom could only be conciliated at an immense sacrifice of the public interest. It is true that a party had the reserved right of rebellion against all this machinery; no one could be punished for treason in so doing otherwise than by losing the favor of his party and being denounced as a traitor; which was almost as efficacious in restraining the refractory as the pains and penalties of treason, the hanging and disembowelling of former times.

My own opinion of the convention system is that it can never be perfect in Illinois without the organization of little township democracies such as are found in New York and New England; that in a State where the people are highly intelligent and not indifferent to public affairs it will enable the people themselves to govern by giving full effect to the will of the majority; but among a people who are either ignorant of or indifferent to the affairs of their government the convention system is a most admirable contrivance to enable active leaders to govern without much responsibility to the people.

By means of the convention system and many exciting contests the two parties of whigs and democrats were thoroughly organized and disciplined by the year 1840. No regular army could have excelled them in discipline. They were organized upon the principles of national politics only, and not in any degree upon those of the State. The first effect of this seemed to be that all ideas of State rights, State sovereignty, State policy and interests, as party questions, were abolished out of men's minds. Our ancestors had greatly relied upon the organization of State sovereignties as checks to anti-republican tendencies and national consolidation. For this purpose all the State constitutions, Illinois amongst the rest, had declared that no person holding an office under the United States should hold an office under the State government. The object of this was to sever all dependence of the State upon the national government. It was not permitted the President to appoint the officers of the State governments for this would at once lay the State governments at the feet of the President. But if the State officers were not appointed by the President they were elected upon a principle which made them, if belonging to his political friends, as subservient to his will as if he had appointed them. The President was the leader of his party in the nation and there was no principle of party in the State but this. Men were elected to office upon the popularity of the President and upon the principles which the President put forth; and they were thus compelled in self-defence to support and defend him through good and evil, right or wrong, as much as if they owed their offices to his gift. Besides this their parties absolutely required them to do so. It may be remarked here as a curious fact that the politicians all over the nation pretending to be most in favor of State rights and State sovereignty have contributed most to overthrow them by forever insisting upon the organization of parties purely upon national questions.

This dependence of State upon national politics and the exclusive devotion of State politicians to national questions was the true cause why so little attention was paid to the policy of the State. These remarks are equally applicable to both political parties. But it is as necessary that the affairs of the United States should be attended to by the people as those of the State, and the misfortunes which a neglect of affairs at home has caused may possibly have been the price of government in the nation.

A new legislature was elected in 1840, which, although they were chosen under the influence of the presidential election of that year, were obliged to think somewhat upon the public condition. The fund commissioners stated the difficulty of meeting the January interest of 1841. As yet the canal had not wholly stopped and the canal men were interested to keep up the credit of the State; and something desperate must be done for that purpose.

The canal contractors had taken their jobs when all prices were high. By the fall of prices they could make a large profit on their work and lose twenty-five per cent. They, therefore, had agreed to take a million of State bonds at par in payment of their estimates. Gen. Thornton was deputed to go to Europe with the bonds and sell them for what they would bring, not less than seventy-five per cent; the contractors suffering the loss. This they could well afford to do; and by this expedient the work on the canal had been continued long after that on the railroads had been abandoned. The canal was not yet looked upon as dead, and a great effort was to be made to raise the means to keep it in life and sustain the credit of the State, without which it was known that the canal would not live an hour.

The time was short, only six weeks until the interest would become due; and many expedients were proposed to raise the money; but the one which met most general favor was a new issue of bonds to be hypothecated for whatever they would bring in market. This was a desperate remedy, and showed the zeal of the legislature in sustaining the public honor. It proposed a plan of raising money which, if pursued as the settled policy of the State, must end in utter ruin. Nevertheless it was but feebly opposed on this ground. The principal ground of opposition was an objection to paying interest at all; and particularly to paying interest upon bonds for which the State had received nothing, or less than par. Now was heard for the first time any very earnest complaints against the acts of the fund commissioners in selling bonds on a credit and for less than their face; and it was seriously and earnestly contended, first, that the State was hopelessly insolvent, that any effort to pay would be ridiculous and futile, and secondly, that the State was not bound to pay interest on more money than had been actually received. An amendment to this effect was offered and strenuously insisted on.

On the other hand it was insisted with reason that the State was bound to do everything in its power to meet its engagements; that if bonds had been erroneously issued it had been done by the State agents, selected and chosen by the State itself; for whose conduct the State must be responsible. It was admitted that if such bonds remained in the hands of the original purchasers, as to them the State would be entitled to a deduction for money not actually received. But it was as earnestly contended that if such bonds had passed into the hands of *bona fide* holders who were no parties to the original deficiency of consideration the State was liable in equity as well as at law to pay the face of the bond. There seems to be an obvious propriety in this view of the case, because the bonds were issued by State agents, appointed by the State, not by its creditors. The constituted authorities of the State ought to have chosen better men for public trusts; and if they did not do so the State is justly responsible for their blunders. It seems to be a principle of law as well as of equity that if the State selects bad men, or those who are incompetent to act as its agents, the State thus abusing its power, and not individuals who had no hand in their appointment, ought to suffer the consequences of its folly or want of devotion to its own interests. This doctrine, if established, will be a lesson to the people and teach them to be considerate and careful in electing their public servants.

These conflicting opinions were near preventing any action on the subject at this session. At last Mr. Cavarly, a member from Greene, introduced a bill of two sections authorizing the fund commissioner to hypothecate internal improvement bonds to the amount of $300,000, and which contained the remarkable provision that the proceeds were to be applied by that officer to the payment of all interest *legally* due on the public debt. Thus shifting from the General Assembly and devolving on the fund commissioner the duty of deciding on the legality of the debt. And by this happy expedient conflicting opinions were reconciled without direct action on the matter of controversy; and thus the two houses were enabled to agree upon a measure to provide temporarily for the payment of the interest on the public debt. The legislature further provided at this session for the issue of interest bonds to be sold in the market for what they would bring; and an additional tax of ten cents on the hundred dollars worth of property was imposed and pledged to pay the interest on these bonds. By these contrivances the interest for January and July, 1841 was paid. The fund commissioner hypothecated internal improvement bonds for the money first due; and his successor in office, finding no sale for Illinois stocks, so much had the credit of the State fallen, was compelled to hypothecate $804,000 of interest bonds for the July interest; on this hypothecation he was to have received $321,600 but was never paid more than $261,500. These bonds have never been redeemed from the holders though eighty of them were afterwards repurchased, and $315,000 of them were received from the Shawneetown Bank for State stock in that institution.

VII

Judicial and Financial Issues, 1838–1842

There were other measures of great interest to the people which came before the legislature of 1840 the principal of which was a bill to reform the Judiciary.

The people of the State at the election of 1840 had sustained Mr. Van Buren, the democratic candidate for President, and both branches of the legislature were largely of the same party. The majority of the judges of the supreme court were whigs. Judge Smith was the only democratic member of the court, whilst Chief Justice Wilson and his associates Lockwood and Brown were of the minority part. It is due to truth here to say that Wilson and Lockwood were in every respect amiable and accomplished gentlemen in private life, and commanded the esteem and respect of all good men for the purity of their conduct and their probity in official station. Wilson was a Virginian of the old sort, a man of good education, sound judgment, and an elegant writer, as his published opinions will show. Lockwood was a New Yorker. He was an excellent lawyer, a man of sound judgment, and his face indicated uncommon purity, modesty, and intelligence together with energy and strong determination. His face was the true index of his character. Brown was a fine, large, affable, and good-looking man, with but little learning or talent,[1] a tolerable share of tact and good sense, a complimentary, smiling and laughing address to all men, and had been elected and continued in office upon the ground that he was believed to be a clever fellow. Two great political questions had been brought before this court, one of which they decided contrary to the views and wishes of the democratic party and the other question was yet pending but it was believed would be decided in the same way.

These were the questions: When Governor Carlin was elected in 1838 he claimed the power to appoint a new Secretary of State. Alexander P. Field was the old Secretary. He had been appointed by Governor Edwards ten years before and had been continued in office without any new appointment under both Reynolds and Duncan. He was a whig and Gov. Carlin was a democrat; and as the Secretary of State is not only a public officer but a sort of confidential helper and adviser of the executive, Gov. Carlin claimed the right of selecting this officer for himself and from his own party. The governor nominated to the senate Mr. McClernand of Gallatin county. The whigs of the senate and some democrats, enough to constitute the majority, decided that the tenure of the office might be defined and limited by the legislature but that until they did so the Secretary could not be removed and a new one appointed. The governor and his friends contended that he had the power of removal and appointment at all times, to be exercised at his discretion. The governor made five or six different nominations, all of which were rejected by the senate.

After the legislature adjourned the governor again appointed Mr. McClernand, who demanded the office of the old Secretary of State and was refused. Mr. McClernand then sued out his writ to try his right to the office. The question was taken to the supreme court and decided against him by Wilson and Lockwood; Judge Smith dissenting and Judge Brown giving no opinion, on account of relationship to Mr. McClernand. This at the time was supposed to be a great question. The ablest counsel in the State were employed, and the decision of the judges is elaborated to such a degree as to show their opinion of its consequences. The decision raised a great flame of excitement and the democrats contended that the odious doctrine of life-officers had been established by it. In 1840 the governor found no difficulty in getting his nomination confirmed. The senate was now largely democratic, probably caused by this decision of the court. But the other great question was still pending; and a fear that it might be decided against the democrats determined that party to reform the Judiciary.

The Constitution provides that all free white male *inhabitants,* over the age of twenty-one years, who have resided in the State for six months, shall be entitled to vote at all general and special elections. The whigs had long contended that this provision did not authorize any but citizens to vote; whilst the practice had been, ever since the Constitution was formed, to allow all to vote, whether citizens or aliens, who had been in the State six months. This question had been much talked of and canvassed in every part of the State. It produced much excitement, as it naturally would when two great parties were arrayed on it, and when it was believed by both parties that the alien vote in the State was sufficient to decide the elections.

In this state of the case two whigs of Galena made an agreed cause to be decided by the circuit court. It was not argued on either side, and the judge, who was a whig, decided that aliens were not entitled to vote.[2] This was all done so quietly that it was near passing without notice. But when the decision was published it threw the leaders of the democratic party into perfect consternation. By this time the alien vote was supposed to be about 10,000 strong, nine-tenths of which was democratic.

The leaders of the party took measures to carry the case to the supreme court. Numerous and able counsel on each side had been heard on it there in December, 1839, and it was continued until the following June. It was universally believed, from certain intimations, that a majority of the judges had determined to decide against the aliens. In June the democratic lawyers succeeded in finding an imperfection in the record which caused another continuance until December, 1840, and until after the presidential election. This was thought to be a great feat of dexterity and management, as by that means the alien vote was secured at all events for one more election, and more particularly for the presidential election of that year. In this, as well as in the other case of the Secretary of State, I think the whigs were clearly wrong. It is a principle in all our constitutions that the appointing power, when exercised by a single person or by a body of men who can conveniently act, must necessarily possess the power of removal from office; and in the other case it was equally clear that the word inhabitant must mean an alien as well as a citizen. But it was also alleged that this provision of our constitution, if construed to allow an unnaturalized alien to vote, would come in conflict with the Constitution of the United States, which gives to Congress the power of passing uniform naturalization laws. It was contended that as no foreigners by those laws could be naturalized without a residence in the country for five years, the State could not confer the elective franchise upon one who had resided in it only six months. The obvious answer to all this is that the Constitution of the United States was never intended to give Congress the power of interfering with the right of suffrage. If it had contained such a provision, so various were the different State Constitutions on this subject at the time it was adopted and so jealous were the States of their sovereignty, that the Constitution of the United States would never have been ratified. Besides this citizenship alone was never construed in any State to confer the elective franchise; there being many citizens in every State, in some more and in others less, who were not allowed to vote. And it seemed to be a legitimate and unanswerable argument that if citizenship alone did not confer the right of voting, the want of it alone could not take it away.

However it was believed that the whig judges, right or wrong would decide with their party. And here I would remark that the highest courts are but indifferent tribunals for the settlement of great political questions, supposing such settlement no longer to rest on physical force, but to rely for its authority upon the conviction of the public judgment. In this sense, such questions can never be settled except by the continued triumph of one party over the other, in which case the minority yields from despair of success. The judges are but men. In all the great questions which arise and which divide the people into parties they will never fail to have their preconceived opinions, as well as others, and those opinions must necessarily be biased by their political predilections. But it is said that party men and politicians ought not to be judges of the courts. It would be better, if this were possible. At a time when the whole people are divided and convulsed by the agitation and discussion of great party measures and principles it would be strange indeed if gifted and talented men could be found with a power of thought making them fit for the office, and yet who have never formed any opinions on such subjects. The most that the judge can do to disarm the public or party prejudice is to conceal his opinions; but the knowing persons of the opposite party are no less certain that he has them. It may, therefore, be said of the ablest and best judges, those most celebrated for dispensing equity and justice in common cases between individuals, that when any great political question on which parties are arrayed comes up for decision, the utmost which can be expected of them is an able and learned argument in favor of their own party, whose views they must naturally favor for the very reason that they prefer one party to the other. Such a decision, therefore, can never be satisfactory to the opposite party, which well knows that if the judges had been of a different political complexion the decision would have been otherwise. And, therefore, no such party decisions, not based upon the power of majorities of the people, can ever be a satisfactory settlement of this description of questions.

As I have said before, the legislature in 1835 had created circuit courts and elected circuit judges, the number of whom had by this time increased to nine. The plan of reform now was to abolish these courts, repeal the judges out of office, and create five additional judges of the supreme court, all of whom were required to hold circuit courts in place of the circuit judges repealed out of office. This arrangement would give the democratic party a majority of two to one on the Supreme bench. The measure was introduced into the Senate by Adam W. Snyder, a senator from St. Clair county; a district containing a larger foreign vote than any other in the State. A long and violent struggle ensued; and at times it was doubtful whether it would pass.

It was confessedly a violent and somewhat revolutionary measure and could never have succeeded except in times of great party excitement. The contest in the Presidential election of 1840 was of such a turbulent and fiery character, and the dominant party in this State had been so badly defeated in the nation at large by the election of Gen. Harrison that they were more than ever inclined to act from motives of resentment and a feeling of mortification. The dominant party therefore came to the work thirsting for revenge, as well as with a determination to leave nothing undone to secure their power in this State at least. Notwithstanding this disposition on the part of the democracy, many members of the legislature belonging to that party were drawn to the support of the measure with a great deal of difficulty; others opposed it outright, and upon no terms and with no appliances of party machinery and discipline could be brought to support it. The fate of some of these democrats affords a melancholy lesson. They were denounced by their friends and turned over to the whigs. But, so far as I know, they have ever since been found acting with the party, though they have never been able to recover its confidence. The excitement has gone by; the party itself has been pretty generally convinced that the system then adopted ought to be abandoned; that the supreme court ought to be constituted as it was before; yet these democrats, many of them, are still under the ban; so true it is that in all party matters a breach of discipline, a rebellion against leaders, is regarded as infinitely more offensive than the mere support of wicked or unwise measures or opposition to good ones. A party never holds its members to account for supporting the worst sort of measures or opposing the best ones unless the leaders have made them the test of fidelity to party; but woe to him whose conscience is so tender that he cannot support, or opposes the measures decreed by his party. Woe to him who is guilty of a breach of discipline, or who rebels against leaders. In all matters of party there are two things to be considered; the principles of the party and its discipline. A man may hold all the principles of the party, but if he does not harmonize with its organization he will not be considered as belonging to it. And he will be allowed much of his natural liberty to think for himself and be forgiven much defection of principle if he will only obey leaders and work in the party harness. A party may entirely change its principles and measures whenever the great leaders say the word; but if it still keeps up the same organization and name and has the same leaders no member is to doubt but that it is the same party it was before. The privilege of changing principles and measures is only the privilege of the great leaders, upon consultation and agreement with the lesser ones; and then all the lesser leaders and members of the party can safeiy follow in the change. But woe to the presumptuous small leader, who sets up to change on his own account; or who undertakes to differ with his great leaders on the adoption of new measures not before thought of in former contests. This, gentle reader, is government by moral means; and it seems, in the present state of civilization, that without this kind of government, imperfect and abhorrent to the freedom of thought as it may be, we are to have our choice between anarchy and a government of stern force. In the democratic party such rebellious, free-thoughted, independent littie leaders, in the slang language of the day, are called *"tender-footed democrats,"* and finally, no democrat, at all; and this I believe to be the case with the other party whenever they have the majority.

The bill was finally passed through both houses and returned by the council of revision with their objections; but was again re-passed through both houses, in the Senate by a large majority, in the House by a majority of one vote. By this means the new Secretary of State was secured in his office and the democratic party was secured in the continued support of the alien vote; for all the new judges elected at this session were as thoroughly satisfied of the right of each governor to appoint his own Secretary of State and of the right of alien inhabitants to vote as the whig judges could be to the contrary.[3]

During the pendency of this question before the legislature the judges decided the alien case from Galena. They, however, did not decide the main question. The case went off upon another point, which it was charged by the democrats that the whig judges had hunted up on purpose to dispose of the case without deciding it, in the hope that when the dominant party could see that they were no longer threatened with a decision contrary to their wishes they would abandon their reform measure. This charge was boldly made by Judge Douglas in a speech in the lobby of the House one evening after an adjournment. Douglas had been one of the counsel for the aliens; and it appeared from his speech that he and Judge Smith had been in constant communication in relation to the progress of the case. Judge Smith (I regret to say it of a man who is no more) was an active, bustling, ambitious, and turbulent member of the democratic party. He had for a long time aimed to be elected to the United States Senate; his devices and intrigues to this end had been innumerable. In fact he never lacked a plot to advance himself or to blow up some other person. He was a laborious and ingenious schemer in politics; but his plans were always too complex and ramified for his power to execute them. Being always unsuccessful himself, he was delighted with the mishaps alike of friends and enemies; and was ever chuckling over the defeat or the blasted hopes of some one. In this case he sought to gain credit with the leading democrats by the part he took, and affected to take, in the alien case, as he had before in the case of the Secretary of State. He it was who privately suggested to counsel the defect in the record which resulted in the continuance in June, 1840; and during the whole time the case was pending, with the same view he was giving out to Douglas and others the probable opinion of the court. He affirmed that the judges at one term all had their opinions written ready to deliver, and all but himself deciding against the aliens; and that the case would have been so decided if he had not discovered the aforesaid defect in the record. Upon his authority Douglas denounced the court and brought all these charges against the whig judges and endeavored to make it appear that they had now only evaded a decision for the time being in the vain hope of stopping the career of the legislature. The judges on their part denied all these charges; and Judge Smith, uniting with the whig judges, published their denial in the Sangamon Journal newspaper at Springfield. Douglas was immediately sustained as to the statements of Judge Smith by the published letters of half a dozen other gentlemen of veracity to whom Judge Smith had made similar statements.

But allowing all that was said to be true, and there is now no doubt that the whole of it was false, it is feared that if the right mode of reformation had been adopted the legislature would have punished an offence which they had themselves caused the court to commit. The judges may possibly have feared being put upon the laborious duty of holding circuit courts, from which they had been relieved for several years; and they may have supposed that the reform measure, as it was called, would be put an end to as soon as the democrats ceased to fear a decision against them in the alien case. If they thought so they had but little knowledge of the spirit and genius of party. The democrats, by a thorough change in the constitution of the court, desired to obtain full security for the future. Independent of this, when a measure once becomes a party measure it cannot be suddenly abandoned. And besides this, again, a party scarcely ever stops at the accomplishment of its wishes unless brought about by its own favorite measures and by something that it has done itself. I have more than once known a party to persist in urging a measure long after its wishes had been accomplished by other means.

Ever since this reforming measure the judiciary has been unpopular with the democratic majorities. Many and most of the judges have had great personal popularity; so much so as to create complaint of so many of them being elected or appointed to other offices. But the bench itself has been the subject of bitter attacks by every legislature since. The two houses have almost come to the opinion that as they are numerous bodies, fresh from the people every two and four years, the other departments of the government, the executive and judiciary, are mere excrescences on the body politic, which ought to be pruned away. As to Judge Smith, he made nothing by all his intrigues. By opposing the reform bill he fell out and quarreled with the leaders of his party. He lost the credit he had gained by being the democratic champion on the bench, and failed to be elected to the United States Senate; and was put back to the laborious duty of holding circuit courts. Thus bringing upon himself, by his active efforts to destroy the character and influence of the court of which he was a member, the just desert of his conduct.

The judges of the supreme court had been withdrawn from holding circuit courts for six years; consequently they had lost their political influence, which now attached itself to the circuit judges, who had a better opportunity of becoming acquainted and making friends among the people. The supreme court, as a co-ordinate branch of government, had become weak; so true is it that the actual power to be exercised by either branch of government depends less upon the powers conferred in the Constitution than upon the moral power of popularity and influence with the people and their representatives. For this reason many believed it to be necessary to restore the judges of the supreme court to circuit duties, in order to give political vigor to the judiciary department; so as to enable them to act with independence and thus preserve the balances of the constitution.

No further attempt was made after July, 1841 to pay interest on the public debt. For want of full knowledge of her condition abroad, and of the condition of other new States, in a short time Illinois and some others in the west became a stench in the nostrils of the civilized world. The people at home began to wake up in terror; the people abroad who wished to settle in a new country avoided Illinois as they would pestilence and famine; and there was great danger that the future emigrants would be men who, having no regard for their own characters, would also have none for that of the State where they might live. The terrors of high taxation were before all eyes, both at home and abroad. Every one at home wanted to sell his property and move away, and but few either at home or abroad wanted to purchase. The impossibility of selling kept us from losing population; and the fear of disgrace or high taxes prevented us from gaining materially.

To add to the general calamity and terror of the people, in February, 1842 the State Bank, with a circulation of three millions of dollars, finally exploded with a great crash, carrying wide-spread ruin all over the State and into the neighboring States and territories. In June following, the bank at Shawneetown "followed in the footsteps of its illustrious predecessor," leaving the people almost entirely without a circulating medium. The paper of these two banks had been at a discount for specie ever since the United States refused to receive it for the public lands and to make the banks depositories of the public moneys. At first the discount was small, two or three per cent, but in two or three years advanced to twelve and fifteen per cent, and then came the crash. The banks, however, managed to make their paper the standard of par; and specie, and other paper of less credit, was above or below par. The discount was sufficient, for three years before, to banish all good money from circulation; so that when the banks failed, the people were left without money until supplied by the course of trade, which, in a country so little commercial as Illinois at that time, was a slow process. When I came into office in 1842 I estimated that the good money in the State in the hands of the people did not exceed one year's interest on the public debt.

That which contributed the last spark to the explosion of the State Bank was the course of some of the State directors, who were contractors to finish the northern cross railroad, and who were to be paid in canal bonds, which at the time were unsaleable. These interested parties, joining with others in the directory, established it as a principle that the bank could not issue an excess of its paper whilst in a state of suspension. This they did to get loans from the bank to carry on their work on the road; and having obtained money themselves upon this principle, they were obliged to vote loans to all others. But experience soon showed that the principle was false, for no sooner was more paper put into circulation than could be sustained by the business of the country than the bank exploded. It may be added to this that the State Bank, to obtain favor from the legislature, was compelled to make loans to the State, and to advance its bills for auditor's warrants for a large amount to defray the ordinary expenses of government; the revenues being again insufficient and the legislature afraid to increase the taxes. When I came into office the State owed the bank on this account two hundred and ninety-four thousand dollars.

A somewhat similar connection with the State assisted much to break the Shawneetown Bank. That bank was first induced to lend the State about $80,000 to finish the State House; and in September, 1839, upon the recommendation and urgent request of Governor Carlin, and upon his promise to deposit $500,000 in internal improvement bonds as collateral security, which promise was never performed, the bank was induced to lend the Commissioners of Public Works the further sum of $200,000, which was never repaid to it.*

Upon the whole, we have heard much said by demagogues about our swindling banks; but it would be an easier matter to show that if the banks had swindled only one quarter as much as they have been swindled by the State and by individuals they would have been perfectly solvent and able to pay every dollar of their debt; and what is most remarkable is that those who have swindled the banks most are the most loud in their cries against them for swindling.

As I have elsewhere said, these banks first suspended specie payments in the spring of 1837. In that year the suspension was legalized to save the canal and internal improvement system. I do not know the reason why this favor was continued by the session of 1838–'9 or any of the following sessions until 1841. But I do know that all or nearly all of the leading democrats opposed the measure. This was a new manifestation of hostility on the part of the democrats to these banks; and this, again, was cause enough to rally the main body of the whigs in their favor, and this, again, was of immense advantage to the banks in sustaining their credit. The merchants and business men all over the country were mostly whigs. They believed that the banks were unjustly persecuted by the democrats, that they were perfectly solvent, and that all the objections of the democrats amounted to no more than senseless clamor.

In the meantime the State Bank had been made the depository of the State revenues. The collectors had been required to pay the revenues arising from taxation into this bank, as into the public treasury. All auditors' warrants were drawn upon the bank, which were paid in its own paper. In this mode the legislature and all public officers were paid in the paper of the bank; for as nothing better was paid in nothing better could be paid out. This gave the bank a decided advantage over the legislature. It was in the power of the bank to send the members home without their pay, except in auditors' warrants at fifty per cent discount, unless something should be done to sustain the credit of its paper. This lever, and a few opportune loans to some democrats, together with the aid of the whigs, commanded relief at the session of 1841. This session was called two weeks earlier than usual for the purpose of providing means to pay the inter-

*See reports of House of Representatives, 1842–'3, pages 203–5.

est on the public debt becoming due in January, 1841. The democrats contended that this early commencement was a special session, and that the regular session must be commenced anew on the first Monday of December following the first meeting. The whigs contended that the two sessions only made one and refused to support a *sine die* adjournment on the Saturday preceding the first Monday in December. This was then supposed to be a very vital question. The democrats supposed that such an adjournment would put an end to the banks, as the previous law had provided for a resumption of specie payments before the adjournment of the next session of the general assembly, or otherwise they were to forfeit their charters. This was a session of much bitterness and personal hatred. The democrats came up from the people inflamed with the highest degree of resentment against the banks and the judiciary; and the whigs came with an equal hatred of the democrats, and a firm determination, as a general thing, to oppose whatever the democrats might favor. I believe it is a principle of all great political parties that they cannot be very far wrong if they disagree to everything proposed by their adversaries. The whigs took ground in favor of the banks, the democrats against them. The question was on the *sine die* adjournment of the special session. The whigs saw that the adjournment would carry. To defeat it, they began to absent themselves from the house, so as not to leave a quorum. A call of the house was made and its officers were sent out to bring in and secure the attendance of the absent members. The doors were closed to prevent further escapes, but nevertheless some of the whigs jumped out of the windows, but not enough to defeat the purpose of the dominant party.[4] The session was adjourned and according to the views of the democrats the banks were at an end. The bank party had been defeated and the democracy had obtained at last a great and glorious victory. But the victory could not be secured; for before the end of the regular session in December the banks obtained a further privilege of suspension, and the State Bank obtained an additional privilege which had never been granted to it before, that of issuing one, two, and three-dollar notes. So much for a democratic victory. This privilege of issuing small notes, it was thought, would aid the banks in making an earlier resumption. They immediately flooded the country with small notes in place of the large ones. This banished the silver dollar from circulation. It destroyed the specie basis all over the country and made it impossible for the banks to increase their stock of precious metals except by purchase. All deposits and payments were made in the only circulation then in the country. The banks might lose specie, but they could not increase it. I think I hazard nothing in saying that this privilege of issuing small notes did as much mischief to the banks themselves as it did to the people at large.

During the whole of this long and angry contest the whigs accused the democrats of making war upon the commerce and the currency of the country. These banks were termed the institutions of the country and war upon them, in the language of the whigs, was war upon the institutions of the country. In whig estimation the democrats were disloyal, destructive, and opposed to government. The whigs, in the estimation of the democrats, were a set of bank vassals, and were frequently called by the democrats the ragocracy. The presidents and directors of banks were called rag barons; bank paper was called bank rags and written or printed lies; whilst the whole body of the whig party were, from an excess of hatred, termed the British-bought, Bank, blue-light, federal, whig party.

Our whig friends contended that the continual and violent opposition of the democrats to the banks destroyed confidence; which, by-the-bye, could only exist when the bulk of the people were under a delusion and believed in a falsehood. According to their views, if the banks owed five times as much as they were able to pay, and the people owed to each other and to the banks more than they were able to pay, and yet if the whole people could be persuaded to believe the incredible falsehood that all were able to pay, this was "confidence," which, if once destroyed, could only be restored by the restoration of a similar general delusion.

VIII

Civil and Religious Discord,
1841–1842

B y the year 1840 the whole State had been settled except some of the wide prairies far from timber. There was no longer any more wilderness. The country in Henry county, though as good as any other part of the State, I believe was the last to be settled in 1838. Several colleges and academies had been built and were in successful operation. The Illinois college at Jacksonville under the direction of the Presbyterians was built by an association of gentlemen of Boston. Shurtleff college at Alton was established under the direction of the Baptists; McKendree college at Lebanon under direction of the Methodists; and McDonough college at Macomb and Knox college at Galesburg were established also by the Presbyterians. The Catholics established a flourishing nunnery at the ancient town of Kaskaskia for the education of females; Bishop Chase, with the aid of contributions from the members of the Episcopal church and others, established Jubilee college in Peoria county; and the Methodists established a flourishing seminary at Mount Morris in the county of Ogle. Besides these there were numerous academies and high schools in many parts of the State. Opportunities for education in the higher branches were good for all who were able and willing to profit by them. Common schools flourished in many places, more than could have been expected when all efficient encouragement to them had been abandoned by the Government.

Chicago, Alton, Springfield, Quincy, Galena, and Nauvoo had become cities before the year 1842. To these has since been added the city of Peoria. Most of the county seats had grown up to be towns of from five to fifteen hundred inhabitants; and there were many other villages in many of the counties containing a population of from one hundred to a thousand souls. The towns contained a good deal of intelligence, polish, and eloquence. It must not be thought that the people of this new country had just sprung up out of the ground with no advantages of education and society. They were nearly all of them emigrants from the old States, being often the most intelligent and enterprising of their population. As such, they were just a slice off of the great loaf of the old States. But they were not apt to be so considered by the latest comers. These always imagined that they were come to a land of comparative ignorance and that they must necessarily be superior to the people already here, until they were convinced to the contrary by finding out that their pretensions had made them ridiculous; and if their pretensions were noticed at all, it was only to be laughed at. It was no uncommon thing to find families of these last newcomers scattered all over the country, forever complaining of the want of good society; and of the many privations they endured in a new country. These complaints were uttered not so much because they were true as to let the people know that those who made them were *somebodies* where they came from. The same kind of people, to show themselves off as something superior to others, were forever uttering sarcasms and slighting remarks of the State and the people. It was no uncommon thing to find them in all the taverns, stage-coaches and steamboats *letting on* that although their destiny compelled them to live in the State, yet they knew how degraded the rest of the people were as well as he who resided in a city, or lived in a palace. Indeed, the bodies only of a great many people and not their minds lived in the State. It was difficult to forget the father-land. Most of the emigrants remembered New York or New England or their other places of nativity with affection and lively interest. A man from Massachusetts took a newspaper from his native town, he watched the progress of politics, the success of men and parties, and the history of government there with as much interest as if he had never removed. And so of the emigrants from other States. It was natural it should be so. But whilst it was so it is to be feared that matters suffered at home. There was but little State pride for Illinois. Illinois could be abused anywhere with impunity. I hope yet to live to see the day in Illinois as it is in Kentucky, Virginia, Tennessee, South Carolina, New York, and New England, that no one will be suffered to abuse the State without being scorned and insulted. It is true that a State pride must be deserved before it can exist. The people must have something to be proud of. The State will never really prosper without this State pride. It is the greatest incentive to excellence in government and in everything else for the people to be proud of their country.*

*It seems to me that the people of Illinois may now justly be proud of their State. They have with great unanimity put down the hideous monster of repudiation; contrary to the instigations of numerous demagogues they have submitted cheerfully to be taxed to pay their just debts; they are about to see their canal, one of the greatest works in America, completed. Their legislatures have improved in knowledge, public spirit and patriotism ever since 1840; which was about the darkest time in public affairs. And when the services of her sons were called for

As new people came in they brought with them their religion and literature. Churches now began to be rapidly established in the towns and in many country places. Pastors were regularly settled and paid; church buildings were erected, divided off into pews, and the sound of the "church-going bell" began to be heard. It soon became fashionable to attend some church, and constant attendance induced many to join as members.

During the previous period of our history our literature was principally confined to mere newspaper writing, which discussed mostly the mere affairs of party or the claims of some man to an office; or the demerit of an opponent. John M. Peck of Rock Spring in St. Clair county published a State Gazetteer, a work of considerable labor and well written. John Russell of Bluff Dale published some fugitive essays and tales in the newspapers which marked him as a man of genius and a fine writer; and Judge James Hall early distinguished himself as a scholar and writer. He published at Vandalia an Illinois monthly magazine of high merit; and an annual called *The Western Souvenir,* a collection of original tales and poetry written principally by himself, evincing such merit as to make him distinguished all over the United States as an author. But there was not sufficient patronage in Illinois at that time for the pursuits of literature; so Judge Hall removed to Cincinnati, where he now resides. But before he left Illinois he had acquired a high reputation as a writer.

The great plenty of money brought here by the work on the canal and the railroads set up a great many merchants all over the country in business; it increased the stocks of goods brought to be sold; created unnatural competition amongst the merchants to sell, who were forced to sell on a credit or not at all. The people were encouraged to buy on credit and when their debts became due, for want of money to pay them they gave their notes to the merchants with twelve per cent interest, which the reader will observe hereafter was the cause of some strange legislation on the collection of debts, and caused the reduction of the rate of interest to six per cent. Until the year 1833 there had been no legal limit to the rate of interest to be fixed by contract. But usury had been carried to such an unprece-

---

in the Mexican war 8,370 of them in a few weeks answered the call, though only 3,720 (four regiments) could be taken. Every one of these regiments afterwards distinguished themselves for unheard-of courage in the severest battles ever fought on this continent. Hardin, Bissell, Weatherford, Morrison, Trail, Warren, are proud names associated with the glorious victory of Buena Vista. Shields, Baker, Harris, Coffey, and others will be remembered as long as the capture of Vera Cruz or the storming of Cerro Gordo are remembered. What did Kentucky ever do more than this?

dented degree of extortion and oppression as to cause the legislature to enact severe usury laws, by which all interest above twelve per cent was condemned. It had been no uncommon thing before this to charge one hundred and one hundred and fifty per cent, and sometimes two and three hundred per cent. But the common rate of interest by contract had been about fifty per cent.

In the year 1839 the people called Mormons came to this State and settled in Hancock county, and as their residence amongst us led to a mobocratic spirit which resulted in their expulsion it is proper here to notice other incidents of this sort in our previous history.

In 1816 and '17, in the towns of the territory, the country was overrun with horse-thieves and counterfeiters. They were so numerous and so well combined together in many counties as to set the laws at defiance. Many of the sheriffs, justices of the peace and constables were of their number; and even some of the judges of the county courts; and they had numerous friends to aid them and sympathize with them, even amongst those who were the least suspected. When any of them were arrested they either escaped from the slight jails of those times or procured some of their gang to be on the jury; and they never lacked witnesses to prove themselves innocent. The people formed themselves into revolutionary tribunals in many counties under the name of regulators; and the governor and judges of the territory, seeing the impossibility of executing the laws in the ordinary way against an organized banditti who set all law at defiance, winked at and encouraged the proceedings of the regulators.

These regulators in number generally constituted about a captain's company, to which they gave a military organization by the election of officers. The company generally operated at night. When assembled for duty they marched, armed and equipped as if for war, to the residence or lurking place of a rogue, arrested, tried, and punished him by severe whipping and banishment from the territory. In this mode most of the rogues were expelled from the country; and it was the opinion of the best men at the time that in the then divided and disorganized state of society and the imperfect civilization which required such proceedings, these measures were not only justifiable, but absolutely necessary for the existence of government.

There yet remained, however, for many years afterwards a noted gang of rogues in the counties of Pope and Massac and other counties bordering on the Ohio river. This gang built a fort in Pope county and set the government at open defiance. In the year 1831 the honest portion of the people in that region assembled under arms in great numbers and attacked the fort with small arms and one piece of artillery. The fort was taken by storm with the loss of one of the regulators and three of the rogues killed in the assault. The residue of the rogues were taken prisoners and tried for their crimes, but I believe were never convicted.

At a later time a number of rogues who had located themselves in the county of Edgar were broken up, whipped and expelled by a company of regulators from the Wabash valley, the present Governor French being a distinguished member of the regulators.

In 1837 a series of mobs took place in Alton which resulted in the destruction of an abolition press and in the death of one of the rioters and one of the abolitionists. This affair has made a great noise in the world and is deserving of a more extended notice. It appears that the Rev. Elijah P. Lovejoy of the Presbyterian church had attempted to publish an abolition paper in St. Louis but his press had there been destroyed by a mob and he himself had been expelled from the city.[1]

Mr. Lovejoy now determined to remove his establishment to Alton. The press for this purpose was landed on Sunday, but during that night was thrown into the river by the citizens. There was much excitement on the subject and a public meeting was called on Monday evening to be held in the Presbyterian church, which was attended by an immense concourse of people.

Mr. Lovejoy first addressed the meeting. He said he came to Alton to establish a religious newspaper. He was pleased with the place, and wished to remain; there most of his subscribers resided in Illinois; and it would best suit his purposes and theirs that he should do so. He disliked St. Louis and he disliked slavery. He regretted that he had met with such a reception at Alton; he presumed that the people had misconceived his object. He was no abolitionist; he believed the abolitionists were injuring the colored race; he had repeatedly denounced them and had been himself denounced by Garrison and others as being in favor of slavery, because he was unwilling to go with the abolitionists in favor of all their measures. He was opposed to slavery to be sure; he had ever been and hoped he always would be opposed to it, and he wished to get away from the evil of it. Whilst at St. Louis where slavery existed he felt bound to oppose it. For so doing his press had been mobbed and himself insulted. He had resolved to come to a free State, and he thanked his God that he was now removed from slavery. He could now publish a religious newspaper without meddling with the subject of slavery; he could entertain his opinions, but being removed from the evil, he would have no cause to express them. Indeed, said he, it would look like cowardice to flee from the place where the evil existed and come to a place where it did not exist to oppose it.

The people understood this to be a pledge of Mr. Lovejoy that he would not mingle the question of slavery with the discussions in his paper; and upon this condition he was permitted to set up the Alton *Observer* without opposition. Time rolled on: the paper extended its circulation, but solely as a religious paper heralding the peaceful gospel of the blessed God, which is peace on earth and good-will to men. After some time slavery was very moderately referred to, and then denounced. Soon after, the paper became moderately abolitionist. Next, some of the most respectable citizens were denounced as being in favor of slavery, and held up to public scorn because they dared to speak their opinions of the abolitionists; and ultimately, in the course of a year, it became decidedly an abolition paper of the fiercest sort and religion was pressed into its service as a mere incident and auxiliary to the main cause of abolitionism.

The mob spirit of Alton became aroused. The people thought that they had nurtured a viper to bite them and destroy their peace. The pledge of Mr. Lovejoy was remembered. He was urged by his friends to desist from his course, but no consideration could shake his inflexible resolution. He only became more violent and his denunciations more personal. A public meeting was called to induce him, by peaceable means if possible, to return to his original pledge. A committee was appointed to wait on him and call his attention to his original promises. He denied making such promises and contended for the freedom of the press and his right to unbounded liberty as one of its conductors. He read to the committee a long homily on mobs; and appeared to think that the action of a mob, by creating sympathy for him, would spread his renown and immortalize his labors. The positive denial of a minister of the gospel of what hundreds had heard him declare increased the rage of the people, which was blown into a consuming fury by a letter which appeared in the *Plain Dealer*, in which the leading men of Alton were denounced because they did not throw themselves into the breach and protect Mr. Lovejoy at the risk of their lives in conducting a press employed to vilify themselves, and to support a cause which they believed to be fraught with injury to all concerned. The people assembled and quietly took the press and types and threw them into the Mississippi. It now became manifest to all rational men that the Alton *Observer* could no longer be published in Alton as an abolition paper. The more reasonable of the abolitionists themselves thought it would be useless to try it again. However, a few of them who were most violent seemed to think that the salvation of the black race depended upon continuing the publication at Alton. They called a private meeting to consult, into which were admitted Messrs. Godfrey and Gilman and the Rev. Mr. Hogan, who were not abolitionists. All expressed their opinions. Some were for re-establishing the press and sustaining it at all hazards. Others thought it would be madness to make the attempt, and they believed that the efforts already made had come near destroying the religious feeling of the community and breaking up the peace and harmony of the churches. Mr. Lovejoy complained that Mr. Godfrey, who was a leading Presbyterian, and the Rev. Mr. Hogan had declared that if the *Observer* were again established they could do nothing to protect it from the mob; but he forgot to state that these gentlemen could not recognize as the cause of God that which had done so much evil. They had seen the effect of abolitionism in the slave States, where, instead of breaking the fetters of the slave it had increased their strength and severity. They conscientiously believed that abolitionism was wrong—they could not risk their lives in its defence.

The majority, however, determined to re-establish the *Observer* as an abolition paper; and as preparatory thereto they put out a call for a convention to be held in Upper Alton on the 26th of October, 1837, of all such persons in Illinois as were opposed to slavery, and in favor of free discussion. The convention assembled; and although the call was for all persons opposed to slavery, yet an attempt was made to exclude all who would not avow themselves to be abolitionists, all others being set down as opposed to free discussion. The trustees of the Presbyterian church would not allow it to assemble in their place of worship unless all were allowed to come who were opposed to slavery. This was finally acceded to, and many such took seats in the convention. A committee was appointed to prepare business and in the afternoon the Rev. Mr. Beecher, then President of Illinois College, was to preach a sermon before the convention. The committee of two abolitionists and one opposed to them made a majority and minority report and President Beecher held forth in a violent harangue against slavery. Mr. Beecher was a man of great learning and decided talents; but he belonged to the class of reformers who disregard all considerations of policy and expediency. He believed slavery to be a sin and a great evil, and his indignant and impatient soul could not await God's own good time to overthrow it by acts of His providence working continual change and revolution in the affairs of men. He contended that slavery was wrong, sinfully and morally wrong, and ought not to be borne with an instant. No Constitution could protect it. If the Constitution sanctioned iniquity

the Constitution was wrong in the sight of God and could not be binding upon the people of this country. For his part, he did not sanction
the Constitution. It was not binding on him; and whilst it tolerated
slavery it could not be. Several other speeches of a like nature were
made on the same side, which were answered by Usher F. Linder, the
Attorney General, and by the Rev. Mr. Hogan.[2]

The next day an abolition society was secretly formed at the
house of the Rev. Mr. Hurlbut in Upper Alton, believed to be the first
ever formed in Illinois. Mr. Beecher was appointed to preach in the
Upper Alton Presbyterian church on the following Sunday. Here his
lectures against slavery were continued until Monday evening. No outbreak had taken place, and Upper Alton was looked upon as conquered. This encouraged a similar effort in the main city on the bank
of the river. Accordingly it was announced that on Tuesday Mr. Beecher would deliver the same lectures in Lower Alton which he had delivered in the upper town. On this day another abolition press was
expected to arrive in a steamboat. The abolitionists announced that
they were organized with a company of forty men armed with muskets, fully determined and prepared to defend it at every hazard. The
people, in a high state of excitement, flocked to the river in great
numbers. The steamboat came but no press was on board. The
evening approached. Mr. Beecher was to deliver his address. The
abolitionists assembled at the church under arms. Armed to the teeth
with muskets and other deadly weapons, they were seen wending
their way to the house of God; and at the close of the service, as the
people returned to their homes, the moonlight was reflected from the
swords and guns of fifteen members of the church, stationed in the
vestibule. Such was religion when made the mere ally and auxiliary
of fanaticism. This was too much. Men could not endure such an
outrage. I do not apologize for mobs, all of which I would crush forever in every part of this free country. But no language can be loaded with sufficient severity for the fanatical leaders who, by their violence, by their utter disregard of honest prejudices, drove a peaceful
community to a temporary insanity and to the commission of enormous crimes.[3]

On Wednesday was to be observed that peculiar calm which indicates an approaching storm. The sayings and doings of Tuesday
were talked over. Many who before had taken no part were now active on the side of the mob. Indignation blazed on every face. As no
outbreak had yet occurred the abolitionists believed that they had
triumphed. In a secret meeting they determined to re-establish the
press at the point of the bayonet. The people could not bear such

threatenings, and now the waves of excitement rolled to the height of mountains. The Rev. Mr. Hogan, in taking the side he did, retained considerable power with the populace. He was appealed to, to allay the threatening storm. He called twenty or thirty of the most moderate on each side to a meeting at his countinghouse. One party seemed willing to compromise matters and bring about an adjustment. Mr. Beecher, at the head of the other, was unwilling to make the slightest concession. He contended for all their abstract rights and demanded all the guarantees of the government and the Constitution at the same time that he and his friends were contending for their right to trample upon both. He invoked the Constitution for his protection. He wanted others to be bound by it, whilst he refused to render it obedience himself. He insisted that all that he claimed should be awarded, to the slightest particular. He would retract nothing, compromise nothing, and no consideration could induce him to accede to other terms. In all this Mr. Beecher displayed that heroic obstinacy which, when accompanied by good sense and powerful talents and working with the natural current of events, has overthrown governments and systems and revolutionized the moral and almost the physical world. But here it was exerted in a cause which could not succeed, at least at that time. This meeting was about to adjourn when it was proposed and resolved to appoint a committee to devise and report some means of adjustment to a meeting to be held next day at 2 o'clock.

The committee met and it was stated to be impossible, after what had transpired, for Mr. Lovejoy to continue his paper. A resolution was passed proposing any other editor, and for Mr. Lovejoy to seek some other field of labor, which was reported to the meeting next day. It is believed that Lovejoy himself would have acceded to this arrangement, but not so with Mr. Beecher and his other friends. Pride and obstinacy were both aroused to demand a triumph in which principle was less considered than victory. Had they made the least concession the scene which followed, resulting in the death of two human beings, would probably never have taken place. The hour of two having arrived, the people assembled in the court-house and the committee, by their chairman, made their report, one calculated to still the troubled elements. Mr. Linder made some remarks calculated to restore peace, and prepared the large meeting then assembled to calmly consider the exceedingly serious matters then before them.

Mr. Lovejoy now arose and commenced his speech, which was very mild and affecting, in which he deprecated the action of the meeting and the report of the committee. He said he had thought of leaving Alton and going elsewhere, but a voice came to him from the east urging him to remain; here he would stay; he could not leave his post without being pursued by the Spirit of God to his destruction. The people might mob him or do anything they pleased; he could not and he would not be driven away; he would live there and die there. The Spirit of God urged him to contend for his rights and for a holy cause. He denied that he had ever given any pledges and called on Mr. Hogan to sustain him in this denial. He never had yielded his rights (he had forgotten his flight from St. Louis), he never would yield them, and he would die contending for them.

Mr. Lovejoy closed his remarks in a state of great excitement and the meeting was quite in an uproar, when Mr. Hogan rose and endeavored to throw some oil on the troubled waters. He said that the meeting had been convened not to consider each man's abstract rights, but to inquire into the doctrine of expediency, and how far we could relinquish the plea of right for the sake of peace. The great apostle had said, All things are lawful for me; but all things are not expedient. If Paul yielded to the law of expediency would it be wrong for them, for Mr. Lovejoy also, following his example? The Spirit of God did not pursue Paul to his destruction for thus acting; but, on the contrary, had commended his course. Paul had never taken up arms to propagate the religion of his master nor to defend himself against the attacks of his enemies. The people of Damascus were opposed to Paul, but did he argue with the populace the question of his legal rights? Did he tell them that he was a Roman citizen and would do and say what he pleased? Did he say, I am a minister of Christ and must not leave the work of my master to flee before the face of a mob? No; he quietly let himself down in a basket outside of the wall and departed for another field of labor. And God commended and blessed him for his wisdom and humility. Mr. Hogan expressed himself strongly in favor of peace and hoped all present would yield something of their determinations to secure it.

The Rev. Mr. Graves next addressed the meeting. He wished to allude to the pledge of Mr. Lovejoy, so much spoken of. Mr. Lovejoy had never given such a pledge; he could not give it, and he appealed to Mr. Hogan to bear him out in the assertion. He commended Mr. Lovejoy for his firmness; he could make no compromise; it was in vain to propose one.

Mr. Hogan then repeated what Lovejoy had said at the first meeting. Mr. Graves admitted that Lovejoy had made such statements, but they were not binding. Mr. Lovejoy was not an abolitionist at the time, nor was he himself one then. Since that time God had opened their eyes to see the great wickedness of slavery. They now felt it a duty to oppose it. If they had given such a pledge they had sinned against God, and ought to repent of it and forsake it. Their decision was unalterably made; they might die, but they could not compromise the performance of duty.

By such specious arguments many good men frequently delude themselves. These men had worked themselves up to a most heroical resolution, and indeed a generous mind finds much to admire in their inflexible obstinacy. It was the self-sacrificing spirit of the martyr and the patriot; and although we may disagree with them, we cannot withhold our admiration from men who are nobly wrong whilst we despise him who is meanly right.

The abolition press was expected to arrive next day after this meeting, but it did not come. An outbreak was now confidently looked for; all business was suspended; nothing was talked of among the populace but the efforts of the abolitionists. These last armed themselves, formed a military company, and elected their officers; and they mounted guard every night in expectation of the arrival of the boat from below with the fatal press. This great matter of discord arrived on the next Monday night and was removed on Tuesday morning to the stone warehouse of Godfrey, Gilman & Co., where its friends were assembled with arms to guard it. On Tuesday every one knew of its arrival, and the citizens were goaded on to madness by the taunts and threats of the abolitionists. They were told that they dare not touch the press, that powder and lead were not mere playthings, that the abolitionists were now organized by authority and were supplied with thirty rounds of cartridges, and that the mob should feel their virtue. These threatenings were doubtless made against the wishes of the leaders, but they served powerfully to augment the spirit of rebellion.

Towards evening the excitement in the city had reached a pitch which made it evident to all that a violent struggle was soon to come, and blood be shed. The press was in the warehouse; the abolitionists and some others who were not abolitionists were assembled with powder and ball to defend it unto death. Between nine and ten o'clock on Tuesday night a mob assembled in front of the warehouse and demanded the press to be given up to them. The night was clear and beautiful, the moon not quite risen, but so clear and bright was the sky that both parties were distinctly visible during the parley. All creation seemed to smile, and everything seemed divine but man, who that beautiful night was converted by his raging and surging passions into a demon of obstinacy on the one side, and of destruction on the other. The assailed party returned for answer that they were well provided with arms and ammunition and would defend the press to the last extremity. The house was then assailed with a shower of stones and the mob endeavored to carry it by storm. Someone in the building fired from the second story. This shot was fatal to a young man by the name of Bishop, producing almost instant death. Some of those in the house afterwards stated that this first shot was fired by Lovejoy. Be this, however, as it may, the result was terrible; for as the populace bore the young man away loud and bitter were their imprecations, and the death of all in the house was boldly threatened by the mob.

Some went to the magazine for powder to blow up the building; others procured ladders to set the roof on fire; but by far the greater number retired to the neighboring grog-shops to re-enforce their courage; and then returned to the assault with their hot blood made hotter still by the power of intoxication. The bells of the city were loudly rung and horns were blown to assemble yet a greater multitude. Armed men everywhere came rushing to the scene of action. Some were urging on the mob and others sought to allay the tumult.

The ladders were placed on the vacant space on the southern side of the building; one man mounted with a torch to fire the roof. There were no windows on this side from which the party within could fire at him as he ascended. At this time Mr. Lovejoy came from the door fronting the river, around the corner of the building, and fired at the crowd. His shot did not take effect and he instantly retreated into the building, where he urged his companions on to an attack, and up-braided them for their cowardice in refusing. A young man by the name of West, seeing the building on fire, ascended the ladder with a bucket of water and extinguished the flames. Whilst he was so engaged Mr. Lovejoy again made his appearance from the same place, again fired without effect, and returned to the building. Meanwhile, several guns were fired by the mob and several by the party in the house through the windows, but all without effect on either side.

The mob still increased. The ferocity grew upon it in proportion to the increase of its numbers and strength. Another attempt was made to fire the house, when Mr. Lovejoy and one of his companions made their appearance from the same door. The former shots from that quarter had drawn attention to this door and when the figures of two men were seen to emerge from it, one of them to raise his gun to fire again, they were fired upon by the mob with fatal precision; one of them being wounded in the leg, and the other, the Rev. Mr. Lovejoy, mortally; having only time to exclaim, "My God! I am shot!"

before he expired. With the fall of the chief or master spirit the sinking courage of his party seemed utterly to die away. A general firing was now kept up by the mob; the roof of the building was in flames, and the party within seemed to expect nothing less than utter destruction. In this extremity they were induced to surrender the obnoxious press. They were permitted to make a hurried escape down the river bank, their retreat being accelerated by several guns fired over their heads. The press was again thrown into the river.

After the violence of feeling had somewhat subsided both parties were indicted for their crimes arising out of these transactions and all were acquitted; making it a matter of record that in fact the abolitionists had not provoked an assault; that there had been no mob; and that no one had been killed or wounded.

Previous to the year 1840 other mobs were rife in the northern part of the State. The people there had settled without title upon the public lands of the United States, which were then neither surveyed nor in market, and they had made valuable improvements on these lands by building mills worth ten thousand dollars, opening farms, frequently of four or five hundred acres, and whole villages of six or eight hundred inhabitants were built on them. By a conventional law of each neighborhood the settlers were all pledged to protect each other in the amount of their respective claims.[4] But there were mean men who disregarded these conventional arrangements. Such as these belonged to that very honest fraternity who profess to regulate all their dealings by the law of the land. Such men had but little regard for public opinion or abstract right; and their consciences did not restrain them from jumping a neighbor's claim if they could be sustained by law and protected against force. It soon became apparent to everyone that actual force was the only protection for this description of property. And although the most of the settlers were from the eastern States; from the land of steady habits, where mobs are regularly hated and denounced, and all unlawful fighting held in abhorrence; yet seeing themselves left without legal protection and subject to the depredations of the dishonorable and unscrupulous they resolved to protect themselves with force. Many were the riots and mobs in every county arising from this state of things. Every neighborhood was signalized by some brawl of the kind. The old, peaceful, staid, puritan Yankee walked into a fight in defence of his claim or that of his neighbor just as if he had received a regular backwoods education in the olden times. It was curious to witness this change of character with the change of position, in emerging from a government of strict law to one of comparative anarchy. The readiness with which our puritan population from the East adopted the mobocratic spirit is evidence that men are the same everywhere under the same circumstances. That which any man will do depends more upon his position upon the laws and government, and upon the administration of the laws, than to mental or physical constitution or any peculiar trait of character or previous training.

Then again the northern part of the State was not destitute of its organized bands of rogues engaged in murders, robberies, horsestealing, and in making and passing counterfeit money. These rogues were scattered all over the north; but the most of them were located in the counties of Ogle, Winnebago, Lee, and De Kalb. In the county of Ogle they were so numerous, strong, and organized that they could not be convicted for their crimes. By getting some of their numbers on the juries, by producing hosts of witnesses to sustain their defence by perjured evidence, and by changing the venue from one county to another, and by continuances from term to term, and by the inability of witnesses to attend from time to time at a distant and foreign county they most generally managed to be acquitted. At the spring term, 1841, seven of them were confined in the Ogle county jail for trial. The judge and the lawyers had assembled at the little village of Oregon preparatory to holding the court.[5] The county had just completed a new courthouse, in which court was to be held for the first time the next day. The jail stood near it, in which were the prisoners. The rogues assembled in the night and set the court-house on fire in the hope that as the prisoners would have to be removed from the jail they might in the hurry and confusion of the people in attending to the fire make their escape. The whole population were awakened at a late hour of a dark and stormy night to see the lurid flames bursting from the roof and windows of their newly-erected temple of justice. The building was entirely consumed, but none of the prisoners escaped.

This produced a great excitement in the country, three of the prisoners were tried, convicted, and sent to the penitentiary for a year. But they managed to get one of their confederates on the jury, who refused to agree to a verdict until the eleven others had threatened to lynch him in the jury room. The other prisoners obtained changes of venue and were never convicted. They all broke out of jail and made their escape. The honest and substantial portion of the people were now determined to take the law into their own hands; they were determined that delays, insufficient jails, changes of venue, hung juries, and perjured evidence should no longer screen the rogue from punishment. And here it is to be remarked that the new counties, such as Ogle, were so poor in revenue and so much in debt, their orders at so great a discount, that they were not able to build good jails; and the other counties which had them refused to receive prisoners from the new counties unless the cost of their keeping were paid in advance. The people formed themselves into regulating companies both in Ogle and Winnebago counties, and proceeding in a summary way they whipped some of the most notorious rogues and ordered others into banishment. Amongst those who had been ordered away were the family of the Driscolls,—the old man and several of his sons. The old man and some of his sons had been in the Ohio penitentiary and made their escape from it. The old man was a stout, well-built, hardened, deliberate man, and his sons had more than common boldness in the commission of crime. This family were determined not to be driven away, and to this end they and several of their confederates held a private meeting in which they resolved to strike terror into the regulators by threatening death to all the leading men in their ranks and by assassinating their captain. Some of the Driscolls went to the house of Capt. Campbell, who was a captain of the regulators, just after dark of a Sunday evening, just as the family had returned from church, and pretending to be strangers inquiring their way they called Capt. Campbell out into his door-yard and there deliberately shot him dead in the presence of his wife and children. Before day next morning the news of the murder had run over the country like lightning. The people early assembled at the house of the murdered man in White Rock Grove in great numbers; and there, seeing the dead victim of this secret assassination, his blood yet fresh upon the ground, his wife and children in frantic agony, they were thrown into a wild uproar of excitement and frenzy, somewhat like that which seizes upon a herd of cattle upon seeing and scenting the blood of a slaughtered bullock. They spread out all over the country in search of the murderers. The actual murderers who had done the deed had escaped, but they seized upon the old man Driscoll, and the people of Winnebago county, coming down next day afterwards, had seized upon two of his sons.[6] The prisoners were taken to Washington Grove in Ogle county for trial. The old man and one of his sons were convicted as being accessories to the murder and the other was acquitted. The trial occupied nearly a whole day before the whole band of regulators, composed of about three hundred men, many of them being magistrates and some of them ministers of the gospel; and is described as having been conducted with much solemnity and seriousness. The condemned were sentenced to be shot within an hour; a minister of the gospel who was present prayed with them and administered to them the consolations of religion; and then they were brought out for execution. They were placed in a kneeling position with bandages over their eyes, and were fired upon by the whole company present, that there might be none who could be legal witnesses of the bloody deed. About one hundred of these men were afterwards tried for murder and acquitted.[7] These terrible measures put an end to the ascendancy of rogues in Ogle county.

There can be no doubt but that the mobocratic spirit originates in two causes. First, the laws fail to provide remedies for great evils. The administration of the laws, owing to the checks and balances in the Constitution, intended for the protection of innocence and liberty against arbitrary power is necessarily slow and uncertain. In framing our governments it seemed to be the great object of our ancestors to secure the public liberty by depriving government of power. Attacks upon liberty were not anticipated from any considerable portion of the people themselves. It was not expected that one portion of the people would attempt to play the tyrant over another. And if such a thing had been thought of the only mode of putting it down was to call out the militia, who are, nine times out of ten, partisans on one side or the other in the contest. The militia may be relied upon to do battle in a popular service, but if mobs are raised to drive out horse thieves, to put down claim-jumpers, to destroy an abolition press, or to expel an odious sect, the militia cannot be brought to act against them efficiently. The people cannot be used to put down the people. The day may unfortunately come when the States, as well as the nation, will be compelled to keep up a regular force.

In fact, the principal strength of government in free countries is that the mass of the people do not need government at all. Each man governs himself and, if need be, assists to govern his neighbor. Religious principles and feelings incline to justice. Industry inclines to peace. Early training begets submission to parents, and then to the magistrates and laws; making government quite possible without much authority in the magistrate. With the assistance of the well-affected honest citizens, who are supposed to make a large majority of the people, the magistrate is able to bring to punishment the lesser sort of rogues, who belong to no great combination, and sometimes succeeds in breaking up the strongest combinations. But if an association of bankers, of public officers who are charged with public affairs to disburse money, swindle the public, or if a number of rogues associate to depredate upon the community we are apt to find the old Athenian definition of law still to be true "that law is a cobweb to catch the small flies, but the great ones break through it." The true reason why the great offenders and combinations of criminals so frequently go unpunished is that they are too strong for the ordinary machinery of government single handed, without a vigorous support of that government by the orderly and well-disposed. The government is too frequently left without this support. The peaceable and orderly many are so engaged in separate and selfish but lawful projects of their own that it is hard to get them to take part in putting down the disorderly few, except when the disorders become intolerable and insufferable; and then the power of the many is exercised as the limbs of the body are exercised, in a spasm which waits for neither law nor government.

The second cause of mobs is that men engaged in unpopular projects expect more protection from the laws than the laws are able to furnish in the face of a popular excitement. They read in the Constitution the guaranty of their rights, and they insist upon the enjoyment of these rights to the fullest extent, no matter what may be the extent of popular opposition against them. In such a case it may happen that the whole people may be on one side and merely the public officers on the other. The public officers are appealed to for protection when it is apparent that, being separated from the strength of the people, they form the mere dead skeleton of a government. The men engaged in projects which may be odious to the people call upon government for that protection which it cannot give. For if government cannot suppress an unpopular band of horse thieves associated to commit crime, how is it to suppress a popular combination which has the people on its side? I am willing enough to acknowledge that all this is wrong, but how is the evil to be avoided? The Alton mob was provoked by the abolitionists. They read in the Constitution that they had a right to print and publish whatever they pleased, being responsible to the laws for the abuse of that right; and they planted themselves here as firmly as if government was omnipotent, or as if they intended, by way of experiment, to test the power of government to put down the people, on whom alone it rests for support. The same may be said of the Mormons. Scattered through the country, they might have lived in peace like other religious sects, but they insisted upon their right to congregate in one great city. The people were determined that they should not exercise this right; and it will be seen in the sequel of this history that in their case, as in every other where large bodies of the people are associated to accomplish with force an unlawful but popular object, the government is powerless against such combinations. This brings us to treat of the Mormons.

The people called Mormons, but who call themselves the Church of Jesus Christ of Latter Day Saints, began to figure in the politics of this State in 1840. They were a religious sect, the followers of a man familiarly called Joe Smith, who was claimed by them to be a prophet. This man was born at Sharon, Windsor County, Vermont, on the 23d of December, 1805. His parents were in humble circumstances, and gave their son but an indifferent education. When he first began to act the prophet he was ignorant of almost everything which belonged to science; but he made up in natural cunning and in power of invention and constructiveness for many deficiencies of education. When he was ten years old his parents removed to Palmyra, Wayne County, New York. Here his extreme youth was spent in an idle, vagabond life, roaming the woods, dreaming of buried treasures, and exerting himself to learn the art of finding them by the twisting of a forked stick in his hands or by looking through enchanted stones. He and his father before him were what are called "water witches," always ready to point out the ground where wells might be dug and water found, and many are the anecdotes of his early life, giving bright promise of future profligacy. Such was Joe Smith when he was found by Sidney Rigdon, who was a man of considerable talents and information. Rigdon had become possessed of a religious romance written by a Presbyterian clergyman in Ohio, then dead, which suggested to him the idea of starting a new religion.[8] It was agreed that Joe Smith should be put forward as a prophet; and the two devised a story that golden plates had been found buried in the earth in the neighborhood of Palmyra, containing a record inscribed on them in unknown characters, which, when deciphered by the power of inspiration, gave the history of the ten lost tribes of Israel in their wanderings through Asia into America, where they had settled and flourished, and where in due time Christ came and preached his gospel to them, appointed his twelve apostles, and was crucified here, nearly in the same manner in which he was crucified in Jerusalem. The record then pretended to give the history of the American Christians for a few hundred years, until the great wickedness of the people called down the judgments of God upon them, which resulted in their extermination. Several nations and people from the Isthmus of Darien to the extremities of North America were arrayed against each other in war. At last the great battle of Cumorah was fought near Palmyra, New York between the Lamanites, who were the heathen of this continent, and the Nephites, who were the Christians, in which battle there was a prodigious slaughter, hundreds of thousands being killed on each side. The nation of the Nephites was destroyed, except a few who had deserted and a few who had escaped into the south country. Among this number were Mormon and his son Moroni, who were righteous men, and who, as was said, were directed by the Almighty to make a record of all these solemn and important events on plates of gold and bury them in the earth, to be discovered in a future age, fourteen centuries afterwards. It is needless to add that the pretended translation of the hieroglyphics said to be inscribed on these pretended plates was no more nor less than the religious romance already spoken of, but which now appeared as the book of Mormon.

The prophet in after-life pretended that at an early age he became much concerned about the salvation of his soul. He went to the religious meetings of many sects to seek information of the way to heaven; and was everywhere told, "this is the way, walk ye in it." He reflected upon the multitude of doctrines and sects, and it occurred to him that God could be the author of but one doctrine, and own but one church; he looked amongst all the sects to see which was this one true church of Christ, but he could not decide; and until he became satisfied, he could not be contented. His anxious desires led him diligently to search the scriptures, and he perused the sacred pages, believing the things that he read. He now saw that the true way was to enquire of God, and then there was a certainty of success. He therefore retired to a secret place in a grove near his father's house, and kneeling down, began to call upon the Lord; darkness gave way, and he prayed with fervency of spirit. Whilst he continued praying the light appeared to be gradually descending towards him; and as it drew nearer it increased in brightness and magnitude, so that by the time it reached the tops of the trees the whole wilderness for quite a distance around was illuminated in a glorious and brilliant manner. He expected the leaves of the trees to be consumed, but seeing no such effect of the light he was encouraged with the hope to endure its presence. It descended slowly until he was enveloped in the midst of it. Immediately he was caught away in a heavenly vision and saw two glorious personages alike in their features; and he was now informed that his sins were forgiven. Here he learned that none of the churches then in being was the church of God; and received a promise at some future time of the fulness of the Gospel and a knowledge of the true doctrine. After this, being still young, he was entangled in the vanities of the world, of which he sincerely and truly repented.

On the 23d of September, 1823, God again heard his prayers. His mind had been drawn out in fervent prayer for his acceptance with God; and for a knowledge of the doctrines of Christ, according to promise in the former vision. While he was thus pouring out his desires, on a sudden a light burst into the room like the light of day, but purer and more glorious in appearance and brightness; the first sight of it was as though the house had been filled with consuming fire; this occasioned a shock felt to the extremities of his body; and then was followed by calmness of mind and overwhelming rapture of joy when in a moment a personage stood before him who, notwithstanding the light, seemed to be surrounded by an additional glory, which shone with increased brilliancy. This personage was above the ordinary size of men, his raiment was perfectly white and had the appearance of being without seam. This glorious being declared himself to be an angel sent to announce the forgiveness of his sins, and to answer his prayers by bringing the glad tidings that the covenant of God with ancient Israel concerning posterity was at last about to be fulfilled; that preparation for the second coming of Christ was speedily to commence; that the fulness of the Gospel was about to be preached in peace unto all nations that a people might be prepared for the millennium of universal peace and joy.

At the same time he was informed that he had been called and chosen as an instrument in the hands of God to bring about some of his marvellous purposes in this glorious dispensation. It was made known to him that the American Indians were a remnant of Israel; that when they first came here they were an enlightened people, having a knowledge of the true God; that the prophets and inspired writers amongst them had been required to keep a true record of their history, which had been handed down for many generations until the people fell into great wickedness; when nearly all of them were destroyed and the records, by command of God, were safely deposited to preserve them from the hands of the wicked, who sought to destroy them. If faithful, he was to be the highly-favored instrument in bringing these records to light.

The angel now disappeared, leaving him in a state of perfect peace, but visited him several times afterwards, instructing him concerning the great work of God about to commence on earth. He was instructed where these records were deposited and required to go immediately to view them. They were found on the side of a hill, slightly buried in the earth, secured in a stone box, on the road from Palmyra to Canandaigua in New York, about three miles from the village of Manchester. The records were said to be engraved on gold plates in Egyptian characters; the plates were of the thickness of tin, bound together like a book, fastened at one side by three rings which ran through the whole and formed a volume about six inches in thickness. And in the same box with them were found two stones, transparent and clear as crystal, the Urim and Thummim, used by seers in ancient times, the instruments of revelations of things distant, past, or future.

When the prophet first saw these things, being filled with the Holy Ghost and standing and admiring, the same angel of the Lord appeared in his presence and said, "look!" and he beheld the devil surrounded by a great train of his associates. He then, after receiving further directions from the angel, started home to his father's house, where he was waylaid by two ruffians. One of them struck him with a club, but was repulsed; but they followed him nearly home when they fled for fear of detection. The news of his discovery got abroad; the new prophet was the sport of lies, slanders, and mobs, and vain attempts to rob him of his plates. He removed to the northern part of Pennsylvania, where he commenced with the aid of inspiration and the Urim and Thummim to translate the plates. He finished a part which is called the Book of Mormon. It is pretended that Mormon hid all the old records up in the hill of Cumorah; but had first made an abridgment of them which was called the Book of Mormon, and which he gave to his son Moroni to finish. Moroni continued to serve his nation for a few years and continued the writings of his father until after the great battle of Cumorah, when he kept himself hid; for the Lamanites sought to kill every Nephite who refused to deny Christ. The story is remarkably well gotten up and may yet unhappily make the foundation of a religion which may roll back upon the world the barbarism of eighteen centuries passed away. Whilst there are fools and knaves there is no telling what may be accomplished by such a religion.

And the prophet was not without his witnesses. Oliver Cowdery, Martin Harris, and David Whitmer solemnly certify "that we have seen the plates which contain the records; that they were translated by the gift and power of God, for his voice hath declared it unto us, wherefore we know of a surety that the work is true; and we declare with words of soberness that an angel of God came down from heaven and brought and laid before our eyes, that we beheld and saw the plates and the engravings thereon." Eight other witnesses certify that Joseph Smith, the translator, had shown them the plates spoken of, which had the appearance of gold; and as many of the plates as the said Smith had translated they did handle with their hands, and they also saw the engravings thereon, all of which had the appearance of ancient work and curious workmanship.

The most probable account of these certificates is that the witnesses were in the conspiracy, aiding the imposture; but I have been informed by men who were once in the confidence of the prophet that he privately gave a different account of the matter. It is related that the prophet's early followers were anxious to see the plates; the prophet had always given out that they could not be seen by the carnal eye, but must be spiritually discerned; that the power to see them depended upon faith and was the gift of God, to be obtained by fasting, prayer, mortification of the flesh, and exercises of the spirit; that so soon as he could see the evidences of a strong and lively faith in any of his followers they should be gratified in their holy curiosity. He set them to continual prayer and other spiritual exercises, to acquire this lively faith by means of which the hidden things of God could be spiritually discerned; and at last, when he could delay them no longer, he assembled them in a room and produced a box, which he said contained the precious treasure. The lid was opened; the witnesses peeped into it, but making no discovery, for the box was empty, they said, "Brother Joseph, we do not see the plates." The prophet answered them, "O ye of little faith! how long will God bear with this wicked and perverse generation? Down on your knees, brethren, every one of you, and pray God for the forgiveness of your sins, and for a holy and living faith which cometh down from heaven." The disciples dropped to their knees and began to pray in the fervency of their spirit, supplicating God for more than two hours with fanatical earnestness; at the end of which time, looking again into the box, they were now persuaded that they saw the plates. I leave it to philosophers to determine whether the fumes of an enthusiastic and fanatical imagination are thus capable of blinding the mind and deceiving the senses by so absurd a delusion.

The book of Mormon pretended to reveal the fulness of the Gospel of Jesus Christ as he delivered it to his people in America. It was to be brought forth by the power of God and carried to the Gentiles, of whom many were to receive it; and after this the seed of Israel were to be brought into the fold also. It was pretended that pristine Christianity was to be restored, with the gift of prophecy and the gift of tongues, with the laying on of hands to cure all manner of diseases. Many were the pretended prophets which this sect brought forth. Many of the disciples spoke an outlandish gibberish, which they called the unknown tongue; others again acted as interpreters of this jargon, for it rarely happened that he who was gifted to speak in the unknown tongue was able to understand his own communications; and many brilliant miracles were pretended to be wrought in the cure of diseases by the laying on of hands and the prayer of faith.

By the 6th of April, 1830 Joe Smith and his associates had made a considerable number of converts to the new religion, who were assembled on that day in the village of Manchester and formed into a church. Their numbers now increased rapidly and in 1833 they removed from New York to Jackson County, Missouri, where they began to build the town of Independence. Here, by pretending that the Lord had given them all that country, and in fact the whole world, they being his saints, and by some petty offences, and by their general tone of arrogance the neighboring people became much excited against them. Some of them were ducked in the river; some were tarred and feathered and others killed; and the whole of them were compelled to remove to the County of Clay, on the opposite side of the Missouri river. They also had a place of gathering together at Kirtland, near Cleaveland, in the State of Ohio. At this last place of gathering Joe Smith established himself; and in 1836 a solemn assembly was held there of several hundred Mormon elders, who, in their own language, "had an interesting time of it, as it appeared by the reports of the elders that the work of God had greatly increased in America, in England, Scotland, and Wales, and in the islands of the sea."

At this place Joe Smith got up a bank, called The Kirtland Safety Bank, of which he was president; and the notes of which were made to resemble the notes of the safety fund banks of New York. The bank failed for a large amount, for want of capital and integrity in its managers; and its failure was accompanied by more than ordinary depravity. The residence of the prophet at this place, after the failure of the bank, became irksome and dangerous. He determined to leave it, and accordingly, accompanied by his apostles and elders, for he had apostles and elders, and the great body of the saints, he shook the dust off his feet as a testimony against Ohio, where he was about to be prosecuted, and departed for Missouri. This time the Mormons settled in Caldwell and Davis Counties in Missouri, far in the northwest part of the State. Here they purchased large tracts of land from the United States and built the city of Far West and many smaller towns. Difficulties again attended them in their new place of residence. They did not fail to display here the usual arrogance of their pretensions, and were charged by the neighboring people with every kind of petty villainy. In a few years the quarrel between the saints and the Gentiles became utterly irreconcilable. The Mormon leaders declared that they would no longer submit to the government of Missouri. The clerk of the circuit court, being a Mormon, was ordered by the prophet to issue no more writs against the saints; and about this time Sidney Rigdon preached before the prophet a Fourth of July sermon, called The Salt Sermon, in which he held forth to the Mormons that the prophet had determined no longer to regard the laws and government of Missouri.[9] The neighboring people of Missouri assembled under arms to drive the Mormons from the State. Armed Mormon parties patrolled the country, robbing and plundering the inhabitants; all the plunder being deposited in one place, called the Lord's treasury. One of these plundering parties met a hostile party commanded by Captain Bogart, who had formerly been a Methodist preacher in Illinois. He had run away from Illinois directly after the Black Hawk war, and was the same Major Bogart heretofore mentioned as commanding a battalion of Rangers in the Black Hawk war, left to guard the frontiers. Bogart's party and the Mormons came to a battle in which the Mormons were defeated. The Mormons, however, burnt and plundered two small towns belonging to their enemies and plundered all the neighboring country. At last Gov. Boggs of Missouri called out a large body of militia and ordered that the Mormons should be exterminated or driven from the State. A large force was marched to their county under Major-Gen. Lucas and Brig.-Gen. Doniphan, where the Mormons were all assembled under arms with the declared intention of resisting to the last extremity. They were soon surrounded in their city of Far West by a much superior force and compelled to surrender at discretion.[10] Much plunder was recaptured and delivered to its former owners. The great body of the Mormons, in fact all except the leaders, were dismissed under a promise to leave the State. The leaders, including the prophet, being arrested, were tried before a court-martial, and sentenced to be shot for treason. But Gen. Doniphan, being a sound lawyer and a man of sense, knowing that such a proceeding was utterly unconstitutional and illegal, by boldly denouncing and firmly remonstrating against this arbitrary mode of trial and punishment saved the lives of the prisoners.*

The leaders were then carried before a circuit judge sitting as an examining court, and were committed to jail for further trial on various charges; such as treason, murder, robbery, arson, and larceny, but finally made their escape out of jail and out of the State before they could be brought to trial. Those who wish to consult a more minute detail of the history of this people, are referred to a volume of

*This is the same Gen. Doniphan who, as Colonel of a regiment of Missouri volunteers, afterwards conquered Chihuahua and gained the splendid victories of Bracito and Sacramento. Among all the officers of the Missouri militia operating against the Mormons, Gen. Doniphan was the only one who boldly denounced the intended assassination of the prisoners under color of law. So true is it that the truly brave man is most apt to be merciful and just.

printed evidence and documents published by order of the legislature of Missouri.

The whole body of the Missouri Mormons came to Illinois in the years 1839 and 1840; and many of the leaders who had escaped came through perils of flood and field which, according to their own account, if written would equal a tale of romance. As they were the weaker party much sympathy was felt and expressed for them by the people of Illinois. The Mormons represented that they had been persecuted in Missouri on account of their religion. The cry of persecution, if believed, is always sure to create sympathy for the sufferers. This was particularly so in Illinois, whose citizens, until some time after this period, were justly distinguished for feelings and principles of the most liberal and enlightened toleration in matters of religion. The Mormons were received as sufferers in the cause of their religion. Several counties and neighborhoods vied with each other in offers of hospitality and in endeavors to get the strangers to settle among them.

At last the Mormons selected a place on the Mississippi river, afterwards called Nauvoo, in the upper part of the county of Hancock, as the place of their future residence. On this spot they designed to build up a great city and temple as the great place of gathering to Zion, and as the great central rendezvous of the sect; from whence was to originate and spread the most gigantic operations for the conversion of the world to the new religion. However, in this history I have nothing to do with the religious, but only the political considerations connected with this people.

In the State of Missouri the Mormons had always supported the democratic party. They had been driven out by a democratic governor of a democratic State; and when they appealed to Mr. Van Buren, the democratic President of the United States, for relief against the Missourians he refused to recommend it for want of constitutional power in the United States to coerce a sovereign State in the execution of its domestic polity. This soured and embittered the Mormons against the democrats. Mr. Clay, as a member of the United States Senate, and John T. Stuart, a member of the House of Representatives in Congress from Illinois, both whigs, undertook their cause and introduced and countenanced their memorials against Missouri; so that when the Mormons came to this State they attached themselves to the whig party. In August, 1840 they voted unanimously for the whig candidates for the Senate and Assembly. In the November following they voted for the whig candidate for President; and in August, 1841 they voted for John T. Stuart, the whig candidate for Congress in their district.

At the legislature of 1840–'41 it became a matter of great interest with both parties to conciliate these people. They were already numerous and were fast increasing by emigration from all parts. It was evident that they were to possess much power in elections. They had already signified their intention of joining neither party, further than they could be supported by that party, but to vote for such persons as had done or were willing to do them most service. And the leaders of both parties believed that the Mormons would soon hold the balance of power, and exerted themselves on both sides, by professions and kindness and devotion to their interest, to win their support.

In this state of the case Dr. John C. Bennett presented himself at the seat of government as the agent of the Mormons. This Bennett was probably the greatest scamp in the western country. I have made particular enquiries concerning him and have traced him in several places in which he had lived before he had joined the Mormons in Ohio, Indiana and Illinois, and he was everywhere accounted the same debauched, unprincipled and profligate character. He was a man of some little talent, and then had the confidence of the Mormons, and particularly that of their leaders. He came as the agent of that people to solicit a city charter; a charter for a military legion; and for various other purposes. This person addressed himself to Mr. Little, the whig senator from Hancock, and to Mr. Douglas, the democratic secretary of State, who both entered heartily into his views and projects. Bennett managed matters well for his constituents. He flattered both sides with the hope of Mormon favor; and both sides expected to receive their votes. A city charter drawn up to suit the Mormons was presented to the Senate by Mr. Little. It was referred to the judiciary committee, of which Mr. Snyder, a democrat, was chairman, who reported it back recommending its passage. The vote was taken, the ayes and noes were not called for, no one opposed it, but all were busy and active in hurrying it through. In like manner it passed the House of Representatives, where it was never read except by its title; the ayes and noes were not called for, and the same universal zeal in its favor was manifested here which had been so conspicuously displaced in the Senate.

This city charter and other charters passed in the same way by this legislature incorporated Nauvoo, provided for the election of a Mayor, four Aldermen, and nine Counsellors; gave them power to pass all ordinances necessary for the peace, benefit, good order, regulation, convenience, or cleanliness of the city, and for the protection of property from fire, which were not *repugnant to the Constitution of the*

United States, or this State. This seemed to give them power to pass ordinances in violation of the *laws* of the State, and to erect a system of government for themselves.

This charter also established a mayor's court with exclusive jurisdiction of all cases arising under the city ordinances, subject to an appeal to the municipal court. It established a municipal court to be composed of the mayor as chief justice and the four aldermen as his associates; which court was to have jurisdiction of appeals from the mayor or aldermen, subject to an appeal again to the circuit court of the county. The municipal court was also clothed with power to issue writs of habeas corpus in all cases arising under the ordinances of the city.

This charter also incorporated the militia of Nauvoo into a military legion, to be called The Nauvoo Legion. It was made entirely independent of the military organization of the State, and not subject to the command of any officer of the State militia except the Governor himself, as commander-in-chief. It was to be furnished with its due proportion of the State arms; and might enroll in its ranks any of the citizens of Hancock county who preferred to join it, whether they lived in the city or elsewhere. This last provision, I believe, was not in the original charter, but was afterwards passed as an amendment to a road law. The charter also established a court-martial for the legion, to be composed of the commissioned officers, who were to make and execute all ordinances necessary for the benefit, government, and regulation of the legion; but in so doing they were not bound to regard the laws of the State, but could do nothing repugnant to the constitution; and finally, the legion was to be at the disposal of the mayor in executing the laws and ordinances of the city. Another charter incorporated a great tavern to be called the Nauvoo House, in which the prophet, Joe Smith and his heirs were to have a suite of rooms forever.

Thus it was proposed to re-establish for the Mormons a government within a government, a legislature with power to pass ordinances at war with the laws of the State; courts to execute them with but little dependence upon the constitutional judiciary; and a military force at their own command, to be governed by its own bylaws and ordinances and subject to no State authority but that of the Governor. It must be acknowledged that these charters were unheard-of, and anti-republican in many particulars; and capable of infinite abuse by a people disposed to abuse them. The powers conferred were expressed in language at once ambiguous and undefined; as if on purpose to allow of misconstruction. The great law of the separation of the powers of government was wholly disregarded. The mayor was at once the executive power, the judiciary, and part of the legislature. The common council, in passing ordinances, were restrained only by the constitution. One would have thought that these charters stood a poor chance of passing the legislature of a republican people jealous of their liberties. Nevertheless they did pass unanimously through both houses. Messrs. Little and Douglas managed with great dexterity with their respective parties. Each party was afraid to object to them for fear of losing the Mormon vote, and each believed that it had secured their favor. These, I believe, were the principal subjects acted on by the session of 1840–'41.

But we will continue a little farther the history of the Mormons. A city government under the charter was organized in 1841. Joe Smith was elected mayor. In this capacity he presided in the common council and assisted in making the laws for the government of the city. And as mayor also he was to see these laws put into force. He was ex-officio judge of the mayor's court and chief justice of the municipal court, and in these capacities he was to interpret the laws which he had assisted to make. The Nauvoo Legion was also organized, with a great multitude of high officers. It was divided into divisions, brigades, cohorts, regiments, battalions, and companies. Each division, brigade, and cohort had its general, and over the whole, as commander-in-chief, Joe Smith was appointed lieutenant-general. These offices, and particularly the last, were created by an ordinance of the court martial, composed of the commissioned officers of the Legion.

The common council passed many ordinances for the punishment of crime. The punishments were generally different from, and vastly more severe than, the punishments provided by the laws of the State.

In the fall of 1841 the governor of Missouri made a demand on Gov. Carlin for the arrest and delivery of Joe Smith and several other head Mormons as fugitives from justice. An executive warrant was issued for that purpose. It was placed in the hands of an agent to be executed; but for some cause unknown to me was returned to Gov. Carlin without being executed. Soon afterwards the governor handed the same writ to his agent, who this time succeeded in arresting Joe Smith upon it. But before this time Mr. Douglas had been elected one of the judges of the supreme court and was assigned to hold circuit courts in Hancock and the neighboring counties. This had given the democratic party the advantage in securing the Mormon vote. Judge Douglas immediately appointed Dr. Bennett a master in chancery. Bennett was then an influential Mormon, and had, before he joined the Mormons, been appointed by Gov. Carlin adjutant-general of the State militia. He had also been elected an alderman of the city and a major-general in the Legion. Upon his arrest, Joe Smith was carried before Judge Douglas upon a writ of habeas corpus and was discharged upon the ground that the writ upon which he had been arrested had been once returned before it had been executed, and was *functus officio*. Whether the decision was right or wrong, Joe Smith was not lawyer enough to know, and was therefore the more inclined to esteem his discharge as a great favor from the democratic party.

The Mormons anticipated a further demand from Missouri, and a further writ from the governor of this State for the arrest of their prophet and leaders. They professed to believe that the public mind in Missouri was so prejudiced against them that a fair trial there was out of the question, and that if their leaders were taken to Missouri for trial and not convicted upon evidence they would be murdered by a mob before they could get out of the State. Some mode of permanent protection, therefore, against the demands of Missouri became a matter of vital importance; and they set their ingenuity to work to devise a scheme of protection by means of their own city ordinances, to be executed by their own municipal court. Gov. Carlin had issued his writ again in 1842. Joe Smith was arrested again, and was either rescued by his followers or discharged by the municipal court on a writ of habeas corpus. The common council passed an ordinance declaring, in effect, that the municipal court should have jurisdiction in all cases of arrests made in the city by any process whatever. The charter intended to give the jurisdiction only in cases where imprisonment was a consequence of the breach of some ordinance. But it was interpreted by the Mormons to authorize the enlargement and extension of the jurisdiction of the court by ordinance. This ordinance will figure very largely in the proceedings of the Mormons hereafter.

In December, 1841 a State democratic convention assembled at Springfield and nominated Adam W. Snyder as the democratic candidate for governor, to be elected in August, 1842. Mr. Snyder was a native of Pennsylvania and a distant relative of Gov. Snyder of that State. In his early youth he learned the trade of a fuller and wool carder. He came to Illinois when he was about eighteen years old; settled in the French village of Cahokia; followed his trade for several years; studied law; removed to the county seat, where he commenced his profession, in which he was successful in getting practice. In 1830 he was elected to the State Senate, and was afterwards elected to Congress from his district; and was again elected to the State Senate in 1840. Mr. Snyder was a very showy, plausible and agreeable man in conversation, and was gifted with a popular eloquence which was considerably effective. He was a member of the senate when the Mormon charters were passed and had taken an active part in furthering their passage. In the spring of 1842 Joseph Duncan, former governor, became the candidate of the whig party for the same office.

In a very short time after the two parties had their candidates fairly in the field Joe Smith published a proclamation to his followers in the Nauvoo papers declaring Judge Douglas to be a master spirit and exhorting them to vote for Mr. Snyder for governor.

The whigs had considerable hope of the Mormon support until the appearance of this proclamation. The Mormons had voted for the whig candidate for Congress in August, 1841. But this proclamation left no doubt as to what they would do in the coming contest. It was plain that the whigs could expect their support no longer, and that the whig party in the legislature had swallowed the odious charters without prospect of reward.

The Mormons, however, were becoming unpopular, nay odious, to the great body of the people. As I have already said, their common council had passed some extraordinary ordinances calculated to set the State government at defiance. The Legion had been furnished with three pieces of cannon and about two hundred and fifty stand of small arms; which popular rumor increased to the number of thirty pieces of cannon and five or six thousand stand of muskets. The Mormons were rapidly increasing by emigration. The great office of Lieutenant General had been created for the commander of the Legion, of higher rank, as was said, than any office in the militia and higher than any office in the regular army. A vast number of reports were circulated all over the country to the prejudice of the Mormons. They were charged with numerous thefts and robberies and rogueries of all sorts; and it was believed by vast numbers of the people that they entertained the treasonable design, when they got strong enough, of overturning the government, driving out the old population, and taking possession of the country as the children of Israel did in the land of Canaan.

The whigs, seeing that they had been outgeneraled by the democrats in securing the Mormon vote, became seriously alarmed and sought to repair their disaster by raising a kind of crusade against that people. The whig newspapers teemed with accounts of the wonders and enormities of Nauvoo, and of the awful wickedness of a party which would consent to receive the support of such miscreants. Governor Duncan, who was really a brave, honest man, and who had nothing to do with getting the Mormon charters passed through the legislature, took the stump on this subject in good earnest and expected to be elected governor almost on this question alone. There is no knowing how far he might have succeeded if Mr. Snyder had lived to be his competitor.

However, Mr. Snyder departed this life, much lamented by numerous friends, in the month of May preceding the election. The democratic party had now to select another candidate for governor. The choice fell upon me. I hope to be excused from saying anything in these memoirs in relation to my own personal qualities and history. If it should ever be thought important that a knowledge of such humble matters should be perpetuated, I will trust the task of doing it to other hands. I will merely mention that at the time I was nominated as a candidate for governor I was one of the judges of the Supreme Court engaged in holding a circuit court on Fox river, in the north. So soon as I heard of my nomination I hastened to the seat of government, resigned the office of judge, and became the candidate of my party. Here permit me to remark, I had never before been much concerned in the political conflicts of the day, and never at all on my own account. It is true that I had been much in office. I had been twice appointed to the office of State's Attorney and four times elected without opposition to the office of judge by the legislature. I had never been a candidate for the legislature, for Congress, or for any office elective by the people and had never wanted to be a candidate for such offices. I had never been an applicant for any office from the General Government, and had always avoided being a candidate for any office which was desired by any respectable political friend.

And here again I must be permitted to indulge in some further reflections upon the practical operation of republican government. The history of my administration but serves to illustrate what has already been demonstrated by two administrations of the federal government. I mean the administrations of Tyler and Polk. Neither of these gentlemen was placed in the office of president because they were leaders of their respective parties. Tyler was accidentally made vice-president by the whigs, and accidentally became president by the death of Gen. Harrison. He had the position as to office to govern, but the moral power of government was in the hands of Henry Clay, the great leader of the whig party and the embodiment of its principles. During all of Tyler's administration he exerted no moral force; government was kept in motion merely by its previous impulse and by the patriotism of Congress, voluntarily subduing so much of its factious spirit as was absolutely necessary to keep government alive. Polk was accidentally nominated by the Baltimore convention after it was ascertained that none of the great leaders of the democratic party could be nominated; and so far during his time the government has been carried on by the mere force of the democratic party, which has been in the majority in Congress, the great leaders, for fear of division in their ranks, uniting sometimes in his support and sometimes dictating to him the policy of his administration. Neither Tyler nor Polk had much distinguished themselves in their respective parties. They had neither of them fought their way in the party contests to the leadership, and to the moral power which the leadership alone can give. So it was with the humble person who was now to be elected governor of Illinois. Mr. Snyder had been nominated because he was a leader of the party. Mr. Snyder died, and I was nominated, not because I was a leader, for I was not, but because I was believed to have no more than a very ordinary share of ambition; because it was doubtful whether any of the leaders could be elected, and because it was thought I would stand more in need of support from leaders than an actual leader would. To this cause, and perhaps there were others, I trace the fact which will hereafter appear that I was never able to command the support of the entire party which elected me.

From such examples as these I venture to assert that the moral power belonging to the leadership of the dominant party is greater than the legal power of office conferred by the Constitution and the laws. In fact it has appeared to me at times that there is very little power of government in this country except that which pertains to the leadership of the party in the majority. Gen. Jackson not only governed whilst he was president, but for eight years afterwards, and has since continued to govern, even after his death.*

*In forming a constitution it is almost impossible to anticipate how much power is delegated to the government, and particularly to the executive branch. The power of the executive branch depends somewhat upon the legal authority with which the officer is clothed, but more upon his personal character and influence. To illustrate this, take the administrations of John Quincy Adams, Gen. Jackson, and John Tyler. These presidents were all clothed with the same identical legal powers. John Quincy Adams, although a man of great abilities, acknowledged the feebleness of his administration, in consequence of not being elected by the people, but by the House of Representatives. Gen. Jackson exercised the power of an autocrat because he was supported by the confidence and affections of the American people. And John Tyler, though a man of very respectable talents, converted the executive department into a kind of anarchy because he had no party in his favor. The election, therefore, of a strong man or a weak one to this office is

When men who are not leaders are put into high office it is generally done through the influence of leaders who expect to govern through them. They are expected to need support more than if they were actual leaders; and are preferred sometimes to actual leaders on account of being more available as candidates, and sometimes because those leaders who cannot get the office themselves hope through them to help to be president or governor, as the case may be. Soon after my election I ascertained that quite a number of such leaders imagined that they, instead of myself, had been elected; and could only be convinced to the contrary on being referred to the returns of the election.

A pusillanimous man, willing to take office upon any terms, is ever disposed to submit to this kind of influence and dictation. He calls it consulting his party when he consults only a few leaders, and this he is obliged to do or find himself without the power to govern. In a government where the democratic spirit is all-powerful this power to govern consists in being able to unite a majority of opinions; but where the people are free, each man to choose for himself, it is extremely difficult to induce a majority to co-operate for the common benefit. Various reasons and passions and prejudices will lead different ways; and very often all reason will be confounded by a combination of clamor and prejudice. It is generally the work of a few leading minds to bring order out of this chaos and to get a majority to think and feel alike. These leaders, therefore, as effectually govern the country as if they were born to rule.

The best and purest mode in which leaders exercise their power is by instruction and persuasion. This kind of government can exist only over a very intelligent and virtuous people. And as a government is always a type of the people over whom it is exercised, so it will be found that when the people are less enlightened and virtuous the means of governing them will be less intellectual. If the people are indifferent to and ignorant of what constitutes good government, the mode which leaders take to unite a majority of them is apt to be as follows: There is in every county, generally at the county seats, a little clique of county leaders who aim to monopolize or dispose of the county offices. Some of them expect to be elected to the legislature, and in time to higher offices. Others expect to be recipients of some

---

equivalent to an amendment of the Constitution by which great powers are given, or withheld, as the case may be. Or, rather, it is more like a revolution by which a dictator is appointed at one time, and at another the authority of the executive omce is so restricted as to convert the government into an anarchy. And yet during the whole time there has been really no change in the fundamental law.

county or State office; or to be appointed to some office by the President through the influence of members of Congress. These lesser leaders all look to some more considerable leader, who is a judge, member of Congress, United States Senator, or Governor of the State. The State leaders again look to some more considerable man at Washington city who is actually president, or who controls the president, or who is himself a prominent candidate for that office. The great leader at Washington dashes boldly out in favor of or against some measure; the class of leaders whose influence, as yet, is bounded by a single State fall into line behind the great leader. These State leaders are kept together by a fear of the opposite party. For instance, if they are democratic leaders they fear that a division amongst themselves will divide the democratic party and thereby cause its defeat and the success of the whigs. They therefore make sacrifices of opinion to keep up unity, the least influential leader having to make the greatest sacrifice.*

The State leaders, whether democrat or whig makes no difference, then give the word to the little cliques of leaders in each county; these county leaders convey it to the little big men in each neighborhood and they do the talking to the rank-and-file of the people. In this way principles and men are put up and put down with amazing celerity. And gentle reader do not be astonished; THIS IS GOVERNMENT! and if there is in point of fact any other sort its existence cannot be proved by me, and yet I have been governor of the State for four years.

*The organization of men into political parties under the control of leaders as a means of government necessarily destroys individuality of character and freedom of opinion. Government implies restraint, compulsion of either the body or mind, or both. The latest improvement to effect this restraint and compulsion is to use moral means, intellectual means operating on the mind, instead of the old mode of using force, such as standing armies, fire, sword and the gibbet to control the mere bodies of men. It is therefore a very common thing for men of all parties to make very great sacrifices of opinion so as to bring themselves into conformity with the bulk of their party. And yet there is nothing more common than for the race of newspaper statesmen to denounce all such of the opposite party as yield their own opinions to the opinions of the majority as truckling and servile. They may possibly be right in this. But undoubtedly such submission is often necessary to the existence of majorities entertaining the same opinion. A little further experience may develop the fact that when this means of securing majorities shall fail the government will fall into anarchy.

Either moral or physical force must be used for purposes of government. When a people are so gross that moral power cannot operate on them physical force must be resorted to. Also, when the officers of government lack talents and moral power physical force may thereby be made necessary; so that it may be said that a people may stand in need of being governed by absolute violence just in proportion to their want of a proper civilization; and sometimes also just in proportion to the want of moral power in the government.

It may be thought that these leaders, of course, are men of great and magnanimous natures. But such is not always the fact. To make a leader nothing more is necessary than a pleasing address, added to zeal for a party and unceasing activity and enterprise. The world is governed by industry more than by talents. True great men are leaders only in times of great trouble, when a nation is in peril. In quiet times the active, talking, enterprising, and cunning manager is apt to be the leader. This kind of leader always claims more than his just share in the benefits and advantages of government. When he has elected some man to high office who is not a leader, he claims every service from him which he has it in his power to render. Many such must have offices which they are not fit for; others have a scheme to make money out of the public; others invoke aid in procuring the enactment of laws for private advantage; and others again require a hundred things which an honest man ought not to do. And if their unreasonable requests are refused; if the true interests of the people are consulted, and the man elected refuses to be a mere instrument in the hands of leaders to make an unequal distribution of the advantages of government, they immediately denounce him, they send out all sorts of falsehoods against him, and, for being honest and devoted to the public interest they get many people to believe that he is a greater rogue than he would really have been if he had done all the villainous things they required him to do. I could relate some amusing instances of this sort in the course of my administration.*

It is no part of my object to overthrow the power of leaders, if I could; for I am persuaded that without it, a governing majority of the

*The condition of a modern governor in party times, is well described in Knickerbocker's history of New York: 'He is an unhappy victim of popularity, who is in fact the most dependent, hen-pecked being in community; doomed to bear the secret goadings and corrections of his own party and the sneers and revilings of the whole world beside. Set up like geese at Christmas holidays, to be pelted and shot at by every whipster and vagabond in the land." From this condition nothing can save a governor but his personal insignificance, the idea that he is not worth making war on. As soon as a governor is elected he receives the congratulations of his friends, and there are generally about ten of these and sometimes more in each county, each one of whom claiming to have elected him. Each one writes to the governor or goes to see him to tell him how well and cunningly he fought and managed and how many sacrifices he made to carry the election. Each one is sure that he did it all himself and claims to be rewarded accordingly. If the governor cannot do everything for everyone as required, the disappointed ones are more earnest in their enmity than they were before in their friendship. Something of this kind has happened to me. I do not complain of it, but merely mention it but to show how difficult it is for a governor to have any policy of his own for the general advantage of the people and pursue it steadily without incurring the censure of such politicians as have no public benefits in view, but merely their own selfish projects.

people would rarely be found. A government of leaders, however defective it may be, is better than no government, upon the same principle that despotism is better than anarchy. But reformation of this power is earnestly desired. For as long as the great body of the people do not investigate, and take so little interest in matters of government, as long as men of influence will endeavor to appropriate the benefits and advantages of government to themselves, and can and do control the people, making it necessary for men in office to lean upon leaders instead of the intelligence of the people for support, there will never be any good government, or if there is the people will not think so.* Fortunate is that country which has great and good men for leaders of parties, upon whose measures a majority of the people can safely unite, and the greater the majority the better. If the power of leaders is ever to be reformed, it will be by beginning with the people themselves. The people, whether good or bad, will have a government which in the main truly represents the state of civilization which they have attained to. The democratic party professes to be the party of progress in matters of government; it has much to reform; but it is sincerely hoped that at no distant day its attention may be directed to the evils of this machinery and correct them. At present the people may be said to govern themselves only by being the depository of power, which they can exercise if they choose; but which for most of the time they choose to give into the hands of their leaders, to be exercised without much responsibility to them. The responsibility is all to attach to their leaders and not to the people.

As soon as I was announced as a candidate for governor the Mormon question was revived against me, as being the heir of the lamented Snyder. But it could not be made to work much against me. I had been as little concerned in the passage of the Mormon charters as my opponent. Of course, in a State so decidedly democratic I

*Just now the public mind is in a great ferment concerning amendments of the constitution, as if amendments of the laws were a cure for every ill that flesh is heir to. Without undertaking to prove, I will venture to assert that there may be a very bad government with very good laws. The laws may be amended, but if human nature is vicious and selfish it will find a way to pervert the best of laws to the worst of purposes. I assert again that if government is to be reformed the work must begin with the people, who are, in a kind of way, the source of power. If it is once given up that the people can never be persuaded to vote wisely and judiciously, to sustain such of their servants as may be faithful and put aside all selfish demagogues who seek to live merely by the profits of office, then we may make up our minds to see government very imperfect in its practical operation under any form of constitution whatever. The Utopians and Perfectionists then will have nothing to do but to lay aside their fine, sun-shiny theories and live in the world the little time that is allotted to them, contented with the imperfections of government as they are obliged to be with the imperfections of everything else.

was elected by a large majority. The banks, the State debt, the canal, and the Mormons, together with the general politics of the Union, were the principal topics of discussion during the canvass. Topics of local interest, however, had but little influence on the result of the election. The people of Illinois were so thoroughly partisan upon the great question of the nation that matters merely of local concern, though of vital importance to the people, were disregarded.

To sum up, then, this was the condition of the State when I came into office as governor. The domestic treasury of the State was indebted for the ordinary expenses of government to the amount of about $313,000. Auditor's warrants on the treasury were selling at fifty per cent discount, and there was no money in the treasury whatever; not even to pay postage on letters. The annual revenues applicable to the payment of ordinary expenses, amounted to about $130,000. The treasury was bankrupt; the revenues were insufficient; the people were unable and unwilling to pay high taxes; and the State had borrowed itself out of all credit. A debt of near fourteen millions of dollars had been contracted for the canal, railroads, and other purposes. The currency of the State had been annihilated; there was not over two or three hundred thousand dollars in good money in the pockets of the whole people, which occasioned a general inability to pay taxes. The whole people were indebted to the merchants; nearly all of whom were indebted to the banks, or to foreign merchants; and the banks owed everybody; and none was able to pay.

To many persons it seemed impossible to devise any system of policy out of this jumble and chaos of confusion which would relieve the State. Every one had his plan, and the confusion of counsels among prominent men was equalled only by the confusion of public affairs.

IX

Financial Ills and Legislative Remedies, 1842

Obstructions to the success of wise policy which would relieve the State from these multiplied evils were to be found in the character, varieties, and genius of the masses of the people; and in the motives, aims, and enterprises of politicians; some account of which is necessary to a right understanding of the future action of government. The State is about four hundred miles long from north to south and about one hundred and fifty miles wide from east to west. This shape of the State naturally divided the legislature into representatives from the south and representatives from the north, and under any circumstances a State so long in proportion to its breadth must contain much of the elements of discord. The southern portion of the State was settled principally by people from the slaveholding States; the north principally from New York and New England. The southern people were generally poor; they were such as were not able to own slaves in a slave State, and who came here to avoid slavery. A poor white man in a slave State is of little more importance in the eyes of the wealthy than the negroes. The very negroes of the rich call such poor persons "poor white folks." The wealthy immigrant from the slave States rarely came here. He moved to some new slave State, to which he could take his negroes. The consequence was that our southern settlements presented but few specimens of the more wealthy, enterprising, intellectual, and cultivated people from the slave States. Those who did come were a very good, honest, kind, hospitable people, unambitious of wealth and great lovers of ease and social enjoyment.

The settlers from the North, not being debarred by our Constitution from bringing their property with them, were of a different class. The northern part of the State was settled in the first instance by wealthy farmers, enterprising merchants, millers, and manufacturers. They made farms, built mills, churches, school-houses, towns, and cities; and made roads and bridges as if by magic; so that although the settlements in the southern part of the State are twenty, thirty, forty, and fifty years in advance on the score of age, yet they are ten years behind in point of wealth and all the appliances of a higher civilization.

This of itself was cause enough for discord between the two ends of the State. The people of the south entertained a most despicable opinion of their northern neighbors. They had never seen the genuine Yankee. They had seen a skinning, trafficking, and tricky race of peddlers from New England who much infested the West and South with tin ware, small assortments of merchandise, and wooden clocks; and they supposed that the whole of the New England people were like these specimens. They formed the opinion that a genuine Yankee was a close, miserly, dishonest, selfish getter of money, void of generosity, hospitality, or any of the kindlier feelings of human nature. The northern people formed equally as unfavorable an opinion of their southern neighbors. The northern man believed the southerner to be a long, lank, lean, lazy, and ignorant animal, but little in advance of the savage state; one who was content to squat in a log-cabin with a large family of ill-fed and ill-clothed, idle, ignorant children. The truth was both parties were wrong. There is much natural shrewdness and sagacity in the most ignorant of the southern people; and they are generally accumulating property as fast as any people can who had so little to begin with. The parties are about equal in point of generosity and liberality, though these virtues show themselves in each people in a different way. The southerner is perhaps the most hospitable and generous to individuals. He is lavish of his victuals, his liquors, and other personal favors. But the northern man is the most liberal in contributing to whatever is for the public benefit. Is a school-house, a bridge, or a church to be built, a road to be made, a school or a minister to be maintained or taxes to be paid for the honor or support of government, the northern man is never found wanting.

This misconception of character was the cause of a good deal of misunderstanding. The great canal itself, from Lake Michigan to the Illinois river, was opposed by some at an early day for fear it would open a way for flooding the State with Yankees. Even as popular a man as the late Lieutenant-Governor Kinney opposed it in a speech in the Senate on this ground. He said the Yankees spread everywhere. He was looking daily for them to overrun this State. They could be found in every country on the globe; and one strong proof to him that John Cleves Symmes was wrong in his theory of the earth was that if such an opening at the north pole as that theory supposed really existed the Yankees would have had a big wagon road to it long before its discovery by Mr. Symmes. This want of concord in the two races of people was unfavorable to the adoption of the wisest means for public relief. In framing a wise policy for the future the success of the canal in the north was one indispensable item. But because it was in the north, and for no other reason that I can discover, it was liable to objection in other quarters.

Another obstacle of a like character was to be found in the motives, aims, and designs of politicians. As yet the people rarely elected members of the legislature with reference to any well defined notions of State policy. As I have said before both parties were so thoroughly partisan upon the great contests upon national questions that local affairs were but little considered. Sometimes some question about the removal of a county seat or the division of a county might influence an election. As between the different parties it seemed to be more important to know whether a candidate for the legislature was for or against a United States Bank, a protective tariff, internal improvements by the federal government, or distributing the proceeds of the public lands; in fine, to know whether he was a whig or a democrat than to know his opinions of State politics. Of all the local questions calculated to influence elections that of the banks, I believe, was the only one which was generally considered.

But the great prevailing principle upon which each party acted in selecting candidates for office was to get popular men. Men who had made themselves agreeable to the people by a continual show of friendship and condescension; men who were loved for their gaiety, cheerfulness, apparent goodness of heart, and agreeable manners. Surly and stubborn wisdom stood no chance for office. The proud and haughty were proscribed. The scripture proverb, "Be humble that ye may be exalted," was understood altogether in a political sense.

One would think that nature herself had fitted out and indicated those who were to be the governors of this country; that in making some men mild, humble, amiable, obliging, and condescending, in other words in fitting some men to be popular and others to be unpopular, Providence itself had selected our rulers. This, however, would be a mistake. There are hundreds of popular men who have none of these gifts by nature. I have known numbers who in spite of nature could be kind, humble, friendly, and agreeable as the best. These are talents which can be acquired by a diligent practice. A friend of mine once informed me that he intended to be a candidate for the legislature but would not declare himself until within a few days of the election, and assigned as a reason "that it was so very hard to be *clever* for a long time at once." This same man by dint of practice afterwards acquired the art of being *clever* all the time. Of all the talents which most recommend a man to his friends is that of being merry, and of laughing agreeably. Even this may be acquired. I have seen hundreds of men who were morose, serious, sour, and even sulky by nature commence by forcing themselves into merriment and laughter, and so go on that in process of time it took the nicest discernment to determine whether their cachinations were genuine or counterfeit.

Politicians generally knew better how to get an office than how to perform its duties. Statesmanship was but little studied; and indeed there is this difference all the world over between a statesman and a mere politician, that the true statesman looks to his whole country; he devises a system of measures, he sees the connection of one measure with another, and he makes them all work together for the common good; whilst the mere politician busies himself altogether in selfish projects to get office without caring much for the policy or measures he advocates after he gets into power. If he dabbles in measures at all he confines himself to something local or temporary or to measures of mere party; he is a one-idea man, for the view of his mind can never take in the whole field of public interest. Hitherto in Illinois the race of politicians has been more numerous and more popular with the people than the race of statesmen. The main reason of this has been that too many people vote to elect men as a favor to the officer, not with a view to require service from them. The elections have been made upon the principle that the officer is to be served, not the people.

Many of these politicians in the legislature made it a rule to vote against all new measures about which the opinions of the people were unknown; shrewdly calculating that if such a measure passed and became popular no one would inquire who had opposed it; but if it turned out to be unpopular, then they could show by the journals that they had voted against it. And if the measure failed of success and became popular the members who opposed it excused themselves to the people by pretending ignorance of the will of their constituents and by promising to be in its favor if again elected.

This kind of policy is said to have originated with John Grammar, long a representative or senator from Union county. He was elected to the territorial legislature about the year 1816 and was continued in the legislature most of the time for twenty years. It is said that when he was first elected, lacking the apparel necessary for a member, he and his sons gathered a large quantity of hazelnuts which were taken to the Ohio Saline and sold for cloth to make a coat and pantaloons. The cloth was the blue strouding used by the Indians for breechcloths. Then it was brought home the neighboring women were assembled to make up the garments of the new member. The cloth was measured every way, cross, lengthwise, and from corner to corner, but still the puzzling truth appeared that the pattern was scant. The women concluded to make of it a very short bob-tailed coat and a long pair of leggins, which being finished and Mr. Grammar arrayed in them, he started for Kaskaskia, the seat of government. Here he continued to wear his leggins over an old tattered garment until the poetry bill (a partial appropriation) passed, when he provided himself with a pair of breeches. Mr. Grammar was a man who could neither read nor write and yet he had the honor to originate a practice which has been much followed by men of more pretensions.

Such demagogism could not succeed in any very enlightened country. The Valley of the Mississippi had so constantly increased in numbers, so far beyond the means of education, that it is doing ourselves no injustice to admit that there is some ignorance amongst us. But this evil must be corrected; education must be more encouraged; knowledge must be made more abundant; more of the people must be taught the power of thinking. An elevated, numerous democracy must be created, which shall destroy the power of the few who monopolize intellect. Intellectual power is power of the most fearful kind; and it is folly to talk of equal rights and equal laws where some few have it and the many have it not. Where this is the case it is folly to talk of self-government. An ignorant people who attempt self-government are, by a fixed law of nature, obliged to fail in the attempt; they may think that they govern themselves when they are only led by the nose by their demagogues. A government of demagogues is only better than anarchy.

The members of the legislature, after having been elected, feeling victorious and triumphant over their adversaries at home, come up to the seat of government in a happy state of exaltation of mind and self-complacency which makes the compliments and flattery with which they are received most soothing and agreeable. The whole world of aspirants for office comes with them. A speaker of the lower house and officers of the two houses are to be elected the first thing. For these offices there are many candidates. I have known more than a hundred candidates for door-keepers of the two houses. Besides these, there are numerous candidates for secretaryships and clerkships. The members exhibit themselves in public places, where they can be approached, complimented, flattered, supplicated, and teased by the several aspirants for office, who fly round from one member to another with great glee and activity, making themselves agreeable, until after the election. After these elections are over there is, in two sessions out of three, a United States Senator to be elected; and every session the legislature elects an auditor of public accounts, State treasurer, public printer, attorney general, and States' attorneys for the several circuits; and fills vacancies on the bench of judges. These elections are not all brought on at once, but a few of them at a time only, so as to keep a number of aspirants at the seat of government during the whole session and husband the importance of the members of the legislature, which in a great measure would be expended and gone by more prompt action in disposing of the seekers for office.

It is during a session of the legislature that all political arrangements are made for the next campaign. Here it is decided who are to be the next candidates for governor and United States Senator, and who to go to Congress from the various districts. It is true that conventions are afterwards held to make the nominations in conformity to what is here agreed; and here too it is determined who are to be recommended for office to the general government. However much the members of the legislature may lack in learning, they are generally shrewd, sensible men, who, from their knowledge of human nature and tact in managing the masses are amongst the master spirits of their several counties. They are such generally as have cultivated the arts of popularity; know how to shake hands with the appearance of cordiality and friendship; are good-natured and social; possess a talent for smiling and laughing in a pleasing way; and of saying agreeable things in conversation. The great majority of them are fired with an ambition either to get back to the legislature or to be elected or appointed to some other office. This puts them upon the alert to preserve their popularity. New measures are considered more with reference to the reception they may meet with at home than to their utility or wisdom. The question in such a case is, how will such a measure take with the people? how can an adversary in his own or the opposite party build an objection on it to the member who has voted for or against it? and how is it to affect his next election, or his party standing? Many members thus guess their way through a whole session; and experience has proved that they have oftener guessed wrong than right; for a fifth part of them never get back to the legislature, and those who do are such as consider the wisdom and soundness of measures, such as have the courage, the ability, and go home with the determination, to defend their acts by an appeal to the judgments of their fellow citizens.

Very many public men for the sake of present popularity do wrong knowingly to secure future power which they may never get. If it were the practice for no one ever to seek or decline office, to be contented without it, and to accept it as a mere duty, then there would be no motive to do wrong, but every motive to do good, during a short continuance of power. But this I fear can never be carried out in practice. The office seeking propensity is wonderful indeed; there seems to be no sufficient reason for it. Office is not clothed with the profit, power, or honor to make it desirable for either. We every day see private men who are more honored and wealthy than any who are in office. In our government the jealousy of liberty disarms all offices of power; the popular notions of economy will not allow them to be profitable; nearly one-half the people in party times, so far from honoring a public officer take a pleasure in despising him; and the leaders among his own political friends, unless he is the great leader of a party, will take care that he shall not have much credit.

The out-door politicians, who are called "lobby members," and who come up to the seat of government for office, are much like the members themselves except that they are more talented and cunning. They are men who take to politics as a trade and business and means of living. They seek to control the legislature in the disposal of offices, and are themselves divided into a hundred little cliques and factions working with or against each other as concurrence or opposition may be most advantageous.

A popular member of the lobby is apt to be some lawyer who practices in several counties. He gets acquainted with the leading men of his party in each county. He aids in getting popular men nominated as candidates for the legislature. He makes speeches for the cause and aids his friends to be elected. As he is naturally superior to them, it is no wonder if they look to him for advice and assistance in performing their arduous duties. By such means he will contrive to control four or five members of the legislature. This he will make known to all the world but the members themselves. He is then looked to as a man of importance. He has so many transferable votes in the legislature. He is courted, caressed, and promised support in his own views in return for his countenance to the projects of others. A lobby member will make but a poor figure without some such capital; and as he comes to the seat of government only as a seeker of office he never troubles himself about measures unless they are strictly of a party character. Other great measures which may make or ruin the country he takes no interest in, unless they can be made helpers to office. In and out of the legislature the machinery of government is more considered than the measures of government. The frequent legislative elections; the running to and fro of the various cliques and factions before each election; the anxiety of members for their popularity at home; the settlement of plans to control future elections, to sustain the party in power on the one side and to overthrow it on the part of the minority, absorb nearly the whole attention of the legislature and leave but little disposition or time to be devoted to legitimate legislation. So much is this the case that the most important measures, such as may have the greatest influence upon the well-being of the present and all future generations, pass through the two houses or are rejected almost without debate and frequently without notice. Of the many common-school laws which have passed our legislature I have never known but one which called forth any general interest.

There are two kinds of professional politicians; though they both aim at the same thing,—the acquisition of office. The one sort are clever, timid, moderate, and accommodating; the other kind are bold, sanguine, and decided. The first sort will agree for the time being to anything and with anybody. These men aim to be affable, pleasant, facetious, and agreeable. They make it a matter of calculation never to contradict, to advocate no opinion, to give no offence, to make no enemies, and to be amiable and agreeable to all. They are called by the others "milk and water men," and are much despised by the bold, decided ultraist. Sometimes the "milk and water" man has the advantage; for as he swims and slides easily and smoothly along, never contradicting, accommodating to all, and friendly to all, he has frequently to be taken up in party contests as the most available candidate. The other sort of professed politicians are the men of energy and action. They are the foremost in the fight with the common enemy. They are the orators for the people; the writers for the newspapers; the organizers and disciplinarians of party; the denouncers of treachery and defection; and work night and day for victory in the party contests. They are always much despised by the opposite party in politics; and are always selected as especial objects of abuse and detraction. The minority party frequently has credit enough to destroy the popularity of a champion of the enemy, even with his own party. He is hated among the best men of his opponents. These opponents may have no direct political influence out of their own ranks; but many of them are credited as gentlemen of veracity; their statements in relation to mere persons are believed, even by political opponents. These statements, though often prompted by political hatred, are uttered boldly and with an appearance of candor by men who are fair dealers, good neighbors, and known to speak the truth in all matters of neighborhood concernment. The popularity of the champion is destroyed. He cannot get all the votes of his own party, and not one from amongst his opponents. He is no longer considered to be an available candidate and has to give place, in all doubtful contests, to his inoffensive milk and water compatriot. For it is a rule with all parties to select only such candidates as can get the largest vote.

A politician, however, of the decided, sanguine kind, if he is a man of sense and tact, if he knows how far to go in the advocacy of his own party and when to stop; if he knows how to abuse the opposite party without giving personal offence; is in the surest road to advancement. This kind of politician is most usually for extreme measures. Nothing moderate will suit him. He must be in advance of everybody else. He aims to be a leader; and to be one he thinks he must be ahead in everything. In the democratic party he is an ultraist; he can hardly find measures sufficiently democratic to suit him. He is a tactician, a disciplinarian; ever belongs to some organization; never bolts a nomination and never votes against his own party. In the whig party he is an old federalist; he has no confidence in the people for self-government; he is in favor of a property qualification for electors and is always against the democrats, right or wrong, and against everything democratic, and firmly believes all the time that the country is just going to be ruined. But in whatever party he may be, whenever that party is dominant he aims to be considered a better party man, to work truer in the party harness than any one else, and if he can so distinguish himself he mounts at once to the leadership. All the active office-seeking tribe are first his allies and afterwards his followers. It is a fact well known that one party is governed by the office-holders and the other by the office-hunters.

Under such circumstances it would be strange indeed if there had been much disposition anywhere to make the future prosperity of the State a consideration paramount to all others.*

Before I came into office the public mind was settled on nothing as the future policy of the State. The people of Bond county, as soon as the internal improvement system passed, had declared in a public meeting that the system must lead to taxation and utter ruin; that the people were not bound to pay any of the debt to be contracted for it; and that Bond county would never assist in paying a cent of it.

---

*When Galena was first settled it is said that the only question asked concerning a newcomer was, whether he would steal or not? If it was answered that he would not steal he was considered a very honest man. So in elections it was now asked only whether a candidate was a whig or a democrat? If the answer to this was satisfactory the candidate was considered to be safe and a great statesman.

Accordingly, they refused to pay taxes for several years. When the system went down and had left the State in the ruinous condition predicted by the Bond county meeting many people remembered that there might be a question raised as to the obligation of payment. Public men everywhere, of all parties, stood in awe of this question; there was a kind of general silence as to what should be done. No one could foresee what would be popular or unpopular. The two great political parties were watching each other with eagle eyes to see that one should not get the advantage of the other. The whigs, driven to desperation by repeated ill success in elections, were many of them in favor of repudiation as a means of bettering their party. The Sangamon *Journal* and the Alton *Telegraph*, the two leading whig newspapers of the State, boldly took ground that the debt never could and never would be paid and that it was of no use to say anything more about it. Very many democrats were in favor of the same course, for fear of losing the power the democratic party already possessed. It was thought to be a very dangerous subject to meddle with. At a democratic convention which nominated Mr. Snyder for governor a resolution against repudiation, offered by Mr. Arnold of Chicago, was laid on the table by an overwhelming vote of the convention, so as not to commit the party one way or the other.[1] It was evident that this was to be a troublesome question; and a great many of the politicians on both sides were as ready to take one side of it as the other; and their choice depended upon which might finally appear to be most popular. The whigs were afraid if they advocated the debt-paying policy the democrats would take the other side and leave the whigs no chance of ever coming into a majority. And the democrats feared that if they advocated a correct policy the other side might be more popular, and might be taken by the whigs. I speak only of the leaders of parties, amongst whom on all sides there was a strong suspicion that repudiation might be more popular than taxation.

It is my solemn belief that when I came into office I had the power to make Illinois a repudiating State. It is true I was not the leader of any party; but my position as governor would have given me leadership enough to have carried the democratic party, except in a few counties in the north, in favor of repudiation. If I had merely stood still and done nothing the result would have been the same. In that case a majority of both parties would have led to either active or passive repudiation. The politicians on neither side, without a bold lead to the contrary by some one high in office, would never have dared to risk their popularity by being the first to advocate an increase of taxes to be paid by a tax-hating people.

Such were the people and such were the great mass of politicians of the State of Illinois in 1842. In general, the legislature meant to do right and to do the best for the country; but here, as everywhere else, there were serious obstacles to contend with before the policy of the country in reference to the deplorable state of public affairs could be settled upon the best footing. I have already said that every one had a plan of his own to restore the State to prosperity; and it may not be improper to devote a page or two to some of them.

All parties proposed some mode of putting the banks into liquidation, except a few whigs and a very few democrats who would have been willing to compel them to a resumption of specie payments and continue their business. Of those who were in favor of winding them up a small portion declared in favor of repealing their charters; of the appointment of commissioners on the part of the State who were to take charge of their specie and other effects, pay their debts, and collect what was due to them. But much the larger portion finally favored a compromise by means of which the State would at once be paid for its stock, or nearly so; and the banks would settle their business and go out of existence under the direction of their own officers. The State Bank held $1,750,000 of State bonds and $294,000 in Auditor's warrants, together with scrip amounting in the whole to $2,100,000, which it was willing to surrender at once and dissolve all further connection with the State. The bank at Shawneetown was willing to surrender a half-a-million immediately and to engage to pay the residue on a short credit. This bank held $469,998 in Auditor's warrants which were to be surrendered as part of the first payment.

There was no party in the legislature 1842–43 in favor of an immediate increase of taxation to pay interest on the public debt. Many there were who wanted to do nothing for five or ten years; and to trust to luck and accident for the means of improvement. There were a very few who were in favor of repudiating the whole debt of the State, who denied the power of the legislature to bind the people by contracting it; and who were in favor of giving up to the public creditor all the property purchased with the borrowed money and all the public works constructed by it, as all that ever could or ought to be done in the way of payment. But the great majority of the legislature held different opinions. Resolutions were passed which clearly stated the inability of the State to meet its engagements and fully recognized our moral and legal obligation to provide for ultimate payment. To pay immediately was out of the question. Heavy taxation then would have depopulated the country and the debt would never be paid.

The State had purchased 42,000 acres of land under the internal improvement system; the United States had given us 210,000 acres more under the distribution law of 1841; we owned 230,467 acres of canal lands and 3,491 town lots in Chicago and other towns on the canal; we owned what work had been done on the canal itself; and various pieces of unfinished railroad in all parts of the State. And we also owned a large quantity of railroad iron and the stock in the banks. This property was our only resource short of taxation to pay the whole debt, and it became us to apply it to the best advantage.

One party proposed that an offer to the public creditors should be made of this property upon condition that they would finish the canal and as many of the railroads as they might choose to finish, and grant an acquittance of the whole debt by a surrender of public securities. It was evident that this plan could not succeed. Many of the State bonds were held in trust for orphans and for charitable purposes. The holders of such could not consent to, and if they did they could not comply with such an arrangement. But the larger portion of our debt was owned by heavy capitalists whose business it was to lend money to States and nations on a mere pledge of the public faith. It was clear that this class could better afford to lose all we owed them than to set the example of such a compromise to the borrowing world. If they made such an arrangement with Illinois they must soon expect similar propositions from all other indebted States. Such an example would be contagious and would put an end to their business of lending by destroying the only security a nation can give— an unsullied public faith.

There were some few persons who were in favor of repudiating the whole debt, of setting the moral sense of mankind at defiance, and of absolutely doing nothing, and worse than nothing; for they proposed that in winding up the banks, by a total repeal of their charters, the public securities held by these institutions and which they were willing to surrender to the State in payment of its stock, should be put into the market and sold as assets; and that if after payment of the debts of the banks anything should be left to be divided among the stockholders, the share coming to the State should be used to purchase an equal sum in bonds.

During the summer of 1842 Justin Butterfield, an eminent lawyer of Chicago, had conversed with Arthur Bronson,* one of the great

*Extract of a letter from George R. Babcock Esq., of the city of Buffalo, N.Y., to Justin Butterfield Esq., of Chicago, Illinois: "I have a distinct remembrance that Mr. Bronson spoke to you in the summer of 1841 at Chicago, on the subject of the unfinished canal; and asked if anything to render available the large expen-

capitalists of New York, who was interested in our State stocks and a large landholder in the northern part of the State. Mr. Bronson was said to be a man of fine talents, deeply skilled in finance, and to possess the confidence of capitalists both in Europe and America. Mr. Butterfield suggested to Mr. Bronson that if the canal property could be conveyed in trust to secure a new advance of money, and if the State creditors could be assured that the State intended to do something by way of taxation or otherwise to sustain its credit, something might be done to obtain money to complete the canal; which was agreed to by Mr. Bronson. Mr. Butterfield repeated this conversation to Mr. Michael Ryan; and Mr. Ryan, being afterwards at New York, became acquainted with Mr. Bronson, Mr. Leavitt, and other wealthy persons of the eastern cities and of London. A plan was then devised, and approved by them, in pursuance of the suggestions of Mr. Butterfield, to the effect that the holders of canal bonds would advance $1,600,000 (the sum reported to be necessary by the chief engineer) to complete the canal. In return for which, the State was to convey the canal property in trust to secure the new loan, as well as for the ultimate payment of the whole canal debt; and was to lay some moderate tax to pay some portion of the accruing interest on the whole debt.

---

diture which had been made upon; and to rescue the credit of the State from the abyss in which it was plunged. You replied, in substance, that the work would sooner or later be resumed; that a State so large and containing such elements of future greatness as Illinois would at some day not distant complete a work so essential to its prosperity, and that the canal and the canal lands would reimburse the cost of its construction. Mr. Bronson seemed gratified to find you so sanguine in your expectations and invited you to meet him at the Lake House that evening to confer farther on the subject of its details. In the evening there was a long discussion, mainly between Mr. Bronson and yourself, of the project, which, as I understand it, has been subsequently carried out by the State and its creditors. The leading feature of the plan, as I recollect it, was to induce the bondholders to advance the funds necessary to complete the canal by a pledge of the canal, its lands, and revenues for the payment of the advance, and a stipulated priority of the payment of the stocks then held by the persons so making the advance; while those creditors who refused to contribute were to be postponed until the preferred debt should be discharged. I cannot say who suggested this plan, as I was not in the room when the conversation commenced. Mr. Bronson frequently expressed fears that the foreign bondholders would regard the offered priority as a lure to obtain more cash, as well as a fraud on those of their fellow sufferers who should not make the required advance. For this reason, I am of opinion that the plan was not suggested by Mr. Bronson. . . .

"GEORGE R. BABCOCK."

It is due to Mr. Butterfield to say, that he mentioned this plan of getting money for the canal, and of the foregoing conversation with Mr. Bronson, some considerable time before Ryan's visit to New York in the fall of 1842. Mr. Butterfield also is entitled to the credit of drawing the canal bill of 1842–43, which was much more perfect when it came from his hands than after it had passed the legislature.

Intimately connected with the success of this plan was the legislation we might adopt on the subject of the banks. If we proceeded with an insane violence, by repealing their charters at the very moment that we were chartering a company and inviting the investment of money to complete the canal, we could expect no less than to frighten capitalists away from the undertaking. We would show them at once that we professed to have the power, and in all probability would exercise it, to repeal the new one as well as the old. But there was a part of the democrats who believed in the right of the legislature to repeal all acts of incorporation, as well private as public. They had been fighting on this question for years and now was a good opportunity for putting it in force. The banks were odious to the people for long continued and repeated delinquencies. It was certain to be popular to be in favor of the most extreme measures against them; so that when it became a question whether they should be strangled to death by slow degrees or delivered over to be scalped and tomahawked with barbarian ferocity many of the professional politicians decided for the most ultra course. This course, was indeed, the best for the politician, but it was the worst for the country. The politician might increase his reputation in his party, he might earn the name of a smashing democrat, but the canal would never be made and nothing would be done to restore the public credit.

Gov. Carlin, my immediate predecessor, though confessedly an honest man in his private dealings, recommended repeal in his valedictory message. When he first came to the seat of government he showed me his message, recommending wise, just, and honorable measures to the banks. He also showed me what he had prepared on the subject of repeal, assuring me that he had decided not to put it in. But shortly afterwards some of the ultraists got hold of him and induced him to alter his message by recommending repeal. This recommendation embarrassed me then and has embarrassed me ever since. Here was a respectable recommendation of something more ultra than I thought was warranted by the best interests of the State. It gave countenance to the ultraists; they could rally around it—win a character for stern and inflexible democrats. It at once put them ahead of the new governor and his friends. By the way, I will here remark that it is the constant trick of the wily, artful politician to affect ultraism. Many of them are without talents or merits of any other sort; and if they were not a little ahead of everybody else in espousing extreme measures there would be nothing of them at all. Gov. Carlin also, in his last message, despaired of the canal. He had not the genius to see how money might be raised to complete it except by petitioning Congress for an increased donation of land, then certain never to be granted.

There was quite a party out of the legislature, expectants of office and others, who hoped that if the banks were repealed out of existence and put into forcible liquidation some of them might be appointed commissioners and put in charge of their specie and effects. It was known that if the bank debts were paid *pro rata,* a large amount of specie would remain on hand for a year or more; the use of which could be made profitable in the meantime. Then there were to be bank attorneys and agents in collecting and securing debts; and the whole would furnish a handsome picking for the buzzards and vultures who hang about lobbies and surround legislatures.

As for myself, I decided at once in favor of a compromise; and I gave notice to all these greedy expectants of office who were hanging around with eyes straining to devour their substance that if the banks were repealed and the appointment of commissioners were vested in me none of them could expect an appointment. This I know cooled some of them.

This was the most important subject which came before the legislature of 1842. State stock to the amount of $3,100,000 was at stake; the canal depended upon it; and it may be worth while to give a short statement of the argument on each side of the question.

It was said in favor of repeal that the banks had so many times baffled the legislature the most decisive steps ought to be taken with them so as to put them to an end at once. The legislature ought to make sure work of it at once, now that they were assembled and had the power. The fact that they had violated their charters was notorious; the decision of which ought not to be left to the doubtful chance of a suit at law in the courts. That the charters ought to be repealed totally, so as forever to prevent the chance of their revival or resurrection by any future legislature. The bonds held by the banks ought to be sold to help pay their debts. The State as a stockholder had no more right than another to be paid for its stock and retire from the concern before the bank debts were paid. The specie would never be paid out *pro rata;* the circulation had been purchased and was now held by private stockholders, who would refuse to present it for payment in hopes that another legislature would renew their charters. The most stringent laws might be passed for the government of the banks, yet experience had shown that as long as they had life they would set all laws at defiance as soon as the Assembly adjourned; and the legislature would have to do at the next session what they had omitted to do now. The compromise proposed was a bad bargain for the State. The stock was worth more than the bonds; the assets of the banks were amply sufficient to pay all their debts and a dividend to the State as a stockholder which would greatly exceed the value of these bonds.

On the side of a compromise it was argued that if the banks had ever baffled the legislature it was in the day of their power when their bills were in credit, and they had money to lend to individuals and to pay the legislature. In the day of their power they had friends, many of whom were the first to desert them in their troubles and weakness. They were shorn of their strength. There were none so poor now as to do them reverence. It was folly to talk of the power of a broken bank in universal discredit with the people. They were too deeply and generally despised for any legislature of any party to revive them. It was just as likely that the internal improvement system would be revived. It would be the height of folly to suffer the bonds held by the banks to be sold. At present they were selling for only fourteen cents on the dollar. If $2,500,000 were added to those already in the market the price must be greatly reduced. If we rejected an offer to get them up at once on such favorable terms and depended on a doubtful dividend to re-purchase them at a discount, if we declared it our policy to go into the market like a common swindler to purchase our own paper at less than its face, the whole world would know that we never intended to pay one cent of the public debt. A sale under such circumstances would be of but little use to the banks or their creditors, but would subject the State to certain loss or disgrace.

The advocates of repeal say that the banks are insolvent and cannot pay their debts if the bonds are not sold; in the next breath they say that the State is making a bad bargain; that the stock is worth more than the bonds, when it is plain that the stock is worth nothing unless the banks pay every dollar of their debt. But the truth is, the banks can pay their debts and will have something left for the stockholders. The creditors are in no danger of eventual loss. But if repeal is to succeed; if their specie and other effects are to be given in charge to public officers; neither creditors nor stockholders may ever get anything. Who are these public officers to be? Are they to be the public officers who mismanaged the old State Bank of 1821 and lost to the State more than its entire capital? Are they to be some of the late fund commissioners, whose blunders saddled the State with a million and a half of dollars in debt for which the first cent was never received? Are they to be the commissioners of the board of public works, whose reckless squandering of the public moneys will be memorable while time lasts? Or are they to be any of the same description of persons? And more particularly, are they to be taken from the hangers-on about the seat of government? We have had enough in our history of the management of money matters by public officers.

The legislature might repeal, but they were not clothed with all the power of this government. The banks were determined to contest their right to repeal. The Supreme Court of the United States had already declared against it in the Dartmouth College case. They would get an injunction from the federal court against our commissioners. The case would be litigated for years at home; it would then be carried to the Supreme Court of the United States. It would be years again before a final decision, and then it was as likely to be against us as for us. In the meantime, if the bank officers were so little to be trusted what security had we that their assets would not be devoured by the expenses of litigation or squandered by dishonesty?

More than all this, repeal was a violent measure. It was calculated to alarm capitalists. We were about to incorporate a company to complete the canal. We were not able to do it ourselves; our only hope was in a company. Capitalists, from whom alone the money to do it could be expected, would reasonably conclude that such a government could not be trusted. They might subscribe to the stock, expend their money, make the canal, and then some hurrah of a popular excitement would result in repealing them out of their rights.

It seemed to me that the arguments in favor of a compromise were conclusive on every point. The villainies charged upon the new owners of the Shawneetown Bank before the compromise bill passed were no worse than what could have been committed before any law whatever could have been passed by this legislature. No such law can be passed in less than six weeks and before the end of such a period a roguish directory could have committed much worse villainies than any which have been charged, and such would most probably have been committed, and no repealing act or after legislation could, as it did not, reach the mischief. But what availed argument or reason against the rapacity of hungry buzzards hunting profitable office, or against the low ambition of the professed politician who ever stands ready to sacrifice the best interest of his country so that he may be reckoned a first-rate party man; one of your "whole hog" fellows; and by such means stand on vantage ground as a candidate for office. Thank God, there were but few such patriots in the legislature.

A bill was brought into the House of Representatives in favor of a compromise with the State Bank and this important measure passed that body by a vote of 107 in the affirmative and 4 against it, on the ayes and noes as follows: Those who voted in the affirmative, were Messrs. Adams, Aldrich, Andrus, Arnold, Bailhache, Bibbons, Bishop, Blair, Blakeman, Bone, Bradley, Brown of Pike, Brown of Sangamon, Browning, Bryant, Burklow, Busey, Caldwell, Canady, Cloud, Cochran, Collins, Compton, Cartwright, Davis of Bond, Davis of Williamson, Dickinson, Dollins, Dougherty, Douglas, Dubois, Edwards, Epler, Ervin, Ewing, Ficklin, Flanders, Fowler, Garrett, Glass, Gobble, Graves, Gregg, Green of Clay, Green of Greene, Haley, Hambaugh, Hannaford, Hanson, Harper, Hatch, Hick, Hicks, Hinton, Horney, Howard, Hunsaker, Jackson of McHenry, Jackson of Whiteside, Jonas, Kendall, Koerner, Kuykendall, Longworthy, Lawler, Lockhard, Logan, McBride, McClernand, McDonald of Calhoun, McDonald of Joe Daviess, McMillan, Manning, Miller, Mitchell, Murphy, Nesbit, Norris, Owen, Penn, Pickering, Pratt, Scott, Sharp, Shirley, Simms, Smith of Crawford, Smith of Hancock, Spicer, Starne, Starr, Stewart, Stockton, Tackerberry, Thompson, Vance, Vandeveer, Vinyard, West, Weatherford, Wheat, Whitcomb, White, Whitten, Woodworth, Yates, and Mr. Speaker—107.

Those who voted in the negative were: Messrs. Ames, Bell, Brinkley, and Loy—4.

This bill was drawn up by myself and agreed to by the bank. It was then shown to Mr. McClernand, the chairman of the finance committee of the lower house. The chairman called a meeting of the democratic members of his committee. Gen. Shields, Judge Douglas, and myself were invited to be present at their meeting. I was desirous of having the measure introduced as a democratic measure and for this reason the whigs of the committee were not invited to be present. The project was stated to the committee and all the members agreed to it but one, and he was soon argued out of his objections by Judge Douglas. The next day it was introduced into the lower house as a report from the finance committee. This circumstance put Mr. McClernand in the position of being its principal advocate; and it was soon known to be a favorite measure of the new administration. It at once met the approbation of all men of sense in the house; and in saying this I say only the truth of those four gentlemen who opposed it, none of whom, though respectable in other matters, to my certain knowledge was capable of entertaining two ideas about public affairs at the same time, of tracing the connection between them, or of conceiving the bare idea of a comprehensive system of State policy.

The opposition to the bill as yet was confined to the out-door hangers-on about the seat of government, many of whom expected, if the banks were repealed and put into forcible liquidation, to get some profitable jobs as commissioners and attorneys. Lyman Trumbull, Secretary of State, put himself at the head of this opposition. In taking this ground Mr. Trumbull was probably less influenced by a hope of pecuniary advantage to himself than by a desire to serve his friends, to be considered a thorough-going party man, and by a hatred of McClernand and Shields, who both favored the measure. His quarrel with McClernand sprung out of his appointment to the office of Secretary of State two years before.

McClernand was a member of the legislature in 1840, but not being an applicant then, Judge Douglas was appointed at the beginning of the session without opposition. But when Douglas was elected a judge of the supreme court towards the end of the session, McClernand incited his friends to get up in his favor a strong recommendation from the members of the legislature for the vacant office. It had been much the practice heretofore for the legislature to dictate to the governor by recommendation. A popular man in former times would be an applicant for an office. He got his friends in the legislature to sign a request that he might have the appointment. The governor was feeble and clothed with but little authority. The legislature came fresh from the people and were clothed with almost the entire power of government. They were soon to return again to their constituents. If the governor refused to oblige them they calumniated and denounced him and endeavored to render him odious to the people after their return home. Besides this, the legislature possessed most of the appointing power themselves. The governor might want some office himself in the future, and he always had a number of friends for whose sake he desired an influence with the assembly. In this view, the governor for the time being himself was usually obliged to be a kind of lobby member; and not infrequently might be classed as one of the hangers-on about the seat of government seeking to control the legislature in the bestowment of offices. He dreaded the anger of the members and would do everything to please them or to avoid their displeasure. In this mode the independence of the executive government was subverted, the two houses were tampered with and controlled, and the two branches of government, intended to be kept separate in their action, were blended and almost amalgamated into one. This will be looked upon as an evil. But as there are three distinct wills to be consulted in all matters of legislation it is perhaps, in the present state of imperfection of human nature, necessary that they should thus mutually operate on each other in order to produce that harmony of action which leads to concurrence in one direction.

It is true that the executive and legislative powers are intended to be kept separate, and although they are in point of fact frequently blended into one, yet on great occasions when the public liberties might be endangered by their union the power of resistance is still capable of being exerted by each department.

But to go back to the quarrel between McClernand and Trumbull. Governor Carlin had already allowed the members of the legislature and his political friends to dictate to him the appointment of McClernand on a former occasion. He had lately yielded to similar dictation in the appointment of Douglas, in opposition to his own wishes; for he had previously promised the office to Isaac N. Morris of Quincy. He had in fact invited Morris to Springfield to receive the appointment. But on the arrival of the governor at the seat of government he was saluted with a legislative recommendation in favor of Douglas which at that time, the beginning of the session, he was unwilling to refuse. Douglas was appointed; and the governor in his turn subsequently used his influence with the legislature to get Morris elected to the office of president of the board of canal commissioners.

But this contest between McClernand and Trumbull took place at the close of the session when the governor had nothing more to hope or to fear from that legislature or any other during the balance of his term. This made him more independent, and he now resolved to resist legislative dictation.

Trumbull was nominated to the Senate; and McClernand and Shields immediately went to work in that body to procure the rejection of his appointment. They came within a vote or two of defeating his nomination.

Ever since this there had been no good feeling between McClernand and Trumbull. As soon as McClernand took his position on the bank question, Trumbull arrayed himself in opposition. He pretended that McClernand's measure was not sufficiently democratic; in fact, that nothing could be democratic in relation to the banks but to tear them up and destroy them root and branch; and he hoped to fasten upon McClernand the imputation of being a "milk and water democrat" and thus lower him in the estimation of the party. At the instance of Ebenezer Peck, the clerk of the supreme court, and some others he put up a notice that he would address the lobby on the subject in the evening after the legislature had adjourned. Most of the members attended to hear his discourse. In this speech he put forth many of the common arguments against banks; and most of the objections heretofore stated to the compromise bill.

The next day McClernand, who possessed a kind of bold and

denunciatory eloquence, came down upon Trumbull and his confederates in a speech in the House; which for argument, eloquence, and statesmanship was far superior to Trumbull's. This speech silenced all opposition thereafter to the bill in the House of Representatives.[2]

The out-door opposition after this, foreseeing a signal defeat in the House, turned their attention to the Senate. This body was composed of fewer members and it was hoped would be more easily managed than a more numerous assembly like the lower House. One of the Senators was put at the head of it who was a man of but a poor education and narrow capacity and had adopted the profession of the law.[3] His first schooling in the practice was as a justice of the peace, in the course of which he learned more of the captious pettifogging arts of his profession than of the science of jurisprudence. He was afterwards elected to the legislature, and here he supported the railroad system. He had been one of the most zealous supporters of that disastrous measure; but he was yet impudently confident in the infallibility of his own judgment, just as though he had never so greatly erred. He was next elected by the legislature to be a judge of the circuit court. As a judge he knew just enough of law and had practiced enough in its quibbles to obliterate from his heart the instinct in favor of natural justice, without supplying its place by the lights of science. In this capacity he seemed to think that the great secret of judicature consisted in giving full effect to quibbles and technical objections, so much so that it was a rare thing for substantial justice to be done in any case before him. An unlearned lawyer or judge with a cramped understanding like his is almost sure to take up the idea that the true way to win a reputation is to show a superior dexterity in finding and giving effect to learned quibbles and trifles, to the total neglect of the great principles of law and justice. He forgets that courts were established to do right between man and man, and only remembers the forms of proceeding. These forms he looks upon as something sacred and holy, and are not to be jostled aside by the demands of natural right. A more enlightened judge places his glory in showing that he is not ignorant of the little sort of learning, and in finding good legal reasons for making it all bend to the great object of all judicature, the administration of substantial justice.

This man was also one of those small-minded men who, as speakers, are always equal on every subject. If he spoke upon a small subject he would raise it and magnify it; if upon a large one, he would reduce it and belittle it to suit his capacity. If he spoke upon a great subject involving the discussion of great principles and the expression of great ideas his mode would make them look small. Any one seeing such things through the medium of one of his speeches would think he saw a large object through a telescope with the little end foremost, which makes objects that are large and near at hand appear to be very far off and very little.

He was elected to the senate in 1840. At that session he voted under executive influence for the bank suspension of that year, and for the State Bank to have the privilege of issuing one-dollar notes. In 1841 he was a candidate for Congress and found himself very unpopular with the democratic party in consequence of this vote, so that he was beaten in his election by a very large majority. In 1842 he undertook to recover the confidence of the party by more than ordinary violence against banks. He must have persuaded himself that as he had lost the confidence of his friends by too much servility to banks, the way to recover it and wipe out the memory of former delinquency was to err as far on the other side by a senseless opposition now that they had lost their power; and the interests of the State required that they should be dealt with upon principles of sound wisdom. His effort, however, did not succeed, for he has never had the confidence of any party since.

In the Senate the whole out-door opposition was let loose upon the bill. Trumbull took his stand in the lobby and sent in amendments of every sort to be proposed by Crain of Washington, Catlin of St. Clair, and others. The mode of attack was to load it down with obnoxious amendments so as to make it odious to its authors; and Trumbull openly boasted that the bill would be so altered and amended in the Senate that its framers in the House would not know their own bantling when it came back to them. From this moment I determined to remove Trumbull from the office of Secretary of State.[4] From the nature of his office he ought to have been my confidential helper and adviser; and when he found that my course was against his principles, if really it was against them, he ought to have resigned. If he did not do so I was bound, in duty to myself and to the public, to remove him and get some other person who would be willing to render this assistance. This was the principle established by the democratic party in the memorable contest between Field and McClernand.

The obnoxious amendments were rejected and the bill passed by a large majority, and was approved by the council of revision. Judge Douglas, notwithstanding he had advised the measure before the finance committee, voted against it in the council. A bill somewhat similar passed in relation to the Shawneetown Bank. By these two bills the domestic treasury of the State was at once relieved and another debt of $2,306,000 was extinguished immediately.

The legislature at this session also passed laws for the sale of State lands and property; for the reception of the distributive share of the State in the proceeds of the sales of the public lands; for the redemption of interest bonds hypothecated to Macalister and Stebbins; and for a loan of $1,600,000 to complete the Illinois and Michigan canal. By these various laws provision was made for the reduction of the State debt to the amount of eight or nine millions of dollars. This was the best that could be done, and it is wonderful, under the circumstances, that so much could be accomplished.

From this moment the affairs of the State began to brighten and improve. Auditors' warrants rose to 85 and 90 per cent. State bonds rose from 14 to 20, 30, and 40 per cent. The banks began to pay out their specie, and within three months' time the currency was restored, confidence was increased in the prospects of the State, and the tide of emigration was once more directed to Illinois.

These were all measures of intrinsic wisdom; but it is amusing to read over the high-sounding titles of the laws which were passed to carry them into effect, as if it were absolutely necessary to humbug the people into the support of the wisest measures of public policy. Accordingly, we read in the statutes of "An act to diminish the State debt, and to put the State Bank into liquidation." "An act to diminish the State debt one million of dollars, and to put the Bank of Illinois into liquidation." "An act to provide for the completion of the Illinois and Michigan canal, and for the payment of the canal debt." "An act to provide for the sale of the public property, and for the payment of the public debt;" and "An act to provide for a settlement with Macalister and Stebbins, and further to diminish the State debt." These high-sounding titles were given to these several laws with a view to set off the strong and anxious desire of the people for the reduction of the State debt against the popular prejudice against the defunct banks, which it was foreseen would be invoked to humbug the people into an opposition to these acts and those who supported them, and to build up the reckless men who had opposed them. It was probably a fair game of humbug against humbug.

The legislature at this session passed a very important law on the subject of the collection of private debts. During the inflation of the bank currency and the credit system, so called, every one had got into debt. The merchants had purchased on a credit and they had again sold on a credit. This system brought a great many goods into the State; more than the people, according to their means, ought to have consumed. But the merchants were anxious to sell and freely credited the people up to about the value of their property. The destruction of the currency made payment impossible. Such a calamity had fallen on the people only about twenty years before; and if a capacity had existed of being profited by experience, it ought now to have been avoided. But it is lamentably true that communities in the aggregate scarcely ever profit by the lessons of experience. The same evils and calamities, and from the same causes, occur again and again and find the people as little expecting them, every time they are repeated, as they were before; and they are every time just as blind about the remedy.

The people in 1820 had brought the same evils on themselves. They then sought a remedy in a State bank with stays of execution. The bank policy was now too odious to be thought of; but the legislature this time adopted a novel expedient which had not been thought of by any former legislature in the world. They passed a law providing that when an execution was levied upon property the property should be appraised by three householders under oath to its value in *"ordinary times;"* and no such property could be sold for less than two-thirds of its value thus ascertained.[5] The Supreme Court of the United States afterwards pronounced this law to be unconstitutional and void. In the meantime it had some good effects. A vast number of debts were paid by arrangements and trades of property voluntarily made between debtor and creditor. It destroyed and checked up unwarrantable credit by alarming the creditor part of the community, and has made them more careful in extending credit in future.

It has appeared to me that there are two modes in which a sound credit may be established. One mode may be to let loose the full vigor and severity of law, as in England, upon the debtor, and thus make mankind afraid to go in debt beyond their ability to pay with ease. The other may be to take away all efficient remedies from the creditor to recover his debt and make him rely upon the honor and integrity of his debtor for payment. In this mode no one would get credit on account of being rich. Credit would be no longer given to the mere possession of property. Because such a one might be a rogue and deny his debt; but if honest, he would never contract for more than he was able to pay; and he would make extraordinary exertions to meet his engagements. In this mode the advantages of credit would be a reward for integrity and punctuality.

The system for the collection of debts by law in Illinois has never been one thing or the other. A kind of inefficient remedy has been held out to the creditor which might succeed in making a debt from an honest man, but never from a rogue. The ease with which it could be evaded put the debtor part of the community under strong temptation to dishonesty. If a creditor, no longer to be put off by fair promises, sues for his debt at law the debtor leaves him to his remedy thus chosen. He satisfies his conscience by a train of reasoning of this sort: "If I had not been sued I would have paid as soon as I possibly could. My creditor is not disposed to rely on my honor, be has sued me at law, and thereby chosen mere legal means to recover his debt. He does not rely upon me any longer. Now let him get his money as soon as the law will give it to him. I feel absolved in conscience from making any further efforts to pay, and will be justified in throwing all the obstacles in his way which the forms and delays of the law can furnish." He immediately goes to work to continue the cause from term to term, to appeal the judgment, when obtained, from court to court; and, as a last resort, he has a favorite mode of defeating his creditor in legal proceedings, as it is generally called, by beating him on the execution. This mode of defence supposes the debtor to make fraudulent sales of his property, or to run it out of the country. All such delusive remedies ought to be abolished immediately. It were better to have none. They can only serve to make rogues and demoralize the people.

X

Politics and Mormonism, 1843–1844

We turn again to the history of the State as connected with the Mormons. This people had now become about 16,000 strong in Hancock county and several thousand more were scattered about in other counties. As I have said before, Governor Carlin in 1842 had issued his warrant for the arrest of Joe Smith, their prophet, as a fugitive from justice in Missouri. This warrant had never been executed and was still outstanding when I came into office. The Mormons were desirous of having the cause of arrest legally tested in the federal court. Upon their application a duplicate warrant was issued in the winter of 1842–43 and placed in the hands of the sheriff of Sangamon county. Upon this Joe Smith came to Springfield and surrendered himself a prisoner. A writ of habeas corpus was obtained from Judge Pope of the federal court and Smith was discharged.

Upon this proceeding the whigs founded a hope of obtaining the future support of the Mormons. The democratic officers in Missouri and Illinois were instrumental in procuring his arrest. He was discharged this time by a whig judge; and his cause had been managed by whig lawyers. As in the case decided by Judge Douglas, Smith was too ignorant of law to know whether he owed his discharge to the law or to the favor of the court and the whig party. Such was the ignorance and stupidity of the Mormons generally that they deemed anything to be law which they judged to be expedient. All action of the government which bore hard on them, however legal, they looked upon as wantonly oppressive; and when the law was administered in their favor they attributed it to partiality and kindness. If the stern duty of a public officer required him to bear hard on them they attributed it to malice. In this manner the Mormons this time were made to believe that they were under great obligations to the whigs for the discharge of their prophet from what they believed to be the persecutions of the democrats; and they resolved to yield their support to the whig party in the next election.

An election for Congress in the Mormon district was to come off in August, 1843. Cyrus Walker was the candidate on the part of the whigs and Joseph P. Hoge on the part of the democrats; both of them distinguished lawyers. The Mormons very early decided to support Mr. Walker, the whig. But owing to causes which I will relate they were induced to change their resolution; and this was the cause in a great measure of that wonderful excitement which subsequently prevailed against that people.

Dr. John C. Bennett, heretofore mentioned as an influential favorite of the Mormon leaders, had been expelled from the Church in 1842. By publications and lectures delivered in various parts of the United States he undertook to expose the doctrines, designs, and government of the Mormons and to do them all the injury in his power. A part of his plan was to get up a new indictment against Joe Smith and Orrin P. Rockwell for an attempt to murder Gov. Boggs in Missouri. An indictment was found in Missouri against Smith and Rockwell on the 5th of June, 1843. On the 7th a messenger from Missouri presented himself to me with a copy of the indictment and a new demand from the governor of Missouri. A new warrant, in pursuance of the constitution of the United States, was issued and placed in the hands of a constable in Hancock.

This constable and the Missouri agent hastened to Nauvoo to make the arrest, where they ascertained that Joe Smith was on a visit to Rock river. They pursued him thither and succeeded in arresting him in Palestine Grove, in the county of Lee. The constable immediately delivered his prisoner to the Missouri agent and returned his warrant as having been executed. The agent started with his prisoner in the direction of Missouri, but on the road was met by a number of armed Mormons who captured the whole party and conducted them in the direction of Nauvoo. Farther on they were met by hundreds of the Mormons, coming to the rescue of their prophet, who conducted him in grand triumph to his own city. Cyrus Walker, the whig candidate for Congress, was sent for to defend him as a lawyer; a writ of habeas corpus was sued out of the municipal court; Mr. Walker appeared as his counsel and made a wonderful exertion in a speech three hours long, to prove to the municipal court, composed of Joe Smith's tools and particular friends, that they had the jurisdiction to issue and act on the writ under the ordinance of their city. Mr Hoge also, the democratic candidate, had gone to Nauvoo seeking the votes of the Mormons. He and Mr. Walker were both called upon in a public assembly of the Mormons to express their opinion as to the legality of this ordinance of the city giving to the municipal court power to issue writs of habeas corpus in all cases of imprisonment, and both of them gave their solemn opinion in favor of the power. Thus the Mormons were deluded and deceived by men who ought to have known and did know better. It was a common thing for this people to be eternally asking and receiving advice. If judicious and legal advice were given to them they rejected it with scorn, when it came in conflict with their favorite projects; for which reason all persons designing to use them made it a rule to find out what they were in favor of and advise them accordingly. In this mode the Mormons relied for advice, for the most part, upon the most corrupt of mankind, who would make no matter of conscience of advising them to their destruction, as a means of gaining their favor. This has always been a difficulty with the Mormons, and grew out of their blind fanaticism, which refused to see or to hear anything against their system, but more out of the corruption of their leaders, whose objects being generally roguish and rotten required corrupt and rotten advisers to keep them in countenance.

The municipal court discharged Joe Smith from his arrest; the Missouri agent immediately applied to me for a militia force to renew it; and Mr. Walker came to the seat of government, on the part of the Mormons, to resist the application. This was only a short time before the election. I was indisposed from the first to call out the militia and informed Mr. Walker that my best opinion then was that the militia would not be ordered; but as many important questions of law were involved in the decision, I declined then to pronounce a definite opinion.

The truth is that, being determined from the first not to be made a party to the contest between Walker and Hoge, and knowing that Walker only wanted my decision to carry back to the Mormons as a means of his success, I ought to have withheld it if for no other reason but this. It was afterwards, upon mature consideration, decided not to call out the militia, because the writ had been returned as having been fully executed by the delivery of Joe Smith to the Missouri agent; after which it was entirely a question between Missouri and Smith, with which Illinois had nothing to do except to issue a new warrant if one had been demanded. The governor in doing what he had done had fulfilled his whole duty under the constitution and the laws. And because Smith had not been forcibly rescued, but had been discharged under color of law by a court which had exceeded its jurisdiction, and it appeared that it would have been a dangerous precedent for the governor, whenever he supposed that the courts had exceeded their powers, to call out the militia to reverse and correct their judgments. Yet for not doing so I was subjected to much unmerited abuse.

However, the democratic managers about Nauvoo, after the usual fashion of managing the Mormons by both parties, terrified them if they voted for the whig candidate, as they were yet determined, with the prospect of the militia being sent against them.

Backenstos, a managing democrat of Hancock county, was sent as a messenger to Springfield to ascertain positively what the governor would do if the Mormons voted the democratic ticket. I happened to be absent at St. Louis, but I heard some weeks after the election that Backenstos went home pretending that he had the most ample assurances of favor to the Mormons so long as they voted the democratic ticket. And I was informed by the man himself, a prominent democrat of Springfield, on the 9th day of October, 1846, for the first time, that during my absence he had given a positive pledge in my name to Backenstos that if the Mormons voted the democratic ticket the militia should not be sent against them.[1] This pledge, however, he took care never to intimate to me until more than three years afterwards. Since the Mormons have become so unpopular and since the most of them have left the State, so that they can no longer be a support to any one, this man, following the example of hundreds of others of a similar class, has joined the anti-Mormon excitement, and has been a strong advocate for the expulsion of the Mormons and all who sought to do them but simple justice. This indicated only that the power in Hancock had got into the hands of the anti-Mormons. The mission of Backenstos produced a total change in the minds of the Mormon leaders. They now resolved to drop their friend Walker and take up Hoge, the democratic candidate. Backenstos returned only a day or two before the election, and there was only a short time for the leaders to operate in. A great meeting was called of several thousand Mormons on Saturday before the election. Hyrum Smith, patriarch in the Mormon Church and brother to the prophet, appeared in this great assembly and there solemnly announced to the people that God had revealed to him that the Mormons must support Mr. Hoge, the democratic candidate. William Law, another great leader of the Mormons, next appeared and denied that the Lord had made any such revelation. He stated that to his certain knowledge the prophet Joseph was in favor of Mr. Walker and that the prophet was more likely to know the mind of the Lord on the subject than the patriarch. Hyrum Smith again repeated his revelation with a greater tone of authority. But the people remained in doubt until the next day, being Sunday, when Joe Smith himself appeared before the assembly. He there stated that "he himself was in favor of Mr. Walker and intended to vote for him; that he would not, if he could, influence any voter in giving his vote; that he considered it a mean business for him or any other man to attempt to dictate to the people who they should support in elections; that he had heard his brother Hyrum had received a revelation from the Lord on the subject; that for his part he did not much believe in revelations on the subject of elections; but brother Hyrum was a man of truth; he had known brother Hyrum intimately ever since he was a boy and he had never known him to tell a lie. If brother Hyrum said he had received such a revelation, he had no doubt it was a fact. When the Lord speaks let all the earth be silent."

This decided the Mormon vote. The next day Mr. Hoge received about three thousand votes in Nauvoo, and was elected to Congress by six or eight hundred majority. The result of the election struck the whigs with perfect amazement. Whilst they fancied themselves secure of getting the Mormon vote for Mr. Walker the whig newspapers had entirely ceased their accustomed abuse of the Mormons. They now renewed their crusade against them, every paper was loaded with accounts of the wickedness, corruptions, and enormities of Nauvoo. The whig orators groaned with complaints and denunciations of the democrats who would consent to receive Mormon support, and the democratic officers of the State were violently charged and assaulted with using the influence of their offices to govern the Mormons. From this time forth the whigs generally, and a part of the democrats, determined upon driving the Mormons out of the State; and everything connected with the Mormons became political and was considered almost entirely with reference to party. To this circumstance, in part, is to be attributed the extreme difficulty ever afterwards of doing anything effectually in relation to the Mormon or anti-Mormon parties, by the executive government.

It appears that the Mormons had been directed by their leaders to vote the whig ticket in the Quincy as well as the Hancock district. In the Quincy district Judge Douglas was the democratic candidate, O. H. Browning was the candidate of the whigs. The leading Mormons at Nauvoo having never determined in favor of the democrats until a day or two before the election, there was not sufficient time, or it was neglected, to send orders from Nauvoo into the Quincy district to effect a change there. The Mormons in that district voted for Browning. Douglas and his friends, being afraid that I might be in his way for the United States Senate in 1846, seized hold of this circumstance to affect my party standing and thereby gave countenance to the clamor of the whigs, secretly whispering it about that I had not only influenced the Mormons to vote for Hoge, but for Browning also. This decided many of the democrats in favor of the expulsion of the Mormons.

No further demand for the arrest of Joe Smith having been made by Missouri, he became emboldened by success. The Mormons became more arrogant and overbearing. In the winter of 1843–44, the common council passed some further ordinances to protect their leaders from arrest on demand from Missouri. They enacted that no writ issued from any other place than Nauvoo for the arrest of any person in it should be executed in the city without an approval endorsed thereon by the mayor; that if any public officer, by virtue of any foreign writ, should attempt to make an arrest in the city without such approval of his process he should be subject to imprisonment for life, and that the governor of the State should not have the power of pardoning the offender without the consent of the mayor. When these ordinances were published thcy created general astonishment. Many people began to believe in good earnest that the Mormons were about to set up a separate government for themselves in defiance of the laws of the State. Owners of property stolen in other counties made pursuit into Nauvoo and were fined by the Mormon courts for daring to seek their property in the holy city. To one such I granted a pardon. Several of the Mormons had been convicted of larceny and they never failed in any instance to procure petitions signed by 1,500 or 2,000 of their friends for their pardon. But that which made it more certain than everything else that the Mormons contemplated a separate government was that about this time they petitioned Congress to establish a territorial government for them in Nauvoo; as if Congress had any power to establish such a government, or any other, within the bounds of a State.

To crown the whole folly of the Mormons, in the spring of 1844 Joe Smith announced himself as a candidate for president of the United States. His followers were confident that he would be elected. Two or three thousand missionaries were immediately sent out to preach their religion and to electioneer in favor of their prophet for the presidency. This folly at once covered that people with ridicule in the minds of all sensible men, and brought them into conflict with the zealots and bigots of all political parties; as the arrogance and extravagance of their religious pretensions had already aroused the opposition of all other denominations in religion.

It seems from the best information which could be got from the best men who had seceded from the Mormon church that Joe Smith about this time conceived the idea of making himself a temporal prince as well as a spiritual leader of his people.[2] He instituted a new and select order of the priesthood, the members of which were to be priests and kings temporally and spiritually. These were to be his nobility, who were to be the upholders of his throne. He caused himself to be crowned and anointed king and priest, far above the rest; and he prescribed the form of an oath of allegiance to himself which he administered to his principal followers. To uphold his pretensions to royalty he deduced his descent by an unbroken chain from Joseph the son of Jacob, and that of his wife from some other renowned personage of Old Testament history. The Mormons openly denounced the government of the United States as utterly corrupt, and as being about to pass away and to be replaced by the government of God, to be administered by his servant Joseph. It is now at this day certain also that about this time the prophet reinstituted an order in the church, called the "Danite band." These were to be a body of police and guards about the person of their sovereign, who were sworn to obey his orders as the orders of God himself. About this time also he gave a new touch to a female order already existing in the church, called Spiritual Wives. A doctrine was now revealed that no woman could get to heaven except as the wife of a Mormon elder. The elders were allowed to have as many of these wives as they could maintain; and it was a doctrine of the church, that any female could be "sealed up to eternal life," by uniting herself as wife or concubine to the elder of her choice. This doctrine was maintained by an appeal to the Old Testament scriptures; and by the example of Abraham and Jacob, of David and Solomon, the favorites of God in a former age of the world.

Soon after these institutions were established, Joe Smith began to play the tyrant over several of his followers. The first act of this sort which excited attention, was an attempt to take the wife of William Law, one of his most talented and principal disciples, and make her a spiritual wife. By means of his common council, without the authority of law, he established a recorder's office in Nauvoo in which alone the titles of property could be recorded. In the same manner and with the same want of legal authority he established an office for issuing marriage licenses to the Mormons, so as to give him absolute control of the marrying propensities of his people. He proclaimed that none in the city should purchase real estate to sell again, but himself. He also permitted no one but himself to have a license in the city for the sale of spirituous liquor; and in many other ways he undertook to regulate and control the business of the Mormons.

This despotism administered by a corrupt and unprincipled man soon became intolerable. William Law, one of the most eloquent preachers of the Mormons, who appeared to me to be a deluded but conscientious and candid man, Wilson Law, his brother, major-general of the legion, and four or five other Mormon leaders resolved upon a rebellion against the authority of the prophet. They designed to enlighten their brethren and fellow-citizens upon the new institutions, the new turn given to Mormonism, and the practices under the new system by procuring a printing press and establishing a newspaper in the city, to be the organ of their complaints and views. But they never issued but one number; before the second could appear the press was demolished by an order of the common council, and the conspirators were ejected from the Mormon church.

The Mormons themselves published the proceedings of the council in the trial and destruction of the heretical press; from which it does not appear that any one was tried or that the editor or any of the owners of the property had notice of the trial or were permitted to defend in any particular. The proceeding was an *ex parte* proceeding, partly civil and partly ecclesiastical, against the press itself. No jury was called or sworn nor were the witnesses required to give their evidence upon oath. The councillors stood up one after another, and some of them several times, and related what they pretended to know. In this mode it was abundantly proved that the owners of the proscribed press were sinners, whoremasters, thieves, swindlers, counterfeiters, and robbers; the evidence of which is reported in the trial at full length. It was altogether the most curious and irregular trial that ever was recorded in any civilized country; and one finds difficulty in determining whether the proceedings of the council were more the result of insanity or depravity. The trial resulted in the conviction of the press as a public nuisance. The mayor was ordered to see it abated as such, and if necessary to call the legion to his assistance. The mayor issued his warrant to the city marshal who, aided by a portion of the legion, proceeded to the obnoxious printing office and destroyed the press and scattered the types and other materials.

After this it became too hot for the seceding and rejected Mormons to remain in the holy city. They retired to Carthage, the county seat of Hancock county; and took out warrants for the mayor and members of the common council and others engaged in the outrage for a riot. Some of these were arrested, but were immediately taken before the municipal court of the city on *habeas corpus* and discharged from custody. The residue of this history of the Mormons, up to the time of the death of the Smiths, will be taken, with such corrections as time has shown to be necessary, from my report to the legislature made on the 23rd of December, 1844.

On the seventeenth day of June following, a committee of a meeting of the citizens of Carthage presented themselves to me with a request that the militia might be ordered out to assist in executing process in the city of Nauvoo. I determined to visit in person that section of country and examine for myself the truth and nature of their complaints. No order for the militia was made; and I arrived at Carthage on the morning of the twenty-first day of the same month.

Upon my arrival I found an armed force assembled and hourly increasing under the summons and direction of the constables of the county, to serve as a *posse comitatus* to assist in the execution of process. The general of the brigade had also called for the militia *en masse* of the counties of McDonough and Schuyler for a similar purpose.[3] Another assemblage to a considerable number had been made at Warsaw, under military command of Col. Levi Williams.

The first thing which I did on my arrival was to place all the militia then assembled, and which were expected to assemble, under military command of their proper officers.

I next despatched a messenger to Nauvoo, informing the mayor and common council of the nature of the complaint made against them; and requested that persons might be sent to me to lay their side of the question before me. A committee was accordingly sent, who made such acknowledgments that I had no difficulty in concluding what were the facts.

It appeared clearly both from the complaints of the citizens and the acknowledgments of the Mormon committee that the whole proceedings of the mayor, the common council, and the municipal court were irregular and illegal, and not to be endured in a free country; though perhaps some apology might be made for the court, as it had been repeatedly assured by some of the best lawyers in the State who had been candidates for office before that people that it had full and competent power to issue writs of *habeas corpus* in all cases whatever. The common council violated the law in assuming the exercise of judicial power; in proceeding *ex parte* without notice to the owners of the property; in proceeding against the property *in rem;* in not calling a jury; in not swearing all the witnesses; in not giving the owners of the property accused of being a nuisance, in consequence of being libelous, an opportunity of giving the truth in evidence; and in fact by not proceeding by civil suit or indictment, as in other cases of libel. The mayor violated the law in ordering this erroneous and absurd judgment of the common council to be executed. And the municipal court erred in discharging them from arrest.

As this proceeding touched the liberty of the press, which is justly dear to any republican people, it was well calculated to raise a great flame of excitement. And it may well be questioned whether years of misrepresentation by the most profligate newspaper could have engendered such a feeling as was produced by the destruction of this one press. It is apparent that the Mormon leaders but little understood, and regarded less, the true principles of civil liberty. A free press well conducted is a great blessing to a free people; a profligate one is likely soon to deprive itself of all credit and influence by the multitude of falsehoods put forth by it. But let this be as it may, there is more lost to rational liberty by a censorship of the press, by suppressing information proper to be known to the people, than can be lost to an individual now and then by a temporary injury to his character and influence by the utmost licentiousness.

There were other causes to heighten the excitement. These people had undertaken to innovate upon the established systems of religion. Their legal right to do so no one will question. But all history bears testimony that innovations upon religion have always been attended by a hostility in the public mind which sometimes have produced the most desolating wars; always more or less of persecution. Even the innocent Quakers, the unoffending Shakers, and the quiet and orderly Methodists in their origin, and until the world got used to them, had enough of persecution to encounter. But if either of these sects had congregated together in one city where the world could never get to know them; could never ascertain by personal acquaintance the truth or falsity of many reports which are always circulated to the prejudice of such innovators; and moreover, if they had armed themselves and organized into a military legion as the citizens of Nauvoo, and had been guilty of highhanded proceedings carried on against the heretical press the public animosity and their persecutions must have greatly increased in rancor and severity.

In addition to these causes of excitement there were a great many reports in circulation and generally believed by the people. These reports I have already alluded to, and they had much influence in swelling the public excitement.

It was asserted that Joe Smith, the founder and head of the Mormon church, had caused himself to be crowned and anointed king of the Mormons; that he had embodied a band of his followers called Danites, who were sworn to obey him as God, and to do his commands, murder and treason not excepted; that he had instituted an order in the church whereby those who composed it were pretended to be sealed up to eternal life against all crimes save the shedding of innocent blood or consenting thereto. That this order was instructed that no blood was innocent blood, except that of the members of the church; and that these two orders were made the ministers of his vengeance and the instruments of an intolerable tyranny which he had established over his people, and which he was about to extend over the neighboring country. The people affected to believe that with this power in the hands of an unscrupulous leader there was no safety for the lives or property of any one who should oppose him. They affected likewise to believe that Smith inculcated the legality of perjury or any other crime in defence, or to advance, the interests of true believers; and that he himself had set them the example by swearing to a false accusation against a certain person for the crime of murder. It was likewise asserted to be a fundamental article of the Mormon faith that God had given the world and all it contained to them as his saints; that they secretly believed in their right to all the goodly lands, farms, and property in the country; that at present they were kept out of their rightful inheritance by force; that consequently there was no moral offence in anticipating God's good time to put them in possession by stealing, if opportunity offered; that in fact the whole church was a community of murderers, thieves, robbers, and outlaws; that Joseph Smith had established a bogus factory in Nauvoo for the manufacture of counterfeit money; and that he maintained about his person a tribe of swindlers, blacklegs, and counterfeiters to make it and put it into circulation.

It was also believed that he had announced a revelation from heaven sanctioning polygamy, by a kind of spiritual wife system whereby a man was allowed one wife in pursuance of the laws of the country and an indefinite number of others to be enjoyed in some mystical and spiritual mode; and that he himself and many of his followers had practiced upon the precepts of this revelation by seducing a large number of women.[4]

It was also asserted that he was in alliance with the Indians of the western territories, and had obtained over them such a control that in case of a war he could command their assistance to murder his enemies.

Upon the whole, if one-half of these reports had been true the Mormon community must have been the most intolerable collection of rogues ever assembled; or, if one-half of them were false, they were the most maligned and abused.

Fortunately for the purposes of those who were active in creating excitement there were many known truths which gave countenance to some of these accusations. It was sufficiently proved in a proceeding at Carthage whilst I was there that Joe Smith had sent a band of his followers to Missouri to kidnap two men who were witnesses against a member of his church then in jail and about to be tried on a charge of larceny. It was also a notorious fact that he had assaulted and severely beaten an officer of the county for an alleged non-performance of his duty, at a time when that officer was just recovering from severe illness.[5] It is a fact also that he stood indicted for the crime of perjury, as was alleged, in swearing to an accusation for murder in order to drive a man out of Nauvoo who had been engaged in buying and selling lots and land, and thus interfering with the monopoly of the prophet as a speculator. It is a fact also that his municipal court, of which he was chief justice, by writ of habeas corpus had frequently discharged individuals accused of high crimes and offences against the laws of the State; and on one occasion had discharged a person accused of swindling the government of the United States, and who had been arrested by process of the federal courts; thereby giving countenance to the report that he obstructed the administration of justice, and had set up a government at Nauvoo independent of the laws and government of the State. This idea was further corroborated in the minds of the people by the fact that the people of Nauvoo had petitioned Congress for a territorial government to be established there, and to be independent of the State government. It was a fact also that some larcenies and robberies had been committed and that Mormons had been convicted of the crimes, and that other larcenies had been committed by persons unknown, but suspected to be Mormons. Justice, however, requires me here to say that upon such investigation as I then could make the charge of promiscuous stealing appeared to be exaggerated.

Another cause of excitement was a report industriously circulated and generally believed that Hyrum Smith, another leader of the Mormon church, had offered a reward for the destruction of the press of the Warsaw *Signal*, a newspaper published in the county, and the organ of the opposition to the Mormons. It was also asserted that the Mormons scattered through the settlements of the county had threatened all persons who turned out to assist the constables with the destruction of their property and the murder of their families, in the absence of their fathers, brothers, and husbands. A Mormon woman in McDonough county was imprisoned for threatening to poison the wells of the people who turned out in the posse; and a Mormon in Warsaw publicly avowed that he was bound by his religion to obey all orders of the prophet, even to commit murder if so commanded.

But the great cause of popular fury was that the Mormons at several preceding elections had cast their vote as a unit; thereby making the fact apparent that no one could aspire to the honors or offices of the country within the sphere of their influence without their approbation and votes. It appears to be one of the principles by which they insist upon being governed as a community to act as a unit in all matters of government and religion. They express themselves to be fearful that if division should be encouraged in politics it would soon extend to their religion and rend their church with schism and into sects.

This seems to me to be an unfortunate view of the subject, and more unfortunate in practice, as I am well satisfied that it must be the fruitful source of excitement, violence, and mobocracy whilst it is persisted in. It is indeed unfortunate for their peace that they do not divide in elections according to their individual preferences or political principles, like other people.

This one principle and practice of theirs arrayed against them in deadly hostility all aspirants for office who were not sure of their support, all who had been unsuccessful in elections, and all who were too proud to court their influence, with all their friends and connections.

These also were the active men in blowing up the fury of the people in hopes that a popular movement might be set on foot which would result in the expulsion or extermination of the Mormon voters. For this purpose public meetings had been called; inflammatory speeches had been made; exaggerated reports had been extensively circulated; committees had been appointed who rode night and day to spread the reports and solicit the aid of neighboring counties. And at a public meeting at Warsaw resolutions were passed to expel or exterminate the Mormon population. This was not, however, a movement which was unanimously concurred in. The county contained a goodly number of inhabitants in favor of peace, or who at least desired to be neutral in such a contest. These were stigmatized by the name of Jack Mormons and there were not a few of the more furious exciters of the people who openly expressed their intention to involve them in the common expulsion or extermination.

A system of excitement and agitation was artfully planned and executed with tact. It consisted in spreading reports and rumors of the most fearful character. As examples: On the morning before my arrival at Carthage I was awakened at an early hour by the frightful report, which was asserted with confidence and apparent consternation, that the Mormons had already commenced the work of burning, destruction, and murder; and that every man capable of bearing arms was instantly wanted at Carthage for the protection of the country. We lost no time in starting; but when we arrived at Carthage we could hear no more concerning this story. Again: during the few days that the militia were encamped at Carthage frequent applications were made to me to send a force here and a force there and a force all about the country to prevent murders, robberies, and larcenies which, it was said, were threatened by the Mormons. No such forces were sent; nor were any such offences committed at that time except the stealing of some provisions, and there was never the least proof that this was done by a Mormon. Again: on my late visit to Hancock county I was informed by some of their violent enemies that the larcenies of the Mormons had become unusually numerous and insufferable. They indeed admitted that but little had been done in this way in their immediate vicinity. But they insisted that sixteen horses had been stolen by the Mormons in one night near Lima, in the county of Adams. At the close of the expedition I called at this same town of Lima and upon inquiry was told that no horses had been stolen in that neighborhood, but that sixteen horses had been stolen in one night in Hancock county. This last informant being told of the Hancock story, again changed the venue to another distant settlement in the northern edge of Adams.

As my object in visiting Hancock was expressly to assist in the execution of the laws, and not to violate them or to witness or permit their violation, as I was convinced that the Mormon leaders had committed a crime in the destruction of the press and had resisted the execution of process, I determined to exert the whole force of the State, if necessary, to bring them to justice. But seeing the great excitement in the public mind and the manifest tendency of this excitement to run into mobocracy, I was of opinion that before I acted I ought to obtain a pledge from the officers and men to support me in strictly legal measures, and to protect the prisoners in case they surrendered. For I was determined, if possible, that the forms of law should not be made the catspaw of a mob to seduce these people to a quiet surrender, as the convenient victims of popular fury. I therefore called together the whole force then assembled at Carthage and made an address, explaining to them what I could, and what I could not, legally do; and also adducing to them various reasons why they as well as the Mormons should submit to the laws; and why, if they had resolved upon revolutionary proceedings, their purpose should be abandoned. The assembled troops seemed much pleased with the address; and upon its conclusion the officers and men unanimously voted, with acclamation, to sustain me in a strictly legal course, and that the prisoners should be protected from violence. Upon the arrival of additional forces from Warsaw, McDonough, and Schuyler similar addresses were made, with the same result.

It seemed to me that these votes fully authorized me to promise the accused Mormons the protection of the law in case they surrendered. They were accordingly duly informed that if they surrendered they would be protected, and if they did not the whole force of the State would be called out, if necessary, to compel their submission. A force of ten men was despatched with the constable to make the arrests and to guard the prisoners to headquarters.[6]

In the meantime Joe Smith, as Lieut.-General of the Nauvoo Legion, had declared martial law in the city; the Legion was assembled and ordered under arms; the members of it residing in the country were ordered into town. The Mormon settlements obeyed the summons of their leader and marched to his assistance. Nauvoo was one great military camp, strictly guarded and watched; and no ingress or egress was allowed except upon the strictest examination. In one instance which came to my knowledge a citizen of McDonough, who happened to be in the city was denied the privilege of returning until he made oath that he did not belong to the party at Carthage, that he would return home without calling at Carthage, and that he would give no information of the movements of the Mormons.

However, upon the arrival of the constable and guard the mayor and common council at once signified their willingness to surrender and stated their readiness to proceed to Carthage next morning at eight o'clock. Martial law had previously been abolished. The hour of eight o'clock came and the accused failed to make their appearance. The constable and his escort returned. The constable made no effort to arrest any of them, nor would he or the guard delay their departure one minute beyond the time, to see whether an arrest could be made. Upon their return they reported that they had been informed that the accused had fled and could not be found.

I immediately proposed to a council of officers to march into Nauvoo with the small force then under my command, but the officers were of opinion that it was too small and many of them insisted upon a further call of the militia. Upon reflection, I was of opinion that the officers were right in the estimate of our force, and the project for immediate action was abandoned. I was soon informed, however, of the conduct of the constable and guard, and then I was perfectly satisfied that a most base fraud had been attempted; that, in fact, it was feared that the Mormons would submit and thereby entitle themselves to the protection of the law. It was very apparent that many of the bustling, active spirits were afraid that there would be no occasion for calling out an overwhelming militia force for marching it into Nauvoo, for probable mutiny when there, and for the extermination of the Mormon race. It appeared that the constable and the escort were fully in the secret, and acted well their part to promote the conspiracy.

Seeing this to be the state of the case, I delayed any further call of the militia to give the accused another opportunity to surrender; for indeed I was most anxious to avoid a general call for the militia at that critical season of the year. The whole spring season preceding had been unusually wet. No ploughing of corn had been done, and but very little planting. The season had just changed to be suitable for ploughing. The crops which had been planted were universally suffering; and the loss of two weeks, or even of one, at that time was likely to produce a general famine all over the country. The wheat harvest was also approaching; and if we got into a war there was no foreseeing when it would end, or when the militia could safely be discharged. In addition to these considerations, all the grist mills in all that section of the country had been swept away or disabled by the high waters, leaving the inhabitants almost without meal or flour and making it impossible then to procure provisions, by impressment or otherwise, for the sustenance of any considerable force.

This was the time of the high waters; of astonishing floods in all the rivers and creeks in the western country. The Mississippi river at St. Louis was several feet higher than it was ever known before; it was up into the second stories of the warehouses on Water street; the steamboats ran up to these warehouses, and could scarcely receive their passengers from the second stories; the whole American Bottom was overflowed from eight to twenty feet deep, and steamboats freely crossed the Bottom along the road from St. Louis to the opposite bluffs in Illinois; houses and fences and stock of all kinds were swept away, the fields near the river, after the water subsided, being covered with sand from a foot to three feet deep; which was generally thrown into ridges and washed into gullies, so as to spoil the land for cultivation. Families had great difficulty in making their escape. Through the active exertions of Mr. Pratt, the mayor of St. Louis, steamboats were sent in every direction to their relief. The boats found many of the families on the tops of their houses just ready to be floated away. The inhabitants of the Bottom lost nearly all their personal property. A large number of them were taken to St. Louis in a state of entire destitution, and their necessities were supplied by the contributions of the charitable of that city. A larger number were forced out on to the Illinois bluffs, where they encamped and were supplied with provisions by the neighboring inhabitants. This freshet nearly ruined the ancient village of Kaskaskia. The inhabitants were driven away and scattered, many of them never to return. For many years before this flood there had been a flourishing institution at Kaskaskia, under the direction of an order of nuns of the Catholic Church. They had erected an extensive building, which was surrounded and filled by the waters to the second story. But they were all safely taken away, pupils and all, by a steamboat which was sent to their relief and which ran directly up to the building and received its inmates from the second story. This school was now transferred to St. Louis, where it yet remains. All the rivers and streams in Illinois were as high, and did as much damage in proportion to their length and the extent of their bottoms, as the Mississippi.

This great flood destroyed the last hope of getting provisions at home; and I was totally without funds belonging to the State with which to purchase at more distant markets, and there was a certainty that such purchases could not have been made on credit abroad. For these reasons I was desirous of avoiding a war if it could be avoided.

In the meantime I made a requisition upon the officers of the Nauvoo legion for the State arms in their possession. It appears that there was no evidence in the quartermaster-general's office of the number and description of arms with which the legion had been furnished. Dr. Bennett, after he had been appointed quartermaster general, had joined the Mormons and had disposed of the public arms as he pleased without keeping or giving any account of them. On this subject I applied to Gen. Wilson Law for information. He had lately been the major-general of the legion. He had seceded from the Mormon party; was one of the owners of the proscribed press; had left the city, as he said, in fear of his life; and was one of the party asking for justice against its constituted authorities. He was interested to exaggerate the number of arms rather than to place it at too low an estimate. From his information I learned that the legion had received three pieces of cannon and about two hundred and fifty stand of small arms and their accoutrements. Of these, the three pieces of cannon and two hundred and twenty stand of small arms were surrendered. These arms were demanded because the legion was illegally used in the destruction of the press and in enforcing martial law in the city in open resistance to legal process and the *posse comitatus.*

I demanded the surrender also on account of the great prejudice and excitement which the possession of these arms by the Mormons had always kindled in the minds of the people. A large portion of the people, by pure misrepresentation, had been made to believe that the legion had received of the State as many as thirty pieces of artillery and five or six thousand stand of small arms, which in all probability would soon be wielded for the conquest of the country; and for their subjection to Mormon domination. I was of opinion that the removal of these arms would tend much to allay this excitement and prejudice; and in point of fact, although wearing a severe aspect, would be an act of real kindness to the Mormons themselves.

On the 23d or 24th day of June Joe Smith, the mayor of Nauvoo, together with his brother Hyrum and all the members of the council and all others demanded, came into Carthage and surrendered themselves prisoners to the constable, on the charge of riot. They all voluntarily entered into a recognizance before the justice of the peace for their appearance at court to answer the charge. And all of them were discharged from custody except Joe and Hyrum Smith, against whom the magistrate had issued a new writ on a complaint of treason.[7] They were immediately arrested by the constable on this charge and retained in his custody to answer it.

The overt act of treason charged against them consisted in the alleged levying of war against the State by declaring martial law in Nauvoo, and in ordering out the legion to resist the *posse comitatus.* Their actual guiltiness of the charge would depend upon circumstances. If their opponents had been seeking to put the law in force in good faith, and nothing more, then an array of a military force in open resistance to *the posse comitatus* and the militia of the State most probably would have amounted to treason. But if those opponents merely intended to use the process of the law, the militia of the State, and the *posse comitatus* as cats-paws to compass the possession of their persons for the purpose of murdering them afterwards, as the sequel demonstrated the fact to be, it might well be doubted whether they were guilty of treason.

Soon after the surrender of the Smiths, at their request I despatched Captain Singleton with his company from Brown county to Nauvoo to guard the town; and I authorized him to take command of the legion. He reported to me afterwards that he called out the legion for inspection; and that upon two hours' notice two thousand of them assembled, all of them armed; and this after the public arms had been taken away from them. So it appears that they had a sufficiency of private arms for any reasonable purpose.

After the Smiths had been arrested on the new charge of treason the justice of the peace postponed the examination because neither of the parties was prepared with his witnesses for trial. In the meantime he committed them to the jail of the county for greater security.

In all this matter the justice of the peace and constable, though humble in office, were acting in a high and independent capacity, far beyond any legal power in me to control. I considered that the executive power could only be called in to assist, and not to dictate or control their action; that in the humble sphere of their duties they were as independent, and clothed with as high authority by the law, as the executive department; and that my province was simply to aid them with the force of the State. It is true that so far as I could prevail on them by advice I endeavored to do so. The prisoners were not in military custody, or prisoners of war; and I could no more legally control these officers than I could the superior courts of justice.

Some persons have supposed that I ought to have had them sent to some distant and friendly part of the State for confinement and trial; and that I ought to have searched them for concealed arms; but these surmises and suppositions are readily disposed of by the fact that they were not my prisoners; but were the prisoners of the constable and jailer, under the direction of the justice of the peace. And also by the fact that by law they could be tried in no other county than Hancock.

The jail in which they were confined is a considerable stone building; containing a residence for the jailer, cells for the close and secure confinement of prisoners, and one larger room not so strong, but more airy and comfortable than the cells. They were put into the cells by the jailer; but upon their remonstrance and request, and by my advice, they were transferred to the larger room; and there they remained until the final catastrophe. Neither they nor I seriously apprehended an attack on the jail through the guard stationed to protect it. Nor did I apprehend the least danger on their part of an attempt to escape. For I was very sure that any such an attempt would have been the signal of their immediate death. Indeed, if they had escaped it would have been fortunate for the purposes of those who were anxious for the expulsion of the Mormon population. For the great body of that people would most assuredly have followed their prophet and principal leaders, as they did in their flight from Missouri.*

*I learned afterwards that the leaders of the anti-Mormons did much to stimulate their followers to the murder of the Smiths in jail, by alleging that the governor intended to favor their escape. If this had been true, and could have been well carried out, it would have been the best way of getting rid of the Mormons.

The force assembled at Carthage amounted to about twelve or thirteen hundred men, and it was calculated that four or five hundred more were assembled at Warsaw. Nearly all that portion resident in Hancock were anxious to be marched into Nauvoo. This measure was supposed to be necessary to search for counterfeit money and the apparatus to make it, and also to strike a salutary terror into the Mormon people by an exhibition of the force of the State, and thereby prevent future outrages, murders, robberies, burnings, and the like, apprehended as the effect of Mormon vengeance on those who had taken a part against them. On my part, at one time this arrangement was agreed to. The morning of the 27th day of June was appointed for the march; and Golden's Point near the Mississippi river and about equidistant from Nauvoo and Warsaw, was selected as the place of rendezvous. I had determined to prevail on the justice to bring out his prisoners and take them along. A council of officers, however, determined that this would be highly inexpedient and dangerous, and offered such substantial reasons for their opinions as induced me to change my resolution.

Two or three days' preparations had been made for this expedition. I observed that some of the people became more and more excited and inflammatory the further the preparations were advanced. Occasional threats came to my ears of destroying the city and murdering or expelling the inhabitants.

I had no objection to ease the terrors of the people by such a display of force, and was most anxious also to search for the alleged apparatus for making counterfeit money; and, in fact, to inquire into all the charges against that people, if I could have been assured of my command against mutiny and insubordination. But I gradually learned to my entire satisfaction that there was a plan to get the troops into Nauvoo and there to begin the war, probably by some of our own party or some of the seceding Mormons taking advantage of the night to fire on our own force, and then laying it on the Mormons. I was satisfied that there were those amongst us fully capable of such

---

These leaders of the Mormons would never have dared to return, and they would have been followed in their flight by all their church. I had such a plan in my mind, but I had never breathed it to a living soul, and was thus thwarted in ridding the State of the Mormons two years before they actually left by the insane frenzy of the anti-Mormons. Joe Smith, when he escaped from Missouri, had no difficulty in again collecting his sect about him at Nauvoo; and so the twelve apostles, after they had been at the head of affairs long enough to establish their authority and influence as leaders, had no difficulty in getting nearly the whole body of Mormons to follow them into the wilderness two years after the death of their pretended prophet.

an act, hoping that in the alarm, bustle, and confusion of a militia camp the truth could not be discovered, and that it might lead to the desired collision.

I had many objections to be made the dupe of any such or similar artifice. I was openly and boldly opposed to any attack on the city unless it should become necessary to arrest prisoners legally charged and demanded. Indeed, if any one will reflect upon the number of women, inoffensive and young persons, and innocent children which must be contained in such a city of twelve or fifteen thousand inhabitants it would seem to me his heart would relent and rebel against such violent resolutions. Nothing but the most blinded and obdurate fury could incite a person, even if he had the power, to the willingness of driving such persons bare and houseless on to the prairies to starve, suffer, and even steal, as they must have done, for subsistence. No one who has children of his own would think of it for a moment.

Besides this, if we had been ever so much disposed to commit such an act of wickedness, we evidently had not the power to do it. I was well assured that the Mormons at a short notice could muster as many as two or three thousand well-armed men. We had not more than seventeen hundred, with three pieces of cannon and about twelve hundred stand of small arms. We had provisions for two days only, and would be compelled to disband at the end of that time. To think of beginning a war under such circumstances was a plain absurdity. If the Mormons had succeeded in repulsing our attack, as most likely would have been the case, the country must necessarily be given up to their ravages until a new force could be assembled and provision made for its subsistence. Or if we should have succeeded in driving them from their city, they would have scattered; and being justly incensed at our barbarity, and suffering with privation and hunger, would have spread desolation all over the country without any possibility on our part, with the force we then had, of preventing it. Again: they would have had the advantage of being able to subsist their force in the field by plundering their enemies.

All these considerations were duly urged by me upon the attention of a council of officers convened on the morning of the 27th of June. I also urged upon the council that such wanton and unprovoked barbarity on their part would turn the sympathy of the people in the surrounding counties in favor of the Mormons, and therefore it would be impossible to raise a volunteer militia force to protect such a people against them. Many of the officers admitted that there might be danger of collision. But such was the blind fury prevailing at the time, though not showing itself by much visible excitement, that a small majority of the council adhered to the first resolution of marching into Nauvoo; most of the officers of the Schuyler and McDonough militia voting against it, and most of those of the county of Hancock voting in its favor.

A very responsible duty now devolved upon me to determine whether I would, as commander-in-chief, be governed by the advice of this majority. I had no hesitation in deciding that I would not; but on the contrary I ordered the troops to be disbanded, both at Carthage and Warsaw, with the exception of three companies, two of which were retained as a guard to the jail and the other was retained to accompany me to Nauvoo.

The officers insisted much in council upon the necessity of marching to that place to search for apparatus to make counterfeit money, and more particularly to terrify the Mormons from attempting any open or secret measures of vengeance against the citizens of the county who had taken a part against them or their leaders. To ease their terrors on this head I proposed to them that I would myself proceed to the city, accompanied by a small force, make the proposed search and deliver an address to the Mormons, and tell them plainly what degree of excitement and hatred prevailed against them in the minds of the whole people, and that if any open or secret violence should be committed on the persons or property of those who had taken part against them that no one would doubt but that it had been perpetrated by them, and that it would be the sure and certain means of the destruction of their city and the extermination of their people.

I ordered two companies under the command of Capt. R. F. Smith of the Carthage Grays to guard the jail. In selecting these companies and particularly the company of the Carthage Grays for this service I have been subjected to some censure. It has been said that this company had already been guilty of mutiny and had been ordered to be arrested whilst in the encampment at Carthage; and that they and their officers were the deadly enemies of the prisoners. Indeed, it would have been difficult to find friends of the prisoners under my command unless I had called in the Mormons as a guard; and this I was satisfied would have led to the immediate war, and the sure death of the prisoners.

It is true that this company had behaved badly towards the brigadier-general in command on the occasion when the prisoners were shown along the line of the McDonough militia. This company had been ordered as a guard. They were under the belief that the prisoners, who were arrested for a capital offence, were shown to the troops in a kind of triumph; and that they had been called on as a triumphal escort to grace the procession. They also entertained a very bad feeling towards the brigadier general who commanded their service on the occasion. The truth is, however, that this company was never ordered to be arrested; that the Smiths were not shown to the McDonough troops as a mark of honor and triumph, but were shown to them at the urgent request of the troops themselves to gratify their curiosity in beholding persons who had made themselves so notorious in the country.

When the Carthage Grays ascertained what was the true motive in showing the prisoners to the troops they were perfectly satisfied. All due atonement was made on their part for their conduct to the brigadier-general and they cheerfully returned to their duty.

Although I knew that this company were the enemies of the Smiths, yet I had confidence in their loyalty and integrity; because their captain was universally spoken of as a most respectable citizen and honorable man. The company itself was an old independent company, well armed, uniformed, and drilled; and the members of it were the elite of the militia of the county. I relied upon this company especially because it was an independent company, for a long time instructed and practiced in military discipline and subordination. I also had their word and honor, officers and men, to do their duty according to law. Besides all this the officers and most of the men resided in Carthage; in the near vicinity of Nauvoo; and, as I thought, must know that they would make themselves and their property convenient and conspicuous marks of Mormon vengeance in case they were guilty of treachery.

I had at first intended to select a guard from the county of McDonough, but the militia of that county were very much dissatisfied to remain; their crops were suffering at home; they were in a perfect fever to be discharged; and I was destitute of provisions to supply them for more than a few days. They were far from home, where they could not supply themselves. Whilst the Carthage company could board at their own houses, and would be put to little inconvenience in comparison.

What gave me greater confidence in the selection of this company as a prudent measure was that the selection was first suggested and urged by the brigadier-general in command, who was well known to be utterly hostile to all mobocracy and violence towards the prisoners and who was openly charged by the violent party with being on the side of the Mormons. At any rate I knew that the jail would have to be guarded as long as the prisoners were confined; that an imprisonment for treason might last the whole summer and the greater part of the autumn before a trial could be had in the circuit court; that it would be utterly impossible in the circumstances of the country to keep a force there from a foreign county for so long a time; and that a time must surely come when the duty of guarding the jail would necessarily devolve on the citizens of the county.

It is true also that at this time I had not believed or suspected that any attack was to be made upon the prisoners in jail. It is true that I was aware that a great deal of hatred existed against them, and that there were those who would do them an injury if they could. I had heard of some threats being made, but none of an attack upon the prisoners whilst in jail. These threats seemed to be made by individuals not acting in concert. They were no more than the bluster which might have been expected, and furnished no indication of numbers combining for this or any other purpose.

I must here be permitted to say also that frequent appeals had been made to me to make a clean and thorough work of the matter by exterminating the Mormons or expelling them from the State. All opinion seemed generally to prevail that the sanction of executive authority would legalize the act and all persons of any influence, authority or note who conversed with me on the subject frequently and repeatedly stated their total unwillingness to act without my direction, or in any mode except according to law.

This was a circumstance well calculated to conceal from me the secret machinations on foot. I had constantly contended against violent measures and so had the brigadier-general in command; and I am convinced that unusual pains were taken to conceal from both of us the secret measures resolved upon. It has been said, however, that some person named Williams in a public speech at Carthage called for volunteers to murder the Smiths; and that I ought to have had him arrested.[8] Whether such a speech was really made or not is yet unknown to me.

Having ordered the guard and left General Deming in command in Carthage and discharged the residue of the militia, I immediately departed for Nauvoo, eighteen miles distant, accompanied by Col. Buckmaster, Quartermaster-General, and Capt. Dunn's company of dragoons.

After we had proceeded four miles Colonel Buckmaster intimated to me a suspicion that an attack would be made upon the jail. He stated the matter as a mere suspicion, arising from having seen two persons converse together at Carthage with some air of mystery. I myself entertained no suspicion of such an attack; at any rate, none before the next day in the afternoon; because it was notorious that we had departed from Carthage with the declared intention of being absent at least two days. I could not believe that any person would attack the jail whilst we were in Nauvoo and thereby expose my life and the lives of my companions to the sudden vengeance of the Mormons upon hearing of the death of their leaders. Nevertheless, acting upon the principle of providing against mere possibilities, I sent back one of the company with a special order to Capt. Smith to guard the jail strictly and at the peril of his life until my return.

We proceeded on our journey four miles farther. By this time I had convinced myself that no attack would be made on the jail that day or night. I supposed that a regard for my safety and the safety of my companions would prevent an attack until those to be engaged in it could be assured of our departure from Nauvoo. I still think that this ought to have appeared to me to be a reasonable supposition.

I therefore determined at this point to omit making the search for counterfeit money at Nauvoo and defer an examination of all the other abominations charged on that people in order to return to Carthage that same night, that I might be on the ground in person in time to prevent an attack upon the jail, if any had been meditated. To this end we called a halt; the baggage wagons were ordered to remain where they were until towards evening, and then return to Carthage.

Having made these arrangements we proceeded on our march and arrived at Nauvoo about four o'clock of the afternoon of the 27th day of June. As soon as notice could be given a crowd of the citizens assembled to hear an address which I proposed to deliver to them. The number present has been variously estimated from one to five thousand.

In this address I stated to them how, and in what, their functionaries had violated the laws. Also, the many scandalous reports in circulation against them, and that these reports, whether true or false, were generally believed by the people. I distinctly stated to them the amount of hatred and prejudice which prevailed everywhere against them, and the causes of it, at length.

I also told them plainly and emphatically that if any vengeance should be attempted openly or secretly against the persons or property of the citizens who had taken part against their leaders that the public hatred and excitement was such that thousands would assemble for the total destruction of their city and the extermination of their people; and that no power in the State would be able to prevent it. During this address some impatience and resentment were manifested by the Mormons at the recital of the various reports enumerated concerning them; which they strenuously and indignantly denied to be true. They claimed to be a law-abiding people and insisted that as they looked to the law alone for their protection, so were they careful themselves to observe its provisions. Upon the conclusion of this address I proposed to take a vote on the question whether they would strictly observe the laws, even in opposition to their prophet and leaders. The vote was unanimous in favor of this proposition.

The anti-Mormons contended that such a vote from the Mormons signified nothing; and truly the subsequent history of that people showed clearly that they were loudest in their professions of attachment to the law whenever they were guilty of the greatest extravagances; and in fact that they were so ignorant and stupid about matters of law that they had no means of judging of the legality of their conduct, only as they were instructed by their spiritual leaders.

A short time before sundown we departed on our return to Carthage. When we had proceeded two miles we met two individuals, one of them a Mormon, who informed us that the Smiths had been assassinated in jail, about five or six o'clock of that day. The intelligence seemed to strike every one with a kind of dumbness. As to myself, it was perfectly astounding; and I anticipated the very worst consequences from it. The Mormons had been represented to me as a lawless, infatuated, and fanatical people, not governed by the ordinary motives which influence the rest of mankind. If so, most likely an exterminating war would ensue and the whole land would be covered with desolation.

Acting upon this supposition, it was my duty to provide as well as I could for the event. I therefore ordered the two messengers into custody and to be returned with us to Carthage. This was done to get time to make such arrangements as could be made, and to prevent any sudden explosion of Mormon excitement before they could be written to by their friends at Carthage. I also despatched messengers to Warsaw to advise the citizens of the event. But the people there knew all about the matter before my messengers arrived. They, like myself, anticipated a general attack all over the country. The women and children were removed across the river; and a committee was despatched that night to Quincy for assistance. The next morning by daylight the ringing of the bells in the city of Quincy announced a public meeting. The people assembled in great numbers at an early hour. The Warsaw committee stated to the meeting that a party of Mormons had attempted to rescue the Smiths out of jail; that a party of Missourians and others had killed the prisoners to prevent their escape; that the governor and his party were at Nauvoo at the time when intelligence of the fact was brought there; that they had been attacked by the Nauvoo legion and had retreated to a house, where they were then closely besieged. That the governor had sent out word that he could maintain his position for two days, and would be certain to be massacred if assistance did not arrive by the end of that time. It is unnecessary to say that this entire story was a fabrication. It was of a piece with the other reparts put into circulation by the anti-Mormon party to influence the public mind and call the people to their assistance. The effect of it, however, was that by ten o'clock on the 28th of June between two and three hundred men from Quincy under the command of Major Flood embarked on board a steamboat for Nauvoo to assist in raising the siege, as they honestly believed.

As for myself, I was well convinced that those, whoever they were, who assassinated the Smiths, meditated in turn my assassination by the Mormons. The very circumstances of the case fully corroborated the information which I afterwards received that upon consultation of the assassins it was agreed amongst them that the murder must be committed whilst the governor was at Nauvoo; that the Mormons would naturally suppose that he had planned it; and that in the first outpouring of their indignation they would assassinate him by way of retaliation. And that thus they would get clear of the Smiths and the governor all at once. They also supposed that if they could so contrive the matter as to have the governor of the State assassinated by the Mormons the public excitement would be greatly increased against that people and would result in their expulsion from the State at least.

Upon hearing of the assassination of the Smiths I was sensible that my command was at an end; that my destruction was meditated as well as that of the Mormons; and that I could not reasonably confide longer in the one party or in the other.

The question then arose what would be proper to be done. A war was expected by everybody. I was desirous of preserving the peace. I could not put myself at the head of the Mormon force with any kind of propriety, and without exciting greater odium against them than already existed. I could not put myself at the head of the anti-Mormon party because they had justly forfeited my confidence and my command over them was put an end to by mutiny and treachery. I could not put myself at the head of either of these forces because both of them in turn had violated the law; and, as I then believed, meditated further aggression. It appeared to me that if a war ensued I ought to have a force in which I could confide, and that I ought to establish my headquarters at a place where I could learn the truth as to what was going on.

For these reasons I determined to proceed to Quincy, a place favorably situated for receiving the earliest intelligence, for issuing orders to raise an army if necessary, and for providing supplies for its subsistence. But first I determined to return back to Carthage and make such arrangements as could be made for the pacification and defence of the country. When I arrived there about ten o'clock at night I found that great consternation prevailed. Many of the citizens had departed with their families and others were preparing to go. As the country was utterly defenceless this seemed to me to be a proper precaution. One company of the guard stationed by me to guard the jail had disbanded and gone home before the jail was attacked; and many of the Carthage Grays departed soon afterwards.

Gen. Deming, who was absent in the country during the murder, had returned; he volunteered to remain in command of a few men, with orders to guard the town, observe the progress of events, and to retreat if menaced by a superior force.

Here also I found Dr. Richards and John Taylor, two of the principal Mormon leaders, who had been in the jail at the time of the attack and who voluntarily addressed a most pacific exhortation to their fellow-citizens, which was the first intelligence of the murder which was received at Nauvoo. I think it very probable that the subsequent good conduct of the Mormons is attributable to the arrest of the messengers and to the influence of this letter.

Having made these arrangements, I departed for Quincy. On my road thither I heard of a body of militia marching from Schuyler and another from Brown. It appears that orders had been sent out in my name, but without my knowledge, for the militia of Schuyler county. I immediately countermanded their march and they returned to their homes. When I arrived at Columbus I found that Capt. Jonas had raised a company of one hundred men, who were just ready to march. By my advice they postponed their march to await further orders. I arrived at Quincy on the morning of the 29th of June about eight o'clock, and immediately issued orders, provisionally, for raising an imposing force when it should seem to be necessary.

I remained at Quincy for about one month, during which time a committee from Warsaw waited on me with a written request that I would expel the Mormons from the State. It seemed that it never occurred to these gentlemen that I had no power to exile a citizen; but they insisted that if this were not done their party would abandon the State. This requisition was refused of course.

During this time also, with the view of saving expense, keeping the peace, and having a force which would be removed from the prejudices in the country, I made application to the United States for five hundred men of the regular army to be stationed for a time in Hancock county, which was subsequently refused.

During this time also I had secret agents amongst all parties, observing their movements; and was accurately informed of everything which was meditated on both sides. It appeared that the anti-Mormon party had not relinquished their hostility to the Mormons, nor their determination to expel them, but had deferred further operations until the fall season, after they had finished their summer's work on their farms.

When I first went to Carthage, and during all this difficult business, no public officer ever acted from purer or more patriotic intentions than I did. I was perfectly conscious of the utmost integrity in all my actions and felt lifted up far above all mere party considerations. But I had scarcely arrived at the scene of action before the whig press commenced the most violent abuse and attributed to me the basest motives. It was alleged in the Sangamon *Journal* and repeated in the other whig newspapers that the governor had merely gone over to cement an alliance with the Mormons; that the leaders would not be brought to punishment, but that a full privilege would be accorded to them to commit crimes of every hue and grade in return for their support of the democratic party. I mention this not by way of complaint, for it is only the privilege of the minority to complain, but for its influence upon the people.

I observed that I was narrowly watched in all my proceedings by my whig fellow citizens, and was suspected of an intention to favor the Mormons. I felt that I did not possess the confidence of the men I commanded, and that they had been induced to withhold it by the promulgation of the most abominable falsehoods. I felt the necessity of possessing their confidence in order to give vigor to my action; and exerted myself in every way to obtain it, so that I could control the excited multitude who were under my command. I succeeded better for a time than could have been expected; but who can control the action of a mob without possessing their entire confidence? It is true also that some unprincipled democrats all the time appeared to be very busy on the side of the Mormons, and this circumstance was well calculated to increase suspicion of every one who had the name of democrat.

XI

The Downfall of Joseph Smith, 1844–1845

It was many days after the assassination of the Smiths before the circumstances of the murder became fully known. It then appeared that, agreeably to previous orders, the posse at Warsaw had marched on the morning of the 27th of June in the direction of Golden's Point with a view to join the force from Carthage, the whole body then to be marched into Nauvoo. But by the time they had gone eight miles they were met by the order to disband; and learning at the same time that the governor was absent at Nauvoo, about two hundred of these men, many of them being disguised by blacking their faces with powder and mud, hastened immediately to Carthage. There they encamped at some distance from the village and soon learned that one of the companies left as a guard had disbanded and returned to their homes; the other company, the Carthage Grays, was stationed by the captain in the public square, a hundred and fifty yards from the jail, whilst eight men were detailed by him, under the command of Sergeant Franklin A. Worrell, to guard the prisoners. A communication was soon established between the conspirators and the company; and it was arranged that the guard should have their guns charged with blank cartridges and fire at the assailants when they attempted to enter the jail. Gen. Deming, who was left in command, being deserted by some of his troops and perceiving the arrangement with the others, and having no force upon which he could rely, for fear of his life retired from the village. The conspirators came up, jumped the slight fence around the jail, were fired upon by the guard, which according to arrangement was overpowered immediately and the assailants entered the prison to the door of the room where the two prisoners were confined with two of their friends, who voluntarily bore them company. An attempt was made to break open the door; but Joe Smith, being armed with a six-barrelled pistol furnished by his friends, fired several times as the door was burst open and wounded three of the assailants. At the same time several shots were fired into the room, by some of which John Taylor received four wounds and Hyrum Smith was instantly killed. Joe Smith now attempted to escape by jumping out of the second-story window; but the fall so stunned him that he was unable to rise; and being placed in a sitting posture by the conspirators below, they despatched him with four balls shot through his body.

Thus fell Joe Smith, the most successful impostor in modern times; a man who, though ignorant and coarse, had some great natural parts which fitted him for temporary success, but which were so obscured and counteracted by the inherent corruption and vices of his nature that he never could succeed in establishing a system of policy which looked to permanent success in the future. His lusts, his love of money and power, always set him to studying present gratification and convenience rather than the remote consequences of his plans. It seems that no power of intellect can save a corrupt man from this error. The strong cravings of the animal nature will never give fair play to a fine understanding, the judgment is never allowed to choose that good which is far away in preference to enticing evil near at hand. And this may be considered a wise ordinance of Providence, by which the counsels of talented but corrupt men are defeated in the very act which promised success.

It must not be supposed that the pretended prophet practiced the tricks of a common impostor; that he was a dark and gloomy person with a long beard, a grave and severe aspect, and a reserved and saintly carriage of his person; on the contrary, he was full of levity, even to boyish romping; dressed like a dandy, and at times drank like a sailor and swore like a pirate. He could, as occasion required, be exceedingly meek in his deportment; and then again rough and boisterous as a highway robber; being always able to satisfy his followers of the propriety of his conduct. He always quailed before power and was arrogant to weakness. At times he could put on the air of a penitent, as if feeling the deepest humiliation for his sins and suffering unutterable anguish, and indulging in the most gloomy forebodings of eternal woe. At such times he would call for the prayers of the brethren in his behalf with a wild and fearful energy and earnestness. He was full six feet high, strongly built, and uncommonly well muscled. No doubt he was as much indebted for his influence over an ignorant people to the superiority of his physical vigor as to his greater cunning and intellect.

His followers were divided into the leaders and the led; the first division embraced a numerous class of broken down, unprincipled men of talents, to be found in every country, who, bankrupt in character and fortune, had nothing to lose by deserting the known religions and carving out a new one of their own. They were mostly infidels who, holding all religions in derision, believed that they had as good a right as Christ or Mahomet or any of the founders of former systems to create one for themselves; and if they could impose it upon mankind, to live upon the labor of their dupes. Those of the second division were the credulous wondering part of men, whose easy belief and admiring natures are always the victims of novelty in whatever shape it may come, who have a capacity to believe any strange and wonderful matter, if it only be new, whilst the wonders of former ages command neither faith nor reverence; they were men of feeble purposes, readily subjected to the will of the strong, giving themselves up entirely to the direction of their leaders; and this accounts for the very great influence of those leaders in controlling them. In other respects some of the Mormons were abandoned rogues who had taken shelter in Nauvoo as a convenient place for the headquarters of their villainy; and others were good, honest, industrious people, who were the sincere victims of an artful delusion. Such as these were more the proper objects of pity than persecution. With them, their religious belief was a kind of insanity; and certainly no greater calamity can befall a human being than to have a mind so constituted as to be made the sincere dupe of a religious imposture.

The more polished portion of the Mormons were a merry set of fellows, fond of music and dancing, dress and gay assemblies. They had their regular dancing parties of gentlemen and ladies and were by no means exclusive in admitting anyone to them on the score of character. It is a notorious fact that a desperado by the name of Rockwell, having attracted the affections of a pretty woman, the wife of a Mormon merchant, took her from her husband by force of arms to live with him in adultery. But whilst she was so living notoriously in adultery with a Mormon bully, in the same city with her husband, she was freely admitted to the best society in the place, to all the gay assemblies, where she and her husband frequently met in the same dance.

The world now indulged in various conjectures as to the further progress of the Mormon religion. By some persons it was believed that it would perish and die away with its founder. But upon the principle that "the blood of the martyrs is the seed of the church," there was now really more cause than ever to predict its success. The murder of the Smiths, instead of putting an end to the delusion of the Mormons and dispersing them, as many believed it would, only bound them together closer than ever, gave them new confidence in their faith and an increased fanaticism. The Mormon church had been organized with a first presidency, composed of Joe and Hyrum Smith and Sidney Rigdon, and twelve apostles of the prophet, representing the apostles of Jesus Christ. The twelve apostles were now absent, and until they could be called together the minds of the saints were unsettled as to the future government of the church. Revelations were published that the prophet, in imitation of the Saviour, was to rise again from the dead. Many were looking in gaping wonderment for the fulfilment of this revelation, and some reported that they had already seen him attended by a celestial army coursing the air on a great white horse. Rigdon, as the only remaining member of the first presidency, claimed the government of the church, as being successor to the prophet. When the twelve apostles returned from foreign parts a fierce struggle for power ensued between them and Rigdon. Rigdon fortified his pretensions by alleging the will of the prophet in his favor and pretending to have several new revelations from heaven, amongst which was one of a very impolitic nature. This was to the effect that all the wealthy Mormons were to break up their residence at Nauvoo and follow him to Pittsburg. This revelation put both the rich and the poor against him. The rich, because they did not want to leave their property; and the poor, because they would not be deserted by the wealthy. This was fatal to the ambition of Rigdon; and the Mormons, tired of the despotism of a one-man government, were now willing to decide in favor of the apostles. Rigdon was expelled from the church as being a false prophet, and left the field with a few followers to establish a little delusion of his own near Pittsburg; leaving the government of the main church in the hands of the apostles, with Brigham Young, a cunning but vulgar man, at their head, occupying the place of Peter in the Christian hierarchy.

Missionaries were despatched to all parts to preach in the name of the "martyred Joseph;" and the Mormon religion thrived more than ever. For a while it was doubtful whether the reign of the military saints in Nauvoo would not in course of time supplant the meek and lowly system of Christ. There were many things to favor their success. The different Christian sects had lost much of the fiery energy by which at first they were animated. They had attained to a more subdued, sober, learned, and intellectual religion. But there is at all times a large class of mankind who will never be satisfied with anything in devotion short of a heated and wild fanaticism. The Mormons were the greatest zealots, the most confident in their faith, and filled with a wilder, fiercer, and more enterprising enthusiasm than any sect on the continent of America; their religion gave promise of more temporal and spiritual advantages for less labor and with less personal sacrifice of passion, lust, prejudice, malice, hatred, and ill-will than any other, perhaps, in the whole world. Their missionaries abroad, to the number of two or three thousand, were most earnest and indefatigable in their efforts to make converts; compassing sea and land to make one proselyte. When abroad, they first preached doctrines somewhat like those of the Campbellites; Sidney Rigdon, the inventor of the system, having once been a Campbellite preacher; and when they had made a favorable impression they began in far-off allusions to open up their mysteries and to reveal to their disciples that a perfect "fulness of the gospel" must be expected. This "fulness of the gospel" was looked for by the dreamy and wondering disciple as an indefinite something not yet to be comprehended, but which was essential to complete happiness and salvation. He was then told that God required him to remove to the place of gathering, where alone this sublime "fulness of the gospel" could be fully revealed and completely enjoyed. When he arrived at the place of gathering he was fortified in the new faith by being withdrawn from all other influences; and by seeing and hearing nothing but Mormons and Mormonism; and by association with those only who never doubted any of the Mormon dogmas. Now the "fulness of the gospel" could be safely made known. If it required him to submit to the most intolerable despotism; if it tolerated and encouraged the lusts of the flesh and a plurality of wives; if it claimed all the world for the saints; universal dominion for the Mormon leaders; if it sanctioned murder, robbery, perjury, and larceny at the command of their priests, no one could now doubt but that this was the "fulness of the gospel," the liberty of the saints, with which Christ had made them free.

The Christian world, which has hitherto regarded Mormonism with silent contempt, unhappily may yet have cause to fear its rapid increase. Modern society is full of material for such a religion. At the death of the prophet, fourteen years after the first Mormon Church was organized, the Mormons in all the world numbered about two hundred thousand souls (one half million according to their statistics); a number equal, perhaps, to the number of Christians when the Christian Church was of the same age. It is to be feared that in course of a century some gifted man like Paul, some splendid orator who will be able by his eloquence to attract crowds of the thousands who are ever ready to hear and be carried away by the sounding brass and tinkling cymbal of sparkling oratory, may command a hearing, may succeed in breathing a new life into this modern Mahometanism, and make the name of the martyred Joseph ring as loud and stir the souls of men as much as the mighty name of Christ itself. Sharon, Palmyra, Manchester, Kirtland, Far West, Adam Ondi Ahmon, Ramus, Nauvoo, and the Carthage Jail may become holy and venerable names, places of classic interest in another age; like Jerusalem, the Garden of Gethsemane, the Mount of Olives, and Mount Calvary to the Christian, and Mecca and Medina to the Turk. And in that event the author of this history feels degraded by the reflection that the humble governor of an obscure State, who would otherwise be forgotten in a few years, stands a fair chance, like Pilate and Herod, by their official connection with the true religion, of being dragged down to posterity with an immortal name hitched on to the memory of a miserable impostor. There may be those whose ambition would lead them to desire an immortal name in history, even on those humbling terms. I am not one of that number.

About one year after the apostles were installed into power they abandoned for the present the project of converting the world to the new religion. All the missionaries and members abroad were ordered home; it was announced that the world had rejected the gospel by the murder of the prophet and patriarch and was to be left to perish in its sins. In the meantime, both before and after this, the elders at Nauvoo quit preaching about religion. The Mormons came from every part, pouring into the city; the congregations were regularly called together for worship, but instead of expounding the new gospel the zealous and infuriated preachers now indulged only in curses and strains of abuse of the Gentiles, and it seemed to be their design to fill their followers with the greatest amount of hatred to all mankind excepting the saints. A sermon was no more than an inflammatory stump speech, relating to their quarrels with their enemies and ornamented with an abundance of profanity. From my own personal knowledge of this people I can say with truth that I have never known much of any of their leaders who was not addicted to profane swearing. No other kind of discourses than these were heard in the city. Curses upon their enemies, upon the country, upon government, upon all public officers were now the lessons taught by the elders to inflame their people with the highest degree of spite and malice against all who were not of the Mormon church or its obsequious tools. The reader can readily imagine how a city of fifteen thousand inhabitants could be wrought up and kept in a continual rage by the inflammatory harangues of its leaders.

In the meantime the anti-Mormons were not idle; they were more than ever determined to expel the Mormons; and being passionately inflamed against them, they made many applications for executive assistance. On the other hand, the Mormons invoked the assistance of government to take vengeance upon the murderers of the Smiths. The anti-Mormons asked the governor to violate the constitution which he was sworn to support by erecting himself into a military despot and exiling the Mormons. The Mormons, on their part, in their newspapers invited the governor to assume absolute power by taking a summary vengeance upon their enemies, by shooting fifty or a hundred of them without judge or jury. Both parties were thoroughly disgusted with constitutional provisions restraining them from the summary attainment of their wishes for vengeance; each was ready to submit to arbitrary power, to the fiat of a dictator, to make me a king for the time being, or at least that I might exercise the power of a king, to abolish both the forms and spirit of free government, if the despotism to be erected upon its ruins could only be wielded for its benefit, and to take vengeance on its enemies. It seems that notwithstanding all our strong professions of attachment to liberty there is all the time an unconquerable leaning to the principles of monarchy and despotism whenever the forms, the delays, and the restraints of republican government fail to correct great evils. When the forms of government in the United States were first invented the public liberty was thought to be the great object of governmental protection. Our ancestors studied to prevent government from doing harm by depriving it of power. They would not trust the power of exiling a citizen upon any terms; or of taking his life without a fair and impartial trial in the courts even to the people themselves, much less to their government. But so infatuated were these parties, so deep did they feel their grievances, that both of them were enraged in their turn because the governor firmly adhered to his oath of office; refusing to be a party to their revolutionary proceedings; to set aside the government of the country and execute summary vengeance upon one or the other of them.

Another election was to come off in August, 1844 for members of Congress, and for the legislature; and an election was pending throughout the nation for a President of the United States. The war of party was never more fierce and terrible than during the pendency of these elections. The parties in many places met separately almost every night; not to argue the questions in dispute, but to denounce, ridicule, abuse, and belittle each other with sarcasm, clamor, noise, and songs, during which nothing could be heard but hallooing, hurrahing, and yelling, and then to disperse through town with insulting taunts and yells of defiance on either side.

In all this they were but little less fanatical and frantic on the subject of politics than were the Mormons about religion. Such a state of excitement could not fail to operate unfavorably upon the Mormon question, involved as it was in the questions of party politics by the former votes of the Mormons. As a means of allaying the excitement and making the question more manageable, I was most anxious that the Mormons should not vote at this election, and strongly advised them against doing so. But Col. E. D. Taylor went to their city a few days before the election and the Mormons, being ever disposed to follow the worst advice they could get, were induced by him and others to vote for all the democratic candidates. Col. Taylor found them very hostile to the governor and on that account much disposed not to vote at this election. The leading whig anti-Mormons, believing that I had an influence over the Mormons, for the purpose of destroying it had assured them that the governor had planned and been favorable to the murder of their prophet and patriarch. The Mormons pretended to suspect that the governor had given some countenance to the murder, or at least had neglected to take the proper precautions to prevent it. And yet it is strange that at this same election they elected Gen. Deming to be the sheriff of the county, when they knew that he had first called out the militia against them, had concurred with me in all the measures subsequently adopted, had been left in command at Carthage during my absence at Nauvoo, and had left his post when he saw that he had no power to prevent the murders. As to myself, I shared the fate of all men in high places who favor moderation, who see that both parties in the frenzy of their excitement are wrong—espousing the cause of neither; which fate always is to be hated by both parties. But Col. Taylor like a skilful politician denied nothing, but gave countenance to everything the Mormons said of the governor; and by admitting to them that the governor was a great rascal; by promising them the support of the democratic party, an assurance he was not authorized to make, but which they were foolish enough to believe, and by insisting that the governor was not the democratic party he overcame their reluctance to vote. Nevertheless, for mere political effect, without a shadow of justice the whig leaders and newspapers everywhere, and some enemies in the democratic ranks, immediately charged this vote of the Mormons to the governor's influence; and this charge being believed by many, made the anti-Mormon party more furious than ever in favor of the expulsion of the Mormons. In the course of the fall of 1844 the anti-Mormon leaders sent printed invitations to all the militia captains in Hancock and to the captains of militia in all the neighboring counties in Illinois, Iowa, and Missouri to be present with their companies at a great wolf hunt in Hancock; and it was privately announced that the wolves to be hunted were the Mormons and Jack Mormons. Preparations were made for assembling several thousand men with provisions for six days; and the anti-Mormon newspapers, in aid of the movement, commenced anew the most awful accounts of thefts and robberies and meditated outrages by the Mormons. The whig press in every part of the United States came to their assistance. The democratic newspapers and leading democrats who had received the benefit of the Mormon votes to their party quailed under the tempest, leaving no organ for the correction of public opinion, either at home or abroad, except the discredited Mormon newspaper at Nauvoo. But very few of my prominent democratic friends would dare to come up to the assistance of their governor, and but few of them dared openly to vindicate his motives in endeavoring to keep the peace. They were willing and anxious for Mormon votes at elections, but they were unwilling to risk their popularity with the people by taking a part in their favor, even when law and justice and the Constitution were all on their side. Such being the odious character of the Mormons, the hatred of the common people against them, and such being the pusillanimity of leading men in fearing to encounter it.

In this state of the case I applied to Brigadier General J. J. Hardin of the State militia and to Colonels Baker and Merriman, all whigs, but all of them men of military ambition, and they, together with Colonel William Weatherford, a democrat,* with my own exertions, succeeded in raising about five hundred volunteers; and thus did these whigs that which my own political friends with two or three exceptions were slow to do, from a sense of duty and gratitude.

With this little force under the command of General Hardin I arrived in Hancock county on the 25th of October. The malcontents abandoned their design and all the leaders of it fled to Missouri. The

---

*Of the officers who were out with me in this expedition General Hardin, Colonels Baker and Weatherford, and Major Warren afterwards greatly distinguished themselves in the Mexican war. Major Warren is noticed by General Taylor in his despatches to the war department as a prudent and gallant officer. Lieutenant-Colonel Weatherford was left a whole day with a few companies to guard the main pass at Buena Vista, where he and his men stood, during all that time, the fire of the Mexican artillery without being allowed to advance near enough to return it. Colonel Baker, after the fall of General Shields, commanded a brigade of two Illinois regiments and one New York regiment in storming the last stronghold of the Mexicans at the battle of Cerro Gordo, in which he and his men behaved most gallantly, carrying everything before them, which completed the entire rout of the Mexican army. General Hardin at the battle of Buena Vista, in command of two Illinois regiments in conjunction with a regiment of Kentucky volunteers, made a most gallant charge upon a large body of Mexican infantry and lancers, five times the numbers of the Americans, which decided the victory on our side—but in which Hardin and many other gallant officers and men lost their lives. But they will live in the affectionate remembrance of their countrymen to the latest time.

Carthage Grays fled almost in a body, carrying their arms along with them. During our stay in the county the anti-Mormons thronged into the camp and conversed freely with the men, who were fast infected with their prejudices, and it was impossible to get any of the officers to aid in expelling them. Colonels Baker, Merriman and Weatherford volunteered their services, if I would go with them, to cross with a force into Missouri to capture three of the anti-Mormon leaders for whose arrest writs had been issued for the murder of the Smiths.[1] To this I assented and procured a boat, which was sent down in the night and secretly landed a mile above Warsaw. Our little force arrived at that place about noon; that night we were to cross to Missouri at Churchville and seize the accused there encamped with a number of their friends; but that afternoon Colonel Baker visited the hostile encampment, and on his return refused to participate in the expedition and advised all his friends against joining it. There was no authority for compelling the men to invade a neighboring State, and for this cause, much to the vexation of myself and several others, the matter fell through.

It seems that Colonel Baker had already partly arranged the terms for the accused to surrender. They were to be taken to Quincy for examination under a military guard; the attorney for the people was to be advised to admit them to bail, and they were to be entitled to a continuance of their trial at the next court at Carthage; upon this, two of the accused came over and surrendered themselves prisoners.

But at that time I was held responsible for this compromise with the murderers. The truth is that I had but little of the moral power to command in this expedition. Officers, men, and all under me were so infected with the anti-Mormon prejudices that I was made to feel severely the want of moral power to control them. It would be thought very strange in any other government that the administration should have the power to direct, but no power to control. By the constitution the governor can neither appoint nor remove a militia officer. He may arrest and order a court martial. But a court martial composed of military officers elected in times of peace, in many cases upon the same principles upon which Colonel Pluck was elected in New York city, is not likely to pay much attention to executive wishes in opposition to popular excitement. So too in Illinois, the governor has no power to appoint, remove, or in anywise control sheriffs, justices of the peace, nor even a constable; and yet the active co-operation of such officers with the executive is indispensable to the success of any effort the governor may make to suppress civil war. If any one supposes that the greatest amount of talents will enable any one to govern under such circumstances, he is mistaken. It may be thought that the governor ought to create a public sentiment in favor of his measures, to sway the minds of those under him to his own course, but if any one supposes that even the greatest abilities could succeed in such an effort against popular feeling and against the inherent love of numerous demagogues for popularity he is again mistaken.

I had determined from the first that some of the ring-leaders in the foul murder of the Smiths should be brought to trial. If these men had been the incarnation of Satan himself, as was believed by many, their murder was a foul and treacherous action, alike disgraceful to those who perpetrated the crime, to the State, and to the governor, whose word had been pledged for the protection of the prisoners in jail, and which had been so shamefully violated; and required that the most vigorous means should be used to bring the assassins to punishment. As much as anything else the expedition under General Hardin had been ordered with a view to arrest the murderers.

Accordingly I employed able lawyers to hunt up the testimony, procure indictments, and prosecute the offenders.[2] A trial was had before Judge Young in the summer of 1845. The sheriff and panel of jurors selected by the Mormon court were set aside for prejudice, and elisors were appointed to select a new jury. One friend of the Mormons and one anti-Mormon were appointed for this purpose; but as more than a thousand men had assembled under arms at the court to keep away the Mormons and their friends, the jury was made up of these military followers of the court, who all swore that they had never formed or expressed any opinion as to the guilt or innocence of the accused. The Mormons had one principal witness who was with the troops at Warsaw, had marched with them until they were disbanded, heard their consultations, went before them to Carthage, and saw them murder the Smiths.[3] But before the trial came on they had induced him to become a Mormon; and being much more anxious for the glorification of the prophet than to avenge his death, the leading Mormons made him publish a pamphlet giving an account of the murder; in which he professed to have seen a bright and shining light descend upon the head of Joe Smith to strike some of the conspirators with blindness, and that he heard supernatural voices in the air confirming his mission as a prophet! Having published this in a book he was compelled to swear to it in court, which of course destroyed the credit of his evidence. This witness was afterwards expelled from the Mormons, but no doubt they will cling to his evidence in favor of the divine mission of the prophet. Many other witnesses were examined who knew the facts, but under the influence of the demoralization of faction denied all knowledge of them. It has been said that faction may find men honest, but it scarcely ever leaves them so. This was verified to the letter in the history of the Mormon quarrel. The accused were all acquitted.

During the progress of these trials the judge was compelled to permit the courthouse to be filled and surrounded by armed bands, who attended court to browbeat and overawe the administration of justice. The judge himself was in a duress, and informed me that he did not consider his life secure any part of the time. The consequence was that the crowd had everything their own way; the lawyers for the defence defended their clients by a long and elaborate attack on the governor; the armed mob stamped with their feet and yelled their approbation at every sarcastic and smart thing that was said; and the judge was not only forced to hear it, but to lend it a kind of approval. Josiah Lamborne was attorney for the prosecution; and O. H. Browning, O. C. Skinner, Calvin A. Warren, and William A. Richardson were for the defence.[4]

At the next term the leading Mormons were tried and acquitted for the destruction of the heretical press. It appears that, not being interested in objecting to the sheriff or the jury selected by a court elected by themselves, they in their turn got a favorable jury determined upon acquittal, and yet the Mormon jurors all swore that they had formed no opinion as to the guilt or innocence of their accused friends. It appeared that the laws furnished the means of suiting each party with a jury. The Mormons could have a Mormon jury to be tried by, selected by themselves; and the anti-Mormons, by objecting to the sheriff and regular panel, could have one from the anti-Mormons. From henceforth no leading man on either side could be arrested without the aid of an army, as the men of one party could not safely surrender to the other for fear of being murdered; when arrested by a military force the constitution prohibited a trial in any other county without the consent of the accused. No one would be convicted of any crime in Hancock; and this put an end to the administration of the criminal law in that distracted county. Government was at an end there, and the whole community was delivered up to the dominion of a frightful anarchy. If the whole State had been in the same condition then indeed would have been verified to the letter what was said by a wit when he expressed an opinion that the people were neither capable of governing themselves nor of being governed by others. And truly there can be no government in a free country where the people do not voluntarily obey the laws.

XII

The Canal Problem and Its Solution, 1843–1845

Having in the last chapter brought down the history of Mormon disturbances to the summer of 1845, we turn again to the civil history of the State. In March, 1843 Col. Charles Oakley and Senator Michael Ryan were appointed agents to negotiate the canal loan; the first of these gentlemen was appointed because the friends of the measure in the legislature insisted on his appointment; Mr. Ryan was appointed because he had commenced the negotiation the year before and having been an engineer on the canal could give explanations as to its progress and statistics which could not so well be given by Colonel Oakley. The first, Col. Oakley, was a man of good sense and middling intelligence, and was patient, gentlemanly, and plausible in his manners; whilst his associate had more mind and ambition, with greater information, but less tact in managing business. The next thing was to raise money, some three thousand dollars, to pay their expenses. There was not a dollar in the treasury and the money had to be taken, a part of it from the school fund, to be replaced in a short time by other moneys coming into the treasury. This was the first charge I had to answer, urged in the south by Trumbull, the lately removed Secretary of State. Messrs. Oakley and Ryan proceeded to New York, but the negotiation was for a time likely to be defeated by partisan editors and letter-writers at home; who, in a desperate effort to make political capital, were anxious that the canal measure might fail in the hands of the dominant party. These writers misrepresented the action of the legislature, revamped the old charge of destructiveness upon the party in power, and boldly asserted that if the creditors of the State advanced the money to make the canal they would be repealed out of their rights by another legislature. This was the first difficulty the agents had to encounter; they commenced a series of publications in the New York papers, many of which were secured to speak favorably of the loan. The legislation of the last winter, the real condition of the State, its future prospects, and the means adopted to reduce the debt by a compromise with the banks and a sale of the public property were truly set forth. Confidence immediately began to revive; our State stocks rose in a week from fourteen to twenty per cent, and in a few weeks more to thirty and forty per cent. This awakened a universal inquiry, and men began to believe that there was some little glimmering prospect that Illinois, lately so low in the slough of universal discredit and contempt, was about to come forth like a phoenix from its ashes. The American Exchange Bank in New York held $250,000 of canal bonds. David Leavitt, the president of this institution, a gentleman of great credit in the financial world, and being a far-seeing and sagacious financier, assisted in calling a meeting of the American bond-holders. At this meeting it was resolved that the American creditors would subscribe for their proportion of the loan.

With this assurance and backed by this expression of confidence at home Messrs. Oakley and Ryan departed for England, carrying letters to Magniac, Jardine & Co. and Baring Brothers & Co. of London, and to Hope & Co. of Amsterdam, who were creditors of the State and amongst the wealthiest capitalists in Europe. These gentlemen were found well disposed to use their great influence in favor of the loan; but they wanted to be thoroughly satisfied as to the value of the canal property as a security for the money, and ultimately for the payment of the whole canal debt of $5,000,000; nor were they willing to abandon the exaction of some legislation manifesting the willingness of the people to submit to taxation, if necessary, to pay some part of the interest on the public debt.

A provisional arrangement was entered into during the summer of 1843, the main articles of which were that Abbott Lawrence, Thomas W. Ward, and Mr. William Sturges of Boston should be a committee to appoint two competent persons in America to examine the canal and canal lands, estimate their value, and the amount of debt already contracted; that if four hundred thousand dollars could be subscribed and if the governor would pledge himself to recommend taxation to the next session of the legislature, this sum should be expended in the meantime, leaving the subscribers at liberty afterwards to increase their subscriptions if they saw proper. With this arrangement Messrs. Oakley and Ryan returned home in November, 1843; the Boston committee appointed Gov. John Davis of Massachusetts and William H. Swift, who was an eminent engineer and a captain in the United States army, to come out to Illinois and make the required examinations. These gentlemen came on early in the winter. The appointment of Gov. Davis was no sooner known than it was fiercely attacked by the *Globe* newspaper at Washington city, the great organ of the democratic party in the United States. Gov. Davis was at that time extensively spoken of as the whig candidate for Vice-

President at the ensuing election; and the zealots of the opposite party pretended to believe that he had been selected by the foreign bond-holders for this particular work so as to give him the power to coerce the government and people of Illinois into the support of the whig party, and to favor the assumption of State debts by the general government or the distribution of the proceeds of the sales of the public lands. As it turned out nothing could have been more basely false and contemptibly ridiculous than this charge, but it was made with such boldness and savage ferocity that if it had been seconded in Illinois it could not have failed to have disgusted our foreign creditors and defeated the negotiation. It seemed that the demon of party on both sides insinuated itself into everything to defeat all rational efforts for the public welfare. To this charge of the *Globe* Senator Ryan published a reply characterized by much boldness and vigor, in which the foreign bond-holders and Gov. Davis were defended with considerable ability and the editor of the *Globe* was castigated for his impertinent interference in our State affairs, with little less ferocity than the charge of the *Globe* itself.

Governor Davis and Captain Swift proceeded with their examinations; found the representations of Messrs. Oakley and Ryan to be substantially true; and in their report, occupying about one hundred pages, strongly recommended the loan. On my part, I agreed to recommend taxation to the legislature; and it was now confidently believed that success would crown our efforts early in the following summer. It became necessary to send an agent back to London to complete the arrangement, but there was no money to pay his expenses. The sum of $1,500 was soon obtained, with my sanction, by Gen. Fry on a pledge of canal scrip, which enabled Senator Ryan to return to London in the spring of 1844. But as the subscription of $400,000 had not been made up according to agreement the foreign bond-holders refused to proceed further with the loan until some substantial evidence should be given by the legislature that the population of the State had some regard to their obligations and to the claims of their creditors, and should make at least a beginning to pay interest on all her debts. It seemed to be the great object of our foreign creditors not so much to secure the amount of their claims as to procure a restoration and practical recognition of the obligation of public faith among States and nations; and in the meantime the London committee sent out to America for Gov. Davis, as, they said, by the details he might give, to inspire with greater confidence the parties from whom subscriptions were solicited. This put off the negotiation until late in the summer; and as it was now near the regular session of the legislature in December, 1844 the London committee broke off the negotiation to await the further action of that body. During the pendency of the last negotiation Col. Oakley had also returned to London; and now both he and Senator Ryan returned home, the unlucky ministers of a broken and discredited State; Oakley to New York to urge further efforts and Ryan to his seat in the Senate.

Ryan was ambitious of political distinction. Whilst he remained in an humble position his manners and pretensions had been humble and amiable; but so soon as he was elevated he became irascible, dictatorial, and overbearing. He placed his heart on getting the money to make the canal; success was to make him the greatest man in the State; failure was to return him to his original obscurity; for this reason he had no patience with the delays incident to this kind of business; every little delay irritated and soured his temper, which he was at no trouble to conceal; so that his demeanor towards the foreign bond-holders was more calculated to disgust than to win their favor. His ambition for exclusive credit had led him, in anticipation of a triumph, to quarrel with and abuse his colleague; but now that both had failed, that there was no credit to quarrel about or divide, he looked around for some convenient person to bear the censure. Instead of coming home to be met with smiles and congratulations, he fancied that he returned only to breast the frowns of an indignant people, and to answer for his bad success. In this extremity he submitted to a weakness which I regret to relate, but as the matter made much noise at the time some account of it is necessary to the completeness of this history. In looking around for a person to throw the blame on he selected Gov. Davis, the man he had defended before against the attacks of the *Globe*. Gov. Davis was a very distinguished whig politician; as such, there was great prejudice against him in the opposite party, which prejudice had been increased by newspaper accounts of his opposition to the war of 1812. He was called an old federalist, which I have already said in another place meant, in the minds of western democrats, everything that was atrocious and abominable. Here then was the very man to attack. Gov. Davis would defend as a matter of course; the people would be divided in the quarrel; the whigs for Gov. Davis and the democrats for Ryan; and thus he would sustain himself, at least with the democracy. This is a trick which, when hard run, unprincipled politicians frequently practise, and cannot be too much condemned by all honorable men. Ryan no sooner arrived in America than he revived the calumnies of the *Globe* newspaper, which he had refuted before, and now openly charged in the New York papers that the Boston committee had sent out Gov. Davis to delay the loan until after the pending Presidential election so as to favor the election of Mr. Clay; and that Gov. Davis did delay it for that purpose. The falsity of this charge is apparent from the following extract of a letter from Baring Brothers & Co. to Ryan himself, a copy of which is now before me: "Since writing what precedes, a copy of the Ottawa *Free Trader* newspaper of September 12 has been put into our hands, with a publication bearing your signature. At this distance we cannot appreciate the party or personal motives which have dictated your statements, nor the effect they may produce on the people of Illinois; but to those who are acquainted with all the circumstances of the case the coarseness of language and the perversion of facts contained in this article will be more prejudicial to the writer than to those whom it is intended to injure. We sincerely regret the appearance of such a manifesto from you on account of the feelings it displays, and of the continued hostility which it seems we must expect from you and your friends to the trustees and to the measures which we believe to be most conducive to the satisfactory completion of the canal; to the ultimate payment of the creditors, and to the general welfare of Illinois. It is more probable that, had we anticipated all your vexatious proceedings, we should have declined all interference with the loan and have left you and Col. Oakley to regret the failure of your negotiation; but having once embarked in the undertaking we shall continue the course which we consider to be in conformity with our duty regardless of unfounded charges and insinuations, from whatever point they may proceed; and we trust and believe that our friends on your side who are entrusted with the administration of the affairs of the canal will pursue the same line of conduct.

"You are incorrect in stating that the subscription for $400,000 was completed, even if the report of Governor Davis and Capt. Swift had proved satisfactory at the time of your departure, after your first visit to this country; and you are further mistaken in supposing that Governor Davis was influenced by any party views in his communications with us, or in his proceedings under our direction. He never advised the delay of the loan on account of the pending presidential election; he never stated that it would be desirable to wait to see whether Mr. Clay, if elected, would support the assumption of State debts by the federal government; he never held out any hope that he would accept the trusteeship, although we were most desirous that he should be appointed; and his advice always was that the canal bond-holders should accept the canal and canal lands in trust and advance the money required, with or without taxation for the payment of interest. But we as universally insisted that before any further sums of money were lent for the public works of Illinois some substantial evidence should be given that the population of the State had some regard for their obligations and to the claims of their creditors. We know very little of the party politics of the United States, and still less of those of your State; and politics never interfere with our dealings either with States or individuals. Our motive for inducing Governor Davis to visit Europe was that he might, by the details he would give, inspire with more confidence the parties from whom subscriptions were solicited; and we still believe that his report and verbal statements were mainly instrumental in preparing us and others for the increased subscriptions to which we agreed during Mr. Leavitt's visit here. As we are anxious that our communications with you should not be exposed to misconstruction, we forward this letter open to Mr. Ward of Boston, to be sent, after perusal and copy, to you."*

*As Ryan may probably attempt to reply to the statements in the text, it may be proper once for all to make a full statement of his conduct. Before he made his charges against Governor Davis he balanced the matter in his mind, whether it would not be better policy to lay the blame of the failure of the canal negotiation on me, but he finally decided that he could attack a whig with more success than a democrat. The grounds upon which he designed to attack me were, first, for appointing Col. Oakley to be his colleague; he alleged that Col. Oakley having formerly been one of the fund commissioners, many of the bond-holders believed him to be dishonest, and to have swindled the State. It is true that Governor Carlin and others had boldly made this charge at home; but it is doing Col. Oakley but simple justice to say that his guilt had never been established to the satisfaction of the people. Secondly, that I had promised to send Ryan a power of attorney in 1844 to negotiate and close the terms of the contract, which was never sent. For which reason he found himself in London confined in his power to negotiate with the bond-holders alone. He alleged that if he had possessed such a power of attorney he could have withdrawn the negotiation from the bond-holders and made application for the money elsewhere, and thereby could have coerced the bond-holders to make a favorable decision before the arrival of Governor Davis. To all which I reply, first, that whether Col. Oakley's appointment was good or bad it was dictated by the friends of the canal, by those most particularly interested in the negotiation; and was recommended to me at the time by Ryan himself. Second, I never promised to send Ryan a power of attorney to negotiate and close the terms of the contract. This is a power which I would have trusted to no one. I always intended that Ryan, or Ryan and Oakley, might negotiate for the loan, but the contract no one should make for the State but myself. I did promise to send Ryan a power of attorney to settle with the estate of Wright & Co., which was sent, and was the only one ever promised. Third, if Ryan had possessed ever so many powers of attorney he could have made nothing by withdrawing the negotiation from the bond-holders. They were the only persons in the wide world from whom there was any chance to get the money; and this was well known to both Ryan and to the bond-holders. The bond-holders had an interest which others had not. We already owed them money which they had no expectation of getting paid to

In the fall of 1844, Mr. William S. Wait of Bond county addressed a letter through the newspapers to the governor against taxation for the payment of the public debt; this gave me a decent pretext for coming before the people with my views in favor of the measure in advance of the meeting of the legislature, then to convene in December following. I knew that nothing could be more unpopular than to favor an increase of taxes; in so doing, I knew that I came into immediate collision with every demagogue and incurred imminent hazard of making myself utterly odious to a tax-hating people. I clearly saw that to be opposed to taxation might be the better for myself, but certainly worse for the State.

The following is the substance of the letter addressed to Mr. Wait, through the newspapers: "I am much pleased that your esteemed favor of September 20th, published in the *State Register* yesterday, has made a proper occasion for some suggestions of mine on the payment of the State debt before the meeting of the next legislature. A deeper interest than what is yet manifest ought to be felt in this subject. It ought to be discussed more than it has been; the people ought to begin to move in it, and make known their will before the meeting of the next legislature.

"You object to increased taxation to pay any portion of interest,

---

them without making a new advance. And yet Ryan pretended to believe that if he had had the power to withdraw the negotiation from them, and threaten them with an application to other capitalists, that they would at once have quailed and closed the contract before the arrival of Governor Davis. Fourth, Oakley afterwards returned to London, he and Ryan were there together, and had a joint power of attorney given the year before which would have authorized them to withdraw the negotiation from the bond-holders and apply elsewhere.

If the money could have been obtained from others, or if the bond-holders could have been alarmed into terms by their threatenings, why now did they not succeed? They both failed in the negotiation with the bond-holders and never pretended to apply elsewhere, or if they did they were bound to fail again, and they knew it; for no man in the whole world would at that time have lent Illinois money without having an interest which compelled him to do it. After the canal bill finally succeeded Ryan wanted to be State trustee; for which reason he made friends with Governor Davis, who was expected to be one of the trustees on the part of the bond-holders. I refused to appoint Ryan, and no sooner did he ascertain this refusal than I found him urging the appointment of Col. Oakley, the man he had charged as being a thief and a swindler whilst he was fund commissioner, a man in whom he said the bond-holders had so little confidence that his appointment to negotiate with them had caused the failure of the negotiation. I have always believed that Ryan had hopes of being appointed chief engineer on the canal if Oakley could be appointed trustee. These statements are made merely to illustrate the civilization of the times, and not at all to affect Mr. Ryan injuriously; for I am well aware that the state of political morals among politicians is such that a man may do many, yes, very many worse things than these and still be very respectable as a politician. God grant that it may not be so long.

believing that the sum within our ability to pay without driving the people to desperation by oppressive taxes will be so small that the effort will be without utility; and also because the general failure of crops for the last two years in a great portion of the State, the high waters of the last spring, the destruction of farms, stock, and crops thereby, and the unprecedented severe sickness of this summer and fall will render it absolutely impossible to collect the present taxes, to say nothing of increased taxation.

"During the last two years many persons have anxiously looked to the next general Assembly, expecting that body to settle forever the question as to what shall be done with the public debt. The question may be postponed; but putting off the evil day will not settle it. It will present itself to every succeeding legislature. We can never get clear of it by postponing it. The men of this day may attempt to throw it upon the future; they may decide to do nothing, but if we decide against the honest claims of our creditors it will be forever rising again to annoy us. The moral sense of the world will be against us and will forever remind us that such a question cannot be settled except in conformity to justice. The fact will stare us in the face that we have had the money of our creditors and that they have had nothing in return. Like the ghost of Macbeth, every time the legislature meets it will rise to glare upon their vision and will not down at their bidding. It will make itself seen, heard, and felt until mankind can eradicate their memories and consciences. There is no possibility of destroying the fact or the question to which it gives rise. All that we can do is to postpone the evil day; and in the meantime we keep ourselves and the world in the fearful apprehension that blighting ruin will sooner or later fall upon this fair land in the shape of high taxes.

"This has been our condition for years past; the mere belief that taxes may be oppressive has lost us many citizens. The high and palmy days once were when we doubled our population in a few years; when if a man had more land than he wanted for cultivation, or if he wanted to leave the country or remove from one part of the State to another, he could sell his land for cash. But those days are gone. What has produced this? has it been high taxes? No! it has been only the fear of them. Is it because industry has been burdened and the country drained of its money to pay either principal or interest of the debt? No! not one cent has yet been paid by taxation. Nevertheless, the people have lived in more alarm than if all the evils they imagined had actually existed. Let us then settle the question and know the worst at once, for the worst can never be so bad as that unmanly fear which blights all enterprise.

"There are but two modes of settling this question; one will be to begin at once a system of taxation which we mean to pursue; the other is by direct repudiation. This last mode will expose us to the merited scorn and contempt of the civilized world. It defies the internal principles of sacred justice, and will establish for us among all men a reputation as odious and detestable as that of a nest of pirates. Mankind will never forget and we can never ourselves forget that we have had the money of our creditors, that we owe them, that they have lost that much; and that with a heaven-daring impudence and scornful defiance of the moral principles of man's nature we deny the debt and refuse to pay it.

"Suppose that the question can be settled in this manner, what better will we be off? It is true that the fear of high taxes would be removed for the present; but will this invite immigration? Will it enable us to sell our property? Men with means to buy would not come to the State. Such persons would never venture themselves here. No man would bring here a good character to be swallowed in our infamy. If any did come, they would be the worthless of mankind; such as we ought to desire to keep away. Our State would become a catchall for passing rogues and vagabonds. The men of character already here would soon lose all self-respect for the character of the State. The State itself would be a place of refuge, where swindlers, horse-thieves, and counterfeiters could resort, to be received and treated as gentlemen. Who of our present population desires to see this? Who desires to raise a family of children in the atmosphere of dishonor, to grow up among swindlers and vagabonds, and leave them at his death an inheritance of infamy? None of us. I am satisfied that all of us, and you in particular, duly appreciate the advantages to a State of a character for honor and uprightness. We look to Kentucky, Tennessee, Virginia, New York, and New England, and why are they great and honorable among States? It is their intelligence, justice, sense of honor, and an all-consoling State pride which make them so. We all wish to see Illinois have a just State pride, let this feeling be cultivated here, let us have something to be proud of, let us vindicate ourselves in our own eyes by acting in such a manner as to deserve to be proud of our State. Until we do this a State pride cannot exist; without this a people may boast, but their boastings will be but the empty swagger of vulgar vice and ignorance, not the complacent, dignified self-respect of the upright citizen. The successful robber exults; and we may exult in the infamy of repudiation, but we cannot exult like a Kentuckian, Virginian, or Yankee. Our sons will never be able to show themselves abroad exulting in the character of their native State, as young men do who are conscious of creditable parentage. This State pride is of great worth to any people. It inspires them to make noble efforts at improvement and excellence, which efforts are totally paralyzed by the contrary feeling of a sense of degradation.

"Many persons regret that this sacred feeling of State pride is not more on the increase in Illinois. We frequently hear strangers speak disparagingly of our people; they do it to our faces in our towns and villages. We ourselves do the same. Every one may speak ill of us with impunity. In Kentucky or Virginia this would not be hazarded. There the perpetrators of such obloquy would be certain to be insulted, and in great danger of physical injury. We are a new State and therefore something of this kind must be expected. Many of our citizens are so recent that as yet they can hardly realize that Illinois is their country. As a new State we have a character to make. We may choose a good or a bad one. But we may be certain that no just State pride can ever exist where it is not really deserved. We have to deserve the good opinion of the world and our own before we can have it. And I do anxiously hope to see the day when Illinois, a State in which I have lived for forty years, may have and deserve a good old-fashioned State pride like some of the older States of the Union; so that her people may feel it, be animated by it to improvement and noble enterprise, and be solaced by it both at home and abroad. I am sure that repudiation of our just debts can never bring us this; but must drag us down like the weight of the nether mill-stone to the abyss of self-abasement, to the great whirlpool of the contempt and scorn of all right-minded and civilized people. It can only degrade us; it can never settle the question of the public debt; that question will arise at every session of the legislature, and in the counsels of every new set of men put into power. The memory of the debt will never be lost; our obligation to pay it is imperishable. We may deny it and plead *non est factum* to our bonds; but like the rogue who seeks to cheat his creditor in private life, we will still owe the debt, the damning consciousness of which, being registered in our hearts and in heaven's high chancery, will stick there to plague us forever.

"Such a settlement of the question, if it could be made, would be of no use, but full of mischief. It would invite neither wealth nor people to come among us. It would not increase the value of our property nor make it more saleable; but in my humble judgment it would debase us and belittle us in our own estimation; make us deserving of the detestation and scorn of the world and fill our State with the low dregs, the scum, the refuse population of other countries—refugees from justice and others, who leave their country for their country's good. How then can this question be settled? I answer that there is but one way, and that is to nerve our hearts and arms and meet it like men. If we can do but little, let us do that little. I am not now in a situation to know how much can be done. The legislature will be the best judge of this when they meet, and as the fear and not the existence of high taxes constitutes our embarrassment, it is hoped that the legislature will provide such a settlement of the question as will ascertain the whole height and depth, length and breadth and thickness of the apprehended evil, for until this is done the fancies, the fears, the imaginations of men will conjure up evils exceeding the reality. The reality, whenever it comes, can never be so terrifying as the undefined, dreamy imaginations of men looking for an unknown and untried evil."

This letter arrived at New York in course of mails, and was very extensively republished in the eastern newspapers. It attracted the attention of Mr. Leavitt and encouraged him and Col. Oakley to return to Europe early in the winter. Upon their arrival in London the letter had preceded them and, Mr. Leavitt informed me, had already produced a very favorable change in the minds of our creditors; as by it they were convinced that the public men in Illinois were not all of them demagogues. It was now agreed by Mr. Leavitt, Magniac, Jardine & Co., and Baring Brothers & Co. to complete the subscriptions to the loan, these gentlemen each subscribing for a much larger share of it than they had originally intended.* Mr. Leavitt and Col. Oakley, with Gov. Davis, hurried on to Illinois and arrived in Springfield about the middle of February, 1845, during the session of the legislature, and about sixteen days before it was to adjourn.

Upon the meeting of the legislature I found that quite an opposition had been organized to the administration. The whigs from party motives were compelled to be against me. The democrats were in a majority of about two-thirds in each house; and here as everywhere else the larger the majority the less is the tenacity of its parts. When majorities cease to fear the minority they are the readier to quarrel amongst themselves. Nothing more promotes union in a party than the fear of defeat; and nothing more promotes anarchy in its mem-

*It is not known in Illinois how much credit is due to Mr. Leavitt for the success of these negotiations. Being a man of great wealth and well-established integrity, and being also himself the owner of $250,000 or more of the Illinois canal stocks, he was able to have an influence with the foreign bond-holders which could have been exerted by no citizen of Illinois. To Mr. Leavitt's visit to Europe and his own liberal subscription are we undoubtedly indebted for the final success of the loan.

bers than over confidence of strength. In my case there was still another cause for a factious opposition. I had within the last two years to make several important appointments; such as two bank commissioners, a Secretary of State, three judges of the supreme court, and one United States Senator. This was just enough of patronage to make the executive more enemies than friends. For these offices there were many applicants; those who were disappointed became bitter enemies; and now a great effort was to be made by these disappointed factionists of the democratic party to defeat the confirmation of the senator and judges before the legislature, and in conjunction with the whigs to oppose and discredit the administration.

It is an easy matter to raise an opposition to any administration. It is only to assume that all men are perfect or ought to be so; that in fact the millennium has already come; and a standard of perfection is to be adopted in judging of all matters of government as if the millennium had come in very deed. It is to turn away your eyes from everything which is right in an administration and to exaggerate all little errors and bring them forward as an evidence of corruption; it is to promulgate falsehood and, if need be, swear to its truth; and in this spirit to find fault with everything and approve nothing. Lies should be uttered boldly, with no appearance of doubt; and in number they should be as legion; for it is a maxim with factionists that where a great quantity of mud is thrown upon a man some of it must certainly stick. As to measures, the administration is obliged to choose some out of many, supposed to be equally well adapted to bring about some result. And in every government there are frequent occasions when it is exceedingly doubtful whether one course or another ought to be pursued. The administration is obliged to decide in favor of one course or one set of measures; the factionist is then to take the other side and as his measures are not to be tried by the test of experiment he has every advantage. If the measure of the administration fail of giving the most perfect satisfaction the difficulties attending them, after they are tried, will be visible to the meanest capacity. But the insufficiencies of rejected measures will never be seen, or at least can never be demonstrated. They may be conjectured, but not proved. The factionist is to make no allowance for all this, but is to charge all the little insufficiencies which too often accompany the most perfect means, and which actual experiment has developed, to imbecility and want of judgment; and is stoutly to insist upon the absolute perfection of other measures and other means not chosen. And this he can do with the greater plausibility as the measures not tried can only be conjectured. An administration in new and difficult positions goes on like men opening a road through heavy timber; all behind can be seen, but all before is hidden from the sight; and it is as easy to conjecture one thing as another of an unknown and unexplored country. The factionist is he who goes before and prophesies evil; and comes after, when the obstructions to sight are removed, and cavils at the small hills and ravines in the way. If fault-finding is the only art of the factionist, he is to imitate the humble genius of the swine, which, although they cannot build fences are sure to find such large cracks and holes in them as have unluckily been left unstopped by the builder.

Upon this plan an opposition was raised to my administration. The disappointed office-seekers succeeded in getting a committee of my personal enemies appointed in the lower house to examine the executive offices.[1] This committee entered into an alliance with a notorious lying letter-writer and pretended to give him information of the enormities which they had discovered in the government, which he wrote out and published for the information of the people.[2] They went sneaking about through the executive offices with the stealthy step of one who wanted to steal, hunting up matters of accusations. I paid no attention to their inquisitorial search, but treated them with perfect contempt, knowing that they would never dare to make a report against me. The committee continued their examination all the session, giving out wonderful accounts to be published in the newspapers, but they never made any report. As they really found nothing to report against they thought it best not to report at all. This was the newest way of discrediting an administration practiced upon me on three different occasions, exclusive right to which ought to be secured to the inventors forever. This opposition amounted to nothing so far as I was concerned myself; but it came near defeating the canal.

The opposition was put on foot principally by Mr. Trumbull,[3] late Secretary of State, who had his private griefs to revenge; and by an ambitious aspirant for the United States Senate[4] who, though often assured to the contrary, would never believe but that I would be a candidate for that office in 1846. Trumbull, being a medium lawyer but no statesman, was literally devoured by ambition for office, and was wholly unfitted to be popular by any natural means with the people amongst whom he resided. He had conceived the opinion that the only means of success was to be a demagogue; and he was unfitted by nature to be a demagogue. He had a remarkably precise, puritanical appearance, without the practices or morals of a Puritan. So far from possessing any appearance of generosity and magnanimity, which so much recommends a man to the people, he was remarkable for a small, lean face, giving promise of narrow, cramped views, great prejudices and industry in finding fault with others. No such man can very successfully play the demagogue; he may manage well with politicians, but he can never establish a broad foundation of support among the people, as there is nothing in such men to blind the people to their true character and motives. Such men might be respectable, acting in accordance with their natural gifts, but must always fall when acting a part for which they were never fitted by nature.

After Trumbull was removed from the office of Secretary of State in the spring of 1843 he hurried off to the Belleville district to be a candidate for Congress, calculating to secure all the rabid democrats who were most hostile to banks to be in his favor. But he failed in getting more than two votes in the nominating convention. The next year he quarrelled with his old friend, Governor Reynolds, for the privilege of being a candidate, and at this session he became a candidate for the United States Senate, but declined before the election as it became evident he would get but a few votes. After that, again he became a prominent candidate for governor, but being again defeated he immediately became a candidate for Congress in the Belleville district, obtained the nomination from his party, and in a district where the democratic party is in a majority of three or four thousand votes he was defeated by more than two thousand majority against him. Up to this time Trumbull was looked upon as a man of great promise in the democratic party. He was believed to be an active, ambitious, and rising man, one who was to possess considerable power. And although without this belief in his favor he would have had no power, yet the idea that he was to be great naturally gave him power. Men love to worship the rising sun and are careful about making enemies of one who either is now, or who it is believed will soon be, great. Politicians estimate the value of such a man as the speculators estimated the value of Chicago lots in 1836. Chicago was then but a village; but it was believed that it would soon be a city, which made lots there sell for more than they are worth now that it has become a city of fifteen thousand inhabitants. Or rather, politicians value such a man as a farmer values a favorite colt; he measures it from the fetlock to the knee and from the knee to the shoulder blade and from thence to the withers and from thence to the loins and around the body, and if he can see in it the promise of a fine horse he asks more for it than he would if it were already a horse. But when Trumbull was defeated for Congress by so large a majority, thus disappointing the popular belief in his destiny, his power and consequence vanished in a moment. It was now certain that the village was not to be a city nor the colt a fine horse. A man's strength is not always real, but greatly depends upon the continued run of a general belief that he is strong, or will be strong some time in his life. For which reason when a public man is once prostrated, right or wrong, he rarely ever rises again. The charm of his power is gone.

The ambitious aspirant for the United States Senate before alluded to became alarmed when I first came into office lest I might be in his way in 1846; and no assurance from me would convince him to the contrary. As I really did not intend to be a candidate I never suspected the system of tactics he put in operation against me. For the amusement of the reader I will state some of his doings. He advised the compromise with the banks to get it introduced into the legislature as an administration measure, and he then opposed it as not being sufficiently democratic. He advised and insisted upon the removal of Trumbull, and when it was done he denounced the act as being an unjustifiable act of power, by means of which he procured Trumbull and his friends to be my enemies and friends to himself. He went to leading men in the south with a view to put them against me by insisting that as I resided in the north I must be the representative of northern interests. To the northern men he insisted that as I had been brought up in the South, with southern feelings and prejudices against Yankees, every northern man was interested in opposing me. One other man desired to make a vacancy for himself in the Lower House of Congress by the election of a member of that body to the Senate; and fearing that I might be in the way of his favorite, this will account for packing a committee against me at the session of 1844–45.[5]

The opposition aimed to defeat my appointments for United States Senator and judges of the supreme court in the elections by the legislature, and to defeat the election of friends of mine who were candidates for public printer, auditor and treasurer; but they were most anxious to get a majority against the measures of the administration. For this purpose the leaders, as usual, opposed everything they supposed the governor was in favor of. The election of United States Senator was first brought on; Trumbull himself was the candidate against my appointment. The election of public printers came next; the election of auditor and treasurer afterwards, and last of all came the election of judges. The plan was to keep the election of judges to the last, and in the meantime to add a little to the opposition strength by gathering the discontented in every preceding election; and then to swell it up again by enlisting such as were opposed to the measures recommended by the executive. My friends were all elected to office; but the opposition came near defeating the canal.[6]

Amongst the most important measures recommended by the governor were the canal bill and a bill to increase the taxes. It has been claimed by Trumbull and his friends that they never opposed the canal, they were only hostile to all canal measures proposed by its friends, without proposing any of their own. As I have said before, about the middle of February Governor Davis and Mr. Leavitt arrived in Springfield, during the session. The opposition were ready to open their eyes and stare with wonder at these envoys of the public creditors. The words federalists, aristocrats, monied kings were freely whispered about. It was given out that a brace of proud aristocrats, the representatives of the monied aristocracy, had arrived to wheedle, coerce, or bribe the legislature as best might suit their purposes. Many who were most active in spreading these dire alarms took sly peeps at the strangers, hoping to find confirmation for their fears; and one or two of them at least with the hope that bribes might be offered. But contrary to their hopes they found Governor Davis and Mr. Leavitt plain, sensible gentlemen; modest and retiring, though kind and familiar when familiarity could be indulged in with propriety. Many of the opposition members took quite a fancy to Governor Davis, to his natural manners, evident kindness of heart, and air of sterling integrity. One of them, after making his acquaintance, was so struck with his good qualities that he offered, if Governor Davis would remove to Illinois, to have him right at once made a justice of the peace; and if he behaved well in that, promised that he should be elevated to higher office, with rapid promotion.

Governor Davis and Mr. Leavitt made the proposition of the public creditors, which was communicated to both Houses through the executive. A bill was prepared by the committee of finance and reported by Mr. Arnold of Chicago proposing some amendments of the canal law of the previous session, and provision for a permanent tax to pay a portion of the interest on the public debt. This bill passed the House by some twenty majority; but whilst there pending, Messrs. Trumbull & Co. arrayed themselves in opposition to it; their main power and art in so doing being to alarm the timid by holding up the terrors of an unpopular vote in favor of taxation. Trumbull took his stand in the lobbies of the two Houses for the purpose of calling out and lecturing members and threatening them with the indignation of the south for showing it the least favor.

Besides this, the whig party were very undecided as to what

course they would take. That party contained in it many ambitious gentlemen of fine talents, well qualified to serve their country in the highest offices; but the overwhelming majorities against them had kept them down. Many of them had become disheartened or embittered to the last degree. Such as these were ready to adopt any expedient for breaking up the thorough organization of the democratic party. This portion of the whig politicians was led on by George T. M. Davis, a whig lawyer and editor, a man of great activity and enterprise; but rather unscrupulous as to the means he employed. A secret meeting of the whig leaders was called. In this Mr. G. T. M. Davis insisted that the whig party should oppose the canal, oppose an increase of taxes, and all measures to pay the public debt. He insisted upon an alliance of the whigs with the southern democrats on these questions as a means of overthrowing the organization of the democratic party; of making a new division of the parties geographically between the north and the south. There was to be a southern party and a northern party and the whigs were to take the side of the south. But N. D. Strong of Alton and Judge Logan, being both of them talented whigs and members of the legislature, had too much self-respect to enter into such a miserable intrigue. They were threatened with expulsion from the whig party for their contumacy. They succeeded, however, in breaking up Davis' arrangement. Judge Logan's support of the canal measures was the means of carrying them through the legislature. To the honor of the south I record the names of four members from that quarter who voted in favor of these measures. These members were Strong of Madison, Adams of Monroe, Janney of Crawford, and Dunlap of Lawrence; one of them a whig and three of them democrats. These gentlemen ought to, and will, be long remembered for their integrity and moral courage. It is due also to Messrs. Gregg and Arnold of the House of Representatives and Messrs. Judd and Mattison of the Senate that their names should be recorded in history and long remembered for their efficient advocacy of these measures.

After the bill had passed the House it was sent to the Senate; here it was defeated two or three days before the close of the session by a single vote. Its enemies now triumphed in a most uproarious manner. Its friends rallied and procured a reconsideration of the vote. It was predicted that nothing but bribery could now carry the bill; and senators were clamorously warned that any change in their votes would subject them to the strongest suspicion of bribery; two of the opposition senators had helped to defeat it in the hope of creating a necessity for the offer of bribes. One old senator who desired to be bribed was as clamorous as the rest. A few of the friends of the canal living in LaSalle and Cook counties made up a subscription of eighty acres of land and some money to bribe him, and would have done so if they had not been advised to the contrary. Such a course towards one senator would have been unjust towards others who lent the measure their honest support, by subjecting them to injurious suspicions.

The vote on the bill in the Senate by which it had been defeated being reconsidered, the bill was referred to a select committee, together with another bill of an unimportant character which had already passed the House of Representatives. It was known that one senator would not vote for the tax and the canal both in the same bill. By their connection the tax was made to appear as a local measure, intended only for the benefit of the north. The committee, therefore, divided the bill. They struck out of the canal bill all that related to a tax, and they struck out all of the bill referred with it and inserted the taxing part into that. And these two bills being now reported back to the Senate, the Senate concurred in their passsage as thus amended by them. They were sent back to the House of Representatives the same hour for the concurrence of the House in the amendments of the Senate, which was given; and thus these important measures passed into laws; or, instead of saying that they passed, I ought rather to say that they wabbled through the legislature. To Thomas M. Kilpatrick, late senator from Scott county, is the honor due of the good management in the Senate, in dividing and amending the measure and thus securing its passage. I give these facts, curious as they may appear, to illustrate the fertile genius of western men, and as a specimen of the modes of legislation in a new country.

The legislature adjourned a day or two after this and the opposition members returned to their constituents in the worst humor imaginable. They threatened a rebellion of the whole south; but, as usual in such cases they were much more excited than their constituents. A few of the disappointed ones, Trumbull amongst the number, threatened to make speeches all around the regular circuit and excite the people against these new measures. But Walter B. Scates, the judge of that circuit, announced his intention to answer them and chastise them as their demagogism deserved, which made them abandon their design. In the summer afterwards two great conventions of the southern people were held, one at Marion and the other at Fairfield, and upon motion of Judge Scates nearly unanimously declared in favor of the canal and of taxation for the payment of the public debt. Thus did the people of the south nobly redeem themselves from the aspersions of the demagogues who misrepresented them in the legislature; and thus perished the last hope of repudiation in Illinois. When Trumbull afterwards became a candidate for governor he was as much in favor of taxation and the canal as any man in the State.

It now only remains to be said on this subject that the canal arrangement was perfected under the laws passed at this session, in June, 1845. Two trustees were elected by the bondholders and one was appointed by the governor; the board was organized, the work on the canal was let to contract, money was obtained as it was wanted; and now there appears to be a moral certainty that the canal will be completed in the course of a year.[7]

At this session the legislature put down the rate of interest on money to six per cent. This was caused by the conduct of the merchants in the middle and southern parts of the State. In the time of bank suspensions, when money was plenty, the merchants well supplied with goods encouraged the people to buy on a credit; the merchants were forced to this by the great amount of goods on hand and the consequent increased competition amongst themselves in their retail business. They readily credited almost any one up to about the value of his property; and when the debtor was unable to pay they took notes at twelve per cent interest, so that nearly the whole people were indebted more than they were able to pay and to save themselves from being sued for their debts they were forced to pay a ruinous rate of interest on them.

At this session, also, the Mormon charters were totally repealed by the legislature. This was then supposed to be a remedy for all the evils of Mormonism.

In 1844–45 also the legislature undertook various reforms and retrenchments. They passed resolutions calling on the governor and judges to relinquish portions of their salaries secured to them by the constitution. The governor and judges refused. The reply of the judges is too long for insertion here; but I will give my own as it was a shorter document: "A resolution of the two houses has been communicated to me requesting the governor and the judges of the supreme court to relinquish to the State such an amount of their salaries as will be equivalent to 25 per cent thereon, to begin with the year 1845.

"The mere matter of money with me is of but little concern. I could perhaps live as much to my satisfaction upon a little as upon a greater amount. And if I could be left to act freely and voluntarily as befits the incumbent of the executive department, one of the independent co-ordinate departments of the government, equal in its sphere to the legislature in theirs; and if I could be assured of payment in good money for the residue of my salary, no member of the legislature would be more willing than I am to make sacrifices of self-interest at the shrine of patriotism. But before I consent to this I have a right to be assured that whatever sum I do agree to receive will be worth something. In fact, I have been acting upon this principle for the last two years, by receiving less salary than was guaranteed by the laws and the constitution. It seems to me that a true economy would consist in providing adequate revenues so as to keep auditor's warrants at par. Everything then for the State could be done cheaper, as in that case no one would have to be shaved by the brokers. I for one would prefer a reduction of salary and thereby save a portion to the State than to suffer loss on auditor's warrants for the benefit of brokers.

"In making these observations I do not intend to be understood as making any kind of promise to relinquish any portion of my salary. This I state for the sake of the principle which I believe is involved in this request of the two houses. I respectfully protest against the right of the legislature to make such a request. There is a principle of constitutional law of free government, of the separation of the powers of government into three departments, of the independence of each one department of the other two, and of the system of checks and balances which all free constitutions must contain, which ought not to allow the governor, even if it were for his advantage, to comply with your resolution. The separation of the powers of government into legislative, judicial, and executive departments, and confiding these departments to separate bodies of magistracy so that each may be exercised independently of the other is justly esteemed to be the grandest discovery in the science of government; and the practical operation of this discovery in modern times has done more for human liberty than all other discoveries put together.

"With a view to secure the independence of the executive and judicial departments, the Constitution has provided that the governor and judges shall receive an adequate salary, which shall not be diminished during their continuance in office. It is true that the legislature does not propose a reduction of salaries without the consent of the incumbents nor does the request of your honorable bodies express on its face any threat to extort this consent, but the moral influence of such a request, coming as it does from a numerous assembly, the immediate representatives of the people, and composed of the principal men in the State, it might have been supposed would carry with it something of coercion to a governor and judges anxious for a good understanding with the legislative power and for the good opinion of their fellow-citizens. In this mode such a request might amount to coercion. There are other modes of coercion besides the employment of physical force. An appeal to the interests, to the fears, or to the love of popularity inherent in each department may be as efficacious in destroying the balances of the Constitution, as violence itself.

"Considering the matter in this light; feeling my obligation under the Constitution to sustain the independence of the executive department, which I have the honor to represent, and being unwilling from any want of firmness on my part to be accessory to a precedent which I believe is now for the first time attempted in the United States, and which, if followed up, may lead to a consolidation of all power in the hands of a single department, I have felt it to be my duty, at the risk of being misinterpreted and of forfeiting somewhat of the good will of my fellow-citizens, respectfully but firmly to resist this temptation now offered to court public favor, that I may thereby preserve the independence of the executive department."*

The legislature then, following up these projects for retrenchment, attempted to remove the judges by address, so that whilst the offices of all of them were vacant their salaries could be reduced. They reduced the salaries of all the other officers of the government and of the judges thereafter to be elected; and they agitated a bill all winter to reduce the fees of the county officers. In this mode they lengthened out the session for more than a month, and increased their own pay about twenty thousand dollars whilst they aimed to save several hundred to the public treasury. The rage for economy was great indeed, the members appearing to think that the State debt might be paid off by stealing small sums from the already small salaries of public officers. There are those in matters of government as well as in religion who tythe annis, mint, and cummin and neglect the weightier matters of the law. Accordingly, the members who were the most fierce for this kind of economy had no capacity to see that the canal measure was a great financial measure for the benefit of the whole State, by means of which five millions of debt will be paid; a sum greater than could be paid by an eternity of such legislation as was proposed by them. If the State debt is ever paid it will not be done by the puny licks of this description of economisers.

---

*The resolution calling upon the governor and judges to relinquish a portion of their salaries was written by Trumbull and put into the hands of N. W. Nunnally, Senator from Edgar county, to be offered to the Senate. Mr. Nunnally, instead of making himself popular, as he supposed he would, could not get the privilege from his party of being a candidate for re-election two years afterwards.

Another subject of interest at this session was the Shawneetown Bank. After the failure of that institution in 1842 the stock in it had been purchased by a company of speculators, who caused themselves to be elected president and directors. After having paid five hundred thousand dollars, it yet owed the State a half a million of dollars for the State stock in it, to be paid in State indebtedness. In anticipation of the passage of the liquidation law of 1842–43 a few favored directors secretly borrowed from it one hundred thousand dollars of its specie with which to purchase State bonds to pay this remaining debt. The money was sent to New York and invested in the purchase of scrip and three hundred and thirty-three thousand dollars of the bonds which had been hypothecated with Macalister and Stebbins in 1841. The reader will remember that $804,000 of these bonds were hypothecated, upon which the State received $261,500. The law authorized them to be sold, but not to be hypothecated. The few favored directors in a secret meeting of the board paid into the bank $100,000 of these bonds, then worth thirty cents on the dollar, in discharge of their notes for the $100,000 in specie previously borrowed. They next paid in another portion of them in discharge of their stock notes; and amongst others Orville Sexton, a member of this legislature and a flaming declaimer against bank corruption, had a note of near $10,000 paid in this way. The whole sum of bonds, being now the property of the bank or of the private stockholders, were tendered to the governor in the spring of 1844 in payment of the debt from the bank to the State. There were then two reasons why they ought to have been refused. To receive them was to defeat the law for a settlement with Macalister and Stebbins; and it was plain that the State was not bound to pay the full amount of their face. They were accordingly refused. But in the fall of 1844 it became fully known that Macalister and Stebbins would never be able to comply with the law for their relief; that the president of the bank was about to return these bonds to New York; and the bank was so insolvent that if they were permanently rejected and suffered to pass out of its hands and beyond its control the State would never get anything for its half million of stock. To keep the bonds at home, subject to the control of the legislature, I entered into a conditional contract with the bank to receive them if the contract was ratified by the legislature. For this prudent and judicious measure I was much abused and denounced at the time by many ultra democrats, who preferred that the State should lose the whole of its stock in this bank than impliedly to sanction the conduct of its officers.

The matter was referred to the committee of the House of Representatives on banks and corporations; of which Dr. Anderson of Lawrence county had been appointed chairman. He was a man who acted partly from spite, but mostly from a selfish policy.[8] He had seen that banks were woefully unpopular with the people; and that many men had successfully ridden the hobby of popular prejudice against them; and he now determined to have his turn of riding also. But there is some art in riding a hobby as well as a horse, and much depends upon the time when you mount it. A man of sagacity discovers a hobby and rides it as long as the popular feeling will carry him; he then throws it aside and gets a new one. The short-lived and variable feelings and prejudices of the public make the life of a hobby a short one. The master spirit rides it only whilst the public mind is in an earnest fervor concerning it. He takes it when it is young and active; and when it becomes old and lame he leaves it for another. In this mode he keeps all the time along with the fervor of the popular mind; and this is the true "tide in the affairs of men, which, taken at the flood, leads on to fortune." The people of Illinois were still much against banks; but the day had passed when hatred to banks was the one idea which ruled the popular mind. In the meantime the Texas and Oregon and tariff questions had arisen and the master equestrians had quit the banks for one or the other or all of these. But not so with the small-fry politicians, who never perceive the advantages of a hobby until it is jaded down by other riders who have ridden to distinction upon it; and then they all mount on and if the animal be not already dead they soon exhaust its remaining vitality; and find themselves again trudging along on foot. On this occasion it was pitiable to see Dr. Anderson and the small geniuses of his tribe ungracefully jolting along upon their worn-out nags, mimicking the airs of accomplished equestrians upon their young and mettlesome steeds. Under such influences, it was at first decided by a majority of both houses to be better to lose the whole amount which the bank owed to the State than to countenance in the least degree the villainy of its officers by receiving these bonds. The people, however, failed to appreciate the vast merits of these members at the next election. Not over a half dozen of them were reelected. Dr. Anderson expected to be sent to Congress at least; but failed to get the nomination of his party even for the legislature of 1846, there not being a half dozen men in his county favorable to his re-election. And shortly afterwards in utter rage against the people and the corruptions of the democratic party he shook the dust off his feet as a testimony against them and departed from the State. The legislature afterwards allowed these bonds to be received at forty eight cents to the dollar, which was a good bargain for the State.

The population of Illinois in 1845, according to the census of that year, amounted to 662,150 souls, being an increase in five years of 183,221.

XIII

Expulsion of the Mormons, 1845–1846

The Mormons next claim our attention. Nauvoo was now a city of about 15,000 inhabitants and was fast increasing, as the followers of the prophet were pouring into it from all parts of the world; and there were several other settlements and villages of Mormons in Hancock county. Nauvoo was scattered over about six square miles, a part of it being built upon the flat skirting and fronting on the Mississippi river, but the greater portion of it upon the bluff's back, east of the river. The great temple, which is said to have cost a million of dollars in money and labor, occupied a commanding position on the brow of this bluff and overlooked the country around for twenty miles in Illinois and Iowa.[1] This temple was not fashioned after any known order of architecture. The Mormons themselves pretended to believe that the building of it was commenced without any previous plan; and that the master builder, from day to day during the progress of its erection, received directions immediately from heaven as to the plan of the building; and really it looks as if it was the result of such frequent changes as would be produced by a daily accession of new ideas. It has been said that the church architecture of a sect indicates the genius and spirit of its religion. The grand and solemn structures of the Catholics point to the towering hierarchy and imposing ceremonies of the church; the low and broad meeting-houses of the Methodists formerly shadowed forth their abhorrence of gaudy decoration and their unpretending humility; and the light, airy, and elegant edifices of the Presbyterians as truly indicate the passion for education, refinement, and polish amongst that thrifty and enterprising people. If the genius of Mormonism were tried by this test, as exhibited in the temple, we could only pronounce that it was a piece of patchwork, variable, strange, and incongruous.

During the summer and fall of 1845 there were several small matters to increase irritation between the Mormons and their neighbors. The anti-Mormons complained of a large number of larcenies and robberies. The Mormon press at Nauvoo and the anti-Mormon papers at Warsaw, Quincy, Springfield, Alton, and St. Louis kept up a continual fire at each other; the anti-Mormons all the time calling upon the people to rise and expel or exterminate the Mormons. The great fires at Pittsburg and in other cities about this time were seized upon by the Mormon press to countenance the assertion that the Lord had sent them to manifest his displeasure against the Gentiles; and to hint that all other places which might countenance the enemies of the Mormons might expect to be visited by "hot drops" of the same description. This was interpreted by the anti-Mormons to be a threat by Mormon incendiaries to burn down all cities and places not friendly to their religion. About this time also a suit had been commenced in the circuit court of the United States against some of the twelve apostles, on a note given in Ohio. The deputy marshal went to summon the defendants. They were determined not to be served with process and a great meeting of their people being called, outrageously inflammatory speeches were made by the leaders; the marshal was threatened and abused for intending to serve a lawful process, and here it was publicly declared and agreed to by the Mormons that no more process should be served in Nauvoo.

Also about this time a leading anti-Mormon by the name of Dr. Marshall made an assault upon Gen. Deming, the sheriff of the county, and was killed by the sheriff in repelling the assault. The sheriff was arrested and held to bail by Judge Young for manslaughter: though as he had acted strictly in self-defence no one seriously believed him to be guilty of any crime whatever. But Dr. Marshall had many friends disposed to revenge his death, the rage of the people ran very high, for which reason it was thought best by the judge to hold the sheriff to bail for something to save him from being sacrificed to the public fury.

Not long after the trials of the supposed murderers of the Smiths it was discovered on a trial of the right of property near Lima in Adams county, by Mormon testimony, that that people had an institution in their church called a "Oneness," which was composed of an association of five persons, over whom "one" was appointed as a kind of guardian. This "one" as trustee for the rest was to own all the property of the association; so that if it were levied upon by an execution for debt the Mormons could prove that the property belonged to one or the other of the parties as might be required to defeat the execution. And not long after this discovery in the fall of 1845 the anti-Mormons of Lima and Green Plains held a meeting to devise means for the expulsion of the Mormons from their neighborhood. They appointed some persons of their own number to fire a few shots at the house where they were assembled; but to do it in such a way as to hurt none who attended the meeting. The meeting was held, the house was fired at, but so as to hurt no one; and the anti-Mormons, suddenly breaking up their meeting, rode all over the country spreading the dire alarm that the Mormons had commenced the work of massacre and death.

This startling intelligence soon assembled a mob. But before I relate what further was done I must give some account of the anti-Mormons. I had a good opportunity to know the early settlers of Hancock county. I had attended the circuit courts there as States-attorney from 1830, when the county was first organized, up to the year 1834; and to my certain knowledge the early settlers, with some honorable exceptions, were, in popular language, hard cases. In the year 1834 one Dr. Galland was a candidate for the legislature in a district composed of Hancock, Adams, and Pike counties. He resided in the county of Hancock, and as he had in the early part of his life been a notorious horse thief and counterfeiter, belonging to the Massac gang, and was then no pretender to integrity, it was useless to deny the charge.

In all his speeches he freely admitted the fact, but came near receiving a majority of votes in his own county of Hancock. I mention this to show the character of the people for integrity. From this time down to the settlement of the Mormons there, and for four years afterwards, I had no means of knowing about the future increase of the Hancock people. But having passed my whole life on the frontiers, on the outer edge of the settlements, I have frequently seen that a few first settlers would fix the character of a settlement for good or for bad for many years after its commencement. If bad men began the settlement bad men would be attracted to them, upon the well-known principle that "birds of a feather will flock together." Rogues will find each other out and so will honest men. From all which it appears extremely probable that the later immigrants were many of them attracted to Hancock by a secret sympathy between them and the early settlers. And so it may appear that the Mormons themselves may have been induced to select Hancock as the place of their settlement, rather than many other places where they were strongly solicited to settle, by the promptings of a secret instinct which without much penetration enables men to discern their fellows.

The mob at Lima proceeded to warn the Mormons to leave the neighborhood and threatened them with fire and sword if they remained. A very poor class of Mormons resided here and it is very likely that the other inhabitants were annoyed beyond further endurance by their little larcenies and rogueries. The Mormons refused to remove; the mob proceeded to burn down their houses; and about one hundred and seventy-five houses and hovels were burnt, the inmates being obliged to flee for their lives. They fled to Nauvoo in a state of utter destitution, carrying their women and children, aged and sick (it was then the height of the sickly season) along with them as best they could. The sight of these miserable creatures aroused the wrath of the Mormons of Nauvoo. As soon as authentic intelligence of these events reached Springfield I ordered Gen. Hardin to raise a force and restore the rule of law. But whilst this force was gathering the sheriff of the county had taken the matter in hand. Gen. Deming had died not long after the death of Dr. Marshall and the Mormons had elected Jacob B. Backenstos to be sheriff in his place.[2] This Backenstos formerly resided in Sangamon county. There he had credit to get a stock of goods, and set up as a merchant. The goods were immediately transferred to his brother, leaving the debt for them unpaid. Here, too, he became acquainted with Judge Douglas, and here commenced that indissoluble friendship between them which has continued inviolate ever since. Douglas was appointed to hold the courts in Hancock county and Backenstos, having broken up in Sangamon, had gone over to Hancock seeking his fortunes. His brother had already married a niece of the prophet and Backenstos immediately attached himself to the interests of the Mormons. Backenstos was a smart-looking shrewd, cunning, plausible man, of such easy manners that he was likely to have great influence with the Mormons. In due time Judge Douglas appointed him to be clerk of the circuit court and this gave him almost absolute power with that people in all political contests. In 1844 Backenstos and a Mormon elder[3] were elected to the legislature; in 1845 he was elected sheriff, in place of Gen. Deming; and finally, to reward him for his great public services, he was appointed a captain of a rifle company in the United States army. But being just now regarded as the political leader of the Mormons, Backenstos was hated with a sincere and thorough hatred by the opposite party.

When the burning of houses commenced the great body of the anti-Mormons expressed themselves strongly against it, giving hopes thereby that a posse of anti-Mormons could be raised to put a stop to such incendiary and riotous conduct. But when they were called on by the new sheriff not a man of them turned out to his assistance, many of them no doubt being influenced by their hatred of the sheriff. Backenstos then went to Nauvoo where he raised a posse of several hundred armed Mormons with which he swept over the county, took possession of Carthage, and established a permanent guard there. The anti-Mormons everywhere fled from their homes before the sheriff, some of them to Iowa and Missouri and others to the neighboring counties in Illinois. The sheriff was unable or unwilling to bring any portion of the rioters to a battle or to arrest any of them for their crimes. The posse came near surprising one small squad, but they made their escape, all but one, before they could be attacked. This one, named McBratney, was shot down by some of the posse in advance, by whom he was hacked and mutilated as though he had been murdered by the Indians.

The sheriff also was in continual peril of his life from the anti-Mormons, who daily threatened him with death the first opportunity. As he was going in a buggy from Warsaw in the direction of Nauvoo he was pursued by three or four men to a place in the road where some Mormon teams were standing. Backenstos passed the teams a few rods, and then stopping, the pursuers came up within a hundred and fifty yards, when they were fired upon with an unerring aim by some one concealed not far to one side of them. By this fire Franklin A. Worrell was killed. He was the same man who had commanded the guard at the jail at the time the Smiths were assassinated; and there made himself conspicuous in betraying his trust by consenting to the assassination. It is believed that Backenstos expected to be pursued and attacked, and had previously stationed some men in ambush to fire upon his pursuers. He was afterwards indicted for the supposed murder, and procured a change of venue to Peoria county, where he was acquitted of the charge. About this time also the Mormons murdered a man by the name of Daubeneyer, without any apparent provocation; and another anti-Mormon named Wilcox was murdered in Nauvoo, as it was believed by order of the twelve apostles. The anti-Mormons also committed one murder. Some of them, under Backman, set fire to some straw near a barn belonging to Durfee, an old Mormon seventy years old; and then lay in ambush until the old man came out to extinguish the fire, when they shot him dead from their place of concealment. The perpetrators of this murder were arrested and brought before an anti-Mormon justice of the peace and were acquitted, though their guilt was sufficiently apparent.

During the ascendency of the sheriff and the absence of the anti-Mormons from their houses the people who had been burnt out of their houses assembled in Nauvoo, from whence, with many others, they sallied forth and ravaged the country, stealing and plundering whatever was convenient to carry or drive away. When informed of these proceedings I hastened to Jacksonville where in a conference with Gen. Hardin, Major Warren, Judge Douglas, and the Attorney-General, Mr. McDougall, it was agreed that these gentlemen should proceed to Hancock in all haste with whatever forces had been raised, few or many, and put an end to these disorders. It was now apparent that neither party in Hancock could be trusted with the power to keep the peace. It was also agreed that all these gentlemen should unite their influence with mine to induce the Mormons to leave the State. Gen. Hardin lost no time in raising three or four hundred volunteers, and when he got to Carthage he found a Mormon guard in possession of the courthouse. This force he ordered to disband and disperse in fifteen minutes. The plundering parties of Mormons were stopped in their ravages. The fugitive anti-Mormons were recalled to their homes and all parties above four in number on either side were prohibited from assembling and marching over the country.

Whilst Gen. Hardin was at Carthage a convention previously appointed assembled at that place, composed of delegates from the eight neighboring counties. The people of the neighboring counties were alarmed lest the anti-Mormons should entirely desert Hancock and by that means leave one of the largest counties of the State to be possessed entirely by Mormons. This they feared would bring the surrounding counties into immediate collision with them. They had therefore appointed this convention to consider measures for the expulsion of the Mormons. The twelve apostles had now become satisfied that the Mormons could not remain, or if they did, the leaders would be compelled to abandon the sway and dominion they exercised over them. They had now become convinced that the kind of Mahometanism which they sought to establish could never be established in the near vicinity of a people whose morals and prejudices were all outraged and shocked by it, unless indeed they were prepared to establish it by force of arms. Through the intervention of Gen. Hardin, acting under instructions from me, an agreement was made between the hostile parties for the voluntary removal of the greater part of the Mormons in the spring of 1846. The two parties agreed that in the meantime they would seek to make no arrests for crimes previously committed; and on my part I agreed that an armed force should be stationed in the county to keep the peace. The presence of such a force and amnesty from prosecutions on all sides were insisted on by the Mormons that they might devote all their time and energies to prepare for their removal. Gen. Hardin first diminished his force to a hundred men, leaving Major Wm. B. Warren in command. And this force being further diminished during the winter to fifty, and then to ten men, was kept up until the last of May, 1846. This force was commanded with great efficiency and prudence during all this winter and spring by Major Warren; and with it he was enabled to keep the turbulent spirit of faction in check, the Mormons well knowing that it would be supported by a much larger force whenever the governor saw proper to call for it. In the meantime they somewhat repented of their bargain and desired Major Warren to be withdrawn. Backenstos was anxious to be again left at the head of his posse to roister over the county and to take vengeance on his enemies. The anti-Mormons were also dissatisfied because the State force preserved a threatening aspect towards them as well as towards the Mormons. He was always ready to enforce arrests of criminals for new offences on either side; and this pleased neither the Mormons nor the anti-Mormons. Civil war was on the very point of breaking out more than a dozen times during the winter. Both parties complained of Major Warren; but I, well knowing that he was manfully doing his duty in one of the most difficult and vexatious services ever devolved upon a militia officer, steadily sustained him against the complaints on both sides. It is but just to Major Warren to say here that he gained a lasting credit with all substantial citizens for his able and prudent conduct during this winter. Of General Hardin, too, it is but just to say that his expedition this time had the happiest results. The greater part of the military tract was saved by it from the horrors of a civil war in the winter time, when much misery would have followed from it, by the dispersion of families and the destruction of property.

During the winter of 1845–46 the Mormons made the most prodigious preparations for removal. All the houses in Nauvoo, and even the temple, were converted into workshops; and before spring more than twelve thousand wagons were in readiness. The people from all parts of the country flocked to Nauvoo to purchase houses and farms, which were sold extremely low, lower than the prices at a sheriff's sale, for money, wagons, horses, oxen, cattle, and other articles of personal property which might be needed by the Mormons in their exodus into the wilderness. By the middle of May it was estimated that sixteen thousand Mormons had crossed the Mississippi and taken up their line of march with their personal property, their wives and little ones westward across the continent to Oregon or California; leaving behind them in Nauvoo a small remnant of a thousand souls, being those who were unable to sell their property or who, having no property to sell, were unable to get away.

The twelve apostles went first with about two thousand of their followers. Indictments had been found against nine of them in the circuit court of the United States for the district of Illinois at its December term, 1845, for counterfeiting the current coin of the United States. The United States Marshal had applied to me for a militia force to arrest them; but in pursuance of the amnesty agreed on for old offences, believing that the arrest of the accused would prevent the removal of the Mormons, and that if arrested there was not the least chance that any of them would ever be convicted, I declined the application unless regularly called upon by the President of the United States according to law.[4] It was generally agreed that it would be impolitic to arrest the leaders and thus put an end to the preparations for removal when it was notorious that none of them could be convicted; for they always commanded evidence and witnesses enough to make a conviction impossible. But with a view to hasten their removal they were made to believe that the President would order the regular army to Nauvoo as soon as the navigation opened in the spring. This had its intended effect; the twelve, with about two thousand of their followers, immediately crossed the Mississippi before the breaking up of the ice. But before this the deputy marshal had sought to arrest the accused without success.[5]

Notwithstanding but few of the Mormons remained behind after June, 1846, the anti-Mormons were no less anxious for their expulsion by force of arms; being another instance of a party not being satisfied with the attainment of its wishes unless brought about by themselves and by measures of their own. It was feared that the Mormons might vote at the August election of that year; and that enough of them yet remained to control the elections in the county, and perhaps in the district for Congress. They therefore took measures to get up a new quarrel with the remaining Mormons. And for this purpose they attacked and severely whipped a party of eight or ten Mormons which had been sent out into the country to harvest some wheat fields in the neighborhood of Pontoosuc, and who had provoked the wrath of the settlement by hallooing, yelling, and other arrogant behavior. Writs were sworn out in Nauvoo against the men of Pontoosuc, who were arrested and kept for several days under strict guard, until they gave bail. Then in their turn they swore out writs for the arrest of the constable and posse who had made the first arrest, for false imprisonment. The Mormon posse were no doubt really afraid to be arrested, believing that instead of being tried they would be murdered. This made an excuse for the anti-Mormons to assemble a posse of several hundred men to assist in making the arrest; but the matter was finally adjusted without any one being taken. A committee of anti-Mormons was sent into Nauvoo, who reported that the Mormons were making every possible preparation for removal;

and the leading Mormons on their part agreed that their people should not vote at the next election.

The August election came on shortly afterwards and the Mormons all voted the whole democratic ticket. I have since been informed by Babbitt, the Mormon elder and agent for the sale of church property, that they were induced to vote this time from the following considerations: The President of the United States had permitted the Mormons to settle on the Indian lands on the Missouri river and had taken five hundred of them into the service as soldiers in the war with Mexico; and in consequence of these favors the Mormons felt under obligation to vote for democrats in support of the administration; and so determined were they that their support of the President should be efficient, that they all voted three or four times each for member of Congress.

This vote of the Mormons enraged the whigs anew against them; the probability that they might attempt to remain permanently in the country and the certainty that many designing persons for selfish purposes were endeavoring to keep them there revived all the excitement which had ever existed against that people. In pursuance of the advice and under the direction of Archibald Williams, a distinguished lawyer and whig politician of Quincy, writs were again sworn out for the arrest of persons in Nauvoo, on various charges. But to create a necessity for a great force to make the arrests, it was freely admitted by John Carlin, the constable sent in with the writs, that the prisoners would be murdered if arrested and carried out of the city. This John Carlin, under a promise to be elected recorder in the place of a Jack Mormon recorder to be driven away, was appointed a special constable to make the arrests. And now the individuals sought to be arrested were openly threatened to be murdered. The special constable went to Nauvoo with the writs in his hands, the accused declined to surrender. And now, having failed to make the arrests, the constable began to call out the *posse comitatus*. This was about the 1st of September, 1846. The posse soon amounted to several hundred men. The Mormons in their turn swore out several writs for the arrest of leading anti-Mormons and under pretence of desiring to execute them called out a posse of Mormons. Here was writ against writ; constable against constable; law against law, and posse against posse.

Whilst the parties were assembling their forces the trustees of Nauvoo being new citizens, not Mormons, applied to the governor for a militia officer to be sent over with ten men, they supposing that this small force would dispense with the services of the civil posse on either side. There was such a want of confidence on all sides that no one would submit to be arrested by an adversary for fear of assassination. This small force it was supposed would restore confidence and order. And here again was a difficulty, who was to be sent on this delicate service. General Hardin, Major Warren, Colonel Weatherford, and Colonel Baker had gone to the Mexican war. These had been the officers upon whom I had relied in all previous emergencies; and they were well qualified for command. And here I must remark that the President in May, 1846 called for four regiments of volunteers from Illinois for the Mexican war. The call was no sooner published in Illinois than nine regiments offered their services. Those of them who were doomed to stay at home were more discontented than men usually are who are drafted into the armies of their country.

And here too I will remark that the laws do not allow the governor to exercise his own best judgment in selecting the most fit person to command. The militia themselves elect their officers, and all the choice which is left to the governor is to select one already elected. In looking round over the State for this purpose, the choice fell upon Major Parker of Fulton county. Major Parker was a whig and was selected partly for that reason, believing that a whig now, as had been the case before with Gen. Hardin and Major Warren, would have more influence in restraining the anti-Mormons than a democrat. But Major Parker's character was unknown out of his own county. Everywhere else it was taken for granted that he was a democrat and had been sent over to Hancock to intrigue with the Mormons. The whig newspapers immediately let loose floods of abuse upon him, both in this State and in Missouri, which completely paralyzed his power to render any effectual service. The constable's posse refused to give place to him and the constable openly declared that he cared but little for the arrests; by which it was apparent that they intended from the first to use the process of the law only as a cover to their design of expelling the Mormons.

The posse continued to increase until it numbered about eight hundred men; and whilst it was getting ready to march into the city it was represented to me by another committee that the new citizens of Nauvoo were themselves divided into two parties, the one siding with the Mormons, the other with their enemies. The Mormons threatened the disaffected new citizens with death if they did not join in the defence of the city. For this reason I sent over M. Brayman Esq., a judicious citizen of Springfield, with suitable orders restraining all compulsion in forcing the citizens to join the Mormons against their will, and generally to inquire into and report all the circumstances of the quarrel.

Soon after Mr. Brayman arrived there he persuaded the leaders on each side into an adjustment of the quarrel. It was agreed that the Mormons should immediately surrender their arms to some person to be appointed to receive them, and to be redelivered when they left the State, and that they would remove from the State in two months. This treaty was agreed to by Gen. Singleton, Col. Chittenden and others on the side of the antis, and by Major Parker and some leading Mormons on the other side. But when the treaty was submitted for ratification to the anti-Mormon forces it was rejected by a small majority. Gen. Singleton and Col. Chittenden, with a proper self-respect, immediately withdrew from command; they not being the first great men placed at the head of affairs at the beginning of violence who have been hurled from their places before the popular frenzy had run its course. And with them also great Archibald Williams, the prime mover of the enterprise, he not being the first man who has got up a popular commotion and failed to govern it afterwards. Indeed, the whole history of revolutions and popular excitements leading to violence is full of instances like these. Mr. Brayman, the same day of the rejection of the treaty, reported to me that nearly one-half of the anti-Mormons would abandon the enterprise and retire with their late commanders, "leaving a set of hare-brained fools to be flogged or to disperse at their leisure." It turned out, however, that the calculations of Mr. Brayman were not realized; for when Singleton and Chittenden retired, Thomas S. Brockman was put in command of the posse. This Brockman was a Campbellite preacher, nominally belonging to the democratic party. He was a large, awkward, uncouth, ignorant semi-barbarian, ambitious of office and bent upon acquiring notoriety. He had been county commissioner of Brown county and in that capacity had let out a contract for building the court-house, and it was afterwards ascertained had let the contract to himself. He managed to get paid in advance and then built such an inferior building that the county had not received it up to Dec., 1846. He had also been a collector of taxes, for which he was a defaulter, and his lands were sold whilst I was governor to pay a judgment obtained against him for moneys collected by him. To the bitterness of his religious prejudices against the Mormons he added a hatred of their immoral practices, probably because they differed from his own. Such was the man who was now at the head of the anti-Mormons,* who were about

---

*To the credit of the Campbellites I record that after this they silenced Brockman from preaching. Before this time he had frequently been a candidate for office without success. In 1847 he thought he could be elected to the convention to

as numerous in camp as ever. After the appointment of Brockman I was not enabled to hear in any authentic shape of the movements on either side until the anti-Mormon forces had arrived near the suburbs of the city and were about ready to commence an attack. The information which was received was by mere rumor of travellers, or by the newspapers from St. Louis. And I will remark that during none of these difficulties have I been able to get letters and despatches from Nauvoo by the United States mail, coming, as it was obliged to do, through the anti-Mormon settlements and post offices.

But soon after the antis had arrived with their force near Nauvoo, and after some little skirmishing, Mr. Brayman came to Springfield with a request for further assistance in defence of the city. It was now too late to call forces from a distance, if they had been ever so willing to come. It was obvious that if any new forces were to be raised they must come from the neighborhood of the conflict. Orders were therefore issued to Major William G. Flood, who was commander of the militia of the adjoining and populous county of Adams, by which he was authorized to raise a sufficient volunteer force in that and the surrounding counties to enforce the observance of law in Hancock. It turned out, however, that great excitement existed in Adams and in all the neighboring country, and Major Flood being of opinion that if he raised a force on the part of the State a much larger force would have turned out in aid of the rioters, declined to act.

To meet such a contingency he had been instructed that if inconvenient for himself to act he was to hand over his authority to some person who would act, and who could be elected to the command of the forces thus to be raised. Major Flood, without handing over his authority to any one in Adams county, went to Nauvoo to use his influence with the contending parties for the restoration of peace; but failing in this, he handed over his authority to the Mormons and their allies, who elected Major Clifford to command them. In issuing this order to Major Flood it was not intended to put the Nauvoo volunteers under any different command than what was specified in the orders to Major Parker, as it had already been declared in those orders that the Mormon force, with the exception of the ten men from Fulton county, were to serve without pay. The order to Major Flood was for an additional force, and not to give a different organization to the force already raised. It is my solemn conviction that no suffi-

---

amend the constitution, from Brown county, upon the glory he had acquired in the Mormon wars. He was nominated by a small meeting of democrats; and in a county of one hundred and fifty majority of democrats he was beaten by a whig by upwards of one hundred and twenty-five majority.

cient force could have been raised to have fought in favor of the Mormons. But there was still another difficulty and every one felt it. No force under our present constitution could more than temporarily have suppressed these difficulties. It has been the practice heretofore for the ring-leaders of rebellion in Hancock to withdraw from the State whenever the State forces were marched over there; and from experience in former trials they had found out that no one could be convicted. The result of former expeditions had been to keep the peace during the presence of the military, but so soon as they disbanded the disorders were renewed. The keeping of the peace, therefore, in that county was some such labor as the work of Sisyphus, who was condemned by the gods throughout eternity to roll a stone up hill and every time he got it nearly to the top it broke loose from him and again came thundering down to the plain below. The former expeditions had shown this to be the case, and now there was a general disposition to let the hostile parties bring matters to a conclusion in their own way; and such was the public prejudice against the Mormons that, ten chances to one, any large force of militia which might have been ordered there would have joined the rioters rather than fought in defence of the Mormons.*

*It has been asked, How did Governor Wright of New York suppress the riots of the anti-renters in 1846? This is easily answered. The anti-rent riots were less generally popular than the riots of the anti-Mormons. The governor there was better supported by public opinion than the governor of Illinois. He had the power, and he exercised it, to appoint and remove sheriffs and other county officers intended for his assistance; and the laws of New York allowed a criminal to be taken without his consent to a distant county for trial. This last advantage was one worth all the rest.

The history of the law concerning the venue in criminal cases is a curiosity. By the ancient common law the jury was to come from the very town or neighborhood where the crime had been committed; and this was because it was supposed that they had a personal knowledge of the circumstances of the crime, and of the character of the criminal and the witnesses. It was to guard against oppression by assuring the accused of a trial by his neighbors and acquaintances, who, if he were a good man, would know it, and deal more gently with him than strangers would. Afterwards, by statute, the jury was to come from the body of the county. Our State constitution, in imitation of the English law, provides that criminals shall be entitled to a jury of the vicinage, which means the same thing. And yet our law says that no man shall be a competent juror who has formed an opinion as to the guilt or innocence of the criminal. If the juror is not to bring his private knowledge, and his bias in favor of the accused, into the jury, but little good is the privilege of having a jury from the vicinage likely to do the prisoner. He might just as well be taken to some other county and tried by strangers as to be tried by strangers in his own county. It is true that the law of Illinois allows the accused to remove his trial for prejudice in the judge or inhabitants, but the State has no right to remove the case without the consent of the prisoner. One of the complaints urged against me, and some men who held themselves out, but rather falsely pretend to be lawyers, have made it, is, that I did not take the Mormon and anti-

The forces under Brockman numbered about 800 men; they were armed with the State arms, which had been given up to them by independent militia companies in the adjacent counties. They also had five pieces of six-pounder iron cannon belonging to the State, which they had obtained in the same way. The Mormon party and their allies, being some of the new citizens under the command of Major Clifford, numbered at first about two hundred and fifty, but were diminished by desertions and removals before any decisive fighting took place to about one hundred and fifty. Some of them were armed with sixteen-shooting rifles—which experience proved were not very effective in their hands—and a few of them with muskets. They had four or five pieces of cannon, hastily and rudely made by themselves out of the shaft of a steamboat.

The Mormons and their allies took position in the suburbs about one mile east of the temple, where they threw up some breastworks for the protection of their artillery. The attacking force was strong enough to have been divided and marched into the city on each side of this battery, and entirely out of the range of its shot; and thus the place might have been taken without firing a gun. But Brockman, although he professed a desire to save the lives of his men, planted his force directly in front of the enemy's battery, but distant more than

---

Mormon prisoners to some foreign county to be tried. Some thought they ought to have been taken before the supreme court and others before the United States court at Springfield, as if either of these courts had the slightest particle of power to try them. Before I heard of these complaints I was not aware that there was so much stupid ignorance in the country, particularly among men who pretend to be lawyers.

There is now no doubt but the power to change the venue in criminal cases, which the constitution of New York vested in the supreme court, to be exercised at discretion, has operated well in all cases of local excitement, and probably saved a war with England, which was likely to grow out of the trial of McLeod for the murder of Durfee and burning the *Caroline* steamboat on the Niagara frontier.

But to return to Gov. Wright. Being supported by public opinion, he put down the anti-renters and protected the property of the wealthy. In return for this favor the wealthy men, at an election a few months afterwards, united with the anti-renters and helped them put Governor Wright down. Governor Wright did all he could to secure the conviction of murderers and assassins amongst the anti-renters, who had raised a rebellion against the laws of property. The men of property immediately helped the anti-renters to defeat Governor Wright's second election, and to elect a man who was pledged to pardon these same murderers and cut-throats out of the penitentiary. The next extensive riot against property in the United States is not likely to be quelled so easily. Public men will hereafter remember the fate of Governor Wright. They will be apt to remember that active efforts against the rioters will make enemies of them without making friends elsewhere. Upon the whole this example of the men of property uniting with the miserable faction of anti-renters to put down such a man as Gov. Wright is one of the worst signs of the times.

half a mile; and now both parties commenced a fire from their cannon, and some few persons on each side approached near enough to open a fire with their rifles and muskets, but not near enough to do each other material injury.

In this manner they continued to fire at each other at such a distance and with such want of skill as that there was but little prospect of injury until the anti-Mormons had exhausted their ammunition, when they retreated in some disorder to their camp. They were not pursued, and here the Mormon party committed an error, for all experience of irregular forces has shown that however brave they may be, a charge on them when they have once commenced a retreat is sure to be successful. Having waited a few days to supply themselves anew with ammunition from Quincy, the antis again advanced to the attack, but without coming nearer to the enemy than before, and what at the time was called a battle was kept up three or four days, during all which time the Mormons admit a loss of two men and a boy killed and three or four wounded. The antis admitted a loss on their side of one man mortally, and nine or ten others not so dangerously wounded. The Mormons claimed that they had killed thirty or forty of the antis. The antis claimed that they had killed thirty or forty of the Mormons, and both parties could have proved their claim by incontestable evidence if their witnesses had been credible.

But the account which each party renders of its loss ought to be taken as the true one, unless such account can be successfully controverted. During all the skirmishing and firing of cannon it is estimated that from seven to nine hundred cannon balls and an infinite number of bullets were fired on each side, from which it appears that the remarkable fact of so few being killed and wounded can be accounted for only by supposing great unskilfulness in the use of arms, and by the very safe distance which the parties kept from each other.

At last, through the intervention of an anti-Mormon committee of one hundred from Quincy, the Mormons and their allies were induced to submit to such terms as the posse chose to dictate, which were that the Mormons should immediately give up their arms to the Quincy committee and remove from the State. The trustees of the church and five of their clerks were permitted to remain for the sale of Mormon property, and the posse were to march in unmolested and to leave a sufficient force to guarantee the performance of these stipulations.

Accordingly the constable's posse marched in with Brockman at their head, consisting of about eight hundred armed men and six or seven hundred unarmed, who had assembled from all the country around from motives of curiosity, to see the once proud city of Nauvoo humbled and delivered up to its enemies and to the domination of a self-constituted and irresponsible power. They proceeded into the city slowly and carefully, examining the way from fear of the explosion of a mine, many of which had been made by the Mormons by burying kegs of powder in the ground, with a man stationed at a distance to pull a string communicating with the trigger of a percussion lock affixed to the keg. This kind of a contrivance was called by the Mormons a "hell's half acre." When the posse arrived in the city the leaders of it erected themselves into a tribunal to decide who should be forced away and who remain. Parties were despatched to hunt for Mormon arms and for Mormons and to bring them to the judgment, where they received their doom from the mouth of Brockman, who there sat a grim and unawed tyrant for the time. As a general rule the Mormons were ordered to leave within an hour or two hours; and by rare grace some of them were allowed until next day, and in a few cases longer. The treaty specified that the Mormons only should be driven into exile. Nothing was said in it concerning the new citizens, who had with the Mormons defended the city.

But the posse no sooner obtained possession than they commenced expelling the new citizens. Some of them were ducked in the river, being in one or two instances actually baptized in the name of the leaders of the mob, others were forcibly driven into the ferry boats to be taken over the river before the bayonets of armed ruffians; and it is believed that the houses of most of them were broken open and their property stolen during their absence. Many of these new settlers were strangers in the country from various parts of the United States who were attracted there by the low price of property, and they knew but little of previous difficulties, or the merits of the quarrel. They saw with their own eyes that the Mormons were industriously preparing to go away, and they knew of their own knowledge that an effort to expel them with force was gratuitous and unnecessary cruelty. They had been trained in the States from whence they came to abhor mobs and to obey the law, and they volunteered their services under executive authority to defend their town and their property against mob violence, and as they honestly believed from destruction. But in this they were partly mistaken for although the mob leaders, in the exercise of unbridled power, were guilty of many enormities to the persons of individuals, and although much personal property was stolen, yet they abstained from materially injuring houses and buildings. The most that was done in this way was the stealing of the doors and the sash of the windows from the houses by somebody; the anti-Mormons allege that they were carried away by the Mormons, and the Mormons aver that the most of them were stolen by the anti-Mormons.

In a few days the obnoxious inhabitants had been expelled, the warlike new citizens with the rest. This class of citizens had strong claims to be treated with more generosity by the conquerors; but a mob, and more especially the mob leaders, inflamed with passion, exasperated by a brave resistance, their vulgar souls seeing no merit in the courage of adversaries, are not apt to show them much favor in the day of success and triumph. The main force of the posse was now disbanded. Brockman returned home. But before he returned, whilst his men were doubly intoxicated with liquor and by the glory of their victory, one hundred of them volunteered to remain to prevent the return of those who had been expelled, or who had fled knowing that they would be forced away and otherwise cruelly treated if they remained to face their conquerors. These, of course, were the lowest, most violent, the least restrained by principle of all the anti-Mormons. The most of them were such vagabonds as had no home anywhere else, no business or employment, and for that reason were the readiest to stay. The posse was finally diminished to about thirty men under Major McCalla, and continued to exercise all the powers of government in Nauvoo, committing many high-handed acts of tyranny and oppression and, as they said, some acts of charity to the suffering women and children, until they heard that a force was coming against them from Springfield.

In the meantime the Mormons had been forced away from their homes unprepared for a journey. They and their women and children had been thrown houseless upon the Iowa shore, without provisions or the means of getting them, or to get away to places where provisions might be obtained. It was now the highest of the sickly season. Many of them were taken from sick beds, hurried into the boats, and driven away by the armed ruffians now exercising the power of government. The best they could do was to erect their tents on the banks of the river and there remain to take their chance of perishing by hunger or by prevailing sickness. In this condition the sick, without shelter, food, nourishment, or medicines, died by scores. The mother watched her sick babe without hope until it died; and when she sunk under accumulated miseries it was only to be quickly followed by her other children, now left without the least attention; for the men had scattered out over the country seeking employment and the means of living. Their distressed condition was no sooner known than all parties contributed to their relief; the anti-Mormons as much as others.

Some of the new citizens who had been driven away had several times attempted to return to look after their property, and were each time driven away with more violence than they were before. The people of the State looked upon these outrages with calm indifference. A few here and there were anxious that something should be done to put an end to them. But such persons were generally moderate men who, because they are not violent themselves, dislike violence in others; and for the same reason, although they desire something to be done, yet never do anything to aid the authorities of the State. These moderate men, if force is necessary to put down force, are always the last whose services can be obtained; and yet they are always the readiest to find fault with the government which they have failed to assist.

They are the first to call upon the governor for prompt action, but the last to bring him any aid; and very many of them tremble at the mere idea of venturing their popularity in such an enterprise. Let no public man in times of excitement depend upon moderate men for support; nor can he in such times justly expect to be supported in moderate measures. All violence is wrong; the moderate course is the right one; the violent men support their measures with energy; the moderate men let theirs perish for want of support. In such a contest a very few, a dozen violent men, are worth a thousand of the moderates. The moderate party never give any efficient support to their leaders. They will coldly approve if, upon a very careful and curious looking into matters, what has been done suits them in the manner and amount of it exactly; but if not suited to the eighth of an inch then they are not sparing in their censure. This is true not only as to excitements which lead to civil war, but as to all excitements attending the contests of party. And it is for this reason that ambitious politicians are always driven to violent courses, to extreme measures, and to eschew all moderation. They know that they can depend upon the men of violence and action for support. And they know, as La Fayette might have known, that the moderate men never give a support worth anything to any one. The wealthy, who stand most in need of protection against violence, very rarely ever volunteer to put it down; most frequently leaving the laws to be enforced, if enforced at all, by obscure men; and many times by such persons as have no business of their own or care for the stability of law and government. Such men as these are the readiest to volunteer in a popular service; some volunteer without considering the merits of the cause; and in civil broils, as they change their minds with the changing winds and have the election of their own commanders, their attachment to the one or the other side is not always to be relied on. Now, as long as the wealthy substantial citizen refuses his aid, the support of government rests upon such feeble helps as these.

But the people had now waked up to reflection; they had seen a mob victorious over the government of the people. The government in a large district was actually put down and trodden under foot. They were willing that the Mormons might be driven away; but they had not anticipated the outrages which followed. A reaction took place, and such is the inconstancy of popular feeling that men who were before outrageous against the governor for making any, even an abortive effort to extend a scanty assistance to an oppressed people, were now no less clamorous against him for not raising a force before one could possibly be raised; and they even went so far as to require that martial law should be declared; and that the rioters should be hung without trial or judgment. Thus they thought that mob violence might be put down by the illegal mob violence of government; and were in favor of converting the government into a mob to put down mobocracy.

There is a vague feeling among the people in favor of martial law on such occasions. I can find no authority in the constitution or anywhere else for the enforcement of martial law outside the lines of a military encampment. The civil law is above the military. But when the civil law shall be utterly disregarded and trampled under foot; when the people become wholly unfit for self-government; when anarchy and disorder shall be forced to give place to despotism; when our forms of government shall be utterly overthrown and abandoned as experiments which have failed, the first dawnings of the reign of tyrants most likely will be preceded by proclamations of martial law, not for the government of armies, but for the government and punishment of a people at once rebellious and deserving to be slaves. The general sentiment in favor of martial law and the disorders calling it forth are fearful evidences of a falling away from the true principles of liberty. Ever since Gen. Jackson on some great occasions, when the fate of half the country was at stake, *took the responsibility,"* the country has swarmed with a tribe of small statesmen who seem to think that the true secret of government is to set it aside and resort to mere force upon the occurrence of the smallest difficulties. It may be well enough on great occasions to have one great Jackson; but on every small occasion no one can imagine the danger of having a multitude of little Jacksons. Jackson's example is to be admired rather than imitated; and the first may be done easier and safer than the last.

Government was obliged to wait for a change in the feelings of the people. As soon as this change was manifested one hundred and twenty men were raised in and near Springfield, and with this small force the governor started to Hancock.[6] Before this force arrived there, it had increased to the number of two hundred. The motive for going over this time was to restore to their homes about sixty families of new citizens, not being Mormons, who had been driven away from their property, most of which had been stolen during their absence. The Mormons could not have been persuaded to return on any terms. The governor had no expectation of being resisted by the great body of antis, although he had attempted to bring some of them to justice for their crimes; yet were they notoriously indebted to him for being recalled to their homes when driven away by the sheriff and his Mormon posse. He had been mainly instrumental in inducing the great body of Mormons to leave the State; he had effectually aided in protecting the county revenue from being collected and most probably squandered by the sheriff, whose only securities were Mormons about to leave the country; he had also given effectual assistance in preventing the Mormon county court from running the county in debt thirty or forty thousand dollars to pay the Mormon posse under Backenstos; and he had, for the space of seven months, obstinately refused to recall Major Warren's force stationed in Hancock for their protection, though their recall was daily insisted upon by the strongest of the governor's political friends. During all this time, he had the anti-Mormons at his mercy; during the dead, cold winter, when their expulsion from their homes would have ruined them. It was only necessary to recall the military and restore the charge of keeping the peace to the sheriff.

But the antis did not feel the least grateful for any of the good which had been done them. They remembered only the evil. It appeared that if they had any gratitude it consisted alone in a lively expectation of future favor. Indeed, during the whole winter that the governor was protecting them in their homes and keeping their lives in their bodies they never ceased cursing and abusing him. But the governor had done these things because they were right, and was too sensible a man to expect any thanks; and they are now mentioned, not to complain, but to illustrate a truth in matters of government, which is this: that he who will preserve the confidence and affection of a faction must be with it every time, through right and wrong. This course the governor is not at liberty to take in a civil war, where both parties seek to trample the government under foot, and where both of them in turn may need restraint. And yet if he does not take one side and keep it, no allowance is made for his position; he is judged of as an individual factionist would be; he is charged with being first on one side and then on the other, and on every side; just as if he had no public duty to perform, but was at liberty to take sides in the quarrel like a private man.

Very much to his astonishment, when the governor arrived in Hancock the anti-Mormons were exceedingly bitter against him. Brockman was sent for; the leaders assembled, and now commenced a series of the most vexatious proceedings. They could hardly find words strong enough to express their unaffected surprise and astonishment at the impudence of the governor and the people of other counties in interfering, as they called it, in the affairs of Hancock. So far had the mob-scenes which they had passed through beclouded their judgments and so far had they imitated the Mormons in their modes of thinking that they really believed that the people of Hancock had some kind of government and sovereignty of their own, and that to interfere with this was to invade their sacred rights. In their long, bitter, and angry contest with the Mormons they had acquired most of the vices of that people, being hurried on by the intensity of bad passions to imitate their crimes, that they might be equal to them in the contest.

This is one of the inevitable effects of long continued faction; and accordingly the presence of the Mormons for six years in that part of the country has left moral blotches and propensities to crime, a total dissolution of moral principle among the remaining inhabitants, which one generation passing away will not eradicate, and perhaps will never be effectually cured until they learn by long and dire experience that the way of the transgressor is hard.

After the arrival of the governor in the county two public meetings were held by the antis, one in Carthage and one in Nauvoo; at both of which it was resolved that they would do nothing whilst the State forces remained; but believing that this force could be kept up only for a short time, they solemnly determined to drive out the proscribed new citizens as soon as the volunteers were withdrawn. As yet they were not aware of the change of opinion against them; they supposed that the people were universally in their favor; and were as arrogant as a mob usually is when they believe themselves able to triumph over their government. Our little force encamped at Nauvoo on the north side of the great temple, protected to the north by a high stone wall. And whilst here our sentinels were fired upon from a tavern near by, kept by a man who had recently kept a house in Illinois town as a place of refuge for the rogues in St. Louis, when hard pressed by the police. At this tavern Backman, the murderer of Durfee; Brath, a swarthy, grim and sanguinary tyrant; Palmer, fresh from the Quincy jail on a charge of rape; Reynolds, who had lately kept a livery stable in St. Louis for the sale of stolen horses; and Van Tuyl, an old, wornout, broken-down, democratic New York politician, took their stand as the anti-Mormon committee of the county to watch our movements.[7] The lines of the encampment were immediately extended so as to include this tavern; martial law was declared, and the inhabitants within the lines of the encampment were notified that if the firing was repeated the offender would be shot or hung, according to the sentence of a court-martial, and that the house itself would be demolished by the artillery. The shooting was not repeated.

Here a laughable matter occurred with a constable and Irish justice of the peace, lately elected by the antis to replace those who had been driven away. These dignitaries broke through the line of sentinels and were put under arrest; but upon giving their word to be forthcoming in the morning to answer for their intrusion they were discharged. Instead of returning to their houses they repaired to the tavern, and having reinforced their courage by additional quantities of liquor they came again to the lines, offering to bribe the sentinels to spike our cannon. They were again arrested and kept until next morning, when Major George R. Weber, now in command, appointed a court-martial to try them. The Irish justice relied much upon his power and consequence as a magistrate, and wanted to be exceedingly noisy and disorderly during the trial. Major Weber ordered him to keep silence until called upon to speak. This the indignant dispenser of justice refused, with a proud swell of importance. With some force Major Weber, taking him by the shoulders, squat him down in a corner; but the magistrate, rising, and still insisting upon his dignity and right to make a noise, was knocked down twice in succession by Major Weber before he could be forced to keep silence. The magistrate and constable were then condemned to be drummed around and out of the camp to the tune of the rogue's march, which was done in good style one very pretty morning. Such a creature as this magistrate was the governor forced by the laws of the State to commission as a justice of the peace; and such officers as these did the anti-Mormons elect to assist him in keeping the peace.

During our stay here Captain Robert Allen, with parts of his company and others, to the number of forty-four men, volunteered to make a secret expedition in the night to Carthage in search of the

State arms, having previously gained intelligence that a large number were concealed in that village. The antis had stationed a committee near us to watch our movements, and as Capt. Allen's men marched on foot intelligence of their coming was conveyed to Carthage and the arms removed to some other place of concealment before their arrival. Whilst this was going on Major Weber, going the rounds outside of the camp, discovered one of the anti-Mormon committee acting as a spy, lying upon a wall, looking into the camp, and tried to arrest him. Major Weber aimed to make the arrest without the taking of life and instead of shooting only struck at him with his pistol. This furnished a new pretext for the old trick of calling out the civil posse against us. Writs were sworn out not only for the arrest of Major Weber, but also for Capt. Allen for stopping some persons in the streets of Carthage whilst searching for arms. These writs were intended to be made the foundation of another call for the posse and for our expulsion from the county. The effort was made, but the mob party failed to enlist more than two hundred and fifty men. We had diminished ours by discharges to one hundred and twenty. But the mob hesitated to attack us without five or six times our number, and accordingly abandoned their design of making the arrests.

After staying in the county seventeen days, being in no danger except from secret assassins, having made diligent search for the five pieces of cannon and other arms belonging to the State without success; and as our officers and men published in a handbill on the ground, having forced the assassins and cut-throats there to endure the presence of the exiled citizens, the principal part of the force was disbanded. Major Jackson and Captain Connelly were left with fifty men to remain until the 15th of December, 1846, before which day the legislature was to assemble, and it was expected that the cold of the winter would by that time put an end to the anti-Mormon agitations. This expectation was realized. Nothing puts an end to the continued enterprises of a mob sooner than the cold of winter.

We did not think it worthwhile to arrest anyone for previous riots, knowing as we did that the State could not change the trial to any other county and that no one could be convicted in Hancock. In fact the antis made their boasts that as they were in the entire possession of the juries and all civil officers of the county no jury could be obtained there to convict them. If Brockman or others had been arrested no justice of the peace would have committed them for trial; if they had been committed they would have been turned loose by the sheriff or the mob. And if they had chosen to stand their trial they were certain not to be convicted. An effort to arrest and prosecute these men would have resulted only in another triumph of the mob over government. In fact there was no way to punish them, as former trials had shown, except by martial law; and this course was utterly illegal. The governor believed that he could not declare martial law for the punishment of citizens without admitting that free government had failed; and assuming that despotism was necessary in its place. He believed that to proceed in such cases by martial law was to overturn the government, institute monarchy, and make himself a dictator. If he erred in this it was an error springing from attachment to the principles of civil liberty. Many were they who wondered that the governor did not do something to punish these men; and held him responsible just as if he actually possessed the power of government; just as if he possessed the power of appointing and removing all the civil and military officers in the disaffected region, who being independent of the governor set up authority against authority; and just as if he had a standing army at command, or with his single arm could make the people put down the people. Let his administration be what it may in these difficulties, yet it illustrates the principle which most of all I desire to illustrate in this history; which is, that government is naturally forced to be a type of the people over whom it is instituted. The people are said to be the masters and public officers the servants, and such is the fact; but with this fact let it be remembered that wherever the relation of master and servant exists the proverb of "like master like man" will apply. If the people will have anarchy there is no power short of despotism capable of forcing them to submission; and the despotism which naturally grows out of anarchy can never be established by those who are elected to administer regular government. If the mob spirit is to continue it must necessarily lead to despotism; but this despotism will be erected upon the ruins of government, and not spring out of it. It has been said that one great party in this country is secretly in favor of monarchy. If this were true that party could not sooner or more effectually accomplish their purposes than to lend their aid in creating a necessity for it. Let them but encourage "every man to do that which seemeth good in his own eyes" and God will give them a king, as he gave one to the Jews for the hardness of their hearts. This simple quotation from Scripture is a vivid description of anarchy; of that state of disorder when men will consent to be slaves rather than without the protection of government; when men fly from the tyranny and misrule of the many-headed monster for protection to the despotism of one man. The giving of a king to the Jews is referred to as a special providence of God. But it is a fundamental law of man's nature from which he cannot escape that despotism is obliged to grow out of general anarchy, as surely as a stone is obliged to fall to the earth when left unsupported in the air. Without any revealed special providence, but in accordance with this great law of man's nature, Cromwell rose out of the disorders of the English revolution; Charles the Second was restored to despotism by the anarchy which succeeded Cromwell; and Bonaparte came forth from the misrule of republican France. The people in all these cases attempted to govern; but in fact did not. They were incapable of self-government; and by returning to despotism admitted that they needed a master. Where the people are unfit for liberty; where they will not be free without violence, license, and injustice to others; where they do not deserve to be free, nature itself will give them a master. No form of constitution can make them free and keep them so. On the contrary, a people who are fit for and deserve liberty cannot be enslaved.

XIV

Crime and Violence in Massac County, 1846

Whilst the Mormons and their adversaries were at war in the county of Hancock a little rebellion, less in numbers but equal in violence, was raging in the county of Massac on the Ohio river.[1] It has heretofore been mentioned that an ancient colony of horse-thieves, counterfeiters, and robbers had long infested the counties of Massac and Pope. They were so strong and so well combined together as to insure immunity from punishment by legal means. In the summer of 1846 a number of these desperadoes attacked the house of an aged citizen in Pope county and robbed him of about $2,500 in gold. In the act of committing the robbery one of them left behind a knife made by a blacksmith of the neighborhood, by means of which he was identified. This one being arrested and subjected to torture by the neighboring people, confessed his crime and gave the names of his associates. These again being arrested, to the number of a dozen, and some of them being tortured, disclosed the names of a long list of confederates in crime scattered through several counties. The honest portion of the people now associated themselves into a band of regulators and proceeded to order all suspected persons to leave the country. But before this order could be enforced the election for county officers came on in August, 1846 and those who were suspected to be rogues all threw their votes one way and, as it was asserted, thereby insured the election of a sheriff and other officers in the county of Massac who were opposed to the proceedings of the regulators, and not over zealous in enforcing the laws. The county of Massac gave about five hundred votes and out of these John W. Read, the successful candidate for sheriff, received about three hundred majority. His opponent was a wealthy citizen and, as it appeared, not very popular, but his influence over his friends was almost unlimited. There was another unsuccessful candidate for county clerk of the same description. These two put themselves at the head of their friends in Pope and Massac. And being assisted by large numbers from Paducah and Smithland in Kentucky, they proceeded to drive out and punish all suspected persons and to torture them to force them to confess and disclose the names of their confederates. By this means the numbers implicated in crime were increased every day. The mode of torture applied to these people was to take them to the Ohio river and hold them under water until they showed a willingness to confess. Others had ropes tied around their bodies over their arms, and a stick twisted into the ropes until their ribs and sides were crushed in by force of the pressure. Some of the persons who were maltreated in this way obtained warrants for the arrest of the regulators. These warrants were put into the hands of the sheriff, who arrested some of the offenders; but the persons arrested were rescued out of jail in a short time by their friends. Shortly after this the regulators ordered the sheriff and county clerk, together with the magistrate who issued the warrants, to leave the country, under the penalty of severe corporal punishment. It appears that by means of torture and bribery some notorious rogues had been induced to accuse the sheriff, the county clerk, and the magistrate of being members of the gang of robbers; and it was upon this pretext that they were ordered to leave the country.

In this condition of things application was made in August, 1846 to the governor for a militia force to sustain the constituted authorities of Massac. This disturbance being at a distance of two hundred and fifty miles from the seat of government and in a part of the country between which and the seat of government there was but very little communication, the facts concerning it were but imperfectly known to the governor, for which reason he issued an order to Brigadier-General John T. Davis of Williamson county to examine into it, and if he judged it necessary, to call out the militia. Gen. Davis proceeded to Massac, called the parties together, and, as he believed, induced them to settle their difficulties; but he had no sooner left the county than violence broke out afresh. The regulators came down from Pope and over from Kentucky and drove out the sheriff, the county clerk, the representative-elect to the legislature, and many others; they committed actual violence by whipping a considerable number, and threatened summary punishment to every one, rogue or honest man, who spoke against their proceedings. This is the great evil of lynch law. The lynchers set out with the moderate and honest intention of exterminating notorious rogues only. But as they proceed they find opposition from many honest persons who can never divest themselves of the belief that the laws of the country are amply sufficient for the punishment and prevention of crime. The lynchers then have to maintain their assumed authority in opposition to law and regular government, and they are apt to be no less arbitrary and violent in so doing than tyranny generally is in maintaining its pretensions.

For this reason they think they must crush all opposition, and in this mode that which at first was merely a war between honest men and rogues is converted into a war between honest men alone, one party contending for the supremacy of the laws and the other maintaining its own assumed authority.

Not long after these events the circuit court was held for Massac. Judge Scates delivered a strong charge to the grand jury against the proceedings of the regulators; the grand jury found indictments against a number of them. Warrants were issued upon the indictments; quite a number were arrested by the sheriff and committed to jail. The regulators assembled from Kentucky and the neighboring counties in Illinois with the avowed intention of releasing the prisoners. They threatened to lynch Judge Scates if he ever returned again to hold court in Massac; and they ordered the members of the grand jury and the witnesses before them to leave the country under pain of corporal punishment. The sheriff set about summoning a posse to secure his prisoners, to resist the regulators, and to maintain the authority of government. But now was the reign of terror indeed. The regulators by their violence had struck terror into all moderate men, who, although they disapproved of their proceedings, were afraid to join the sheriff for fear of being involved in the fate of the horse thieves. These moderate men who disapproved of the proceedings of the regulators were in a majority of three to one in the county; but such is the inefficiency of moderate men that one bold daring man of violence can generally overawe and terrify a dozen of them. For this reason the sheriff failed to raise a force among the reputable moderate men of the county and was joined only, for the most part, by sixty or seventy men who had been ordered to leave the country, many of whom were known to be notorious rogues.

The regulators marched down to Metropolis city, the county seat of Massac, in much greater force. A parley ensued between the sheriff's party and the regulators; and it was finally agreed that the sheriff's party should surrender under a promise of exemption from violence. The regulators then took possession of the jail, liberated their friends confined in it, carried several of the sheriff's posse along with them as prisoners, and murdered some of them by drowning them in the Ohio river. The sheriff and all his active friends were again ordered to leave, and were driven out of the country.

The sheriff, the representative to the legislature, and another gentleman then proceeded to see the governor, who was then at Nauvoo in Hancock county with a military force endeavoring to reinstate the exiled citizens of Hancock. As he was now within twenty days of the expiration of his office he was loath to begin measures with the Massac rioters which he feared might not be approved or pursued by his successor. Besides this, from all former experience he was perfectly certain that it would be entirely useless to order out the militia for the protection of horse-thieves. He well knew that the militia could not be raised for such a purpose. He therefore issued an order to Dr. William J. Gibbs of Johnson county authorizing him to call upon the militia officers in some of the neighboring counties for a force to protect the sheriff and other county officers, the magistrates, the grand jury and the witnesses before them, and the honest part of the community. Dr. Gibbs proceeded to Massac, and calling to his assistance two justices of the peace, he required the regulators to come before them and establish their charges so that he could know who were and who were not rogues, to be put out of the protection of law. The regulators declined appearing before him, wherefore the doctor adjudged that there were no rogues in Massac county and that all were entitled to protection against the regulators. He proceeded to call for the militia of Union and other counties; but notwithstanding the doctor had adjudged that there were no rogues in Massac the militia knew to the contrary, and as was foreseen by the governor the militia refused to turn out for their protection. Thus the regulators were again left undisputed masters of the county. They now assembled themselves together, caught a number of suspected persons, and tried them by a committee; some were acquitted, others convicted, and were whipped or tarred and feathered. The numbers implicated with the counterfeiters increased rather than diminished. Many persons who had before been considered honest men were now implicated, which increased the excitement. Many who were formerly in favor of the regulators now left them and disapproved of their conduct. The one party was called Regulators, the other Flatheads.

A party of about twenty regulators went to the house of an old man named Mathis to arrest him and force him to give evidence of the guilt of certain persons of the neighborhood, and of some who had been inmates of his house. He and his wife resisted the arrest. The old woman, being unusually strong and active, knocked down one or two of the party with her fists. A gun was then presented to her breast, accompanied by a threat of blowing her heart out if she continued her resistance. She caught the gun and shoved it downwards, when it went off and shot her through the thigh. She was also struck several blows on the head with the gun-barrel, inflicting considerable wounds, knocking her down in her turn. The party captured the old man Mathis and carried him away with them, since which time he has not been heard of, but is supposed to have been murdered. The regulators say that the shooting of the old lady was accidental. She made the proper affidavit for the purpose of having the perpetrators of the crime arrested. The proper authorities succeeded in arresting about ten of them. They were carried to the Metropolis house in Metropolis city and there placed under a guard while search was made for the old man Mathis, who was desired as a witness against the prisoners. The news of their arrest having gone abroad, it was rumored all over the country that the Flatheads intended to put them to death if they failed to convict them. This brought out a large force of regulators for the avowed purpose of rescuing the prisoners. They marched to Metropolis city, where they found the sheriff with a party about as numerous as their own. Various attempts to compromise the difficulty without the effusion of blood were made; but this could be effected only by the unconditional release of the prisoners. After getting their friends from the sheriff's party the regulators arrested several of the sheriff's guards and delivered them to the Kentuckians to be dealt with as they saw proper. In attempting to arrest one man they fired at him twice without injury, when he surrendered; and as he was led down stairs he was stabbed from behind by one of the regulators; and he having screamed murder in consequence of his wound, a Methodist preacher who commanded one of the regulating companies exclaimed, "Now they are using them as they should be."* The wounded man was said to be respectable, and upon good authority was represented to be an honest, industrious young man. The man who stabbed him had before had a personal difficulty with him and sought this means of getting revenged. Thus it is when regular government is prostrated and the laws trampled under foot, apparently for the best of purposes, men will avail themselves of the prevalent anarchy to revenge their private quarrels; in a short time the original purpose for which force is resorted to will be forgotten; and instead of punishing horse-thieves and robbers those who drop the law and resort to force soon find themselves fiercely contending to revenge injuries and insults, and to maintain their assumed authority.

The prisoners taken away by the Kentuckians were mostly suspicious characters; one of them resided in LaSalle county near the Illinois river, but had resided several months at Metropolis in settling the affairs of an estate, and whose only offence was that he had taken an active part in arresting and securing the prisoners just now released. He was tied, together with the other prisoners, and all of

*See volume of Illinois Reports for 1846–47, p. 96, Senate Documents.

them taken off towards Paducah. Letters were received from the regulators by their friends in Springfield in which they gave an account
of what they had done with several of these persons. They wrote that
several of them had gone to Arkansas, by which was understood that
they had drowned their prisoners in the Ohio river and left their bodies
to float with the current in the direction toward Arkansas. On the 23d
of December, 1846 a convention of regulators from the counties of
Pope, Massac, and Johnson met at Golconda and ordered the sheriff of Massac, the clerk of the county court, and many other citizens
to leave the country within thirty days. The sheriff and many others
left the country and were absent all winter. The new governor and
the legislature then in session were busy all winter in devising measures to suppress these disturbances; but nothing effectual was done.
The legislature passed a law, the constitutionality of which was doubted by many, authorizing the governor when he was satisfied that a
crime had been committed by twenty persons or more to issue his
proclamation; and then the judge of the circuit was authorized to hold
a district court in a large district embracing several counties. By this
means it was sought to evade the constitution and take the trial out
of the county where the crime was committed, against the will of the
accused. In other words, it was believed that in this indirect mode
the State could entitle itself to a change of venue in criminal cases
against the will of the prisoner. Our former experience had abundantly
showed that when crimes had been committed by powerful combinations of men the guilty never could be convicted in the counties in
which the crimes had been committed. I have never learned whether
any proceedings have taken place under the law; but so it is, no one
has yet been punished; the disturbances in Massac have died away.
And whether they died away naturally, being obliged like everything
else to come to an end, or whether the rioters were deterred by the
provisions of the foregoing act of the legislature is unknown to the
author.

In the conclusion of this history the author must be permitted
to indulge in a slight retrospection of the past. In 1842, when he came
into office, the State was in debt about $14,000,000 for moneys wast-
ed upon internal improvements and in banking; the domestic treasury of the State was in arrears $313,000 for the ordinary expenses
of government; auditors' warrants were freely selling at a discount
of fifty per cent; the people were unable to pay even moderate taxes
to replenish the treasury, in which not one cent was contained even

to pay postage on letters to and from the public offices; the great canal, after spending five millions of dollars on it, was about to be abandoned; the banks, upon which the people had relied for a currency, had become insolvent, their paper had fallen so low as to cease to circulate as money, and as yet no other money had taken its place, leaving the people wholly destitute of a circulating medium and universally in debt; immigration to the State had almost ceased; real estate was wholly unsaleable; the people abroad, terrified by the prospect of high taxation, refused to come amongst us for settlement; and our own people at home were no less alarmed and terrified at the magnitude of our debt, then apparently so much exceeding any known resources of the country. Many were driven to absolute despair of ever paying a cent of it; and it would have required but little countenance and encouragement in the then disheartened and wavering condition of the public mind to have plunged the State into the irretrievable infamy of open repudiation. This is by no means an exaggerated picture of our affairs in 1842.

In December, 1846, when the author went out of office, the domestic debt of the treasury, instead of being $313,000 was only $31,000, with $9,000 in the treasury; auditors' warrants were at par or very nearly so; the banks had been put into liquidation in a manner just to all parties, and so as to maintain the character of the State for moderation and integrity; violent counsels were rejected; the notes of the banks had entirely disappeared and had been replaced in circulation by a reasonable abundance of gold and silver coin and the notes of solvent banks of other States; the people had very generally paid their private debts; a very considerable portion of the State debt had been paid also; about three millions of dollars had been paid by a sale of the public property and by putting the bank into liquidation; and a sum of five millions more had been effectually provided for to be paid after the completion of the canal; being a reduction of eight millions of the State debt which had been paid, redeemed, or provided for whilst the author was in office. The State itself, although broken, and at one time discredited and a by-word throughout the civilized world, had to the astonishment of every one been able to borrow on the credit of its property the further sum of $1,600,000 to finish the canal; and that great work, at one time so hopeless and so nearly abandoned, is now in a fair way of completion.

The people abroad have once more begun to seek this goodly land for their future homes. From 1843 until 1846 our population rapidly increased; and is now increasing faster than it ever did before. Our own people have become contented and happy; and the former discredit resting upon them abroad for supposed wilful delinquency in paying the State debt no longer exists.

It is a just pride and a high satisfaction for the author to feel and know that he has been somewhat instrumental in producing these gratifying results. In this history he has detailed all the measures of the legislature which produced them; and if these measures did not all originate with him, he can rightfully and justly claim that he supported them with all his power and influence and has faithfully endeavored to carry them out with the best ability he could command. For so doing he has had to encounter bitter opposition to his administration; and enmities have sprung up personally against himself which he hopes will not last forever. For although he wants no office, yet is he possessed of such sensibility that it is painful to him to be the subject of unmerited obloquy; and for this reason, and this alone, he hopes that when those of his fellow-citizens who disapproved of his administration in these particulars have time to look into the merits of these measures and see how they have lifted the State from the lowest abyss of despair and gloom to a commanding and honorable position among her sisters of the Union, they will not remember their wrath forever.

Notes

Chapter I

1. When running for governor in 1842, Ford stood in opposition to an effort in the far northern counties of Illinois that were claimed by Wisconsin to annex to that territory in order to escape liability for Illinois's huge internal improvement debt. Wisconsin proponents of the measure, of course, claimed title to the area on the grounds of the terms of the Northwest Ordinance and continued to do so after the Illinois agitation had abated.

2. Under Illinois's first state constitution, that of 1818, the governor lacked an effective veto power, and his legislative authority was correspondingly weak. The responsibility for reviewing legislation was given instead to a Council of Revision comprised of the governor and justices of the state's supreme court. Any bills returned to the General Assembly by the Council of Revision could be repassed by a simple majority of both houses. See "Constitution of 1818," in Emil Joseph Verlie, comp., "Illinois Constitutions," *Collections of the Illinois State Historical Library* 13 (1919): 34–35.

Chapter II

1. George Forquer, who is almost always mentioned with approval in this book, was Thomas Ford's older half-brother, surrogate father, and political mentor.

2. Alexander Pope Field of Union County was well known as a foe of the circuit court system in 1826–27. *Illinois Intelligencer* (Vandalia), December 16, 1826, January 6, 1827.

3. A son of Alexander Hamilton, William S. Hamilton had been involved in the Survey of the Illinois Military Tract. He surveyed the town plat of Peoria, where a major street bears his name. He later was active in the Lead Region north of Galena and participated in the gold rush to California, where he died. David McCulloch, *Historical Encyclopedia of Illinois and History of Peoria County* (Chicago, 1902), 205.

4. The governor of Illinois in 1844 was Thomas Ford.

5. A Jo Daviess County tradition has it that James Johnson, possibly the brother of Richard M. Johnson, vice president of the United States under Van Buren, brought slaves to work in the Galena mines in

1822. One James Johnson obtained a federal permit to mine lead at Galena in 1823. It is a fact that a brother of Richard Johnson with that name had supplied federal garrisons on the Mississippi and Missouri rivers in 1819 and 1820 and had obviously come to know the area. *The History of Jo Daviess County, Illinois* . . . (Chicago, 1878), 236–38, 244, 257.

6. Ford's admiration of Daniel Pope Cook rose in part from personal indebtedness. Cook had taken an interest in Ford when the latter was a fatherless youth, and Ford later had studied law under Cook's direction.

7. A system of general taxation for the creation of a permanent Illinois school fund was prescribed by the Illinois General Assembly the year after the first publication of Ford's *History*, in 1855. See *Laws of Illinois*, 1855, 51–91.

Chapter III

1. Abner Field, although not the incumbent, was the incensed "unsuccessful candidate" referred to here. At least three of his "opponents" can be identified: Thomas Reynolds (later to be governor of Missouri), David Blackwell, and John Reynolds. Thomas C. Browne to Henry Eddy, February 11, 1827, S. H. Kimmel to Eddy, February 11, 1827, Henry Eddy Papers, Illinois Historical Survey, Urbana.

Chapter IV

1. The Military Tract, an area of 3,500,000 acres occupying approximately the triangle enclosed between the Illinois and the Mississippi rivers, was set aside by Congress as bounty lands for soldiers of the War of 1812. The bounty rights were largely bought by eastern speculators at a low price because individual soldiers were unable or disinclined to settle their respective tracts. Such absentee ownership provoked deep-seated animosity in the minds of the actual settlers of Illinois, and individuals as well as local and state governments cheerfully exerted themselves to despoil the nonresident proprietors. See Thomas Ford, *A History of Illinois*, ed. Milo Quaife, 2 vols. (Chicago, 1945–46), 1:142.

2. Ford's memory of the electoral impact of the Wiggins Loan seems inflated. The enabling act authorized the governor, John Reynolds, to contract for the loan. It passed the 1830–31 house without a recorded vote. A roll call was taken in the senate, where six of the nine who voted in favor of the loan sat in the next General Assembly, whereas of the seven who opposed it, only one returned. Any blame for the loan should have gone to Reynolds, who at all events constitutionally could not succeed himself as governor. *Laws of Illinois*, 1830–31, 92–94; Illinois *House Journal*, 1830–31, 299; Illinois *Senate Journal*, 1830–31, 297; 1832–33, 3–4.

3. There is reason to believe that the so-called Little Bull Law had

the effect that the author describes. That act was passed in the second session of the Ninth General Assembly (1835–36), and its repeal was one of the first acts of the Tenth General Assembly a year later. The bill was passed without a recorded vote in the senate, but a roll call was taken in the House. Of the twenty-four who voted in favor, seventeen (70 percent) did not return the next year; of those, ten ran but were not reelected. Of the sixteen who voted against it, nine (56 percent) did not return to the legislature; of those, six ran but were not reelected. The Ninth General Assembly had 81 members; the Tenth General Assembly contained 131. Because of this unusual political mortality and the expansion of the legislature, the Tenth General Assembly contained an extraordinary complement of new and inexperienced members, many of whom enthusiastically helped saddle the state with its ultimately ruinous internal improvement obligation. See 124ff. Illinois *House Journal*, 1835–36, 344; 1836–37, 3–5; Illinois *Senate Journal*, 1835–36, 220; *Laws of Illinois*, 1836–37, 49.

4. The Kentuckian was James M. Strode of Galena.

5. Governor Ford presents as good an exculpation of the disgraceful affair of Stillman's defeat as possible, but it is not free from contemporary bias. Instead of seven hundred warriors, Black Hawk had but forty. He was not expecting a battle and had sent his emissaries into Stillman's camp under a flag of truce to beg for peace. If they had been received with reasonable common sense and decency, the war would have ended at this point instead of being prolonged to its miserable conclusion at Bad Axe, with all of the intervening slaughter and horror. See Ford, *History of Illinois*, ed. Quaife, 1:175.

6. Henry Gratiot had mined in the Galena region since 1823. His settlement was at Gratiot's Grove, fifteen miles from Galena in what was then Michigan Territory. It was there that the ransom of the Hall sisters took place. *History of Jo Daviess County*, 245, 284.

7. It may be doubted whether General Whiteside shot the Indian leader. In describing the action Stevens observes, "During the thickest of the fight the apparent leader of the Indians, mounted on a white horse, rode backward and forward, urging his men on with shouts and gestures; but the intrepid volunteers were pouring lead into the ranks of the Indians with such deadly effect that they were gradually forced back. After a little the white horse was seen leaving the field without a rider." Frank E. Stevens, *The Black Hawk War* (Chicago, 1903), 179. See Ford, *History of Illinois*, ed. Quaife, 1:182.

8. A scion of a numerous and famous fur-trading family, Felix St. Vrain was the unfortunate agent for the Sacs and Foxes at Rock Island.

9. This is Ford's only reference to Stephenson, who, like many veterans of the Black Hawk War, carried his military reputation into politics. He served in the Illinois senate in 1834–35, became register of the Galena Land Office, and was the Democratic nominee for governor in 1838 when it was discovered that he was in default to the land office in

the amount of $40,000. He withdrew from the gubernatorial race, to be replaced by Thomas Carlin, who was elected. Theodore Calvin Pease, *The Frontier State, 1818–1848* (Chicago, 1922), 249–50.

10. The Four Lakes were Kegonsa, Waubesa, Monona, and Mendota, connected by the Yahara or Catfish River, which is merely the upper extension of Rock River. Between and around Monona and Mendota (still locally known also as Third and Fourth Lakes) lies the city of Madison. See Ford, *History of Illinois*, ed. Quaife, 1:193.

11. At the site of Beloit, Wisconsin; Governor Ford, who seems to have depended upon Wakefield for this statement, is again in error. On June 30, the army camped on Rock River, about seven miles south of the state boundary, arriving at Beloit about noon of July 1. Ibid., 195.

Chapter V

1. The ridge-and-valley country of the Driftless Area of southwestern Wisconsin is indeed rough and picturesque, especially near the Mississippi, but Ford, who was never there, exaggerates its character. It is certainly not "alpine in all its features."

2. The reference is to the third of the Four Lakes, Lake Monona. The march the next day was through the present site of the city of Madison, Wisconsin.

3. At Stillman's Run, Black Hawk's peace overture was defeated by the undisciplined stupidity of the Illinois volunteers; at Wisconsin Heights, by the unfortunate absence of the Winnebago scouts and the inability of the whites to understand the message to which they were listening. The speaker was Neapope, Black Hawk's principal lieutenant, who apart from other qualities possessed an extraordinary voice. Wakefield relates that the white soldiers supposed him to be issuing directions to the warriors for an attack upon their camp, and while the red orator poured out his mournful appeal for peace and mercy General Henry delivered an eloquent counterappeal to his men to repel the attack that was momentarily expected: "Stand firm my brave Suckers," he concluded, "until you can see the whites of their eyes before you discharge their muskets, and then meet them with a charge as you have before done, and that too with great success." In 1832 as in the War of 1812, the discharge of volleys of high-powered oratory was a common prelude to the volleys of musketry. See Ford, *History of Illinois*, ed. Quaife, 1:220.

4. This battle, known ever since as the battle of Wisconsin Heights, was a rear-guard action that Black Hawk fought to hold back the army long enough for women, children, and remaining warriors to escape across the wide-flowing Wisconsin. In this most difficult operation he was entirely successful. Governor Ford's explanation of the disparity in losses between the two armies is of doubtful validity, as are the figures given for the loss sustained by the Indians. Black Hawk himself claimed he

lost but six men and believed the white loss was proportionately far greater than his own. "Whatever may be the sentiments of the white people in relation to this battle," he concluded, "my nation, though fallen, will award me the reputation of a great brave in conducting it." Most modern historians seem disposed to accept his estimate. Ibid., 1:221.

5. In the second printing of the 1854 edition of Ford's *History,* from which most extant copies originated, this phrase has been changed to "unworthy artifices used to deprive him."

There were six such alterations of text between the first printing and the second one. Almost all copies of the first printing contain six tipped-in leaves on which the alterations appear; the second printing contains all the corrections and no tipped-in pages. The first printing is also distinguished by an error on the title page: The date of the state's commencement is given as 1814 instead of 1818. This mistake was corrected in the second printing. Almost invariably these text changes reduced the acerbity of Ford's assessments of several Illinois public men. There is reason to believe that the text changes were done at the behest of Ford's literary executor, James Shields, because pencil corrections that were made in the unaltered copy of the first printing that resides at the Illinois State Historical Library, are in a hand that bears great similarity to that of Shields. Information inside the rear cover of this copy identifies it with Ivison & Phinney, the New York associate of the Chicago publisher S. C. Griggs & Co. Because the book was printed in New York, it appears that this copy may have been the one on the basis of which changes were made between the first and second printings.

6. Governor Ford's statement is considerably inaccurate. Following his return from his eastern tour in 1833, Black Hawk lived in retirement, his rival Keokuk, leader of the peace party among the Sauk, having been made responsible for his good behavior. During these years he acquired a certain degree of popularity with the whites, the tendency being to regard him as a fallen martyr. In his declining years he was cared for by his squaw, As-shaw-e-qua or Singing Bird, and his daughter Nam-e-qua, both of whom were fastidiously neat. He died at his lodge on the bank of the Des Moines River on October 3, 1838, and was buried near his cabin "in a suit of military clothes given to him when in Washington City by General Jackson, with hat, sword, gold epaulets, etc." A year later, a certain Dr. Turner robbed the grave of the body and other contents to place it on public exhibition. This indecent act was repudiated by Governor Lucas of Iowa, who recovered the bones and ultimately placed them in the collection of the Burlington Geological and Historical Society. In 1855 they were consumed in the burning of the society's building. As-shaw-e-qua accompanied her tribe to the new reservation in Kansas, where she died at the age of eighty-five in the summer of 1846. Whether any descendants of Black Hawk still survive is unknown. See Ford, *History of Illinois,* ed. Quaife, 1:253.

Chapter VI

1. Ford does not mention that he was one of the defense attorneys in Judge Smith's impeachment trial. Illinois *Senate Journal*, 1832–33, Appendix, 3–91; "Speech of Thomas Ford, In Defense of the Hon. Theophilus W. Smith, Before the Senate of Illinois, Sitting as a Court of Impeachment, January 29 and 30, 1833," Vandalia, 1833.

2. It seems likely that this senator was G. W. P. Maxwell of Schuyler County, who was very interested in the opening of roads in the Military Tract but whose position on the state's banks was decidedly lukewarm until the time came for the passage of both bills. Illinois *Senate Journal*, 1834–35, 170, 332–33, 354, 360.

3. John Dougherty of Union County was elected a state's attorney at this session. He took a consistently antibank position in the house, other than to favor at last the passage of the bill incorporating the State Bank of Illinois. Illinois *House Journal*, 1834–35, 356, 359, 504–5, 508, 511–12, 521–25, 553–54.

4. Godfrey and Gilman's Galena agent was Hezekiah H. Gear, a successful lead mine developer. Once well established, he financed other mining operations in the Lead Region. *History of Jo Daviess County*, 248–49.

5. Ford seems to have originated the legend of the logrolling activity of Sangamon County's "Long Nine." There is almost no documentary evidence that originated before the publication of Ford's *History* to corroborate this account, and such trading is difficult to establish from a perusal of the house and senate journals. On the other hand, the story is plausible; logrolling was frequently the means of doing business in the Illinois General Assembly. Although Ford professes outrage here at the Long Nine's activities, there is no reason to believe that any of the Sangamon delegation felt discredited by Ford's accusations. None denied them or even responded to them, although other parts of this book generated considerable controversy at the time of publication.

6. This entire sentence has been deleted from the second printing of the 1854 edition.

7. From about 1837 to 1860, the Democratic party was called by its opponents the Loco-Foco party. The name is supposed to have originated in New York City in 1835, when, during a factional squabble at Tammany Hall, a radical faction seized control of the city caucus. The opposition then turned off the gas by which the room was lighted, produced candles, and lit them with locofoco matches, continued the meeting. See Ford, *History of Illinois*, ed. Quaife, 1:311.

8. To the end of the paragraph, this clause has been deleted from the second printing of the 1854 edition. Peck had been a political ally of Shields, if not of Ford. This excision, and other changes to be noted, may have derived at least tacitly from an effort on the part of Stephen A. Douglas and James Shields, both in the U.S. Senate in 1854, to main-

tain good feeling among leaders and factions in the Illinois Democratic party. Such a short-lived period of conciliation did indeed exist between the election of Franklin Pierce to the presidency and the introduction of the Kansas-Nebraska Act. Robert W. Johannsen, *Stephen A. Douglas* (New York, 1973), 379–80.

9. Ford's reference to "The Lobby" here is to the unofficial "Third House" of the Illinois Legislature. It convened for at least ten years during the 1830s and 1840s and was made up of legislators, lawyers, and office-holders and office-seekers around the capitol; they met at night and deliberated current issues, sometimes facetiously, while the Legislature was in session. At other times, Ford writes of "The Lobby" as the literal lobby of each legislative chamber, from which the proceedings were watched and occasionally influenced by interested outsiders who commented on the activity and sometimes sent in legislative proposals. Rodney O. Davis, "Lobbying and the Third House in the Early Illinois General Assembly," *The Old Northwest* 14 (1989) [1991]: 267–84.

Chapter VII

1. This phrase is deleted from the second printing of the 1854 edition. Browne was a Whig, but Shields had served with him on the Illinois supreme court.

2. The circuit justice who made the controversial decision in the alien voting case was Dan Stone, earlier one of Sangamon County's Long Nine.

3. One of the beneficiaries of the reorganization of the judiciary in 1841 was Thomas Ford himself; he was one of the five new judges chosen by the General Assembly.

4. By leaping out a window of the hall, three House Whigs tried to prevent a quorum, defeat the sine die adjournment, and thus relieve the state's banks of the burden of specie resumption. The three men were Asahel Gridley of McLean County, Joseph Gillespie of Madison County, and Abraham Lincoln. Joseph Gillespie to William H. Herndon, January 31, 1866, mss. 2453–54, Herndon-Weik Collection, Library of Congress.

Chapter VIII

1. Lovejoy's St. Louis *Observer* had become an abolition paper, but Lovejoy's expulsion from Missouri by mob action did not immediately arise from his abolitionism. It instead followed his attack in the *Observer* on Missouri Judge Luke Lawless, who had instructed a grand jury to return no indictment after the lynching of a free black man in St. Louis if the jury should conclude that the lynching had been an act of an irrational multitude seized by an "almost electric frenzy." Such an act, Lawless had said, "transcends your jurisdiction—it is beyond the reach of human law." To Lovejoy, such an instruction seemed to condone mob violence against unpopular victims; he condemned it and was accordingly so harassed

that he had to leave St. Louis. Merton L. Dillon, *Elijah P. Lovejoy, Abolitionist Editor* (Urbana, 1961), 87–89.

2. Ford's discussion of the Alton antislavery convention is excessively abbreviated. The minority report was made by Usher F. Linder, attorney general of Illinois, who the next day was able to pack the convention with an antiabolitionist majority. That majority resolved that not even slave states possessed the right to abolish slavery and then adjourned the convention sine die. At that point Lovejoy and Beecher concluded to organize a state antislavery society in privacy in order to avoid such intrusion and diversion of their intentions. Dillon, *Elijah P. Lovejoy*, 134–39.

3. Something, no doubt, may be said in defense of Governor Ford's argument, yet members of the Mormon church can hardly desire, or themselves frame, a more powerful defense of the action of Joseph Smith in destroying the press of the Nauvoo *Expositor* described in chapter X. See Ford, *History of Illinois*, ed. Quaife, 2:22.

4. What Ford calls the "conventional law of each neighborhood" in western regions where public land was not yet available for legal entry was usually enforced by claims associations or clubs. These were generally comprised of the earliest-arriving settlers and their friends, among whom the sanction of numbers protected their extralegal land claims. Frequently, land-seeking latecomers or nonmembers of claim clubs were regarded either with suspicion or as outright claim-jumpers. Allan G. Bogue, *From Prairie to Corn Belt* (Chicago, 1963), 31–39; Allan G. Bogue, "The Iowa Claim Clubs: Symbol and Substance," *Mississippi Valley Historical Review* 45 (1958): 231–53.

5. The presiding judge at this Ogle County trial late in March 1841 was Thomas Ford, whose exasperation with the defendants was notorious at the time.

6. David and Taylor Driscoll were the actual murderers of Captain John Campbell. Their father, John Driscoll, and their brother William were killed by the Ogle County vigilantes; their brother Pierce was released. *The History of Ogle County, Illinois* (Chicago, 1878), 350–70.

7. Ford presided over the murder trial of the Regulators in September 1841 and found the outcome of the trial most satisfactory.

8. Some early critics of Mormonism alleged that the Book of Mormon was based on an earlier manuscript composed in upstate New York by Solomon Spaulding. The Spaulding theory was based on the presumption that Joseph Smith was incapable of composing the Book of Mormon, and it has few defenders in the twentieth century, even among doubters of Joseph Smith's prophetic status. Leonard J. Arrington and Davis Bitton, *The Mormon Experience* (New York, 1979), 15; Fawn M. Brodie, *No Man Knows My History: The Life of Joseph Smith, the Mormon Prophet* (New York, 1946), 419–33.

9. Rigdon delivered the Salt Sermon, in which the Mormons were described as the "salt of the earth," on June 19, 1838. On July 4 he delivered an inflammatory sermon at Far West, in which the "Mormon

Declaration of Rights" was proclaimed. F. Mark McKiernan, *The Voice of One Crying in the Wilderness: Sidney Rigdon, Religious Rebel, 1793–1876* (Lawrence, Kans., 1971), 85–86, 87–89.

10. The Mormons' last stand in Missouri was conducted with much less credit to Missourians than to the Latter-Day Saints. Ford hardly alludes to the violence that lasted from August through October of 1838, culminating with the massacre of seventeen Mormon men and boys at Haun's Mill on October 30. Smith's surrender at Far West followed shortly after because he expected a manyfold repetition of Haun's Mill otherwise. F. Mark McKiernan, "Mormons on the Defensive: Far West," in *The Restoration Movement: Essays in Mormon History*, ed. F. Mark McKiernan et al. (Lawrence, Kans., 1973), 133–34.

Chapter IX

1. There is no record of this resolution being offered by Isaac Arnold in the proceedings of the 1841 Democratic state convention. But Arnold was an ally of Ford in the General Assembly between 1842 and 1845; he was a foe of repudiation there, and he coauthored the plan for the reduction of the state debt. *Illinois State Register* (Springfield), December 17, 1841.

2. This exchange illustrates how legislative debate could cross the boundaries dividing official bodies from unofficial ones in early Illinois politics. Trumbull's antibank speech was delivered to the lobby and then answered in the house by McClernand. Trumbull in turn responded to the lobby. On occasion, legislators had to attend all sessions of the "Third House" to be apprised of the whole of a dialogue. Alton *Telegraph*, December 31, 1842, February 19, 1843.

3. The unnamed subject of Governor Ford's merciless castigation was James H. Ralston, who in 1841 was defeated in the congressional election by John T. Stuart by a vote of 21,698 to 19,553. See Ford, *History of Illinois*, ed. Quaife, 2:133.

4. Ford endured this opposition from Trumbull, his secretary of state, until the end of the legislative session. Only then did he remove him from office.

5. *Laws of Illinois*, 1842–43, 186–89.

Chapter X

1. William Backenstos, the sheriff of Hancock County, was known as a "Jack Mormon," or Mormon sympathizer. The "prominent democrat of Springfield" was probably Mason Brayman, a Springfield lawyer and political ally of Ford. Marvin S. Hill, *Quest for Refuge: The Mormon Flight from American Pluralism* (Salt Lake City, 1988), 131–32.

2. Mormon anticipation of the Millennium is manifest in the formal organization in the spring of 1844 of the political Kingdom of God at

Nauvoo. The kingdom was to be administered by the Council of Fifty, also established then. Apparently at the same time Joseph Smith had himself ordained as "King on Earth." Klaus Hansen, *Quest for Empire: The Political Kingdom of God and the Council of Fifty in Mormon History* (East Lansing, 1967), passim and 65–66, 155–58.

3. The general of the militia brigade was Minor R. Deming.

4. Here Governor Ford errs through understatement. Although strenuously denied at the time (and even yet by the Reorganized Church of Latter Day Saints), Smith and his chosen intimates were indulging extensively in polygamy. Although the precise number of Smith's wives is unknown, Fawn Brodie, in *No Man Knows My History*, lists the names of forty-nine, and Brigham Young on one occasion stated that he had sealed "dozens" of women to Smith. They ranged in age from girls in their teens to women in their late fifties. Many were married women whose husbands were living; several were sisters; and two were mother and daughter, the marriage of the latter being kept a secret from the former. Nor were the relations thus enjoyed "mystical and spiritual"; on the contrary, they were commonplace and carnal. See Ford, *History of Illinois*, ed. Quaife, 2:169–70.

5. There were numerous allegations of the abuse and harassment of non-Mormons in Nauvoo, including one of the caning of a Warsaw citizen named Bennett by Joseph Smith. No account of a physical attack by Smith on a Hancock County official has come to light, however. Warsaw *Message*, September 27, 1843.

6. Constable David Bettisworth was sent on such a mission to Nauvoo as is described here but earlier, on June 12. Dallin H. Oaks and Marvin S. Hill, *Carthage Conspiracy: The Trial of the Accused Assassins of Joseph Smith* (Urbana, 1975), 15–16.

7. The magistrate was Robert F. Smith, who was also a captain of the Carthage Grays, a local militia unit mentioned subsequently.

8. At the trial of the accused assassins of Joseph Smith in 1845, it was asserted that Levi Williams, a Warsaw militia leader, had called for volunteers to go to Carthage on June 27 from among members of the Warsaw militia who had been discharged at Golden's Point on that date. Oaks and Hill, *Carthage Conspiracy*, 117–18.

Chapter XI

1. The three anti-Mormon leaders who were to be arrested were Levi Williams, Thomas Sharp, editor of the inflammatory Warsaw *Signal*, and Joseph H. Jackson, allegedly a leader of the mob who had earlier lived in Nauvoo. Oaks and Hill, *Carthage Conspiracy*, 38.

2. Prosecutors willing to remain in the unpopular case against Smith's accused assassins were hard to come by and retain, especially if they possessed political ambitions. Murray McConnel of Jacksonville investigated the initial charges. William Elliot, newly elected attorney for

the Fifth Judicial Circuit prosecuted the case before the grand jury, but he took no part in the murder trial. James H. Ralston was named circuit attorney pro tem by Judge Young, but the actual prosecution of the defendants before a trial jury was done by Josiah Lamborn, lately attorney general of Illinois. Oaks and Hill, *Carthage Conspiracy*, 37–38, 51, 70, 77.

3. This was William Daniels, a militiaman who participated in the mobbing of the Smiths. Soon afterward he became a convert to Mormonism, and his story of the shooting is incorporated in the *Correct Account of the Murder of Generals Joseph and Hyrum Smith* published at Nauvoo in 1845. According to it, God miraculously intervened to strike powerless the arm of the lyncher who rushed forward with a bowie knife, intent upon cutting off Smith's head. The like paralysis extended to the four militiamen who had fired the final shots and whose guns now fell clattering to the ground. One can only wonder why this miraculous protection was not extended in time to save Smith's life instead of merely to spare his corpse from desecration. See Ford, *History of Illinois*, ed. Quaife, 2:235–36.

4. Unlike the prosecution in the Smith murder trial, the defense was both enthusiastic and stellar. Browning, Skinner, Warren, and Richardson were engaged to defend the accused assassins, along with Archibald Williams and Thomas Morrison. Browning and Williams were well-known Whig lawyers and politicians from Quincy. The reputation of Richardson, a Jacksonian from Rushville, was comparable; he had just served a term as speaker of the Illinois house, where he was frequently at odds with Ford. At the murder trial Lamborn found himself contending against six defense counselors. Oaks and Hill, *Carthage Conspiracy*, 79–84.

Chapter XII

1. The committee was comprised of John S. Zieber, William G. Anderson, and Stephen T. Logan of the house and Joel A. Matteson and Ferris Forman of the senate. All were Democrats but Logan, whom Ford lauds below for his support of the Illinois and Michigan Canal. Indeed, Ford considered Logan's role decisive in securing the passage of the canal bill. Matteson also supported that measure. Illinois *House Journal*, 1844–45, 87; Illinois *Senate Journal*, 1844–45, 83.

2. George T. M. Davis, junior editor of the Whig Alton *Telegraph*, attended the proceedings of the 1844–45 General Assembly and wrote highly partisan weekly letters to his newspaper about them. He also corresponded over the name "Virginius" with the St. Louis *Republican*. In both capacities he was severely critical of Thomas Ford and was correspondingly attacked by Democratic journals.

3. This entire paragraph was substantially altered in the second printing of the 1854 edition, undoubtedly to lessen the acrimony that Ford

had felt toward Lyman Trumbull. Although Trumbull and Shields had been political adversaries, and early in 1855 Trumbull would win the U.S. Senate seat that Shields had occupied, Ford's language may have seemed too harsh for one Democrat to use against another. The altered paragraph is repeated in full herewith:

"The opposition was put on foot in part by Mr. Trumbull, late Secretary of State, who had his private griefs to assuage; and by an ambitious aspirant for the United States Senate, who though often assured to the contrary, would never believe but that I would be a candidate for that office in 1846. Trumbull being a good lawyer, but no statesman was literally devoured by ambition for office, and was rather unfitted to be popular by any natural means, with the people amongst whom he resided. He seemed to have the opinion that the only means of success, was to be a demagogue; and he was unfitted by nature to be a demagogue. So far from possessing that appearance of generosity and magnanimity, which often recommends a man to the people, his manners were precise, and his appearance would be called by many *puritanical.* He was a man of strong prejudices, and not remarkable for liberal views. No such man can very successfully play the demagogue; he may manage well with politicians, but he can never establish a broad foundation of support among the people, as there is nothing in such men to attract the people to their opinions and character. Such men might be respectable, acting in accordance with their natural gifts, but must always fall when acting a part for which they were never fitted by nature."

4. The allusion is to Stephen A. Douglas, with whom it was widely believed that Ford would contend for a U.S. Senate seat in 1846. Johannsen, *Stephen A. Douglas,* 188.

5. William A. Richardson was accused of such a scheme as this at this time. He was speaker of the house of representatives in 1844–45 and practically sovereign in making committee assignments. Pease, *The Frontier State,* 299.

6. James Semple was elected to the U.S. Senate over Lyman Trumbull. William Walters and George Weber of the *Illinois State Register* in Springfield were returned as public printers, having defeated John S. Zieber, a Peoria editor and chair of the joint committee to examine the executive office, in the Democratic caucus. The victorious candidates for state auditor, treasurer, and the three vacant judgeships, were William L. D. Ewing, Milton Carpenter, James Shields, Jesse B. Thomas, and John D. Caton. Who their opponents were in the Democratic caucus is unrecorded. Illinois *House Journal,* 1844–45, 57, 199, 456–457; Illinois *Senate Journal,* 1844–45, 49, 177, 328–29; *Illinois State Register* (Springfield), January 17, 1845.

7. The canal was completed and the first boat passed through on April 23, 1848, approximately a year after this forecast was made. Begun on July 4, 1836, it had cost the state of Illinois a dozen years of effort and the expenditure of millions of dollars. Its construction had a tre-

mendous effect upon the further growth and prosperity of Chicago and Illinois. Somewhere in the great city a fitting memorial to the man whose courage and foresight made its completion possible should have been created long since. See Ford, *History of Illinois*, ed. Quaife, 2:278–79.

8. Ford's ire at Anderson was twofold; Anderson had been an active member of the committee to examine the executive office. Illinois *House Journal*, 1844–45, 87, 97.

Chapter XIII

1. More than a year after Ford had completed his manuscript, on October 9, 1848, the Nauvoo temple was gutted by an arsonist's fire. The walls soon after blew over in a great windstorm.

2. Jacob B. Backenstos and his brother William were both controversial sheriffs of Hancock County, William elected in 1842 and Jacob in 1845. Thomas Gregg, *History of Hancock County* (Chicago, 1880), 449–50.

3. Almon W. Babbitt was the Mormon elder who accompanied J. B. Backenstos to the General Assembly from Hancock County in 1844–45. Illinois *House Journal*, 1844–45, 4.

4. Stinson H. Anderson, a Democratic wheelhorse and a Polk appointee, was U.S. marshal for Illinois in 1845. *Illinois State Register* (Springfield), April 4, 1845.

5. The deputy marshal took William Miller of Nauvoo into custody, thinking him to be Brigham Young. Only after reaching Carthage did he realize that he was the victim of a Mormon hoax. Oaks and Hill, *Carthage Conspiracy*, 204.

6. This last expedition, called a fool's errand at the time, lasted from October 28 through November 14, 1846, during the waning weeks of Ford's term as governor. The governor endured personal insult while in Hancock County and also the derision of the state's Whig press. A contemporary observer noted truthfully that "the governor, whatever he may do, in reference to Mormon affairs, seems doomed to condemnation." *Illinois State Register* (Springfield), October 30, 1846.

7. The names of Backman, Brath, Palmer, and Reynolds have all been stricken from the second printing of the 1854 edition and replaced with asterisks.

The names of J. H. Sherman, J. W. Brattle, and Abram Van Tuyl were signed to an anti-Mormon address defending recent efforts to expel Mormons and new citizens from Nauvoo. The address was issued at Carthage and published in the Quincy *Whig* on December 2, 1846.

Chapter XIV

1. His brief treatment of the Massac County vigilantism reveals Ford's preoccupation with Hancock County affairs at the time of the outbreak

of southern Illinois violence and also the brevity of the remainder of his term as governor. Massac County would be a problem for Ford's successor, Augustus French, during the next two regular sessions of the General Assembly and for a special session called in October 1849. Not until 1850 were the Massac County troubles finally quieted. James A. Rose, "The Regulators and Flatheads in Southern Illinois," *Transactions of the Illinois State Historical Society for 1906,* 108–21.

Index

Abolition: unpopularity of, 17, 18

Abolitionists, 161–69

Absentee owners: hostility to, 67, 115. *See also* Land, Military tract

Adams, Capt. John G.: in Stillman's Run battle, 79–80

Adams, John Quincy: administration of, 188; election to presidency, 15, 39–40, 47–48

Agriculture: pioneer methods of, 23–24

Alexander, Gen. Milton K.: in Black Hawk War, 83–108

Aliens: contest over suffrage, 146–52

Allen, Capt. Robert: and militia, 306

Alton: Lovejoy riots and, 160–69; rivalry with St. Louis, 119–21, 127

Alton *Observer:* in Lovejoy riots, 162–69

Alton *Telegraph:* on repudiation, 203

American Bottom: defined, 13; flooding and, 234–35

Anderson, Stinson H. (U.S. marshal), 329n

Anderson, Dr. William G.: on bank settlement, 281–83; Ford administration and, 327n

Apple River Fort: attack on, 84–85

Appointive power: contest over, 145–46; constitutional provisions, 11–13

Archer, William. B. (canal commissioner), 123

Arnold, Isaac: canal loan bill and, 275–76; on repudiation, 325n

Ashawequa (wife of Black Hawk), 111

Atkinson, Gen. Henry: in Black Hawk War, 78–111

Babbitt, Almon W. (Mormon elder), 292; election to legislature, 329n

Babcock, George R.: letter quoted, 205–6

Backenstos, Jacob B.: Mormons and, 222–23; as sheriff, 287–88, 290

Backenstos, William (Hancock County sheriff), 325n

Backman: and murder of Mormon, 288

Bailey, Maj. David: in Stillman's Run battle, 78

Baker, Col. E. D.: in Mexican War, 293; in Mormon War, 256–57

Ballot: in elections, 55–56

Banks: charter of, 25–26, 114–15; failure of, 153–55; pioneer, 24–28; as political issue, 196, 204–5, 207–16, 281–82; sale of bonds, 129–32, 134. *See also* Internal improvements, Kirtland Safety Bank, Shawneetown Bank, State Bank

Baptists: founding of college, 157

Baring Bros. and Co.: in canal loan negotiation, 261, 263–65, 270

Battle of Bad Axe, 104–8

Battle of Pecatonica, 85

Battle of Stillman's Run, 78–80

Beardstown: army rendezvous at, 77

Beecher, Rev. Edward: in Lovejoy crusade, 163–66

Belleville: duel at, 28

Belmont (capital of Wisconsin), 88

Beloit, 87

Bennett, Dr. John C.: anti-Mormon crusade, 220; Nauvoo career of, 181–85; Nauvoo Legion and, 235

Bennett, Wm. (duelist), 28

Berry, Elijah C., 12–14

Bettisworth, David: mission to Nauvoo, 326n

Birkbeck, Morris: as antislavery lead-

er, 32–33; career of, 32; death of, 45–46
Bishop, Lyman: death of, 168
Black Code, 16–18
Blacks: early laws concerning, 16–18. *See also* Slavery
Black Hawk: in Black Hawk War, 71–111; campaign of 1832, 77–108; captivity of, 107–11; characterized, 72–73; death of, 111; invasion of Illinois, 77; seizing and burning of village, 71–71, 76
Black Hawk War: campaign of 1831, 73–77; campaign of 1832, 77–107; origin of, 71–74;
Blackwell, David (antislavery leader), 32–33; opposition to Field, 318n
Blue Mounds: army rendezvous at, 104
Boards of Public Works: operations of, 125–26. *See also* Fund comissioners, Internal improvements
Bogart, Samuel: in Mormon War, 180; rangers and, 83
Boggs, Gov. L. W.: expulsion of Mormons, 180
Bond, Gov. Shadrach (first state governor), 12–13; as party leader, 46–47; death of, 46; refusal of pardon, 28; slavery and, 33; on State Bank, 129
Bonnets: women's adoption of, 61
Book of Mormon: origin of, 174–78
Boots: pioneers' adoption of, 61
Boyle, Chief Justice John: career of, 39
Brattle, J. W.: on expulsion of Mormons, 329n
Brayman, Mason: in Mormon War, 293–95, 325n
Breese, Sidney: on railroad proposal, 112
Bribery: legislators and, 275–76
Brockman, Thomas S.: characterized, 294; in Mormon War, 295, 297–300
Bronson, Arthur: canal loan and, 205–6
Brown, Judge Thomas C.: election of, 13, 34; slavery and, 30–33; in supreme court contest, 145–52

Browning, O. H.: accused Smith murderers and, 259; congressional campaign of, 223
Bucklin, James M. (canal engineer), 122
Buckmaster, Nathaniel: in Black Hawk War, 74; in Mormon War, 242
Bulls, legislation concerning, 70–71
Burnt Village: army occupation of, 88–90
"Butcher-Knife boys," 57
Butterfield, Justin: on canal loan, 205–6

Caldwell, Billy, 87
Caldwell County, Mo.: and Mormons, 179
Campbell, Capt. John: death of, 171
Campbell, Thompson: report on schools, 37
Canals. *See* Illinois and Michigan Canal
Carlin, John: in Mormon War, 292
Carlin, Gov. Thomas: arrest of Joseph Smith and, 184–85, 219; election as governor, 131; bank loan and, 153–54; Col. Oakley and, 165; contest over appointment, 145–47; legislative overrides of, 213; on repeal of bank charters, 207–8
Carpenter, Milton: election as state treasurer, 328n
Carthage: as anti-Mormon center, 226–59
Carthage Grays: flight of, 257; in murder of Smiths, 240–43; 246, 248–49
Casey, Zadoc, Lieut. Gov., 87
Catfish River, 87, 95
Catholics: founding of nunnery, 157; in French Illinois, 20; at Kaskaskia, 235
Caton, John D., 328n
Cavarly, Alfred W.: and finance bill, 144
Central Railroad: proposal for, 112
Chase, Bishop Philander, 157
Cheater: Black Hawk and, 107–9
Chicago: described, 19; land boom in, 114–15, 123; town lot boom in, 273–74; visit of army to, 110

Chippewa Indians: in Winnebago War, 42

Chittenden, Col. John B. (militia leader), 294

Cholera: in army, 109–10

Chouteau, Auguste, 71

Churches: in Lovejoy crusade, 161–69

Churchill, George (antislavery leader), 32–33

Circuit courts: reform of, 148–52

Cities: growth of, 157

Claims associations, 324n

Clark, Gen. William, 73

Clay County, Mo.: activities of Mormons in, 179

Clay, Henry: as advocate, 55; aid to Mormons, 181; presidential candidacy of, 40, 47, 264–65

Clifford, Maj. Benjamin, 295

Coats: pioneers and, 61

Coles County: naming of, 45

Coles, Gov. Edward: as antislavery leader, 30–33; freeing of slaves, 35–36; leaves state, 45–46

Colleges: founding of, 157

Collins, Col. James: in Black Hawk War, 93–107

Commerce: in pioneer Illinois, 24, 63–66

Common schools: progress of, 157, 195

Connelly, Capt. (militia officer), 306

Constitution of 1818: provisions of, 11–12

Conway, Joseph: political career of, 35

Cook County: naming of, 47

Cook, Daniel P.: as antislavery leader, 30–33; career of, 46–47; death of, 46; as office holder, 14

Coon-skin caps, 61

Corporations: repeal of charters, 210

Costumes: of pioneers, 61

Council of Fifty, 325n

Counterfeiting: by Massac-Pope County gangs, 309, 312; by Mormons, 229, 238, 243, 291

Courts-martial: at Nauvoo, 305

Covenanters, 11

Cowdery, Oliver (witness to Book of Mormon), 177–78

Craig, Capt. James, 92

Crain, John: political rewards of, 133

Cranberry Lake, 94

Crawford, Wm. H.: presidential candidacy of, 15, 30, 39–40, 47–48

Crime: legislation concerning, 71; in northern Illinois, 169–72; in pioneer Illinois, 52–55, 160; in southern Illinois, 309–14. See also Lovejoy, Elijah P., Mobs, Mormons

Croghan, Maj. George (hero of Fort Stephenson), 114

Crozier, Samuel, 59

Culture: progress toward noted, 157–59

Daniels, William (witness of Smith murders), 258

Danites, 225, 228

Dartmouth College case, 210

Daubeneyer, Andrew: death of, 288

Davenport, Col. George (partisan of Black Hawk), 73

Davis County, Mo.: Mormons and, 179

Davis, Gen. John T.: in Massac County rebellion, 310

Davis, George T. M.: canal bill and, 276; on Ford administration, 327n

Davis, Gov. John: attack of Globe and, 262–63; canal loan and, 261–65, 270, 275

Davis, William, 81–82

Dawson, John: political rewards of, 133

Debts: collection of, 216–18

Decori (Winnebago chief): captures Black Hawk, 107–9

Dells of Wisconsin: Chief Black Hawk and, 107–9

Dement, Maj. John: as candidate for state treasurer, 71; in Kellogg's Grove battle, 86–87.; political rewards of, 133

Deming, Gen. Minor R.: death of, 287; Dr. Marshall and, 285; election as sheriff, 255; militia career of, 242, 246, 248

Democratic party: on banks, 121, 207; canal loan and, 262, 263–66,

270–71, 276; origin of, 137; relations with Mormons, 181–86, 219–24, 255–56, 292, 293; state-debt issue and, 203, 207; in supreme court purge, 145–52. *See also* Banks, Internal improvements

Despotism: origin of, 307–8

De Witt, Col. A. B., 77

Dixon, John: career of, 81

Dixon, 77–78, 110

Dodge, Gen. Henry: in Black Hawk War, 72–111; military merit discussed, 98–103; in Pecatonica battle, 85–86; in Winnebago War, 43; in Wisconsin battle, 97–98

Doniphan, Gen. Alexander: in Mormon War, 180

Dougherty, John: political rewards of, 132–33, 322n

Douglas, Stephen A.: congressional campaign of, 223; on judiciary, 150–51; Mormons and, 182–86; in Mormon War, 289; nomination for Congress, 139; political rewards of, 132, 134; senatorial aspirations of, 272, 274, 328n; State Bank bill and, 211; on state nickname, 43; supreme court career of, 212–13

Driscoll family: criminal career of, 171

Duncan, Joseph: candidacy for governor, 186–87; career of, 48–49, 113–14; death of, 46; on internal improvement bill, 129; on support of schools, 36

Dunn, Capt., 242

Dunn, Judge Charles, 88, 91

Durfee, Edward, 288, 305

Early, Capt. Jacob M.: spy company and, 89

Eddy, Henry (antislavery editor), 32

Education: promoted by preachers, 61; progress of, 157; sale of school lands, 50–51; status in pioneer Illinois, 21, 36–37

Edwards County: founding of, 32; naming of, 45; outlawry in, 161

Edwards, Cyrus, 131

Edwards, Gov. Ninian: career of, 14,

39–40; death of, 45; election as governor, 38, 40; as party leader, 46; as political rewards of, 133; as proslavery leader, 30–33; September 1815 treaty and, 71; on State Bank, 40–42

Edwardsville: establishment of bank, 24; establishment of newspapers, 32; naming of, 45

Elections: of 1822, 30; of 1826, 38–40; of 1827, 52; of 1830, 67–70; of 1840, 135; drinking habits at, 68; pioneer methods of, 56–59; of state treasurer, 71

Elizabeth: as site of Apple River fort, 84

Elkin, William. F.: political rewards of, 133

Elliot, William: Smith murderers and, 326–27n

Episcopalians: founding of college, 157

Eustis, Col. Abram: Black Hawk and, 111

Ewing, Col. William. L. D.: in Black Hawk War, 88–107; election as state auditor, 328n

Executions: of Bennett, 28; of Green, 53–54

Farmers: bank credit and, 121

Federalists: local hatred of, 46

Field, Abner (unsuccessful candidate), 318n

Field, Alexander P.: on circuit courts, 317n; removal from office, 145–46

"Flatheads" (Massac County faction), 312–13

Flood of 1844: described, 234–35

Flood, Maj. William G.: in Mormon War, 295

Ford, Gov. Thomas: achievements as governor, 315–16; career of, xvii, xix–xx, xxiii–xxvii; on collection laws, 217–18; defeat of repudiation, 203, 260–78; early life, xvii–xix; and *History*, xx–xxx; nomination for governor, 187–88, 192; Ogle County regulators and, 324n; relations with Mormons, 220–59, 303–6; role at

Smith impeachment, 322n; on salary reduction, 278–80; and school reform, 317n; Shawneetown Bank and, 215, 281–82; state bank bill and, 208–15;

Ford, Mrs. Thomas (Frances Hambaugh), xviii

Forman, Ferris: investigation of Ford administration, 327n

Forquer, George, xviii; as antislavery leader, 33; death of, 46; railroad proposal of, 112; report on state loan, 122

Fort Armstrong: described, 76–77

Fort Hamilton: garrisoning of, 91; Indian attack on, 85

Fort Stephenson: attack on, 114

Fort Winnebago: army visits to, 91; description of, 91–91

Foster, William. P.: career of, 14; election as judge, 13

Four Lakes: army traverse of, 95–96; described, 87; as objective of army, 87

Fox River: described, 91–92

French, Augustus C.: political rewards of, 133, 134; and regulators, 161

French: in Illinois, characterized, 19–20

Fry, Gen. Jacob: in Black Hawk War, 77–107

Fund commissioners: operations of, 125–35, 143–44

Gaines, Gen. Edmund P.: in Black Hawk War, 118–20

Galena: anecdote about, 202; in Black Hawk War, 84–85; early history of, 43; lead speculation at, 120

The Galenian, 98

Galland, Dr. Isaac: characterized, 286

Gatewood, William Jefferson: on convention system, 139

Gear, Hezekiah H. (Godfrey and Gilman agent), 322n

Gibbs, Dr. William. J.: in Massac County rebellion, 312

Gillespie, Joseph: and sine die adjournment, 323n

Gilman, Winthrop S., 163, 167

Godfrey, Benjamin: in Lovejoy crusade, 163, 167

Godfrey Gilman and Co.: in bank contest, 118–21

Golden's Point, 238, 248

Government: limits upon power of, 172–73, 237, 253–54, 257, 293, 296–97, 307; republican, characterized, 187–92

Grammar, John: political career of, 197–98

Gratiot, Henry: ransom of Hall sisters and, 319n

Graves, Rev. Frederick W.: in Lovejoy crusade, 166

Green, Eliphalet: anecdote about, 53–54

Green Plains: in Mormon War, 285

Gregg, David L.: on canal bill, 276

Gridley, Asahel: and sine die adjournment, 323n

Grundy, Felix, 55

Hackelton, Maj. Samuel: in Stillman's Run battle, 78, 80

Hall family: Indian captivity and massacre of, 81–82

Hall, James: as candidate for office, 71; election as judge, 34; literary work of, 159

Hamilton, Col. William. S.: in Black Hawk War, 90; career of, 36

Hamilton's Diggings: founding of, 36

Hancock County: Mormons in, 219; political control of, 221; settlers characterized, 286. See also Mormons

Hanson, Nicholas: in slavery contest, 31–32

Happy, William. W.: political rewards of, 133

Hardin, Gen. John J.: in Mexican War, 293; in Mormon War, 256, 287, 289–90

Harris, Martin (witness of Book of Mormon), 177

Harrison, William. H.: election of, 149; negotiation of Indian treaty, 71; as presidential candidate, 135

Hartford Convention, 46
Hats: pioneers and, 61
Haun's Mill massacre, 325n
Hell's Half Acre: explanation of, 299
Henry County: settlement of, 157
Henry, Gen. James D.: in Bad Axe battle, 105–7; in Black Hawk War, 74–107; military achievements of, 98–103; quelling of mutiny, 93
Hogan, John: in Lovejoy crusade, 163–66; political rewards of, 133
Hoge, Joseph P.: congressional campaign of, 220–23
Hooking timber, 116
Hope and Co., 261
Horses: disabled, 92; of French settlers, 20; stampede, 91
Hubbard, Adolphus F.: candidacy for governor, 38
Hubbard, Gurdon S. (canal commissioner), 123
Hurlbut, Rev. Thaddeus B., 164

Illinois: admission to statehood, 7–28; Black Code, 16–18; boundary issue, 7–10; claim of U.S. lands, 45; Convention of 1818, 10–13; cultural growth of, 159; during Ford administration, 314–16; educational progress of, 157; in 1818, 18–24; failure of banks, 153–56; Indian Wars, 20–21, 42–44, 71–111; internal improvement issue, 112–44, 205; judicial reform, 145–52; Lovejoy riots, 161–69; merchants of, 159–60, 193, 278; mobs, 169–72, 285–89, 309–14; in Mexican War, 158, 293; Mormons in, 187–86, 219–38; pioneer elections, 68; pioneer justice, 52–55; pioneer religion, 60–63; pioneer violence, 55–57; repudiation and, 260–78; sectional differences, 194–96, 274, 276; slavery issue, 30–33; State Bank issue and, 204, 210–15; state debt, 203–16; state pride, 157–59, 269
Illinois College, 157, 163
Illinois and Michigan Canal: appropriation of land for, 47; bonds for, 153;

canal loan struggle, 205–6, 216; 260–66, 270, 275–78; completion of, 278, 315, 328n; debate over construction, 13; history of, 122, 125; opposition to, 195–196; progress of, 134; railroad and, 112; reasons for building, 10
Illinois River: early steamboats on, 63; improvement of, 124–34
Illinois State Bank: struggle over, 204, 210–15. *See also* Repudiation
Impeachment: of Judge Theophilus W. Smith, 112–13
Independence, Mo., 179
Indian Creek, 81–82
Indian Wars, 20, 42–44, 72–11
Interest rates, 159–60, 278
Internal improvements, 112–44

"Jack Mormons": explained, 231; plot against, 255–56
Jackson, Andrew: creation of political party, 137; declaration of martial law, 302; Gov. Duncan on, 113–14; influence in Illinois politics, 67, 70; interview with Black Hawk, 110–11; leadership of, 188; presidential candidacy of, 39, 47–49
Jackson, Joseph H. (anti-Mormon mob leader), 326n
Jackson, Maj. J. E.: and militia, 306
Jenkins, Lt. Gov. Alexander M., 112
Johnson, Col. James (founder of Galena), 42
Jonas, Capt.: and militia, 246
Jones, Col. Gabriel, 97–98
Jubilee College: founding of, 157
Judd, Norman B.: on canal bill, 276
Judges: pioneer, 52–55; courts organized, 34–35, 145–52

Kane County: naming of, 11
Kane, Elias K.: career of, 10–11; death of, 46; as office holder, 32–33; and party, 46–47
Kaskaskia: as first capital of Illinois, 13–14; flood and, 235; newspaper established at, 32; nunnery at, 157; removal of, 18
Kaskaskia River: improvement of, 125

Keelboats: abandonment of, 63; as army transports, 77; Indian attacks on, 42; on Mississippi, 24

Kellogg's Grove battle, 86–87

Kentuckians: in Massac County rebellion, 309–13

Keokuk (chief): as leader of peace party, 77; as rival of Black Hawk, 110–11

Kilpatrick, Thomas M.: on canal bill, 277; on common schools, 36

Kingdom of God: at Nauvoo, 324–25n

Kinney, William C. (proslavery leader), 32–33; campaign for governor, 67–69; contest over state treasurership, 71; on Gov. Edwards, 44; on Yankees, 195

Kirtland Safety Bank, 179

Knox College, 157

Lake Kegonsa, 87

Lake Koshkonong: army at, 88; erection of fort, 91

Lake Mendota, 87

Lake Waubesa, 87

Lamborne, Josiah, 259

Land: absentee ownership of, 67, 115; appropriation for canal, 47; government sale of, 24; granted to schools, 50–51; quality of, 204–5, 216; speculation in, 114; state claims for, 45

Law, William, 222, 225–26

Law, Wilson: and Nauvoo Legion, 235; and rebellion, 225–26

Lawless, Judge Luke: and St. Louis lynching, 323n

Lawrence, Abbott, 261

Lead mines: early settlement of, 42–43; in Winnebago War, 43

Leadership: importance of, 187–92

Leavitt, David: on canal loan, 206, 261, 270, 275

Le Claire, Antoine, 73

Legislature: appointive powers of, 12, 145–46; appointments and, 212–13; assault of members, 52; characterized, 15–16, 197–201; contest over slavery, 31–33; courtship of Mormons, 182–84; creation of State Bank, 25–26; impeachments in,

112–13; intrigues of, 57–59; log-rolling in, 126–29; override of constitution, 125; reorganization of judiciary, 35, 145–52; salaries of, 278–80; sale of school lands, 50–51. See also Debts, Illinois and Michigan Canal, Illinois State Bank, Internal improvements

Leib, Col. Daniel M.: in Black Hawk War, 74

Lemon (Lemen), James (pioneer), 23–24

Lima: in Mormon War, 285–86

Lincoln, Abraham: political rewards of, 133; and sine die adjournment, 323n

Linder, Usher F.: in Lovejoy crusade, 164, 324n; political rewards of, 133

Lippincott, Thomas (antislavery leader), 32

Liquor: influence on mob, 168; and pioneers, 68

Little Bear (chief), 84

Little Bull Law, 71, 318–19n

Little, Sidney: and Mormons, 182–84

Little Thunder (chief), 94

Lobbyists: conduct described, 200–201

Lockwood, Judge Samuel D.: as antislavery leader, 33; election of, 34; prosecution of duelists, 28; report of law code, 37; in supreme court contest, 145–51

Loco-foco party: origin of name, 137, 322n

Logan, Judge Stephen T.: on canal bill, 276; investigation of Ford administration, 327n

Log-rolling: in state legislature, 126–29

"Long Nine": activities of, 127

Lovejoy, Elijah P., 161–69

Lucas, Gen. Samuel D.: in Mormon War, 180

Lynch law, 310

MacAlister and Stebbins, 281

Magniac, Jardine and Co.: in canal loan negotiation, 261, 270

Manchester: Mormon associations with, 177–78

Manitou Village, 92
Marshall, Dr. Samuel, 285
Martial law, 302
Massac County rebellion, 160, 309–14
Mather Lamb and Co., 63
Mather, Thomas (antislavery leader), 33; in bank contest, 118–20
Mathes family, 312–13
Matteson, Joel A.: on canal bill, 276; investigation of Ford administration, 327n
Maxwell, G. W. P.: on banks and roads, 322n
McBratney, Samuel, 288
McCalla, Maj. (militia leader), 300
McClernand, John A.: Lyman Trumbull and, 212–13; political rewards of, 133; on state bank bill, 211, 213
McConnell, Maj. Murray: actions against Smith murderers, 326n; in Black Hawk War, 94–107
McDonough College: founding of, 157
McDougall, J. A. (attorney general), 289
McKendree College: founding of, 157
McLean, John: career of, 27; death of, 46; party and, 46–47; as proslavery leader, 33
McLeod, Alexander: trial of, 297
McRoberts, Judge Samuel: death of, 46; election of, 35; as proslavery leader, 32; revision of laws, 37; State Bank and, 121; unpopular decision of, 35–36
Memphis Convention, 126
Menard, Col. Pierre: anecdote about, 26; eligibility for office, 11–12
Merchants, pioneer: activities of, 159–60, 193, 278; methods of, 63–66
Merino sheep: introduction of, 32
Merriman, E. H.: in Black Hawk War, 94, 99, 101; in Mormon War, 256–57
Metropolis City: lawlessness in, 311–13
Mexican War: role of Illinois in, 158, 293
Military Tract: described, 67; taxation of, 50, 115–16

Militia: in Black Hawk War, 73–107; in Winnebago War, 43–44
Miller, John S., 75–76
Miller, William, 328n
Mills, Benjamin, 112
Minshall, William. A.: political rewards of, 133
Missionaries: Mormon, 224, 251–52, 253
Mississippi River: flood of 1844, 234–35
Missouri: Mormon activities in, 178–87; seizure of Joseph Smith in, 184–86, 219–21; and slave holders, 30–31
Mobs: causes of, 172–73; claim jumpers and, 169–70; in early Illinois, 160–61; in Lovejoy riots, 161–69; Ogle County outlawry, 170–72. See also Massac County rebellion, Mormons
Moderates: characterized, 301–2; futility of, 311
Money: in pioneer Illinois, 24–28, 64–66
Moore, Gen. James B.: political campaign of, 30
Moore, John: political rewards of, 133
Mormons: accusations against, 228–32, 284–85; and building of temple, 284; career in state, 219–59; characterized, 219–21, 249–50, 251–53; early history of, 173–78; expulsion from Illinois, 284–308; in Missouri, 178–87; numbers of, 252; political maneuvering of, 219–24; profanity of leaders, 253; as project for temporal rule, 224–25; rebellion of followers, 225–26; removal to Illinois, 181–86; spiritual wife doctrine of, 225;
Mormon Battalion, 291
Morrison, Thomas: and Smith murderers, 327n
Mount Morris Seminary: founding of, 157
Musical standards: of pioneers, 222–23

Naper, Joseph, political rewards of, 132–33

Nauvoo: authority of council at, 224, 225–26; authority of court at, 220–21; capture of by Gentiles, 295, 297–300; Mormon experience at, 219–59; Mormon expulsion from, 284–306; Mormons remove to, 181–86; temple built, 284. *See also* Mormons

Nauvoo charter, 182–86; repeal of, 278

Nauvoo House, 183

Nauvoo Legion, 182–83, 184, 235–36

Nauvoo University, 182

Neale, Gen. Tom M.: in Winnebago War, 43

Neapope: appeals for peace, 98; as captive, 110; 320n

New Englanders: business habits of, 66

New Orleans, as commercial outlet, 64–65

Newspapers: establishment of, 32; promotion of party differences, 136–37

New York banking system, 131

Noel, Capt. Thomas, 90

Northern Cross Railroad: financial operations of, 153

Nunnally, N. W.: on salary reduction, 280

Oakley, Col. Charles (canal loan agent), 160–266, 270

Ogle County: outlawry in, 170–72

Ohio River: outlaws on, 310, 312, 313–14

Old Man's Creek. *See* Battle of Stillman's Run

Oratory: pioneer ideals of, 66

Ordinance of 1787: provisions on state boundaries, 7–9

Oregon: outlawry in, 170–72

Ottawa, 82; platting of, 122

Palestine Grove, 220

Palmyra: Mormon associations with, 174–78

Paquette, Pierre: career of, 93

Parker, Maj. James R.: in Mormon War, 193

Paul, René (canal engineer), 122

Pawpaw Grove, 82

Peck, Ebenezer: and convention system, 139

Peck, Rev. John M.: career of, 60; literary career of, 159

Penitentiary system: introduction of, 71

Perkins, Maj. Isaac: in Black Hawk War, 79–80

Personal politics: merits of, 34; operations of, 138; in pioneer Illinois, 33. *See also* Political parties

Pettigrew, William: massacre of family, 81–82

Philleo, Dr. Addison, 96–97; on Gen. Dodge, 98–99, 101

Phillips, Judge Joseph: career of, 13–14; leaves state, 45; as proslavery leader, 30–33

Pioneers: characterized, 20–24; concept of government, 56–59; dress of, 61. *See also* Crime, Elections, Liquor, Religion, Schools

Plum River, 87

Political conventions: origin of, 138–42

Political parties: activities of, 135–43, 145–52; merits of, 33–34; organization of, 46–50; responsibilities of, 116

Politicians: characterized, 187–92, 196–202

Polk, President James K., 187–88

Polygamy: Mormons and, 229; Reorganized Church and, 252

Pope County: outlawry in, 160–61, 309–14

Pope, Nathaniel: in admission of Illinois, 7–10, 11; as party leader, 46; 219

Posey, Gen. Alexander: in Black Hawk War, 83–107

Post, Justus (canal engineer), 122

Potawatomi Indians: in Black Hawk War, 77, 83, 87

Prairie du Chien: in Black Hawk War, 105–9

Prairies: settlers' attitude on, 67

Pratt, Mayor Bernard, Jr., 234

Preachers: characterized, 21–22. *See also* Religion

Presbyterians: founding of colleges, 157; role in Lovejoy crusade, 161–69

Press: in early Illinois, 159; suppression of, 161–69, 226–28, 259

"The Prophet," 107–11

Prophet's town: army rendezvous at, 78

"Pukes": origin of name, 43

Quincy: and Mormon vote, 223; in Mormon War, 244–47

Railroads: early charters of, 112; mania for building, 125–31; as substitute for canal, 122. *See also* Internal improvements

Ralston, James H.: Ford on, 325n; political rewards of, 133–34; on state bank bill, 133;

Rawlings, M. M. (Shawneetown fund commissioner), 130

Read, John W., 309–10

Red Bird: in Winnebago War, 42, 44

Regulators: in Ogle County, xxvii, 170–72; pioneer activities of, 160; in Pope and Massac counties, 309–14. *See also* Mobs, Mormons

Religion: in Military Tract, 116; in pioneer Illinois, 60–63. *See also* Catholicism

Repudiation: debated, 143–44; as political issue, 203–16, 260–78

Reynolds, Gov. John: in Black Hawk War, 73–82; characterized, 69; chastised, 318n; election as governor, 67–69; election as judge, 13; as proslavery leader, 33; state treasurer contest and, 71; Wiggins loan and, 318n

Reynolds, Thomas (proslavery leader), 32–33; chastised, 318n; death of, 46

Richards, Dr. Willard, 246

Richardson, William A.: congressional aspirations of, 328n; Smith murderers and, 259

Rigdon, Sidney: as cofounder of Mormonism, 174–75; Salt Sermon and, 180, 324n; as successor to Joseph Smith, 250–51

Rivers: improvement of, 125–26; settlers and, 67

Roads: taxes for, 36

Rock Island, 76, 110

Rockport, 74

Rock River: beauty of, 94; Black Hawk War and, 71–111; improvement of, 124

Rockwell, Orrin P., 220, 250

Russell, John: literary career of, 159

Ryan, Michael: on canal loan, 206, 260–66

St. Louis: commercial dominance of, 119; expulsion of abolitionists from, 161; flood of 1844 and, 234; rivalry of Alton merchants and, 119–20; treaty of 1804 and, 77

St. Vrain, Felix, 84

Sangamon County: legislative delegation of, 127

Sangamon *Journal:* on repudiation, 203

Sauk and Fox Indians: divisions among, 77; treaty with, 110. *See also* Black Hawk War

Sawyer, John York: death of, 46; as judge, 34; revision of laws, 37

Scates, Judge Walter B.: on canal bill, 277; outlaws and, 311

Schools: founding by churches, 61; land for, 50–51; legislation on, 36–37; pioneer, 21

Scott, Gen. Winfield: in Black Hawk War, 110

Secretary of state: contest over appointment as, 145–46

Sectionalism, 13, 194–96, 274, 276

Semple, Gen. James: bravery of, 83; political rewards of, 133; senate seat and, 328n

Settlers: characterized, 157–58, 194–96

Sexton, Orville, 281

Sharp, Thomas (Warsaw *Signal* editor), 326n

Shaubanie (Pottawattomie war chief), 87

Shaw, John: in slavery contest, 31–32
Shawneetown: antislavery newspaper in, 32
Shawneetown Bank, 24, 114–15, 118, 129, 135; debt of, 204; liquidation of, 215, 281–82; misconduct of owners, 210. *See also* Illinois State Bank, Internal improvements, Repudiation
Sherman, J. H.: on expulsion of Mormons, 329n
Shields, Gen. James: election as judge, 328n; and Ford's *History*, 1–2, 321n; political rewards of, 133, 211
Shurtleff College: founding of, 157
Singleton, Capt. James (militia leader), 236, 294
Skinner, O. C., 259
Slavery: Black Code and, 16–18; Convenanters on, 11; in Illinois, 30–33; Lovejoy crusade, 161–69
Sloe, Thomas C.: candidacy for governor, 37, 40
Sloo and Co., 119
Smith, Lt. Col. Jeremiah, 93
Smith, Capt. Robert F. (militia leader), 240–41, 243; as Carthage magistrate, 326n
Smith, Joseph: accusation of treason and, 236; characterized, 249; death of, 243–46, 248; as despot, 225–26; efforts to arrest, 184–85, 219–21; founding of Mormon church, 174–78; imprisonment of, 236–43; in Nauvoo, 181–86, 219–49; polygamy and, 229; presidential candidacy of, 224; as temporal ruler, 224–25; trial of murderers, 258–59
Smith, Judge Theophilus W.: accusations against, 40–41; in bank contest, 118–21; as canal commissioner, 121; election as judge, 34; impeachment of, 112–13; law code and, 37; party and, 46; as proslavery leader, 32–33; political intrigues of, 150–52; in supreme court contest, 145–52
Smith, Robert: political rewards of, 133

Snyder, Adam W.: battle with Indians, 83; candidacy for governor, 185–86; introduction of judiciary bill, 148
Spaulding, Solomon, 324n
Specie circulars, 24
Speculation: mania for, 123–35; in pioneer Illinois, 24–28. *See also* Banks, Internal improvements, Land
Spiritual wifery: Mormon practice of, 225, 229
Springfield, 127
S. S. Griggs and Co., xiii–xv
Starr, Judge Henry: revision of laws, 37; 45
State Bank: charges against, 40–42; failure of, 153–56; and notes, 70–71; operations of, 27–28, 116–21; organization of, 25–26, 114–15
State pride, 157–58, 269
State sovereignty, 142
State treasurer: election of, 108
Steamboats: for canal, 134; introduction of, 63; the *Warrior*, 105, 109
Stephenson, Col. James W.: in Black Hawk War, 80, 86; as nominee for governor, 139
Stewart, Alphonso, 28
Stewart, John J. (John T. Stuart), 99
Stillman, Maj. Isaiah: defeat of, 78–80
Stone, Capt. Clark, 84
Stone, Dan: alien case and, 323n; political rewards of, 133
Stone Manning and Co., 119–20
Street, Gen. Joseph M.: and Indian captives, 108–9
Strode, Col. James M., in Black Hawk War, 79–80, 85, 319n; introduction of loan bill, 122
Strong, N. D.: on canal bill, 276
Stuart, John T., 181
Sturges, William, 261
"Suckers": origin of name, 43
Suffrage, 146–52
Supreme court: judges and law code, 37; reformation of, 145–52
Swift, William H., 261–64
Symmes, John Cleves, 195–96

Taxation, struggle over, 202–3, 204,

261–62, 266–70. *See also* Repudiation

Taxes: on Military Tract, 115

Taylor, Col. E. D., 255

Taylor, John (Mormon leader), 246, 248

Taylor, Zachary: in Black Hawk War, 90, 99, 109

Theft: by Gentiles, 300; by Mormons, 224, 226, 230, 232, 284, 288; by Pope County Gang, 309

Thomas, Jesse B.: career of, 14; leaves state, 45; as proslavery leader, 30–33

Thomas, Jesse B. Jr., 328n

Thomas, John, 77, 83

Thomas, Judge William: in Black Hawk War, 75, 78, 81; party and, 46; on school bill, 36

Thompson, Col. Samuel M., 77

Thornton, William F. (canal commissioner), 123

Throckmorton, Capt. John, 105

Tillson, John, Jr., 118–19

Torture: in Massac County rebellion, 309–10

Trumbull, Lyman: candidacy for governor, 277; on canal loan bill, 260, 272–75, 277; on salary reduction bill, 280; on State Bank bill, 212–15

Turney, James: as attorney general, 34; prosecution of murderer, 54

Twelve Apostles, 250–51, 289–91

Twiggs, Gen. David E., 110

Tyler, President John, 187–88

United States Bank: expiration of charter, 115; influence on pioneer trade, 64; as political issue, 196

Van Buren, Martin, 135, 145

Van Tuyl, Abram (anti-Mormon leader), 305; on expulsion of Mormons, 329n

Vandalia: as location of capital, 18; newspaper in, 32; removal of capital from, 127; State Bank and, 25–28

Vandruff's Island, 74–76

Vincennes, 14

Wabash River: improvement of, 124

Wait, William S.: on taxation, 266

Walker, Cyrus, 219–23

Walters, William, 328n

War of 1812: Illinois settlers in, 20–21

Ward, Thomas W., 261

Warren, Calvin A.: on Smith murderers, 259

Warren, Hooper: as antislavery editor, 32–33

Warren, Maj. William B.: in Mexican War, 293; in Mormon War, 289–90

Warsaw: as anti-Mormon center, 244, 246. *See also* Mormons

Warsaw *Signal*, 230

Washington Grove, 171–72

Wattles, James O.: election as judge, 34

Weber, George, 328n

Weed, H. M.: on common schools, 36

West, Emanuel J., 35

West, Henry H.: at Lovejoy riot, 168

Whig party: associations with Mormons, 181–86, 219–23, 291–93; on banks, 121; canal loan and, 262, 264–66, 270, 275–76; on convention system, 138; and Gov. Ford, 247; origin of, 113, 137; on repudiation, 203; in supreme court contest, 145–52

White Pawnee (chief), 93

White Rock Grove, 171

Whiteside, Gen. Samuel: in Black Hawk War, 74–83

Whitewater River, 88

Whitmer, David (witness of Book of Mormon), 177

Wiggins loan, 70–71

Wiggins, Samuel: in bank contest, 118–20

Wilcox, Phineas, 288

Wiley, Rev., 11

Will, Conrad: bank bill and, 115

Will County: naming of, 115

Williams, Archibald (anti-Mormon leader), 292, 294; Smith murderers and, 327n

Williams, Levi, 326n

Winnebago County: outlawry in, 170–72

Winnebago Indians: in Black Hawk
  War, 77–110
Winnebago War, 42–44
Wisconsin: and boundary controver-
  sy, 8–9; Black Hawk War and, 85–
  110
Wisconsin Heights battle, 97–98
Wisconsin River: battle at, 97–98;
  Black Hawk and, 107–9; crossing
  of, 104; described, 91–92
Woodbridge, W. W., 94
Worrell, Franklin A., 248, 288
Wright, Gov. Silas: and antirent riots,
  296–97

Wright and Co., 131
Wright, John S.: on common schools,
  36–37

Yahara River. *See* Catfish River
Yankees: in mobs, 169; southern
  ideas on, 195, 274
Young, Brigham: on polygamy, 225;
  as successor of Joseph Smith, 251
Young, Richard M.: election as judge,
  34; on State Bank, 27

Zieber, John S.: on Ford administration, 327n